The Commonalities of Global Crises

Christian Karner • Bernhard Weicht
Editors

The Commonalities of Global Crises

Markets, Communities and Nostalgia

Editors
Christian Karner
University of Nottingham
Mühlheim, Germany

Bernhard Weicht
Department of Sociology,
University of Innsbruck
Innsbruck, Austria

ISBN 978-1-137-50271-1   ISBN 978-1-137-50273-5   (eBook)
DOI 10.1057/978-1-137-50273-5

Library of Congress Control Number: 2016937329

Printed on acid-free paper

This Palgrave Macmillan imprint is published by Springer Nature
The registered company is Macmillan Publishers Ltd. London

Contents

Notes on Contributors

Giorgos Bithymitris holds a PhD from Panteion University of Social and Political Sciences. His research focuses on union movement theory, social movements, collective identities, ideology and framing processes in crisis contexts. He is a post-doctoral researcher at Panteion University, exploring collective identities among the working class of West Piraeus in the context of crisis and de-industrialization. He also works as an employment counsellor at the Network for Employment & Social Care (DAKM). Giorgos is a member of the Policy Advisory Board of the EU FP7 Project "Cultural Pathways to Economic Self-Sufficiency and Entrepreneurship".

Seppe De Blust is a sociologist and urban planner doing a PhD in Planning & Development, KU Leuven on the strategic positioning of spatial professionals in neighbourhood redevelopment processes. Seppe is also cofounder of Ndvr, an office for socio-spatial research, design consultancy and process guidance.

Julia O'Connell Davidson is Chair of Social Research in the School of Sociology, Politics and International Studies at the University of Bristol. She has researched and written on employment relations, prostitution, "trafficking", childhood, and currently holds a Leverhulme Major Research Fellowship for a project on "modern slavery". She is author of *Modern Slavery: The Margins of Freedom* (Palgrave Macmillan 2015).

Tim Devos is an architect doing a PhD in social geography at the Department of Earth and Environmental Sciences, KU Leuven, on the involvement of local stakeholders in participatory planning processes. Tim is also cofounder of Ndvr.

Bernhard Forchtner is a lecturer at the Department of Media & Communication, University of Leicester. Previously he was Marie Curie Fellow working on far-right ecological risk communication. He has published in the field of memory studies, in the interface of sociological theory and critical discourse analysis, and on prejudice and discrimination. Recent publications include "The Nature of Nationalism. Populist Radical Right Parties on Countryside and Climate" in *Nature & Culture* and "Embattled Vienna 1683/2010: Right-Wing Populism, Collective Memory and the Fictionalisation of Politics" in *Visual Communication*.

Raimundo Frei holds a PhD in sociology from the Humboldt-University of Berlin. His dissertation offers a narrative approach to generational memories. He is currently a researcher at Chile UNDP (United Nations Development Programme), focusing on cultural mechanisms in the reproduction of social inequalities. He also leads a comparative project sponsored by the University of Chile to research narratives and memories of inequalities in Argentina and Chile.

John Holmwood is Professor of Sociology at the University of Nottingham. During the academic year 2014–15, he was a member of the Institute for Advanced Study in Princeton. His research interests include social inequality, the public university and democratic knowledge. He is the editor of *A Manifesto for the Public University* (2011) and one of the founding editors of the free online magazine of social research, commentary and policy analysis, *Discover Society*.

Amal Treacher Kabesh is Associate Professor in the School of Sociology and Social Policy at the University of Nottingham. She is currently completing a book entitled *Egyptian Revolutions: Conflict, Repetition, Identification* (Rowman & Littlefield) that draws upon postcolonial and psychosocial theory to analyse the troubling socio-political processes that take place in Egypt. Her extensive publications focus on subjectivity, gender and ethnicity, the relationship between the Middle East and the West, and relationships between self and other.

Christian Karner is Associate Professor of Sociology at the University of Nottingham and he has been a Research Associate in the Center for Austrian Studies at the University of Minnesota. His research and publications relate to the negotiations of local, ethnic and national identities in the context of contemporary globalization. Christian's books include *Writing History, Constructing Religion* (co-edited with James Crossley, 2005), *Ethnicity and Everyday Life* (2007), *Negotiating National Identities: Between Globalization, the Past and "the Other"* (2011), and *The Use and Abuse of Memory* (co-edited with Bram Mertens, 2013).

José Julián López is Associate Professor in the School of Sociological and Anthropological Studies at the University of Ottawa. His current work is concerned with developing sociological approaches to the study of human rights, and the human right to food. His previous research explored modes of ethical regulation of new technologies and the social-discursivity of metaphors.

Bruno Meeus is a geographer, Innoviris postdoctoral research fellow at the Faculty of Architecture, Campus Sint-Lucas Brussels of the KU Leuven, and project manager at the Cosmopolis Centre for Urban Research at VUB. His research interests revolve around migration, urban inequality and action-oriented ethnography.

Frédéric Moulène is Associate Researcher at the University of Strasbourg and Teaching Fellow at the University of Besançon. His PhD offered a sociological contribution to the study of performative political discourse. He is a specialist in the sociology of language and a member of the research committee "Language and Society" within the International Sociological Association. His other research relates to urban sociology, the anthropology of space, and economic sociology.

Barbara Samaluk is a postdoctoral Research Fellow in the Work and Employment Research Unit at the University of Greenwich Business School. Her research interests include transnational labour migration, cultural political economy, commodification and marketization in postcolonial and post-socialist contexts, diversity and anti-discrimination. Her publications feature in edited volumes and journals, including *Work, employment and society*. Her current research explores the effects of marketization. Barbara's research is underpinned by years of human rights and anti-discrimination advocacy work in various post-socialist countries.

Bernhard Weicht is Assistant Professor in the Department of Sociology at the University of Innsbruck. He holds a PhD from the University of Nottingham where he researched the construction of care for elderly people. He continued his work at Utrecht University with a project on the intersections of care and migration regimes. Bernhard has published on the construction of care, ageing, dependency, migrant care workers and the intersection of migration and care. Most recently, his monograph *The Meaning of Care* was published by Palgrave Macmillan (2015). He is chair of the European Sociological Association Research Network "Ageing in Europe".

List of Tables

Markets, "Communities" and Nostalgia

Christian Karner and Bernhard Weicht

At least since the financial crisis of 2007/2008, deep socioeconomic turmoil has been all around us in Europe and other parts of the Global North. As our futures seem increasingly precarious, contemporary circumstances challenge Fukuyama's proclamation (1992) of not very long ago that the collapse of communism had brought about an irreversible and crisis-free victory of free-market capitalism and democracy that were tantamount to an "end of history". Two decades later, we are facing heightened local and global inequalities, environmental catastrophes, and newly hardening cultural boundaries. Concurrently, emerging markets leave established superpowers anxious about their future standing, while nation-states generally find themselves at the mercy of global financial markets and their auxiliary institutions. As significantly, the economic realities of the twenty-first century are met by prominent local, regional, national and transnational counterreactions, many of which revolve around questions of belonging and the entitlements group membership bestows.

With a series of case studies, this volume throws such developments, crises, and the political and ethical issues they raise into sharp relief. As analyses of contrasting responses to current tensions, our individual

C. Karner (✉) • B. Weicht
University of Nottingham, Nottingham, United Kingdom

University of Innsbruck, Innsbruck, Austria

© The Editor(s) (if applicable) and The Author(s) 2016   **1**
C. Karner, B. Weicht (eds.), *The Commonalities of Global Crises*,
DOI 10.1057/978-1-137-50273-5_1

contributions demand and offer careful socioeconomic contextualization. Some of the reactions thus discussed may be described as politics of nostalgia and solidarity, which variously delineate boundaries of group membership and its associated rights, opportunities and support structures. Avoiding forms of economic reductionism we will argue that the competing reactions to our era of global markets and globalizing pressures cannot be deduced from their economic base in any straightforward or sufficient manner. Instead, nuanced discussions of the complex interplay of social and economic forces are required. Before turning to existing theoretical strands that facilitate such analyses, more needs to be said about what is at stake in the diverse contexts examined in our later chapters, and what they have in common.

That Which Lies Beyond Markets...

Separated by more than two centuries in time and thousands of miles in geographical space, the very different historical moments captured in the following scene-setting quotations share a common denominator. They alert us to context-specific acts of resistance against a common foe: unrestricted markets and their (perceived) social costs and dislocations. E.P. Thompson describes such resistance in his analysis of eighteenth-century English food riots and the "confrontations ... over access (or entitlements) to 'necessities'" they revealed:

> [A]lmost every eighteenth-century crowd action [was] ... informed by the belief that [people] were defending traditional rights and customs... a popular consensus as to what were legitimate and... illegitimate practices in marketing, milling, baking etc. This... was grounded upon a consistent traditional view of ... the proper economic functions... within the community, which... can be said to constitute the moral economy... An outrage to these moral assumptions, quite as much as actual deprivation, was the usual occasion for direct action. (Thompson 1991: 337; 188)

Our second quotation is taken from the *Occupy Handbook* and relates to what has been described (Brucato 2012: 77) as the "first worldwide postmodern uprising":

The rich are getting richer ... the poor are being left behind, without decent jobs, income security ... or a political voice ... The Occupy movement['s] ... cause is the reform of the political economy of global capitalism ... While there is no single platform to arise from the global movement, the main demands are clear enough: Politics in the hands of the 99 percent, not of the 1 percent that control the large corporations ... Rebuilding a mixed economy with a proper balance of markets and governments ... Shifting public funds into training and education so that young people can develop the skills needed for gainful employment ... Taxing the rich and the financial sector ... [R]ebuilding a social safety net and active labor market policies ... Reinventing ... health and education, to bring them within reach of everybody. (Sachs 2012: 466; 473)

While these two moments can certainly only be understood in their respective contexts, they both involve the discursive and institutional reassertion of a "community" that claims to be bonded by more than economic rationality, market forces and interactions. We here encounter two otherwise very different historical snippets, in which the all-too-common reduction of social life to the profit-maximizing behaviour ascribed to *homo oeconomicus* appears to run into its outer limits. And the latter in turn are invoked and insisted upon by people self-describing as members of a community allegedly defined by crucial extraeconomic dimensions, whether a shared history, ethnic, national or religious commonalities, or a cosmopolitanism of universal rights and entitlements.

At this point, and this is part of the crux of what follows, a hefty, doubledose of sociological scepticism is in order. Whilst daily life and key events in the early twenty-first century provide ample reason to be deeply concerned about the damage unfettered market forces can evidently cause, we may need to be just as wary of (some of) the "communities" invoked by some of those resisting or opposing markets. Sociologically speaking, we know that most, arguably all, communities are "imagined" (Anderson 1983), that is, they are ideologically reified constructs with often far-reaching consequences, including the discursive and institutional exclusion of perceived "others". Our critical task, then, is twofold: to be equally attentive, first, to the consequences of the growing colonization of ever-widening aspects of life by markets and, second, to the ideological naturalization (Barthes 1993: 129) of boundaries affected by most, if not all communities, arguably even those claiming to speak in universal terms.

This edited collection explores interrelated hunches, which our contributors' wide-ranging analyses will elevate to the epistemologically firmer status of social scientific hypotheses requiring further, urgent attention at our current historical juncture. The first of these hunches relates to the highly plausible possibility that the diverse phenomena examined across the following chapters indeed share the crucial dimension highlighted here: they all revolve around the fundamental ethical and political question as to what, if anything, is, can or should be outside the reaches of economic markets. Or put more emotively, we are about to examine a series of cases challenging us to consider if there may be core aspects of life—whether particular rights, entitlements, social relationships, resources or inalienable qualities such as dignity—that cannot be commodified, and hence, bought or sold, without fundamentally undermining the conditions of possibility for a potentially more just, inclusive and humane life. Needless to say, for now the jury is—and, at the outset of this interdisciplinary project, needs to be—"out" on this question. Similarly obvious is the need to disentangle the judgments, interpretations and positions captured in the following chapters from their authors' analytical commentaries on those voices. Whilst the two can, of course, and at times do overlap substantially, both their interrelationships and differences are still most helpfully portrayed in Anthony Giddens' (1984: 284) definition of the "double hermeneutic", the distinctly social scientific process of developing second-order interpretations of the preinterpreted, prelived social realities as articulated and experienced by the people whose lives we record and seek to understand. One of the implications, in the present context, of such an understanding of social scientific work is that readers should not assume a uniformity of political positions across the following chapters, or indeed between the social actors described in these chapters and the social scientists providing the second-order interpretations.

Our second hunch relates back to the confluence of historical distance and recurrence jointly, albeit inadvertently, transmitted by E.P. Thompson and the Occupy Movement. If tension between increasingly unconstrained market forces and attempts to recurb those forces indeed recurs not only synchronically, as suggested across the ensuing chapters, but also diachronically, as suggested by our two scene-setting quotations, important questions follow. Such potential historical recurrence opens the possibility of there being established, perhaps partly forgotten theoretical leads that responded to earlier periods of market-induced social change and that can now help illuminate the trials, tribulations and challenges of our globally interrelated lives in the twenty-first century. In parts of what follows, we turn to some such previous attempts to comprehend the relationship between the social and the economic in order to explore their relevance to the present. This entails an engagement with seminal contributions to economic history and economic anthropology from our current historical vantage point. If our suspicion of there being some transcontextual recurrence is thereby strengthened, then we may be justified in postulating that the interactions between markets and various self-defined communities hold a crucial analytical key for social scientists and historians, whatever their respective areas of interest. Putting this very boldly indeed, we would like to entertain the possibility that the market-versus-community trope may need to be added to some of the (heuristic) oppositions that have most enduringly shaped the social sciences, such as those between "mechanical" and "organic" solidarity, between the bourgeoisie and the proletariat, between "charismatic" and "bureaucratic" authority, between the *id* and *superego*, or between "system" and "life-world".

The analyses contained in this collection offer thought-provoking reflections on how, in the context of the here and now, people respond to current tensions between markets and communities. While defining oppositions between the political left and the right persist, of course, there, and this reflects our third hunch, can also be challenging overlaps: although the character and boundaries of "the communities" they invoke continue to differ profoundly, *in responding* to and often *rejecting* market forces and their impacts on individuals, groups, localities, areas, relationships and lives, the left and the right sometimes move on similar grounds. This is a chief reason why we propose to build a conceptual bridge from looking at markets and their social consequences to examining *competing politics of nostalgia and solidarity*. This analytical move enables a fresh understanding of contemporary politics and ideological oppositions, the profound differences as well as partial and complex entanglements of political opponents. Between them, our chapters demonstrate that a joint focus on, first, the widening reach of market forces *and*, second, on the various narratives of nostalgia and shared belonging underpinning different defensive reactions is required for such a fresh understanding to emerge.

Moral Economies, (Dis)Embeddedness, and "Double Movements"

To contextualize the following discussions, we first want to sketch three theoretical terrains—to do with the relationship between the economy and its social contexts, with (widening) commodification, and with the politics of nostalgia and solidarity respectively—within which this volume is embedded and to which it contributes. These terrains can be read against the backdrop of what Carrier and Miller (1999: 24) have described as a century-long "battle" between economics and other social sciences, a battle clearly dominated by the former, over "the academic representation of social relations". What is at stake, then, exceeds the contextual particularities illuminated by any one empirical case study. Instead, we are confronting larger questions about the relationship between economic practices and interactions on one hand, and political structures, cultural ideas, and historical contexts, on the other.

E.P. Thompson's previously-cited idea of a "moral economy" provides a first glimpse of a(n alternative) conceptualization of markets as part of something larger, rather than their conventional definition as self-contained domains subject to unalterable, universal principles and rules. This derives further plausibility from ethnographic studies of moral economies, most notably James Scott's work (1977) on Southeast Asian subsistence farmers, which point toward a locally taken-for-granted "right to survive" serving as a standard of legitimacy, and applied to the performance of political elites, that outweighs economic considerations of profit maximization. The most enduring momentum to this argumentative strand is provided by Karl Polanyi's seminal study *The Great Transformation*. First published in 1944, Polanyi's most influential work has received high-profile praise as "the most powerful critique yet produced of market liberalism" (Block 2001: xviii), for "expos[ing] the myth of the free market", revealing the inevitable and "complex intertwining of politics and economics", and for focusing on values "more basic" than the "ideology of the self-regulated market" (Stiglitz 2001: xiii; xv; xvi).

The three central ideas in Polanyi's magnum opus are of immediate relevance to the analyses contained in the present volume. The first of these is the idea of a "disembedding" of the economy and the historical schema it reveals. According to Polanyi (2001: 71; 3; 43), the "absorption" of the economy in the social system was an anthropological constant, up until the watershed brought about by the "stark utopia" of economic liberalism (and its idea of a "self-adjusting market") and the Industrial Revolution:

> [T]he change from regulated to self-regulating markets at the end of the eighteenth century represented a complete transformation in the structure of society. A self-regulating market demands … the institutional separation of society into an economic and a political sphere…Nineteenth century society, in which economic activity was isolated and imputed to a distinctive economic motive, was a singular departure. (Polanyi 2001: 74)

The second, closely related idea, which is of particular relevance to our later discussion of commodification, was Polanyi's observation (2001: 44; 75) that nineteenth-century civilization first replaced the previously dominant economic "motive of subsistence" with a new motive, that of "gain"; this entailed a radical extension of "the commodity concept", or of "objects produced for sale on the market". In this context, Polanyi postulates, three central factors of production—*labour, land* and *money*—were turned into "fictitious commodities", thereby ultimately threatening human relations and "natural habitat[s]":

> None of them is produced for sale. The commodity description of labor, land, and money is entirely fictitious. Nevertheless, it is with the help of this fiction that the actual markets for labor, land, and money are organized; these are being actually bought and sold on the market; their demand

and supply are real magnitudes… Undoubtedly, labor, land, and money are essential to a market economy. But no society could stand the effects of such a system of crude fictions … unless its human and natural substance as well as its business organization was protected against the ravages of this satanic mill. (Polanyi 2001: 76–7)

This leads to Polanyi's third central proposition, which resonates most immediately with our earlier mention of, and later elaborations on, the tensions between widening market forces and political reactions against them. This is Polanyi's concept of the "double movement", through which he seeks to explain a wide variety of social and historical phenomena that reacted against the effects of self-regulating markets and the "commodity fiction". These "countermoves"—born of the realization that "leaving the fate of soil and people to the market would be tantamount to annihilating them" (Polanyi 2001: 137)—ranged from the development of modern central banking, new legislation and "protective institutions, such as trade unions, factory laws" as well as "land laws and agrarian tariffs" (Polanyi 2001: 81; 138), all the way to the large, mutually exclusive political counterreactions to economic liberalism that were socialism and fascism, respectively. Polanyi's central point about the latter, and therefore his notion of the "double movement" overall, are echoed in our earlier-stated aim: to trace *both* the common structural contexts *and* the defining ideational differences of competing political positions. In Polanyi's case, this manifested in his observations (2001: 162; 248; 267–8) that "in a crisis 'responses' might point toward mutually exclusive solutions", that "fascism, like socialism, was rooted in a market society that refused to function", but that they differed fundamentally in "moral or religious" terms: in contrast to economic liberalism, both fascism and socialism rediscovered and accepted "the reality of society" but, crucially, they called for very different ways of re-embedding the economy; while socialism "upholds freedom", fascism's "degenerative bent" consists of a "relinquishing [of] freedom and a glorifi[cation of] power".

While the secondary literature (for example Dale 2010: 2) attests to the contemporary resonance of Polanyi's ideas in "speaking to the condition of neoliberal globalization", it also highlights weaknesses in the theoretical framework and historical schematization that define *The Great*

Transformation. Polanyi's concepts of "the self-regulating market" and "fictitious commodities" are therefore shown to be subject to contrasting uses and interpretations; his chronological order has been taken to task for overlooking the arguably much older seeds of market society; and the Marxist criticism—formulated by Maurice Godelier—of the lack of a theory of exploitation in Polanyi's work, and associated "charges of functionalism", need to be taken seriously (Dale 2010: 72–84; 132; 122).

These blind spots in Polanyi's conceptual edifice notwithstanding, subsequent, critical elaborations on it—which have famously included Mark Granovetter's (1985) social network analysis and the "new institutionalism" (for example DiMaggio and Powell 1983)—as well as on the previously-mentioned notion of a moral economy, have made considerable theoretical headway and offer important empirical insights relevant to our later discussions (also see Burawoy 2014). Thus, for example, William Booth has argued that the idea of an *embedded moral economy*, despite its intrinsic and potentially problematic "romanticism", makes two important points. First, it develops an alternative, distinctly ethical "framework, within which to think about the economy", confronting systems of production, distribution and consumption with the basic, yet all-too-widely ignored question as "to what end ... we do the things called economic"; second, Booth derives an alternative historical reading from the transformation of moral economies into market economies that is less rose-tinted about the former: instead, it illuminates the "shift from status to contract", with markets entailing a "new form of moral embeddedness" that reflected a move from a hierarchical community of ascribed subject positions and economic positions to a "society in which a certain equality and autonomy were accorded primacy". (Booth 1994: 663; 661) Fred Block has similarly observed (2003: 275) that due to Polanyi's "changing theoretical orientations", essentially a gradual distancing from Marxism that accompanied his writing of *The Great Transformation*, Polanyi "glimpses", though does not "name or elaborate" the concept of "the always embedded market economy". Jointly, these contributions condense interrelated insights that recur throughout our volume. Economic systems, including the neoliberal, rapidly globalizing variety, are "always embedded" somehow, socially, institutionally and in cultural assumptions and normative idea(l)s. A key part of our challenge, then, is to illuminate the context-specific political and ethical embeddedness of any given economy.

Also relevant are empirical studies that have gone some way toward redressing over-romanticized conceptions of moral economies. Marcel Fafchamps (1992), for instance, offers game theoretical corroboration of the thesis that peasants' self-interested economic behaviour and wider "solidarity systems", or their market transactions and moral economies, can be mutually sustaining rather than contradictory. Oliver de Sardan (1999) provides further conceptual disenchantment by showing a particular moral economy—one grounded in various cultural "logics" of gift-giving, solidarity, "predatory authority", negotiation, and "redistributive accumulation"—to underpin and reproduce corruption in Africa. The dangers of a potential neo-Orientalism in such arguments aside, they warn us of the perils of uncritically equating moral economies with equality, justice or inclusiveness. Translated into the terms of our volume, such arguments remind us not to take the claims and constructions of the politics of nostalgia to be examined here at face value; as we will see, a close examination of the solidarity structures such politics often uphold or advocate can provide the required critical purchase.

Within economic anthropology, part of Polanyi's early legacy was the formulation of a *substantivist* counterposition to the *formalist* paradigm. The latter considered profit maximization to define and exhaust all economic activity regardless of its cultural setting and historical context. Substantivists, by contrast, postulated a fundamental discontinuity between premodern ("socially embedded") economic systems and capitalist social formations, considering the tenets of (Western) economic theory to only apply to industrializing or (post) industrial societies (see Karner 2011: 122). In empirical-historical and methodological terms, one may critically reflect on the debate as follows: is the substantivist position a form of economic-cum-cultural relativism justified by the historical and anthropological records? Or, alternatively, might substantivism help perpetuate images of premodern, preindustrial "noble others"—before their assumed fall from grace and corruption by the forces of modernity—that, as James Clifford (1986) has suggested, have spurred forms of "salvage" ethnography? Powerful substantivist arguments have certainly endured, such as Marshall Sahlins' insistence (1972: 4; 39) that scarcity as defined in the modern world was only created by the "market-industrial system" and that "paleolithic techniques" had long been sufficient in meeting "the economic problem", until the fateful creation of "the unattainable: infinite needs". Yet, over time, the theoretical pendulum seemed to swing backward in a distinctly formalist direction (Dale 2010: 127).

It is against this backdrop that Maurice Bloch and Jonathan Parry's attempted synthesis (1989) of the two rival perspectives in economic anthropology can be read. Historically, Bloch and Parry argue, economic systems have combined two coexisting spheres: a "short-term transactional order" of competition and individual acquisition; and a "long-term moral order", to which the former is considered subordinate and which is articulated through discourses of social reproduction (for example of the household, the "community", or the nation). Yet, Bloch and Parry also suggest (1989: 29–30) that contemporary capitalism is arguably "entirely different" insofar as it displays a dominance of individualized economic practice that is no longer related, let alone subordinated, to a long-term, "transcendental order" of social or "cosmic" reproduction. A not entirely dissimilar argument, at least in relation to Bloch and Parry's conceptualization of noncapitalist economies, appears in Stephen Gudeman's outline of *Economy's Tension*. This refers to a defining, constitutive, yet contextually variable dialectic between markets and the realm of "mutuality". Providing conceptual momentum for our later analyses, Gudeman elaborates:

> Economy is made up of a contradiction…Shot through with … competition and mutuality, with antagonism and community, economy encompasses more than most economists … allow, and is more complex than most anthropologists realize … In part, individuals live from the competitive trade of goods, services and money … I term this mode *impersonal trade or market* … But people also live from goods and services that make, mediate, and maintain social relationships. Through *mutuality or community* things and services are secured and allocated, [through] continuing ties, such as taxation and redistribution; through cooperation in kinship groups, households, and other groupings … peo-

ple also keep what they produce and transfer it through mutual relationships. Such transfers, guided by heterogeneous values and lasting social connections, offer temporal certitude but can be violated or turn oppressive. (Gudeman 2012: 4–5)

Markets and mutualities assume different forms, explaining—in Gudeman's view—the changing and "shifting" manifestations of the dialectic that constitutes any economy. And "communities", Gudeman confirms in alerting us to the possibility of their turning "oppressive", should indeed not be reified as inevitably harmonious social units that shelter all individuals in their reach. What we thus encounter is arguably another extension of Polanyi's notion of the "double movement", here played out synchronically rather than across the large historical distances that preoccupied Polanyi in *The Great Transformation*, between the forces of marketization and various social counterreactions. In what follows, we ask how this dialectic manifests at our historical juncture and across a range of highly pertinent and heterogeneous empirical settings.

In their reflections on the turmoil on both sides of the Atlantic since 2008, Manuel Castells, João Caraça, and Gustavo Cardoso similarly emphasize (2012: 13) that "all economies are culture" before introducing another crucial variable—that of "crisis"; a systemic crisis in the economy, they argue, also implies a cultural crisis that indicates the "nonsustainability of certain values" and calls for simultaneously cultural and economic change. Without citing Polanyian literature, Castells et al. also seemingly describe an "always embedded economy". What is more, their contextualization of change as resulting from crisis inadvertently enables a further theoretical link: to Pierre Bourdieu's powerful, if little used observation (1977: 168–9) that crises transform *doxa*, or cultural "commonsense", into realms of reflection, discursive contest and politicization. How, we ask in later chapters, does this play out in the context of the current crisis, one that is indeed both economic and cultural? Which competing "moral orders", in elaboration on Bloch and Parry's terminology, are mobilized in particular empirical contexts and against the backdrop provided by current crises? Before starting our explorations of these defining questions of our era, there is more theoretical groundwork to be done.

Between "Triple Movements" and the Commodification of Everything?

Polanyi's *double movement thesis* raises the problem as to whether the "protective countermovements" reacting against the commodifying and disembedding effects of markets includes too heterogeneous a range of ideological formations and legal-structural adjustments. Gareth Dale makes this point (2010: 218–20) in relation to a particular argument that regards "campaigns to restrict immigration as 'Polanyi-esque movements of self-protection … [which supposedly] express workers' resistance to their treatment as fictitious commodities". Comparing this with other critical, though politically very different reactions to neoliberalism, Dale rightly questions if it makes "sense to lump together the alterglobalization movement with xenophobic reactionaries". Or translating this into terms even more directly relevant to the present volume: are the very different politics of nostalgia and solidarity examined in later chapters similar enough, although clearly *not* in ideological terms but perhaps in relation to the wider social dislocations they react against, to be subsumed under a singular heading?

A similar, very productive line of critical engagement with Polanyi has been opened up by Nancy Fraser's transformation of the notion of a double movement into that of a "triple movement". This implicates, first, the "marketization championed by neoliberals"; second, "social protection … [of] various forms, some savory, others unsavory"; and third, calls for "emancipation" for and by diverse groups and individuals who experience inequality and exclusion *either* in the realm of the market *or* within the social structures upheld by protectionists (Fraser 2012a: 25). Echoing Booth's observation (1994: 660) that embedded (premodern) economies also tended to be "suffused with hierarchy", Nancy Fraser returns to the previously mentioned charge of romanticism levelled against Polanyi's framework. The structural arrangements that embed markets and whose preservation or rebuilding some protectionists advocate can, as Fraser shows (2012a: 14), be steeply hierarchical and deeply exclusionary—in short, they can be the very "entrenched disparities in … status, political voice, and access to resources … [that] emancipatory movements often direct their struggles against". Acknowledging that for some among the traditionally disenfranchised markets can offer "emancipatory moments", Fraser offers a subtle, though unelaborated crossreference to Bourdieu's previously mentioned model of the consciousness-raising effects brought about by crises and some of the political reactions they spur: by "making explicit" and "subjecting to critique" the normative, traditionally hegemonic claims made by (some) protectionist movements, emancipation "transform[s] taken-for-granted doxa into an object of political contestation" and brings "matters previously immersed in what Polanyi called 'society' into ... the public sphere of civil society" (Fraser 2012a: 15). With regard to the present volume, this offers considerable methodological scope for locating and capturing the constitutive, mutually contesting forces of what indeed appear to be "triple movements" evident today.

Elsewhere, Fraser elaborates on a "neo-Polanyian" position by juxtaposing what she describes as the original "ontological interpretation" of fictitious commodification to her alternative, "structural interpretation". The former, Fraser reiterates (2012b: 7–8), is "essentialist, ahistorical and insensitive to domination" insofar as it assumes a supposedly "original condition", disregarding how in premodern social formations *land, labour and money* typically implicated hierarchical structures of inequality and exclusion (for example. in the case of feudalism, slavery and patriarchy it was the very construction of labour as a "noncommodity" that enabled institutional reproduction). By contrast, Fraser's "structural interpretation" of fictitious commodification is presented as tuned into changing and complex historical circumstances and the central role played by domination in those:

> [W]e might define fictitious commodification as the attempt to commodify the market's conditions of possibility ... [like] a tiger that bites its own tail. For structural reasons ... society cannot be commodities all the way down ... [T]he structural interpretation of fictitious commodification ... directs attention to the tendency of unregulated markets to destroy their own conditions of possibility ... It [also] reminds us that what commodification erodes is not always worth defending ... Freed from the communitarian bias of the ontological reading, the structural interpretation makes possible a more complex critique of capitalist crisis. (Fraser 2012b: 8)

Fraser's argument is powerful and pertinent to our volume. First, it alerts us to the different "strands" of the current crisis, each of which reappears in some of our later chapters: an "ecological" strand; a "financialization strand" to do with the contemporary power of "global market forces" and comparative disempowerment of even the wealthiest of nation-states; and a third "strand pertaining to social reproduction" under neoliberal conditions, as reflected in our contemporary management of "care or affective labor" (Fraser 2012b: 11; 4). Second, Fraser's insistence that the notion of "fictitious commodification", if read structurally rather than ontologically, holds a key to illuminating, and critiquing, present crises enables us to establish wider and productive conceptual bridges to other relevant scholarship—on *commodification* and its simultaneously economic and cultural significance in the early twenty-first century.

In elaboration of Polanyi's ideas concerning the commodification of land, labour and money, William Booth has observed (1994: 656) that "the magnitude of the market's reach can be measured by the extent of commodification", including the transformation of "nature and persons ... into objects of sale". Before turning to scholarship that critically engages with the personal, cultural, political and environmental implications of such widening commodification, some conceptual remarks are needed. In other words, how—and in opposition to what—have "commodities" been defined?

A relevant sociological-anthropological perspective on this is offered by a seminal collection of essays, whose editor—Arjun Appadurai—advocates a decisive analytical shift: away from a focus on commodities, conventionally understood as "objects of economic value", towards thinking about "*the commodity situation in the social life of any 'thing'* ... [*and*] *defined as the situation in which its exchangeability (past, present or future) for some other thing is its socially relevant feature*" (Appadurai 1988: 3; 13; original italics). What we encounter here is an insistence on contextualization, to avoid our interpretative complicity in reified understandings of particular objects as supposedly intrinsic commodities and to move, instead, towards an illumination of the social forces that transform various things, entities or beings into exchangeable objects in particular historical circumstances and cultural settings. In the same collection of essays, Igor Kopytoff develops the argument for understanding "commoditization as process" through an exploration of "the cultural biography of things" further:

> [T]he production of commodities is also a cultural and cognitive process: commodities must be not only produced materially as things, but also culturally marked as being a certain kind of thing. Out of the total range of things available in a society, only some … are considered appropriate for marking as commodities. Moreover, the same thing may be treated as a commodity at one time and not at another … In contemporary Western thought, we take it … for granted that … physical objects and rights to them represent the natural universe of commodities. At the opposite pole we place people, who represent the natural universe of individuation and singularization. This conceptual polarity of individualized persons and commoditized things is recent and … exceptional. (Kopytoff 1988: 64)

Kopytoff builds on this (1988: 73) by defining *culture*—here understood in Durkheimian fashion as a force that "sacralizes" and "singularizes" parts of its surroundings and materials—as a "counterdrive" to commoditization and its homogenization of (exchange) value; and in response to the obvious question as to what exactly particular social-cultural formations define as *set apart, forbidden* and hence precluded from commodification, Kopytoff includes "public lands, monuments, state art collections, the paraphernalia of political power, royal residences, chiefly insignia, [and] ritual objects". As we discover in some of our chapters, this list can easily be expanded to include, for example, water, Mediterranean islands, or the right to food as being widely asserted—in conflict with their possible or actual marketization—to lie beyond the realm of commodification.

As early as a quarter of a century ago, however, Kopytoff went on to question the likely success of such cultural struggles in an era he described with reference to "commoditization and monetization … invad[ing] almost every aspect of existence, be it openly or by way of a black market" (1988: 88). This sceptical, *kulturpessimistische* tone recurs in much of the more recent literature on commodification, in which unrestrained marketization—or the ever-widening colonization of previously noncommodified domains and "social things"—is associated with profound cultural, political and environmental crises. By comparison, a relatively optimistic position on the reach and likely outer limits of commodification emerges from Robert Bocock's argument (1993: 116) that although "consumerism has become the practical ideology ... legitimat[ing] capitalism... to millions ... [among] the affluent and the poor, both in the West and elsewhere", there are noticeable countertendencies. Bocock lists ecologists and "religious discourses... [potentially] allied with environmentalism" as the most likely opposition to the juggernaut of marketization: the world religions, he contends, can instil an attitude of "caring ... towards nature, and for providing a critique of capitalist consumption patterns ... before the damage to the planet is too great" (Bocock 1993: 117–9). With the benefit of hindsight, Bocock's relative optimism may need to be read as being a "child of its times", as articulated before some very different, infamously violent uses of religion became too prominent to miss, and as insufficiently aware of the possible commodification of the religious realm in today's "spiritual supermarket".

Articulating a more sceptical position, Fredric Jameson's seminal argument (1991) that late- or multinational, consumer-focused capitalism is characterized by the relentless commodification of previously extra-economic realms must be mentioned in this context (see Karner 2008). Jameson (1991: 36) detects a "prodigious expansion of capital into hitherto uncommodified areas", triggering a "new and historically original ... colonization of Nature and the Unconscious". This line of argument has been developed further in Zygmunt Bauman's wide-ranging analyses of the manifold implications and manifestations of such ever-widening commodification. These include, Bauman has argued (1992, 1998, 2000, 2002, 2003), our historically novel structural interpellation as consumers, rather than producers; social reproduction operating through "consumerist seduction" that instils political docility and depletes the public sphere of active citizenship; the commodification of human relationships, with formerly enduring bonds being replaced by a "best before mentality" demanding "instant gratification" from those (currently) closest to us; as well as a profound psychodynamic shift from repression and the resulting neuroses, as diagnosed in Freudian psychoanalysis, to the anomic "absence of ideals... and mental depression—... [an] inability to act ... as the emblematic malaise of our ... postmodern times" (Bauman 2001b: 43). Common to such arguments is the postulate of a profound watershed in recent history, brought about by, or at least closely associated with, the power and ever-growing reach of consumerism.

A further theoretical node, whose complexity space does not permit us to do full justice to in the present context, is provided by Jean Baudrillard. More particularly, Baudrillard's historical schema and its juxtaposition of some of the most famous economic-symbolic practices recorded by anthropologists, such as the Trobrianders' *kula* or the *potlatch* of the North-West Americas, to contemporary consumerism, enable the construction of a conceptual bridge to our third and final set of theoretical preliminaries. In Mike Gane's paraphrasing (1993: x), "for Baudrillard Marx was not sufficiently radical ... it was not use-value which should have been contrasted with exchange value, but symbolic exchange which should have been contrasted with commodity exchange ... Like Mauss, Baudrillard suggests the superiority of the symbolic order over the semiotic order (the obligation of gift over the cash nexus) while witnessing the apparent destruction of the former by the latter." Baudrillard himself summarizes this rupture between an original, now (largely) vanished symbolic order (in which individualized consumption is subordinate to, or embedded in, the larger socio-political order) and our hyperindividualized, consumerist era as follows:

> Alluding to primitive societies is undoubtedly dangerous—it is nonetheless necessary to recall that originally the consumption of goods ... does not answer to an individual economy of needs but is a social function of prestige and hierarchical distribution ... Goods and objects must necessarily be produced and exchanged ... in order that the social hierarchy be manifest. Among the Trobriand islanders (Malinowski) the distinction between economic function and sign function is radical: there are two classes of objects upon which two parallel systems are articulated—the Kula, a system of symbolic exchange founded upon circulation ... about which a social system of values and status is organised—and the Gimwali, the commerce of primary goods. In our societies this segregation has disappeared. (Baudrillard 1981: 30)

Elsewhere, Baudrillard (1993: 1) qualifies this radical historical break, stressing that although "symbolic exchange" no longer acts as the "organizing principle" of modern society, the latter is still haunted by "the symbolic"—in the form of various "radical utopias". Arguably, we here encounter a social theoretical equivalent of some of the politics of nostalgia, to which we turn next and in some of our later chapters: the proposition that our consumption-focused society is built upon a profound loss; the loss of particular kinds of "communities", which is simultaneously a loss of older (/invariably hierarchical) structures.

This can be further connected with recent literature on various antiglobalization movements. Premised on the obvious but important observation that (post)modernity and the "global empire" produce a diversity of "disenfranchised subjectivities" (Kirtsoglou 2013: 174), such scholarship has analysed how "local discontent with globalizing and homogenizing processes", the financial crises and growing inequalities (Theodossopoulos and Kirtsoglou 2013: ix) is in itself a global phenomenon; resulting antiglobalization movements implicate local actors who often use the very information technologies that sustain our era's "network society" and "space of flows" (Castells 2000) in order to imagine, and speak on behalf of, a "wider community in discontent" (Theodossopoulos 2013: 15). As we will discover, such antiglobalization-, antineoliberal discourses come in many forms, certainly not all of which offer such "subversive cosmopolitanisms". Fraser's more fine-grained distinction between "emancipation" on one hand, and both "savoury and unsavoury" forms of social protectionism, on the other, will therefore prove to be useful.

Before turning to our individual analyses, a final set of issues remains to be flagged up. "The politics of belonging," observes Nira Yuval-Davis (2006: 213), "has come to occupy the heart of the political agenda almost everywhere on the globe." Building on our engagement with the debates reviewed here, two further, interrelated questions need to be raised: first, do those seminal conceptualizations of the relationship between economics and the social, and of commodification, help illuminate the structural contexts, out of which such politics of belonging have emerged? Second, how do discourses of belonging articulate and intersect with equally prominent politics of nostalgia and solidarity? While the first question will be left for our individual contributors to address, the second requires additional conceptual work, to which we turn in the final section of our introduction.

The Politics of "Community" and Nostalgia

Criticism of neoliberalism often invokes solidarity and an imagined condition (relatively) free from the pressures of market competition. More generally, invocations of "community" are a crucial feature of—or, more accurately, a reaction to—modernization and capitalist development. Bauman (2001a: 1–2) locates such communities' strength in the creation of perceived safety in a hostile world. The changes of modernity, by contrast, are experienced as alienating individuals from each other and their wider groups, as an ethic of individualization, a "duty to oneself" (Beck and Beck-Gernsheim 2001: 38), has arguably replaced a historically older reliance on social networks. Several aspects comprise the discursive construction of "community". In a discussion of the "imagined traditional community" typically thought to be threatened and in demise, Jane Jones (2008: 34) demonstrates that ideas of rurality, for example, reinforce the symbolic power of community. The rural is identified with the safety of close and enduring social relations. Most famously, Tönnies's definition of *Gesellschaft* as "formed and fundamentally conditioned by rational will" is contrasted to such (imagined) communities, *Gemeinschaften*, "in which natural will predominates" (1955: 17). This opposition between modern (bureaucratic, capitalist) societies to purportedly primordial communities also resonates in Thompson's (1991: 85) account of local struggles against capitalist development, showing people to be "defending their own modes of work and leisure … rituals … satisfactions and view of life". While local communities may thus often be seen as answers to contemporary risks and pressures, Manuel Castells helpfully introduces more nuance: such communities are indeed "defensive reactions against the impositions of … uncontrollable, fast-paced change. They do build havens, but not heavens." (Castells 1997: 64).

It has become commonplace to argue that the "traditional family" and communities are threatened by economic developments that define our current era of globalization (for example Robertson 1995: 30). In such accounts "community" is constructed as an ideological extension of family, and the neighbourhood in which community happens as an extension of people's homes, both providing safety and comfort (for example Bauman 2004: 61). "Community" thus reflects a moral ideal, an image of "the good society", often constructed in opposition to the market and presumed to require altruism and mutual responsibility (Firth 2007; Jones 2008; Nisbet 1966). The positive connotations triggered by "community" are imagined as reminders of a better past (for example de Certeau et al. 1998: 142). Political projects building on such taken-for-granted notions have been shown to often be "constructed defensively in relation to outside threats" (Sprigings and Allen 2005: 407). Importantly, such projects can assume rather different forms. For example, while Barrera (2008) sees particularly the church and theological ethics as moral counterweights to the individualizing market, Dench et al. (2006: 232) propose a general rediscovery of "small groups as a source of civic virtues" (that is, families and localities).

Discourses of community thus often implicate nostalgic idealizations of the past, a myth that "bring[s people] together and reinforce[s] social solidarity" (Coontz 1992: 6). This needs to be understood in relation to present circumstances found wanting, hostile, or atomizing, whether in the context of the "retreat of tradition and custom" (Giddens 1998: 36) or the displacement of "kinship support" by "impersonal welfare provisions" (Dench et al. 2006: 4). However, such nostalgia sits uneasily with the counterrealization that "the pre-industrial family was a union born of necessity and compulsion" (Beck and Beck-Gernsheim 2001: 129–130). In the US context Coontz (1992: 9) similarly demonstrates that the idealized image of (white, middle class) families is "an ahistorical amalgam of structures, values, and behaviors that never co-existed in the same time and place".

While nostalgic idealizations of "community" provide the possibility of counterimages to forces of individualization and commodification, literature on nostalgia reveals additional features. Feelings and expressions of nostalgia rest on a longing for a better situation and a perceived ideal which, discursively, is tied to the past. Derived from this, nostalgia entails feelings of loss and decline in the face of societal changes. Nostalgia, describing both an individual psychological disposition (Zhou et al. 2012; Pourtova 2013) and a social configuration (Bookman 2008; Mand 2006) can fuel both resistance to change, for example in organisational contexts (McDonald et al. 2006; Strangleman 2012; Green et al. 2011) or by contrast, be vital for progressive social transformation (Brenner and Haaken 2000: 334). Looking at its respective foci more closely, nostalgia's discursive and affective characteristics revolve around the imagination of temporal distance and spatial displacement (Boym 2001). The temporal dimension as a yearning for the past can relate to idealizations of concrete periods, such as the phenomenon of postcommunist nostalgia (Todorova and Gille 2010; Hann 2012; Bartmanski 2011). More often, however, the temporal relates to undefined periods, revealing mythical constructions of a past that never was but that is juxtaposed to the insecurities and threats of the present (for example Boym 2001: 8). With regard to its spatial dimensions, nostalgia also manifests as a longing for an (exotic) "elsewhere", referring either to "anthropological places" (Augé 1995), very specific localities (for example Watson and Wells 2005), or the more generic, imagined defence of the local against the global (Massey 2007). Unsurprisingly, the earlier mentioned distinction between the rural and the urban can play an important role here. Lefebvre (2000: 190), for instance, argues that the very concept of urban society is based on an imagined historical trajectory, with "[u]rban society [seen as] rising from the ashes of rural society" (2000: 189). In relation to idealizations of "old urban working class communities" imagined to have resembled rural networks, Williams (1973: 289) argues that the contrast between country and city "is one of the major forms in which we become conscious of … our experience and of the crisis of our society". Overall, Alleyne's (2002) description of the construction of communities as being displaced in time and space shows the temporal and the spatial dimensions of nostalgia to be intertwined. While nostalgia is a longing for another time and space that evade modernity's pressures and challenges, it also includes an element of recognition of the impossibility of this endeavour. As such, nostalgia can be described as an impossible utopia situated in the past (for example Rubenstein 2001: 4).

As already mentioned, intrinsic to such nostalgic imaginations are feelings of personal and social loss and the criticism of (perceived) societal decline they articulate (for example Sprigings and Allen 2005). This suggests a close link between the discursive construction of "community" and the experience of melancholia (for example Tate 2007: 3). Nostalgia thus expresses a feeling of homelessness, of insecurity and the desire for certainties and a refuge (Duyvendak 2011). In this edited volume we understand nostalgia in its potential to reveal collective uneasiness with existing circumstances. Nostalgia's temporal focus on the past entails a critique of social change and is therefore a criticism of the situation *in situ* (Duyvendak 2011), revealing a loss of faith in the notion of progress (for example Pickering and Keightley 2006) and in existing social institutions. Yet, the social critique implicit in nostalgia need not be singularly preoccupied with the past only (for example Beck 1998: 34). Instead, nostalgia can spur new definitions of community and create solidarity. For our investigations, nostalgia's potential in formulating or channelling social critique, thus sometimes acting as a "necessary myth" (Bonnett 2010), is particularly important. Or, in Fraser's earlier-quoted terminology, we need to interrogate if and how nostalgia can drive "emancipation" rather than (intrinsically conservative, often steeply hierarchical) "social protectionism".

Longing for other times and places does of course not automatically entail critical social engagement, as shown, for example, by nostalgia's uses to consumer capitalism (Özyürek 2006; Smith et al. 2011). This, then, raises the question if nostalgia includes a *potential* for social critique and a yearning for inclusive solidarity, how can such a progressive politics of nostalgia crystallize? In this respect, the distinction between two different kinds of nostalgic expression is helpful. In a discussion of nationalist nostalgia, Boym (2001; also see Duyvendak 2011) separates *restorative-* from *reflective nostalgia*: the former constitutes an "antimodern mythmaking of history", through which people imagine a romanticized past ideal and argue for its revival. Conversely, reflective nostalgia, according to Boym, self-critically reconstructs select elements of the past. It is this latter version that offers the potential for progressive interventions in the here and now. This second, reflective form of nostalgia includes elements of comparison with (perceived) contemporary injustices and can therefore be characterized as utopian rather than melancholic (Pickering and Keightley 2006). The longing for community and its solidarity structures is thus intrinsically ambiguous, insofar as a "community" can be a much-needed counterforce to atomizing commodification as much as a reactionary mechanism of exclusion. Put differently, the meanings, manifestations and social effects of both "community" and nostalgia can only be understood in specific contexts. What is more, nostalgia's intrinsic ambivalence leads to it being embraced by both conservative and progressive forces, while at the same time it is rejected by others on both the right and the left for its potential anti-modernism (Bonnett 2010). Several of our chapters touch on the potential of certain nostalgic discourses to productively use historical narratives in the service of emancipatory interventions. Parts of the present volume thereby explore *how*—discursively and organizationally—such "productive nostalgias" (Blunt 2003) capitalize on imagined and idealized versions of the past to evaluate (see Hutcheon 1998) and respond to the present, making use of a "retrospective utopia" (Velikonja 2009). Boym (2001) describes such uses of the past to imagine a different, more just future as "creative nostalgia" (as opposed to "prefabricated nostalgia").

The recurring issues meandering through this book therefore include a key question raised by Brenner and Haaken (2000), namely how to distinguish between regressive and progressive elements of utopian nostalgia; or, in bell hooks' terms (1990: 147), how to separate a mere longing for times gone past from a "remembering that serves to illuminate and transform the present". Boym summarizes nostalgia's possibilities and ambivalences by pointing towards the "different turns" it can take: the past may "increase emancipatory possibilities ... offering multiple imagined communities and ways of belonging that are not exclusively based on ethnic or national principles. [Yet, i]t can also be politically manipulated through ... practices of national commemoration with the aim of re-establishing social cohesion, a sense of security and an obedient relationship to authority." (Boym 2001: 42) As some of our contributors show, both these reactions can spur discursive and practical interventions in times of hyper-commodification. Identifying their shared target(s) of critique, while illuminating their very different ideological trajectories, ranks amongst our chief aims.

In summary, the processes of ever-widening and expanding commodification are met by various communal attempts of embedding and re-embedding markets and by politics of nostalgia and solidarity. Having sketched the bodies of literature, to which our volume contributes, let us conclude this introduction with a brief anticipation of the discussions of these three dimensions of the commonalities of crises that are offered by the following individual contributions.

The theoretical framing provided in this introduction is followed by four contributions that explore the dimensions and limits of marketization and commodification. Frédéric Moulène explores the political dimension of this discussion with an examination of how marketization has gained support in France, even though the country has historically been amongst the most reluctant to embrace neoliberalism. The starting point to Moulène's reflections is the socialist government's recent *Responsibility and Solidarity Pact*, which provides generous tax cuts to companies in return for their contributions to job creation. The chapter builds on Polanyian theoretical concepts to develop an original analysis of political communication in the wider context of pertinent French experiences and debates.

Barbara Samaluk's chapter contextualises postsocialist, central and eastern European labour migration to the UK within their broader histories in order to explore how neoliberal restructuring has reshaped subjectivities to impose *the work ethic* and how this affects migrant workers' strategies in the UK. Samulak's comparative perspective exposes how distinctive histories and different, national neoliberalization processes inform Polish and Slovenian migrant workers' strategies of (self)disciplining and resistance.

Questions of rights and agency are also central to Julia O'Connell Davidson's critical examination—through "the lens of slavery"—of Nancy Fraser's marketization/social protection/emancipation schema. With her meticulously researched accounts of transatlantic slavery or, more accurately, of both abolitionist and proslavery discourses at the time, as well as of extreme exploitation and the antislavery movement today, Julia O'Connell Davidson adds a vital *longue durée* perspective to our volume. Her chapter thereby combines historical depth with extraordinary timeliness, whilst offering further theoretical refinement in the process.

Theoretical refinement is also provided by Bernhard Weicht's exploration of the possibilities and limits for commodification processes, focusing specifically on recent policy changes to the elderly care systems in four European countries. Basing his discussion on very different political and institutional contexts enables Weicht to identify the moral and social challenges to the marketization of inherently human activities. The chapter thereby emphasises the characteristics and specificities of moral economies within the Polanyian concept of fictitious commodities.

The volume then continues with four contributions that examine reactions of and within communities and attempts at (re-)embedding markets. This section begins with a theoretically focused chapter by John Holmwood, which—adopting a strategy of conceptual "provincializing"—reveals *race* as a lacuna in Polanyian and neo-Polanyian scholarship. Alongside its wide-ranging theoretical reflections, Holmwood's discussion is extraordinarily timely, engaging with US "race relations" and the current "asylum crisis" in large parts of Europe, as well as with wider currents of marketization.

This is followed by Giorgos Bithymitris' ethnographic study of the biographical narratives and everyday identifications amongst workers and the unemployed in deindustrialized and acutely crisis-stricken West Piraeus. Against the backdrop of Greece's severe socioeconomic crisis and the growing popularity of the extreme right, Bithymitris examines the reconstruction of workers' identities and the competing and changing national- and occupational self-images in a former "working-class citadel" west of Athens.

In a chapter focused on Austria, a national context that still ranks amongst the comparatively more affluent and structurally resilient, Christian Karner examines diverse public discourses formulated in the context of the global and European economic crises since 2008 and their local impact; the economy's perceived "disembedding" and hyper-commodification are shown to lie at the heart of current Austrian concerns, further entrenching a clash between nationalist nostalgia and inclusive multiculturalism respectively.

We end this section with a chapter by José López, in which he builds on his research on the human right to food to offer a critical and highly productive re-engagement with Polanyi's opposition between "embeddedness" and "disembeddedness". López's conceptual refinement of (neo-) Polanyian scholarship and its defining opposition revolves around a crucial, second dimension of "embeddedness": the question of individuals' social and moral recognition as fully participating members of a political community or, conversely, of their exclusion from it.

The third group of contributions then focuses on various types of reactions against commodification and marketization processes, by exploring the competing politics of nostalgia and solidarity. In a timely contribution with a very local focus, Tim Devos, Bruno Meeus and Seppe De Blust examine the multiple and contradictory ways in which nostalgia is mobilized by various actors involved in the redevelopment of a former slaughterhouse area in the Antwerp neighbourhood "den Dam". By exploring the political strategies of both institutional politics and local social movements the authors provide an insightful demonstration of the meanings which the concepts of nostalgia and authenticity can acquire.

This is followed by Bernhard Forchtner's analysis of a discourse of environmental crises by the British National Party. While both environmental crises and the rise of the far right have been extensively discussed, academic and public debates have seldom asked how the environment is appropriated by contemporary far-right actors, for example through nostalgically constructing "rural harmony" and "communal purity" in attacks on commodification and the logic of the market.

Raimundo Frei then examines "modalities of nostalgia" by means of a generational approach in Chile and Argentina. Based on narrative interviews among two age groups, the chapter reveals how different collective templates of nostalgia are employed in life stories when linking public memories of authoritarian dictatorships to current insecurity and renewed criticism of neoliberal policies by the last wave of youth political activism.

The rallying calls during the Egyptian Revolution of 2011 were "Bread, Freedom, Social Justice", which resonated with most of the Egyptian population who had suffered under the Mubarak regime. The Muslim Brotherhood and the Salafi movement gained widespread support partly due to their pledge to social welfare provision. These movements, based on a particular interpretation of Islam, also uphold the principles of Islamic Finance (a fiscal system based on Shari'a law). In her chapter, Amal Treacher Kabesh explores what motivated Egyptian citizens to endorse these movements, including widespread nostalgia and perceptions of this alternative financial system as resisting international capital and corruption.

In our epilogue we then bring these perspectives back together and discuss the implications of the various analyses for both political discourses and theoretical conceptualizations.

In this introduction we have covered large conceptual terrains that stretch from "moral economies", the "always embedded economy", "double-" and "triple movements", to (hyper-) commodification, and the politics of nostalgic communities. While these inter-related concepts and the social realities they depict provide the shared context to all our chapters, our respective contributors set themselves different empirical tasks that demand different theoretical foci, methodological approaches, and conceptual emphases. Common to all of them is the realization of how much there is at stake, politically and ethically, in the complex intertwining of the social and economic forces that are shaping the early twenty-first century. As we are writing these closing lines, news headlines report that the global economic prognoses for the year(s) ahead are again more pessimistic than a recent and rare moment of (post-crisis) hope had led us to believe. At the same time, there is much talk about what, if anything, can and should temper the worst effects of economic crises, marketization, and austerity. And all along we have been witnessing the renewed salience of both neo-nationalist politics and of, at times, strongly discriminatory networks of social solidarity, within which ethnic, religious or national "others" are constructed as less deserving than the imagined in-group. This volume is an attempt to contextualize and understand particular manifestations of some of the defining pressures and phenomena of our era. Such understanding, in turn, is a necessary precursor to being able to decide how to best respond to those pressures and phenomena.

References

Alleyne, B. (2002). An idea of community and its discontents: Towards a more reflexive sense of belonging in multicultural Britain. *Ethnic and Racial Studies, 25*(4), 607–627.

Anderson, B. (1983). *Imagined communities*. London: Verso.

Appadurai, A. (1988). Introduction: Commodities and the politics of value. In A. Appadurai (Ed.), *The social life of things* (pp. 3–62). Cambridge: Cambridge University Press.

Augé, M. (1995). *Non-places: Introduction to an anthropology of supermodernity.* London: Verso.

Barrera, A. (2008). Globalization's shifting economic and moral terrain: Contesting marketplace mores. *Theological Studies, 69*(2), 290–308.

Barthes, R. (1993 [1972]). *Mythologies.* London: Vintage Classics.

Bartmanski, D. (2011). Successful icons of failed time: Rethinking post-communist nostalgia. *Acta Sociologica, 54*(3), 213–231.

Baudrillard, J. (1981). *For a critique of the political economy of the sign.* St. Louis: Telos.

Baudrillard, J. (1993). *Symbolic exchange and death.* London: Sage.

Bauman, Z. (1992). *Intimations of postmodernity.* London: Routledge.

Bauman, Z. (1998). *Globalization.* Cambridge: Polity.

Bauman, Z. (2000). *Liquid modernity.* Cambridge: Polity.

Bauman, Z. (2001a). *Community.* Cambridge: Polity.

Bauman, Z. (2001b). *The individualized society.* Cambridge: Polity.

Bauman, Z. (2002). *Society under siege.* Cambridge: Polity.

Bauman, Z. (2003). *Liquid love.* Cambridge: Polity.

Bauman, Z. (2004). *Identity.* Cambridge: Polity.

Beck, U. (1998). *Democracy without enemies.* Cambridge: Polity.

Beck, U., & Beck-Gernsheim, E. (2001). *Individualization.* London: Sage.

Bloch, M., & Parry, J. (1989). Introduction. In J. Parry & M. Bloch (Eds.), *Money and the morality of exchange* (pp. 1–32). Cambridge: Cambridge University Press.

Block, F. (2001). Introduction. In K. Polanyi (Ed.), (2001 [1944]). *The great transformation* (pp. xviii–xxxviii). Boston: Beacon Press.

Block, F. (2003). Karl Polanyi and the writing of the 'The great transformation'. *Theory and Society, 32*(3), 275–306.

Blunt, A. (2003). Collective memory and productive nostalgia: Anglo-Indian homemaking at McCluskieganj. *Environment and Planning D: Society and Space, 21*(6), 717–738.

Bocock, R. (1993). *Consumption.* London: Routledge.

Bonnett, A. (2010). *Left in the past: Radicalism and the politics of nostalgia.* New York: Continuum.

Bookman, A. (2008). Innovative models of aging in place: Transforming our communities for an aging population. *Community, Work & Family, 11*(4), 419–438.

Booth, W. J. (1994). On the idea of the moral economy. *The American Political Science Review, 88*(3), 653–667.

Bourdieu, P. (1977). *Outline of a theory of practice.* Cambridge: Cambridge University Press.

Boym, S. (2001). *The future of nostalgia.* New York: Basic Books.

Brenner, J., & Haaken, J. (2000). Utopian thought: Re-visioning gender, family and community. *Community, Work & Family, 3*(3), 333–347.

Brucato, B. (2012). The crisis and the way forward: What we can learn from Occupy Wall Street. *Humanity & Society, 36*(1), 76–84.

Burawoy, M. (2014). Sociology as a vacation: Moral commitment and scientific imagination. *Current Sociology, 62*(2), 279–284.

Carrier, J. G., & Miller, D. (1999). From private virtue to public vice. In H. Moore (Ed.), *Anthropological theory today* (pp. 24–27). Cambridge: Polity.

Castells, M. (1997). *The power of identity.* Oxford: Blackwell.

Castells, M. (2000). *The rise of the network society.* Oxford: Blackwell.

Castells, M., Caraça, J., & Cardoso, G. (2012). The cultures of the economic crisis: An introduction. In M. Castells, J. Caraça, & G. Cardoso (Eds.), *Aftermath: The cultures of the economic crisis* (pp. 1–14). Oxford: Oxford University Press.

Clifford, J. (1986). On ethnographic allegory. In J. Clifford & G. Marcus (Eds.), *Writing culture* (pp. 98–121). Berkeley: University of California Press.

Coontz, S. (1992). *The way we never were: American families and the nostalgia trap.* New York: Basic Books.

Dale, G. (2010). *Karl Polanyi.* Cambridge: Polity.

De Certeau, M., Giard, L., & Mayol, P. (1998). *The practice of everyday life* (Vol. 2). Minneapolis: University of Minnesota Press.

de Sardan, O. (1999). A moral economy of corruption in Africa? *The Journal of Modern African Studies, 37*(1), 25–52.

Dench, G., Gavron, K., & Young, M. (2006). *The New East end.* London: Profile Books.

DiMaggio, P., & Powell, W. (1983). 'The iron cage revisited': Institutional isomorphism and collective rationality in organizational fields. *American Sociological Review, 48*, 147–160.

Duyvendak, J. W. (2011). *The politics of home.* New York: Palgrave Macmillan.

Fafchamps, M. (1992). Solidarity networks in preindustrial societies: Rational peasants with a moral economy. *Economic Development and Cultural Change, 41*(1), 147–174.

Firth, A. (2007). Transcending the 'merely material': Secular morality and progressive politics. *History of the Human Sciences, 20*(1), 67–81.

Fraser, N. (2012a). *Marketization, social protection, emancipation: Toward a neo-Polanyian conception of capitalist crisis.* http://sophiapol.hypotheses.org/files/2012/02/Texte-Nancy-Fraser-anglais.doc. Accessed 22 July 2013.

Fraser, N. (2012b). *Can society be commodities all the way down?* Working Papers Series, Fondation Maison des sciences de l'homme. http://halshs.archives-ouvertes.fr/docs/00/72/50/60/PDF/FMSH-WP-2012-18_Fraser2.pdf. Accessed 22 July 2013.

Fukuyama, F. (1992). *The end of history and the last man.* London: Hamish Hamilton.

Gane, M. (1993). Introduction. In J. Baudrillard (Ed.), *Symbolic exchange and death* (pp. viii–vxii). London: Sage.

Giddens, A. (1984). *The constitution of society.* Cambridge: Polity.

Giddens, A. (1998). *The Third Way.* Cambridge: Polity.

Granovetter, M. (1985). Economic action and social structure: The problem of embeddedness. *American Journal of Sociology, 91*(3), 481–510.

Green, J., Durand, M. A., Hutchings, A., & Black, N. (2011). Modernisation as a professionalising strategy: The case of critical care in England. *Sociology of Health & Illness, 33*(6), 819–836.

Gudeman, S. (2012). *Economy's tension: The dialectics of community and market.* New York: Berghahn.

Hann, C. (2012). Transition, tradition, and nostalgia: Postsocialist transformations in a comparative framework. *Collegium Antropologicum, 36*(4), 1119–1128.

hooks, b. (1990). *Yearning: Race, gender, and cultural politics.* Boston: South End Press.

Hutcheon, L. (1998). *Irony, nostalgia, and the postmodern.* http://www.library.utoronto.ca/utel/criticism/hutchinp.html. Accessed 10 Oct 2013.

Jameson, F. (1991). *Postmodernism, or the cultural logic of late capitalism.* London: Verso.

Jones, J. (2008). 'The good old days': In-migration, social control and the decline of the 'imagined' community in a North Wales market town. *Community, Work & Family, 11*(1), 19–36.

Karner, C. (2008). The market and the nation: Austrian (dis)agreements. *Social Identities, 14*(2), 161–187.

Karner, C. (2011). *Negotiating national identities.* Farnham: Ashgate.

Kirtsoglou, E. (2013). Conclusion: United in discontent. In D. Theodossopoulos & E. Kirtsoglou (Eds.), *United in discontent* (pp. 168–179). New York: Berghahn.

Kopytoff, I. (1988). The cultural biography of things: Commoditization as process. In A. Appadurai (Ed.), *The social life of things* (pp. 64–91). Cambridge: Cambridge University Press.

Lefebvre, H. (2000). *Everyday life in the modern world*. London: Continuum.

Mand, K. (2006). Social relations beyond the family? Exploring elderly South Asian women's friendships in London. *Community, Work & Family, 9*(3), 309–323.

Massey, D. (2007). *World city*. Cambridge: Polity.

McDonald, R., Warring, J., & Harrison, S. (2006). At the cutting edge? Modernization and nostalgia in a hospital operating theatre department. *Sociology, 40*(6), 1097–1115.

Nisbet, R. (1966). *The sociological tradition*. London: Heinemann.

Özyürek, E. (2006). *Nostalgia for the modern: State secularism and everyday politics in Turkey*. Durham: Duke University Press.

Pickering, M., & Keightley, E. (2006). The modalities of nostalgia. *Current Sociology, 54*(6), 919–941.

Polanyi, K. (2001[1944]). *The great transformation: The political and economic origins of our time*. Boston: Beacon Press.

Pourtova, E. (2013). Nostalgia and lost identity. *Journal of Analytical Psychology, 58*(1), 34–51.

Robertson, R. (1995). Glocalization: Time-space and homogeneity-heterogeneity. In M. Featherstone, S. Lash, & R. Robertson (Eds.), *Global modernities* (pp. 25–44). London: Sage.

Rubenstein, R. (2001). *Home matters: Longing and belonging, nostalgia and mourning in women's fiction*. New York: Palgrave.

Sachs, J. D. (2012). Occupy global capitalism. In J. Byrne (Ed.), *The occupy handbook* (pp. 462–474). New York: Back Bay Books.

Sahlins, M. (1972). *Stone age economics*. New Brunswick: Transaction.

Scott, J. (1977). *The moral economy of the peasant*. New Haven: Yale University Press.

Smith, R. J., Heley, J., & Stafford, I. (2011). Woolworths and Wales: A multi-dimensional analysis of the loss of a local brand. *Sociological Research Online, 16*(1). doi:10.5153/sro.2284.

Sprigings, N., & Allen, C. (2005). The communities we are regaining but need to lose: A critical commentary on community building in beyond-place societies. *Community, Work & Family, 8*(4), 389–411.

Stiglitz, J. E. (2001). Foreword. In K. Polanyi (2001 [1944]), *The great transformation* (pp.vii–xvii). Boston: Beacon Press.

Strangleman, T. (2012). Work identity in crisis? Rethinking the problem of attachment and loss at work. *Sociology, 46*(3), 411–425.

Tate, S. (2007). Translating melancholia: A poetics of Black interstitial community. *Community, Work & Family, 10*(1), 1–15.

Theodossopoulos, D. (2013). Introduction: United in discontent. In D. Theodossopoulos & E. Kirtsoglou (Eds.), *United in discontent* (pp. 1–19). New York: Berghahn.

Theodossopoulos, D., & Kirtsoglou, E. (2013). Editors' preface. In D. Theodossopoulos & E. Kirtsoglou (Eds.), *United in discontent* (pp. ix–ix). New York: Berghahn.

Thompson, E. P. (1991). *Customs in common*. London: The Merlin Press.

Todorova, M., & Gille, Z. (2010). *Post-communist nostalgia*. Oxford: Berghahn.

Tönnies, F. (1955). *Community and association*. London: Routledge.

Velikonja, M. (2009). Lost in transition: Nostalgia for socialism in post-socialist countries. *East European Politics and Societies, 23*(4), 535–551.

Watson, S., & Wells, K. (2005). Spaces of nostalgia: The hollowing out of a London market. *Social & Cultural Geography, 6*(1), 17–30.

Williams, R. (1973). *The country & the city*. London: Chatto & Windus.

Yuval-Davis, N. (2006). Belonging and the politics of belonging. *Patterns of Prejudice, 40*(3), 197–214.

Zhou, X., Wildschut, T., Sedikides, C., Chen, X., & Vingerhoets, A. (2012). Heartwarming memories: Nostalgia maintains physiological comfort. *Emotion, 12*(4), 678–684.

France in Times of the "Responsibility and Solidarity Pact": "Neoliberal Normalization" or a Laboratory of New Resistance?

Frédéric Moulène

It is worth asking whether Karl Polanyi (2001 [1944]) would have seen the "Conservative revolution" initiated by Ronald Reagan in the United States and Margaret Thatcher in Great Britain in the early 1980s as a new phase of "disembedding". If this new economic agenda was exported to the European continent thereafter, but at different speeds and rarely explicitly, the French example is particularly interesting. Indeed, France has been known for its mixed-economy model since at least World WarII: in this country, the *trente glorieuses* were probably made easier by a skilful blend of capitalism and economic planning, with big state-owned companies and a welfare system almost as generous as the Nordic ones. However, France has not been spared neoliberal changes, as shown, for instance, by a shifting focus on high profits and macroeconomic balances in 1983, a first wave of privatizations in 1986 and a second one at the end of François Mitterrand's era; and by gradual flexibility measures on the labour market and pension reforms since 1993. Lastly, the national stage has been dominated by a policy shift in favour of reinforced budgetary discipline and competitiveness, known as the "Responsibility and Solidarity Pact" advocated by François

F. Moulène (✉)
University of Strasbourg, France

© The Editor(s) (if applicable) and The Author(s) 2016   **35**
C. Karner, B. Weicht (eds.), *The Commonalities of Global Crises*,
DOI 10.1057/978-1-137-50273-5_2

Hollande, from the Socialist Party in the Fifth Republic. This political milestone has been largely denounced by his party's left wingers, reflecting a climate of tension similar to the rifts within New Zealand's Labour Party in the mid-1980s, or those experienced by Britain's or Germany's Social Democrats ten years later (Halimi 2006). France—often seen as the most reluctant country to embrace free-market policies—seems to get closer to the neoliberal model or at least to what Anthony Giddens (2000) has called the "Third Way". My aim here is not just to trace the extension of the market's scope in French society. I propose to look at this issue from the perspectives of a critical discourse analysis and neo-Polanyian studies (Moulène 2015), in order to ask: how has this change crystallized rhetorically, how is it justified and argued for in the case of the "pact" in question? Do we find in relevant political speeches evidence of Polanyi's double movement (that is, marketization and protective countermovements)? Do both appear at the same time and in the same kinds of speeches? If so, how does such rhetoric handle the risk of being seen as contradictory and thereby losing credibility? And can it be shielded from such a charge?

These political risks and questions are particularly pertinent now that France's main parties are more divided and less popular than ever, facing pressures from different forces on opposite ends of the political spectrum. The first one is the National Front, among the most powerful far-right parties, which set off a political earthquake by coming out ahead in the last European elections in France; the other source of pressure is being exerted by a recent alliance between the declining Communist Party and the new Left Party (that is, the "Left Front"). In this context, further questions arise: to what extent is there evidence of "nostalgia" for an idealized past, more specifically, for the era of Keynesian-Fordist state regulation? Do these mutually opposed forces, the far left and the extreme right, overestimate the violence of marketization? Do they foster, in their own agendas, other sources of oppression? And are they able to point toward what Nancy Fraser calls "emancipation" (knowing that social disruption does not just come from markets)? To address these questions, I examine a wide range of pertinent political speeches to discuss the issue, indirectly highlighted by Polanyi, of language performativity (Austin 1962; Brisset 2012) in economic realms. After outlining the national political context, I successively investigate how the government defends its policy against the charge of "a neoliberal shift", and what kinds of discursive resistance the other groups formulate.

The Responsibility and Solidarity Pact and the Fictitious "French Exception"

The End of a Persistent Misunderstanding

France continues to be regarded as the most state-regulated country in Western Europe, and even the French elites often share this view. This has become more pronounced since the ideological watershed of the early 1980s, when Thatcher and Reagan were starting to implement their neoliberal agenda, and France took a very different path by voting in the candidate of the Socialist Party (PS), Mitterrand, supported by the communists, in May 1981. A discourse about "the French exception", often involving a systematic "comparison with neighbouring countries" (Guilbert 2011: 93) is common both in the media and in academic literature (Smith 2004[1]). A particularly striking example was provided by the British liberal weekly *The Economist* reporting on the French elections campaign of 2007. The front page of the 26 October 2006 issue rhetorically asked, "*What France needs*", suggesting a response by showing Thatcher with the French flag. The ensuing lead article was symptomatic (but far from unique, see Malm 2015) of the discourse in question:

> It will always be hard to get reforms past the gauntlet of France's street protesters ... Look across the Channel: in the 1970s Britain was suffering from declinism too. Many said that the trade unions were too strong, that reform was impossible... And yet after 1979, Margaret Thatcher showed that a determined government could shake up a sclerotic economy. The real issue is ... whether there is a Madame Thatcher who has the courage to take on vested interests. The prognosis is not encouraging ... Yet [Sarkozy] was an interventionist finance minister with no apparent love for free markets, and has recently sounded softer on the need for radical reform. ("What France needs")

---

[1] Smith (2004), professor of history, has articulated several *clichés*, in semi-journalist style, bemoaning "French dogmatism" and claiming to detect opposition to reform systematic of anti-globalization behaviour, and an alleged inability to question the national model.

Continuing along these lines, it was here argued that France, highly reluctant to embrace "marketization", would have difficulties in proceeding with neoliberal reforms that other developed countries had implemented. The article assigns responsibility to "resistance forces", namely unions and political activism, knowing that in France the right has a long-standing tradition of interventionism and the left is often compared to the British Labour Party prior to Tony Blair.

It is true that the Jacobinist tradition has left a legacy of centralization and a strong state. The French welfare system is still generous and employment laws provide a high level of social protection, therefore France's labour market is often seen as one of the most rigid of the world, diametrically opposed in this respect to the United States, Britain, Australia, Japan and Switzerland (OECD 2015). However, it is unfortunate that such texts ignore the fact that France has also been affected by the transnational, neoliberal trend since the 1970s, when Keynesianism encountered a new economic crisis. Further, French liberals had been influential even in the "Thirty Glorious Years" (Gaïti 2014)—the clearest example of this was provided by Pinay's austerity plan of 1958, which owed its name to the Minister of Finances and Economic Affairs appointed by de Gaulle at this time. But like their British counterparts, French (neo)liberals had to await the damaging consequences of the first oil shock to break the postwar consensus. In 1976, France took a monetarist turn with Prime Minister Raymond Barre, before Mitterrand's victory five years later. The latter's socialist agenda was ambitious (that is, nationalizations, general wage increases, a fifth week of annual vacation) but did not last long: in 1983 the economic situation (that is, unemployment, trade deficit and deficit spending) forced a new austerity plan and led the socialists to defeat in the 1986 legislative elections. Since that time, three rounds of privatizations (in 1986, 1993, 1997[2]) have reduced the proportion of the public sector in relation to the national economy to 2 % of GDP in 2000 compared to 21 % in 1986, and the share of the labour force employed in the sector decreased from 20 % to 2 % in the same period (Loiseau 2002:

---

[2] In 1997, the left governed France but for its new government there was no question of going back to 1981. This refutes the idea that the PS of today had not changed its agenda and resembles Labour before Blairism.

3). The reforms have not spared many areas of social protection and some benefits are being eroded, although they generally remain at a high level. In this way, the introduction of a user-fee system in the national health system (*ticket modérateur*, 1983) has significantly increased patients' contributions; and a quarter of public hospital beds disappeared between 1981 and 2008 (Benkimoun 2008: 8).

Sarkozysm (2007–12) was surely not as radical as Thatcherism, but it promoted further reforms toward marketization and withdrawal of economic intervention: tax cuts for companies (*Loi de modernisation de l'économie*, 2007) and households (*Bouclier fiscal*, 2007), limitations on the right to strike (*Minimum service act*, 2007), a reform of the pension system by increasing the retirement age (2010). This political commitment to "change" was notable in Sarkozy's rhetorical strategies and "spin doctoring" (Calvet and Véronis 2008). Moreover, the conservative president built his successful campaign and policies on a denouncement of the "bad sides" of the "French exception":

France[3] is not just the country of the 35 hours law,[4] illegal immigrants, burnt-out buses and RMI.[5] ("Nicolas Sarkozy, discours à Saint-Etienne...", 2006)

It is fascinating to see how France wants to be the only one country whose taxes work. And at the same time, we look surprised when many companies decide to go abroad! ("Nicolas Sarkozy, discours à Toulouse", 2007)

At the same time, Sarkozy and the French right have always defended a "third way" between radical laissez-faire (associated with Anglo-Saxon capitalism) and statism purportedly supported by the traditional left:

---

[3] All translations are the author's.

[4] In 2000, the socialist government of Lionel Jospin adopted a measure to decrease the working week from 39 hours to 35. The principle was intended to yield a better division of labour and reduce unemployment.

[5] The Revenu Minimal d'Insertion (created in 1988 under Mitterrand) provides support for people without any income who are of working age but not entitled to access the unemployment compensation system.

This is the miracle of France which combines such an elevated vision of state and an equal passion of freedom. ("Nicolas Sarkozy, discours à Périgueux", 2006)

It would be naïve, though, to consider this speech as additional evidence of a French aversion to liberalism. Indeed, the merits of Polanyi's work include its deconstruction of the myth of a market without state intervention by "revealing the inevitable and complex intertwining of politics and economics" (Stiglitz 2001: xv). This includes the following suggestion:

> For as long as [the system of a self-regulating market] is not established, economic liberals must and will unhesitatingly call for the intervention of the state in order to establish it, and once established, in order to maintain it. (Polanyi 2001: 155).

An example of this is provided by restrictive French strike legislation aiming to protect markets from the unions' power (Moulène 1998: 2). At this point, we ought to seriously question the conventional notion that automatically assumes the state to be in opposition to companies' interests. Thus, neoliberalism does not at all involve a complete disembedding, for even Thatcherite Britain and Reaganomics knew that markets, far from emerging spontaneously, had to be organised by state intervention. In this regard, the French right's discourse on liberalism (combining the state *and* markets) seems more in touch with economic realities than the libertarian fiction (opposing market *versus* state).

Since 2012, France has been governed by the socialists again who have recently brought in the Responsibility and Solidarity Pact (RSP). This offers an opportunity to show how the French left has changed its tune about the market and the state.

From the Context to the Text of the Pact: Is French Socialism Aging?

Hollande's election as the second socialist president of the Fifth Republic has not had the same historical importance as Mitterrand's victory in 1981. However, the electoral victor of 2012 promised his voters that "now, it's time for change" (*Le changement, c'est maintenant!*), a campaign slogan clearly addressed to Sarkozy. But when he came to power, Hollande took but small steps: a weak increase of the minimal wage (+2 %) and a further increase to the RSA[6]: +10 % over five years, but the rise was, until 2014, similar to what Sarkozy had implemented (RSA 2015). At the same time, the government promised 150 000 "jobs for the future" (*Emplois d'avenir*) for young people struggling to find employment, notably in deprived areas. Meanwhile, the Solidarity Tax on wealth[7] (*Impôt de solidarité sur la fortune*) has been revised to be more redistributive and the marginal rate of taxation has increased from 41 to 45 %. But many other promises were quickly broken: in the 75 % tax plan for millionaires; there was a renegotiation of the Stability and Growth Pact with the supporters of austerity in Europe. Above all, a new pension reform has increased social security contributions (by 0.3 points from 2014 to 2017) and again extended working years required for a full pension (that is, 43 years in 2035 instead of 41.5 as before). Some of the main trade unions (CGT, FO[8]) have strongly denounced the risk of social regression, although the government stresses that it did not change the retirement age to 62, thereby resisting the conservatives' agenda. In March 2014, the socialists lost the municipal elections and Hollande decided to change the government with Manuel Valls as new Prime Minister. In socialist circles Valls is known as an unofficial leader of the party's internal right wing. Hollande had already made and announced the decision to the French on television three months earlier (that is, on 31 December 2013). As shown in a speech analysed below, the Responsibility Pact—not in the original socialist manifesto of 2012—foresees a reduction of employers' tax contributions in return for creating new jobs.[9] This policy is based on the

---

[6] The Revenu de Solidarité Active was aimed at encouraging low-income people to earn more by working while receiving welfare benefit.

[7] The ISF was created in 1981, after Mitterrand's electoral victory. It is an annual property tax for households with assets in excess of €1,300,000. (Date: 1 January 2014).

[8] The Confédération Générale du Travail (CGT), previously close to the Communist Party, still has clear left-leaning positions. By contrast, the Force Ouvrière (FO) was anti-communist during the Cold War and had cordial relations with the right but adopted a critical tone in the 1990s.

[9] Since the first days of Hollande's presidency several measures presaged fiscal exemptions to companies committed to hiring workers. (for example crédit d'impôt pour la compétitivité et l'emploi, 2012).

diagnosis that the deterioration of the French balance of trade since the early 2000s (and its negative impact on employment) is linked to labour costs, traditionally considered high in France. It is symptomatic that *Les Echos*, the daily economic newspaper, has supported the Pact, providing a comparison of French and German balances: a deficit of € 61.2 billion for France against a surplus of € 198.9 billion for Germany in 2013 (Benhamou 2014). The article explains the strength of German trade not only through its specialization on high-value-added goods (that is, their reputation for quality) but also with reference to downsizing of labour costs under G. Schröder and the Hartz plan.[10] So while French goods had been cheaper than the German ones before 2000, the latter were now 14 % less expensive. Once again, it is significant that a "comparison with neighbouring countries" is made to support a harmonization process with those and to argue for marketization (see below).

In March 2014, the MEDEF (Mouvement des Entreprises de France), the largest employers' federation and three important unions (CFDT, CFTC, CFE-CGC[11]) signed the pact, but the CGT and the FO did not. This is probably why Hollande added a "Solidarity pact" that underlines the counterobligation on the part of companies in return for tax reduction; that is, job creation and the inclusion of young people in the labour market.

We have traced the political context in which the Pact was established. It shows the deep transformations of the French Socialist party since the 1980s. In 1999, it did not support the Blair-Schröder Manifesto[12] but

---

[10] Between 2003 and 2005, Schröder based his reforms of the German labour marked on the recommendations of a commission led by Peter Hartz. In summary, this implemented a "welfare to work principle" through reduction of unemployment benefits, reinforced incentives to work and so on.

[11] The Confédération Française Démocratique du Travail, after being a "self-managed socialist movement" in the 1960s and 1970s, replaced the FO in the 1990s as the negotiating partner of employers and governments. The Confédération Française des Travailleurs Chrétiens supports the social Christian tradition and seems to be the employers' favoured partner. The Confédération Générale des Cadres (CFE-CGC) is a moderate union for executives.

[12] Blair and Schröder agreed on the manifesto "Europe: The Third Way/Die Neue Mitte" in 1999 when they were in power. They wanted to renew the agenda of European social democracy by reconciling social justice and economic dynamism. In France, Jospin rejected this approach: "if the third way seeks to be placed between social-democracy and liberalism, I do not associate myself with comments like that." (See "Le socialisme européen", 1999: 47).

it is conceivable that Valls would do so today: he thinks that "the word *socialist* is probably obsolete and refers to an idea from the nineteenth century" (Rovan 2014). But like in Britain, where Blair's "New Labour" would not have been possible without his predecessors Neil Kinnock and John Smith, the changes of the PS started after the shift of 1983. And it is significant that the *Financial Times* (1990) recognized Mitterrand as "the monetarist of the year 1990", as recalled Loriaux (1996: 120):

> In the intervening decade, the government abolished the selective credit controls that had given the state extensive influence over the allocation of credit by banks, it created a money market that was made to function much like its liberal American and British counterparts, it established a financial futures market to rival that of Chicago, it abolished exchange controls, it cut back dramatically on the allocation of loan subsides to industry by public and semi-public financial institutions, and all the while it encouraged one of the most dramatic bull markets ever to hit the Paris stock exchange.

Surely, the sixth strongest economy in the world cannot sidestep global change altogether. And the French left has not been immune to the ideological shifts seen elsewhere, although this has often been delayed, unstable or ambiguous. Ultimately, the Responsibility and Solidarity Pact seems to complete the "normalisation process" of the PS within European social democracy.

The Pact as Discourse on Markets and Social Protection

Responsibility and Solidarity: A Coherent and Balanced Double-Movement?

Like other social domains, political life engages language. Political communication is not restricted to spreading information to citizens about new measures or particular situations. For politicians, speeches are a means of acting, of shaping their agenda, gaining trust, and being believed and followed (Charaudeau 2005: 12–17). And for Hollande's Responsibility Pact, the challenge has been crucial: after one and a half years in power without signs of success (in terms of unemployment, the budget deficit, unpopularity), Hollande had to react. We thus turn to the forms of talk the president used when he announced the Pact on 31 December 2013. Let's recall his first speech on the matter:

> I'd like to speak to you about what we have in common and what we hold most dear: namely, our country. 2013 was intense... because the government embarked on reforms to rebalance our public accounts, improve companies' competitiveness, modernize the labour market and consolidate our pensions, while taking into account the gruelling nature of some jobs. It gave priority to education ... and opened up marriage for all. But 2013 was also difficult for many of you and for the country, because the crisis proved to be longer and deeper than we ourselves had predicted ... The very state of the country justified my asking you to make an effort. I know what this represents. Taxes have become heavy, too heavy, after accumulating for many years. In 2013, unemployment remained at a high level... I repeat to you this evening: I have only one priority, only one goal, only one commitment: namely, employment! ... That's why I'm offering companies a responsibility pact. It's based on a simple principle: fewer burdens on work, fewer constraints on their activities and, in exchange, more recruitment and more industrial dialogue. I also pay tribute to the employers and unions, who at the beginning of the year had already succeeded in reaching an agreement on making employment more secure ... 2014 will also be the year of strong decisions ... Firstly, I want to reduce public spending. We must make savings wherever they're possible. And I'm certain we can do better by spending less. That goes for the state, which must concentrate on its essential missions, but also for the local authorities... and for the welfare system, our most precious asset, which must end excesses[13]—we're aware of them—and abuses, because they call into question the very idea of solidarity. We must spend less in order to reduce our deficit but also to be able, ultimately, to cut taxes. (Embassy of France 2013)

Two weeks later, the president justified his strategy at a press conference:

---

[13] Sarkozy, for his part, had strongly denounced "those who commit welfare fraud" ("Nicolas Sarkozy: discours à Périgueux", 2006).

Why this pact? Because the time has come to solve France's main problem: its production. Yes, its production. We need to produce more, and better. Action is therefore needed on supply. Yes, supply! This is not contradictory with demand. Supply even creates demand. This pact has four main dimensions. The first is continuing to reduce the cost of labour... The second dimension is giving businesses visibility. Investment is impossible if the framework is unclear or if the rules change... My wish is for modernization of corporate taxation and a reduction in the number of taxes... The third dimension of the responsibility pact is simplification. The number of regulations needs to be reduced ... The fourth dimension is what businesses do in return ... It will involve numerical targets for recruitment, employment of young people and seniors, the quality of work, training and the opening of negotiations on pay and the modernization of social dialogue. (Embassy of France 2014)

Two and a half months later, the socialist defeat at the municipal elections led Hollande to focus on the social counterpart. The Responsibility Pact is here transformed into a Responsibility *and Solidarity* Pact:

A Solidarity pact must be associated with the one for responsibility. Its first cornerstone is education, training of young people, its second one is social security, with the priority given to health, and lastly, the third one is buying power that will be obtained through tax cuts for the French by 2017 and a fast reduction of employee contributions. ("Hollande dévoile...", 2014)

With the new government put in place, Manuel Valls (instead of the unpopular Jean-Marc Ayrault) confirmed the Pact in his statements of policy intent of 8 April and 4 November:

In a globalised economy, our companies have to face global competition that gives us no respite. So we must to protect them. ... [Y]es, we will encourage firms to support R&D and innovation, to enhance the functioning of the labour market, to reduce the costs and simplify administrative procedures and to promote social dialogue at each level. With a main requirement: the companies have responsibilities towards their managers, employees and workers. They contribute to the wealth of the firms. The principle of the responsibility and solidarity pact is simple: everyone must commit to creating jobs. It is a pioneer initiative in our country: learning to dare [to be] positive and fruitful compromises. The divergence of interests is real, the key issue is not to erase this problem but rather to overcome it. That's what modernity means ... The Pact concerns solidarity and it has to improve the purchasing power of low-paid workers. The best way to achieve this is through action on social contributions so as to increase net wages. ("L'essentiel de la déclaration...", 2014)

Our country makes considerable efforts: more than €40 billion over three years to help companies, namely employers, bosses, engineers, managers, workers. This is a tremendous effort aimed at ensuring the recovery of the country. But this effort is not aimed at benefitting shareholders: it must be a vehicle for investments and employment, for job creation. ("Pacte de responsabilité: un effort à faire...", 2014)

These speeches emphasise that everybody's efforts have to converge on the priority given to employment, which is seen as a factor of economic wealth and social inclusion. The RSP is presented as coherent and balanced, and tax reductions and administrative simplifications are predicted to give more opportunities for investing and creating jobs. At the same time, business is expected to contribute to social protection by delivering guarantees in matters of training, employability and working with unions. From a Polanyian perspective, the first tendency points towards marketization (that is, smaller tax contributions, less stateregulation); but the second thrust engages social protection, knowing that without any state regulation, markets have the potential to deepen social inequalities. Therefore, in this speech, the insistence on a counterpart to marketization is not a detail but an essential element without which marketization is assumed to fail.

Responsibility Versus Solidarity: A Senseless and Dramatic Double Bind?

Even if it is still too soon to assess the outcomes of the RSP, it seems that the government has become more sceptical. In December 2014, Emmanuel Macron, the Minister of Economics, admitted a "failure" in this regard (see "Macron pointe...", 2014). And the Prime Minister conceded that "the effort has been insufficient in too many branches."("Pacte de responsabilité: Manuel Valls rappelle...", 2015).

While supporters of the RSP are themselves developing doubts on the measure, its opponents—on both ends of the political spectrum—have articulated strong criticisms, albeit ones informed by contrasting reasons. The left has been divided between a pro-RSP camp (a socialist majority) and the contra-camp, that is, the far leftwing and radical left, most of the Green party, a significant minority of *"frondeurs" within the PS*—the name invokes the "Fronde" (1648–1653), the protests against Louis XIV and the rebellious spirit of the groups involved in this period of social unrest. The socialist partisans have supported Hollande and Valls. But there are numerous dissenting voices, which corroborates the existence of a "social-liberal" split within the party. In April 2014, 41 socialist MPs refused to vote for the budget stability programme submitted by Valls to the Assemblée Nationale (Bekmezian and Bonnefous 2014) and some weeks later, the number of frondeurs rose to one hundred:

In several years, people will wonder how a left-wing government gave €41 billion to employers who constantly refuse any counterparts... In July [2014], one hundred MPs put out a call against the Manuel Valls' budget cuts. But only about twenty supported the policy of the Prime minister. Between the two groups there are some 170 deputies who are getting more and more sceptical. (G. Filoche [former labour inspector and member of the left wing of the PS], quoted in Vaillant 2014)

Valls can make all publicity stunts he wants, the reality is a massive tax grab on employees, on the middle-class (in favour of companies), at the expense of purchasing power. The reality is that money will be used for things that are not priority for France. I give you an example: the non-indexation of pensions and family allowances [author's note: more exactly, the government decided to delay rather than delete the indexation, until October 2014 instead of April of the same year (Castagnet and Rouden 2014: 8–9)] provide savings of €2 billion, but on the other side €3 billion will be given to supermarket chains, starting this year. But it is clear that ... [this] doesn't create jobs: the tax advantage ... is funded by people who can no longer consume ... It is economic nonsense and socially unacceptable. This approach has been followed in Southern Europe and led these countries to disaster. (Marie-Noëlle Lienemann, quoted in "Le Pacte de responsabilité: une 'aberration'...", 2014)

The other leftist parties responded even more strongly to the RSP. The two Green ministers, Cécile Duflot and Pascal Canfin quit the government and the majority of their party voted against the Pact with the radical left. The founder of the Left Party, resulting from a split within the PS in 2008, Jean-Luc Mélenchon stated his categorical disagreement:

> I think that it is just a fool's bargain. Mr Gattaz [the leader of the MEDEF] promised the unions ... one million jobs. What a joke! Because the French economy creates mechanically 200,000 jobs in a year, so he promised them that the sun will rise tomorrow ... I think that the approach is flawed from the start: we give something to companies and they answered, "we will see later about counterparts". (Quoted in "Pacte de responsabilité: Jean-Luc Mélenchon dénonce...", 2014)
>
> This is a right-wing policy and everybody knows that ... This is not a policy for companies but rather a policy for shareholders who are given by the state a gift of about €30 billion. But ... it does not work and will never do! Because this policy is followed everywhere in Europe and leads us to a general recession! (ibid.)

This charge utilizes a rhetorical device known as "acceptability making" (Faye 1973). The demanded guarantee of counterparts is a semantic stratagem, without which the Pact would be refused, especially by unions. Vague promises, it is argued, will not commit companies in any way, leading to repeated accusations of "corporate handouts" against Hollande that had also been levelled against previous conservative governments. However, Mélenchon seemingly contradicted himself in the two excerpts: in the first one, he denounced the "gift" to companies in general, in the second one, he argued that the RSP would favour shareholders rather than companies themselves. This shift can plausibly be interpreted as having been due to journalists' pressure who pointed out that firms created jobs, leading this leftist leader to change his rhetorical target. Lienemann and Duflot, meanwhile, criticised the one-sidedness of companies benefitting from the reduced tax while their businesses would flourish.

These speeches reflect traditional Keynesian premises, attacking the RSP because it would lead to an unfair redistribution from households to companies: in other words, that this would mean marketization *without* social protection. This criticism probably prompted Hollande and Valls to add the solidarity side of the Pact, which has not been enough to reassure its opponents on the left.

The right's response, meanwhile, was to detect a socialist turn to liberalism. Indeed, it is significant that a few conservative and centre-right leaders, particularly Sarkozy, expressed their views on the Pact. They hesitated between supporting the socialist acceptance of market competition and performing their role as opposition:

> It seems that there is a general consensus on the necessity to reduce the labour costs. ... François Hollande is just implementing Nicolas Sarkozy's policy, but with less talent, less energy and without a parliamentary majority. And a year and a half after having broken and destabilized our economy. (Baroin [Republican Senator], interviewed in "Hollande applique...", 2014)
>
> The President has strongly asserted the primacy of supply-side policy in an unprecedented way... He has understood that the reversal of the unemployment trend requires more job creation by firms, more investment and confidence in their shares ... Now, it seems to me that François Hollande is making the same policy as every social-democrat and liberal party in Europe. (Raymond Soubie [Republican and former social affairs advisor to Nicolas Sarkozy], in Chastang 2014: 8)

And Jean-Pierre Raffarin, a Republican senator, considered "this discursive change [to be] welcome ... The president is finally adopting a realistic vision of the international economic situation." Not dissimilarly, Alain Juppé, potential Republican candidate for the presidential elections in 2017, saluted the "Copernican revolution" of the left (see "Juppé estime que...", 2014).

The Pact Seen from a Polanyian Perspective: The Power and Limits of Speech

The Rhetorical Devices of the Pact-Discourse: An Ongoing Normalization of the French Debate?

The French context provides some corroboration for the claim that "current events confirm the thinking of Polanyi ... [and his] vigilance against soothing speeches on the [purported] convergence between market[s] and democracy: disembedding threatens the substance of society … [and yet] disembedding calls [forth] re-embedding [that] may take two directions: one is authoritarian, the other one is emancipatory." (Hillenkamp-Laville 2013: 20).

To fully mobilize Polanyi for an analysis of the RSP and its implications, we thus must adopt a critical position vis-à-vis claims that less regulation for companies will inevitably increase general prosperity. The Polanyian objection is that the extension of markets and a climate of *laissez-faire* is often disastrous for citizens: it is the reason why states intervene to prevent or limit the detrimental effects of market forces. This is the double movement: between marketization and social protection against economic downturns and their wider consequences (that is, unemployment, poverty, political apathy or distrust of democracy).

How can the pro-RSP speeches be situated in relation to the Polanyian paradigm? Some recurring claims and topoi warrant further commentary:

a) *The Pact as a matter of consensus*: the initiative is justified by the collective interest, national solidarity and community. "The people" are portrayed as one and the same, a united group with identical aims ("we'll need *everyone* to play an active role to win this battle"). Therefore, there is no vision of social and class antagonism, but an insistence on social partners ("employers *and* unions") agreeing. Occasionally, speakers admit to difficulties "for many" citizens without giving any detail about their social profile. Seen from this angle, there is a striking similarity between Hollande and Blair, calling for an application of Fairclough's (2000) approach to "New Labour" to the French context (Moulène 2011: 315).

b) *"Naturalization" and common sense*: some of the political speeches highlighted present the crisis as an uncontrollable, "natural" force (Fairclough 2000: 24). This involves rhetorical devices such as "naturalization", "evidentialization" and "depolitization" (Moulène 2011: 319–326), whereby speakers present the Pact as "obvious" and beyond political debate. The problem is that this presupposes a background of theoretical assumptions that Hollande does not state: it is assumed that one of the main causes of unemployment is structural rigidity (for example concerning regulations and taxes regarding the labour market), which implies a neoliberal framework; and "such [a] presupposition can be called ideological" (Fairclough 2000: 27). President Hollande thereby takes a big risk of being seen as a genuine liberal and of coming very close to Sarkozy and the right by emphasizing the "excesses" and "abuses" by the recipients of social benefits. Statements like "we're aware of them" do not leave any doubt about Hollande's suspicions.

c) *The Pact as a matter of modernisation*: a further prominent discursive feature concerns voluntarism and energy ("I want to", "strong decision"), with the government thus conveying a sense of a recovery ("rebalance", "improve", "consolidate"). There is, so the argument goes, neither an alternative ("we must make", "we have to") nor doubt as to its success ("I am certain"). This is a rhetoric of reform and modernization that is almost ubiquitous in political speech today and transcends the right/left divide (Fairclough 2000: 119–120; Moulène 2011: 253–258).

d) *The Pact as a matter of economic* and *social convergence*: we also here find a rhetorical trope of "squaring of the circle" (Fairclough 2000: 9) with Hollande, like Blair before him, presupposing compatibility between market efficiency and social justice. Although the wording may be different (Blair often used "yet also", Hollande prefers lists presented in a "both... and ..." pattern), for both economic elements precede social ones (for example Hollande mentions pensions *after* discussing budget balance and competitiveness, exactly like in the Blairist formula "enterprise as well as fairness"). "Potentially fatal contradictions" between economic power and social protection never appear in such a discourse: "It is a rhetoric of denial of expectations— things are not as they have been thought to be." (Fairclough 2000: 11) The Pact foregrounds responsibility and companies before moving on toward solidarity (for example, with households). The "social is always bracketed with [the] *economic*" (Barthes 1997: 107), as if the addition of a social element provides an "alibi", a veneer of respectability to the apparent priority given to economic purposes (Guilbert 2011: 123). An analysis of such discursive features can be complemented by the

Polanyian discussion of fictitious commodities and their negative social impact (Polanyi 2001, Karner and Weicht's introduction to the present volume). By contrast, discourse on the alleged social virtues of economic efficiency resembles proclamations of faith rather being premised on solid argument.

The economic content of the pro-Pact plea is indeed very revealing. In his political turnaround, Hollande assumed a production-driven view by asserting that "France's main problem" is "its production". What is remarkable is that he thereby endorsed, and again naturalized, J.-B. Say's law of markets by explicitly stating that "supply even creates demand". In doing so, Hollande took even more clearly the risk of being seen as neoliberal and self-contradictory. His position ventured onto dangerous ground, being pulled in different directions—its socialist label (with its emphasis on Keynesian, demand-side economics) and its apparent neoliberal change of direction. The semantic precautions taken ("this is not contradictory with demand") do not put the president out of range of the potential charge of ideological treason, all the more so as he advocated the idea that "supply even creates demand", the famous quote attributed to Say.[14] Moreover, Hollande even suggested that taxes may "cost more to collect than they contribute" (Embassy 2014). This corresponds to the *perversity thesis* defined by A.O. Hirschman as "any purpose action to improve some feature of the political, economic or social order [that is taken] to exacerbate [what] one wishes to remedy" (1991: 7). This subsumes the proposition that taxes may be unable to fulfil their objectives (*futility thesis*) or even turn against their beneficiaries (*jeopardy thesis*). While Hollande does not extend this charge to the welfare state (unlike the classical conservative position), all these discursive elements suggest an ongoing neoliberal "normalization" of the French debate. The times of France's "national exceptionism" may indeed be over.

---

[14] Many liberals (for example Ludwig von Mises 1950) state that Keynes rephrased Say in order to defend his alternative theory. The Keynesian reformulation is a fact but it is not certain that Keynes consciously tried to distort the original meaning of Say's principle.

Resistance to the Pact: Nostalgic Reaction or Emancipatory Aims?

The first pro-Pact speech put strong emphasis on key measures implemented by the socialist government, including education policy and "marriage for all" (allowing "gay marriage"). This is also comparable with "New Labour"[15]: contemporary social democrats tend to focus on reforms regarding lifestyles—personal and family issues, sexual freedom, gender equality and civic rights (Dixon 2008). But this seems to happen at the expense of economic reforms, an area in which the left has internalised many elements of neoliberalism:

> This confinement within the standard vision of economics is symptomatic of the neoliberal order, but it marks also the drama of the attempt to revive social democracy in the sense of Giddens' Third Way (1998) by promoting reforms on societal issues and endorsing the neoliberal economic agenda. It has caused widespread distrust as unemployment and social exclusion have increased. (Hillenkamp-Laville 2013: 19).

This consideration brings us closer to Fraser's attempt (2012) to develop the Polanyian framework by moving from a "double movement" to a "triple" one, involving marketization, social protection, and emancipation. The criticism Fraser addresses to *The Great Transformation* is that the latter "occult[s] non-market-based forms of injustice" or "oppressive forms of social protection". Overly simplistic readings of Polanyi posit that marketization triggers social turmoil, while social protection invariably has a positive impact. Hence, so such readings go, at the end of the "great transformation" stood the emergence of the welfare state in the twentieth century. Fraser finds fault with the over-romanticization of the past intrinsic to such readings, but also encountered among the "traditional" left and many unions that import a "nostalgia" without properly acknowledging the hierarchies and exclusions of the past and its "social

---

[15] Dixon mentions Blair's progressive discourse and policy regarding the House of Lords Act 1999 (that reduced the power of hereditary peers), devolution of the Scottish parliament (1998), new rights given to gays and lesbians (1997) in contrast with the conservative aspects of its economic measures.

protection". How, if at all, do such debates map onto forms of resistance against the RSP?

If the Pact is presented by its supporters as a necessary modernizing reform, it does not follow that its opponents refuse it on behalf of the past. This particular debate is not at all between progressives and nostalgics. However, it is true that among Hollande's and Valls' adversaries, there are prominent positions that argue against "emancipation", in Fraser's sense, opting for "social protection" instead. Le Pen's far-right discourse provides an illustration of this:

> What the government wants to do is to kill the demand so as to stimulate the supply. It is stupid. The essential question is: who is going to pay for this policy? Because if we implement compensation taxes and transfer the cost of this measure to customers, the middle-class, we will kill [companies]. And the best way to kill companies is to kill customers ... The euro causes a big competitiveness disadvantage, we have to tackle the question of unbridled competition but we need clever protectionism for that ... If we want to go back to employment, we have to stop the ultraliberal model which is ever in favour of emerging countries and bad for us. Economic patriotism, a strategic state, reducing the public deficit by facing the immigration problem, fighting fraud ... Moreover, the companies of the CAC40 [the French equivalent of the FTSE100] firms do not create jobs like the little and middle companies and also the very little ones, [but] each tax cut to the CAC40 firms will be done without any counterpart. (see "Marine Le Pen: 'Le Pacte...'", 2014)

The composite nature of this speech is remarkable: there are neoliberal references (tax cuts, denunciation of welfare fraud); some Keynesian ones (demand-side economics, a link made between RSP and austerity, state regulation); a distinction between (affluent) multinational companies and small firms (presumed to be under threat); overall, a mix of the political agendas of the right and the radical left, with the latter often criticizing the impact of the strong euro on trade and calling for protectionist measures. But above all, Le Pen's interpretation includes anti-immigration rhetoric even when she is just asked about economic issues. In Fraser's terminology, this anti-Pact discourse shows little, if any, evidence of an emancipatory thrust. According to Fraser, "social protection commands support in various forms, some savoury, some unsavoury—

from nationally oriented social-democrats and trade-unionists to anti-immigrant populist movements, etc." (2012: 25). The FN's refusal of the Pact is couched in defensive social protection (although other voices in the party sound much more liberal), that is *restricted to nationals* (or EU members?). By contrast, the pro-Pact discourse may be read through Fraser's categories as adding some emancipatory aims, such as cutting tax excess and bureaucracy, to its marketization agenda. This can only be persuasive if solidarity guarantees are effective, which seems very uncertain at present. Fraser herself acknowledges, with Eisenstein (2005), the problem of "dangerous liaisons" between marketization and some aspects of an emancipatory project.

Conclusion

The example of the Responsibility and Solidarity Pact shows the power of marketization in these first decades of the twenty first century. Although it did not originate in a radical neoliberal agenda, it involves tax cuts and policies of deregulation in a country renowned for its traditional state intervention and currently governed by the socialists. But beyond the context and the concrete effects of this policy, my aim here has been to study how political discourse tries to explain and justify the measures and how opponents have reacted. On the basis of Polanyi's works and particularly its relevance to critical discourse analysis, I have tried to track down the "crude fictions" of the all-powerful market (Polanyi 2001: 76–77). A key question here concerns the performativity (Austin 1962) of a political speech, "which may be capable of acting on this world by acting on agents' representation of it" (Bourdieu 1993: 128). The question as to whether and to what extent citizens are persuaded by the discourses at hand remains the object of important future work. In any case, the rhetorical efforts made by politicians to justify their positions are considerable. Polanyi's observation of "how crippling the effect of the sound currency postulate was on popular policies" between the World Wars (2001: 237) is still relevant in light of how "new" social democrats are today giving priority to companies. And even if the Pact insists on social counterparts, its background assumption is that unemployment is caused by high labour costs and can be solved by supply-side policies. In reaction, new forms of resistance are forming in an unfavourable historical context: a far cry from the successful social movement of 1995, every wave of protests since 2002 (in 2003, 2010, 2013) has been defeated by successive governments. The latter demonstrated their strong will and ability to keep pressure on the unions whose traditional strategies, efficient over many decades, have declined in the face of a political rhetoric that justifies the reforms and stigmatises dissenters as "irresponsible" (Moulène 2011: 146) and in "a society that discourage[s] even the idea of radical alternatives to the status quo", as Marcuse anticipated in the 1960s (Tally 2010: 6). Meanwhile, "new resistance" challenges to the two-party system (that is, Socialists/Republicans) includes both the National Front and a new radical left. If the conservatives are the favourite for the presidential elections of 2017, their position is awkward: they are the main opposition, yet they share the socialist discourse of a "win-win" principle (that is tax cuts *but also* job creation), and they stand firm on immigration and security under the pressure of the FN. The risk for the PS is to be seen as being too similar to the right, while they push the conservatives to overstate their agenda in order to look different. So when a dominant party changes its discourse, it allows or forces its adversaries to change theirs: we also see this in the FN trying to hijack Keynesian rhetoric that the PS seems to surrender. Maybe the Pact will not have any success, but we already have to fear that its disorienting and surprising discourse contributes to a general loss of political bearings in France today.

References

Austin, J. L. (1962[1957]). *How to do things with words*. Oxford: Clarendon Press.

Barthes, R. (1997). *The Eiffel Tower and other mythologies*. Berkeley: University of California Press.

Bekmezian, H. & Bonnefous, B. (2014). PS: L'heure de vérité des 41 députés 'frondeurs'. *Le Monde*, 7 June. http://www.lemonde.fr/politique/article/2014/06/07/ps-l-heure-de-verite-des-41-deputes-frondeurs_4434078_823448.html. Accessed 4 July 2015.

Benhamou, A. (2014). France-Allemagne : la dérive incessante des balances commerciales. *Les Échos*, 7 February. http://www.lesechos.fr/idees-debats/cercle/cercle-90999-france-allemagne-la-derive-incessante-des-balances-commerciales-1003319.php. Accessed 24 Nov 2015.

Benkimoun, P. (2008). La qualité de l'hôpital public mise en accusation. *Le Monde*. 30 December. http://www.lemonde.fr/societe/article/2008/12/30/la-qualite-de-l-hopital-public-mise-en-accusation_1136314_3224.html. Accessed 24 Nov 2015.

Bourdieu, P. (1993). *Language and symbolic power*. Cambridge: Harvard University Press.

Brisset, N. (2012). Retour sur le désencastrement. Polanyi ou la science économique vue comme une institution influençant l'évolution des systèmes économiques. *European Journal of Social Sciences, 50*(1), 7–39.

Calvet, L.-J., & Véronis, J. (2008). *Les mots de Nicolas Sarkozy*. Paris: Seuil.

Castagnet, M. & Rouden, C. (2014). 'Le gouvernement gèle les allocations et les retraites'. *La Croix*, 16 April. http://www.la-croix.com/Actualite/France/Le-gouvernement-gele-les-allocations-et-les-retraites-2014-04-16-1137321. Accessed 24 Nov 2015.

Charaudeau, P. (2005). *Le discours politique. Les masques du pouvoir*. Paris: Vuibert.

Chastand, J.-B. (2014). Le Pacte de responsabilité est bon dans son principe. *Le Monde*, 15 January. http://www.lemonde.fr/politique/article/2014/01/15/le-pacte-de-responsabilite-est-bon-dans-son-principe_4348225_823448.html. Accessed 24 Nov 2015.

Dixon, K. (2008). *New labour and devolution*. https://halshs.archives-ouvertes.fr/halshs-00317916/PDF/Dixon_New_Labour_and_Devolution_Textes_et_Contextes_n_1_2008.pdf. Accessed 17 Apr 2015.

Eisenstein, H. (2005). A dangerous liaison? Feminism and corporate globalization. *Science and Society, 69*(3), 487–518.

Embassy of France in London. (2013). *Gaïti, people*, 31 December. http://www.ambafrance-uk.org/Francois-Hollande-s-New-Year,23174. Accessed 4 July 2015.

Embassy of France in London. (2014). *Presidential conference in Paris*, 14 January. http://www.ambafrance-uk.org/President-Hollande-speaks-to-the. Accessed 4 July 2015.

Fairclough, N. (2000). *New labour, new language*. London: Routledge.

Faye, J.-P. (1973). Languages totalitaires. *Critique de la raison et de l'économie narrative, Paris: Hermann.*.

Fraser, N. (2012). *Marketization, social protection, emancipation: Toward a neo-Polanyian conception of capitalist crisis*. http://sophiapol.hypotheses.org/files/2012/02/Texte-Nancy-Fraser-anglais.doc. Accessed 3 July 2015.

Gaïti, B. L'érosion discrète de l'État-providence dans la France des années 1960. Retour sur les temporalités d'un 'tournant néolibéral'. *Actes de la Recherche en Sciences Sociales* 201-2, March. pp. 58–71.

Giddens, A. (2000). *The Third Way & its critics*. Cambridge: Polity.

Guilbert, T. (2011). *L'"évidence" du discours néolibéral. Analyse dans la presse écrite*. Le Croquant: Bellecombe-en-Bauges.

Halimi, S. (2006). *Le Grand bond en arrière*. Paris: Fayard.

Hillenkamp, I., & Laville, J.-L. (2013). Introduction. In I. Hillenkamp & J.-L. Laville (Eds.), *Socioéconomie et démocratie. L'actualité de Karl Polanyi* (pp. 7–36). Erès: Toulouse.

Hirschman, A. O. (1991). *The rhetoric of reaction: Perversity*. Belknap: Futility, Jeopardy, Cambridge.

Hollande applique la politique de Sarkozy 'avec moins de talent'. *Le Point,* 9 Feb 2014. http://www.lepoint.fr/politique/baroin-hollande-applique-la-politique-de-sarkozy-avec-moins-de-talent-09-02-2014-1789781_20.php. Accessed 4 July 2015.

Hollande dévoile le pacte de solidarité. (2014, 1 April). https://www.youtube.com/watch?v=N9-uKjjvV8w. Accessed 4 July 2015.

Juppé estime que Hollande a effectué une 'révolution copernicienne' de sa pensée. (2014). *Le Parisien,* 15 January. http://www.leparisien.fr/bordeaux-33000/juppe-estime-que-hollande-a-effectue-une-revolution-copernicienne-de-sa-pensee-15-01-2014-3498985.php. Accessed 15 Nov 2015.

L'essentiel de la déclaration de politique générale de Manel Valls. (2014, September 16). http://www.gouvernement.fr/l-essentiel-de-la-declaration-de-politique-generale-de-manuel-valls. Accessed 4 July 2015.Le Pacte de responsabilité: une 'aberration' selon Marie-Noëlle Lienemann, 2014, Apr 16. https://www.youtube.com/watch?v=sdURFcMn61A. Accessed 25 Apr 2015.

Le socialisme européen. 1999. *La Revue socialiste, 1.*(Spring 1999).

Loiseau, H. (2002). 1985–2000: quinze ans de mutations du secteur public d'entreprises. *INSEE Première*, 860, July. http://www.insee.fr/fr/themes/document.asp?id=879. Accessed 24 Nov 2015.

Loriaux, M. M. (1996). Socialist monetarism and financial liberalization in France. In M. M. Loriaux (Ed.), *Liberalizing finance in interventionist state*. Ithaca: Cornell University Press.

Macron pointe la responsabilité du patronat dans l' 'échec' du pacte de responsabilité. Le Monde (2014, December 2). http://www.lemonde.fr/economie/article/2014/12/02/pacte-de-responsabilite-macron-denonce-le-faible-nombre-d-accords-signes_4532589_3234.html. Accessed 25 Apr 2015.

Malm, S. (2015). France needs its own Margaret Thatcher to tackle chaos caused by militant trade unions. *Daily Mail*, 25 June. http://www.dailymail.co.uk/news/article-3138627/France-needs-Margaret-Thatcher-tackle-chaos-caused-militant-trade-unions-says-British-transport-secretary.html. Accessed 3 July 2015.

Marine Le Pen: 'Le Pacte de responsabilité sera inefficace'—L'invité de RTL. (2014, June 30). https://youtube.com/watch?v=gxtW2-kgpC4. Accessed 4 July 2015.

Mises, L. von (1950). *Lord Keynes and Say's law. The Freeman*, 30 October. https://mises.org/library/lord-keynes-and-says-law. Accessed 24 Nov 2015.

Mitterrand: Monetarist of the year. (1990). *Financial Times*. 20 Apr 1990.

Moulène, F. (1998). L'essence du néolibéralisme. *Le Monde diplomatique, 531*, 2.

Moulène, F. (2011). *Les électeurs face à la thématique de la "rupture" dans la campagne présidentielle française de 2007: loyauté ou résistance? Une contribution sociologique à l'étude de la performance des discours politiques*. Ph.D Thesis. Université de Strasbourg, Unpublished.

Moulène, F. (2015). Penser la force du discours libéral avec Karl Polanyi. In C. Grenouillet & C. Vuillermot-Febvet (Eds.), *La langue du management et de l'économie à l'ère néolibérale: formes sociales et littéraires* (pp. 81–92). Strasbourg: Presses Universitaires de Strasbourg.

Nicolas Sarkozy, discours à Périgueux. 2006, October 12. http://sites.univ-vprovence.fr/veronis/Discours2007/transcript.php?n=Sarkozy&p=2006-10-12&e=miracle&e2=#n4. Accessed 2 July 2015.

Nicolas Sarkozy, discours à Saint-Etienne. 2006, November 9. http://sites.univ-provence.fr/veronis/Discours2007/transcript.php?n=Sarkozy&p=2006-11-09&e=bus&e2=#n1. Accessed 4 July 2015.

Nicolas Sarkozy, discours à Toulouse. 2007, April 12. http://sites.univ-provence.fr/veronis/Discours2007/transcript.php?n=Sarkozy&p=2007-04-12&e=seulpays&e2=#n2. Accessed 2 July 2015.

Organisation for Economic Co-opération and Development [OECD]. (2015). *Economic surveys France, overview (March)*. http://www.oecd.org/eco/surveys/France-2015-overview.pdf. Accessed 24 November 2015.

Pacte de responsabilité: Jean-Luc Mélenchon dénonce une 'méthode viciée'. 2014, March 6. http://videos.lexpress.fr/actualite/politique/video-pacte-de-responsabilite-jean-luc-melenchon-denonce-une-methode-viciee_1497836.html. Accessed 4 July 2015.

Pacte de responsabilité: Manuel Valls rappelle à l'ordre le patronat. 2015 April 8. In http://www.francetvinfo.fr/politique/manuel-valls/pacte-de-responsabilite-manuel-valls-rappelle-a-l-ordre-le-patronat_871575.html. Accessed 4 July 2015.

Pacte de responsabilité: un effort à faire pour l'emploi, dit Valls. 2014, November 4. http://www.dailymotion.com/video/x29bgto_pacte-de-responsabilite-effort-a-faire-pour-l-emploi-dit-valls_news. Accessed 4 July 2015.

Polanyi, K. (2001[1944]). *The great transformation: The political and economic origins of our time*. Boston: Beacon Press.

Rovan, A. (2014). *Valls déclare la guerre aux 'passeistes' du PS*. Le Figaro, 23 October. Accessed 24 Nov 2015.

RSA, *Evolution montant RSA*. (2015). http://rsa-revenu-de-solidarite-active.com/evolution-rsa.html. Accessed 24 Nov 2015.

Smith, T. B. (2004). *France in crisis. Welfare, inequality and globalization since 1980*. Cambridge: Cambridge University Press.

Stiglitz, J. E. (2001). Foreword. In K. Polanyi (2001 [1944]). *The great transformation: The political and economic origins of our time*. (pp. vii–xvii). Boston: Beacon Press.

Tally, R. T. Jr. (2010). Sartre, Marcuse and the Utopian project today. *Comparative Literature and Culture* 12.1. http://docs.lib.purdue.edu/cgi/viewcontent.cgi?article=1572&context=clcweb. Accessed 24 Nov 2015.

Vaillant, G. (2014). Pacte de responsabilité: 'vers une vraie révolte' au PS?. *Lejdd*. 11 August. http://www.lejdd.fr/Politique/Pacte-de-responsabilite-vers-une-vraie-revolte-au-PS-679762. Accessed 24 Nov 2015.

What France needs. *The Economist*. (2006, October 26). http://www.economist.com/node/8080753. Accessed 24 Nov 2015.

Neoliberal Moral Economy: Migrant Workers' Value Struggles Across Temporal and Spatial Dimensions

Barbara Samaluk

Introduction

This chapter focuses on Polish and Slovenian migrant workers' value struggles in the UK and across spatial and temporal dimensions. Following a brief outline of the historical and socioeconomic contexts that characterise these migrant workers' trajectories, this chapter explores the workings of a moral economy embodied in Polish and Slovenian workers' histories and its changes enacted through structural and migration processes. Poland and Slovenia share a history of socialism and subsequent transition to a market economy that profoundly changed everyday life and work in postsocialist countries, often bearing high social costs visible in deepening social stratification, poverty and emigration (Samaluk 2014a, b, 2015; Śliwa 2009; Stenning et al. 2010). Although these two countries have a common history, they were nevertheless characterised by diverse forms of socialism and transitional Europeanization and neoliberalisation processes (Bohle 2006; Bohle and Greskovits 2012). This shared, yet

B. Samaluk (✉)
University of Greenwich, London, UK

© The Editor(s) (if applicable) and The Author(s) 2016   **61**
C. Karner, B. Weicht (eds.), *The Commonalities of Global Crises*,
DOI 10.1057/978-1-137-50273-5_3

diverse embodied history affects the way Polish and Slovenian workers are received in the UK and the way they reevaluate their new place.

In UK policy and economic–/public discourse, workers from postsocialist central and eastern European (CEE) countries are, on one hand, constructed as a threat to the welfare state and, on the other, praised for their distinctive work ethic and utilised for low-skilled and low-paid jobs (Anderson et al. 2006; MacKenzie and Forde 2009; Samaluk 2014a, 2014b; Wills et al. 2010). In this regard, various authors argue that for UK policymakers, CEE labour migration was not about exercising EU citizenship rights of free movement, but about substituting migrant workers from outside the EU/EEA area in order to fill labour shortages at the lower end of the economy (Anderson et al. 2006; Ciupijus 2011; McDowell 2009a; Wills et al. 2010).

This evidence suggests that contemporary systems of transnational migration do not only have economic, but also symbolic, cultural and moral dimensions and are central to "self-" and "class-making" (Skeggs 2004a, b). This can include discourses about the West that guide CEE workers' self-making and migration strategies (Samaluk 2015). This chapter focuses on Polish and Slovenian workers' perspectives in order to explore how their value struggles and strategies in the UK are informed by their diverse embodied histories, structural changes and conditions they encounter in the UK. This perspective enables an analysis of struggles for value in economic terms and, at the same time, of struggles over shared dispositions, practices and orientations (Skeggs and Loveday 2012: 476).

Neoliberal Moral Economy

Neoliberalism started with economic restructuring in the 1970s, and can be defined as a form of political, economic and cultural hegemony that is characterised by globalised markets, transnationalised production and consumption, deregulation, flexibilisation and the rise of the global and mobile precariat (Appadurai 1996; Bohle 2006; Harvey 2005; Samaluk 2014a, b; Standing 2011; Wills et al. 2010). The global expansion of neoliberalism is also associated with attacks on and fundamental changes of the welfare state and its moral economy (Peck 2002; Sayer 2000). In this regard, Sayer argues that there is a need to put the analytical focus upon "'moral economy' as a way of thinking about the normative issues posed by contemporary advanced economies" (Sayer 2000: 80). These should go beyond the issues of equality and justice and question the basic needs and ends of economic activity in order to determine how economic activities are justified by moral-political norms, how they legitimize unequal power relations and affect people's lives and agency. It is therefore important to understand the perspectives, values and exchanges that hide within themselves a complex cultural history, that create divisions and make the economy possible (Skeggs 2004a: 13).

In this regard, one needs to take into account the links between moral and cultural values. Although moral values are not necessarily culture-bound, they are culturally mediated and thus also central in economic exchange, in class- and self-making (Sayer 2000; Skeggs 2004a, b). Within the individualising logic of (neo)liberal theory, culturally mediated values are in their economic guise turned "into subjective individual preferences realized through making contracts with others" (Sayer 2000: 96). This has also led to a "contractualization of citizenship" that turns the principle of noncontractual citizenship rights and obligations into a contractual quid pro quo market exchange (Somers 2008: 2). This moral economy places the responsibilities for exchange on individuals who now have the moral duty to pursue their self-interest and compete on the market (Skeggs 2004b: 31).

"Moral citizens" should, in this discursive logic, not be dependent on state provision, but rather take individual responsibility for their own condition. Work has thus been culturally and morally revalued in relation to welfare, and therefore participation in the labour market has become a civic virtue (Haylett 2001). The neoliberal moral economy demands increasing subordination of people's private lives to their working lives and increasingly blurs the boundaries between work and life (Fleming and Spicer 2004; Lewis 2003). The politics of time, such as the acceptable length of the working day or work-life balance policies, are also closely related to moral economy (Sayer 2000). This type of moral economy creates, on the one hand, work-rich and time-poor knowledge workers, and, on the other, service workers who provide commodified services in low-paid and insecure jobs (McDowell 2009b). Moreover, it turns a person into "a key unit of value that does not just sell its labour, but comes to exchange already loaded with capacities" (Skeggs 2011: 508).

The focus on moral economy can thus expose a taken-for-granted knowledge production that constructs groups and determines the normative "subject of value", through which individuals are judged, categorised, (self)disciplined and upon which also struggles of resistance emerge (Bourdieu 1977, 1987; Skeggs 2004a, 2011). This research leans on Skeggs' conceptualisation of value that is, unlike in Marx's commodity form, "generated from the power, perspective and relationship that make exchange possible in the first place" (Skeggs 2004a: 12). This conception realises that workers' value struggles are informed by the embodied histories migrant workers "carry with them" from their places of origin and which are transformed by their migration trajectories. For that we have to take into account that migrant workers embody different time/space vectors that make them perceive and value things differently and cannot be explained "by an epistemology developed from an understanding situated in entirely different materialities or from theoretical abstractions, rather than alternative, lived and emplaced practices" (Skeggs 2011: 508).

In order to take into account the epistemologies developed from a postsocialist space, this chapter draws from postcolonial perspectives on postsocialism that, among other things, expose the neocolonial relations linked with the global expansion of neoliberalism and enacted in CEE through transition and Europeanisation processes (Böröcz 2001; Buchowski 2006; Samaluk 2014a, b, 2015, 2016; Stenning and Hörschelmann 2008). In order to understand the neoliberal expansion into CEE, there is a need to take into account the colonial interests of global powers, and their hegemonic discursive claims of there being "no alternative", and to recognise that neoliberalisation extends market rules to other spheres of life and translates into variegated forms in different places (Stenning et al. 2010).

Since the fall of the Berlin Wall, postsocialist CEE countries have become one of the biggest laboratories for the expansion of neoliberal hegemony. During EU accession and the transition process, postsocialist CEE countries were evaluated through various means and assigned a homogeneous, ideological and obsolete socialist history that needed to be overcome by a purportedly nonideological, inevitably capitalist market economy that shifted toward its neoliberal form (Bohle 2006; Böröcz 2001). The policies advocated by the EU and other transnational actors, and often embraced and promoted by domestic politics, were teleological and reductionist and have, under the guise of modernisation and the narratives of a "return to Europe", placed strong emphasis on changes to be implemented by CEE countries in order for them to reach the "standards" of advanced economies (Kuus 2004; Močnik 2002; Stenning et al. 2010).

This relates to a neoliberal colonial logic that is grounded within the binary division of West and East, capitalism and socialism, which also uses a (self-)colonising "catching up model" that legitimises the framing of neoliberalism as the modernising project (Samaluk 2016). Among other things, this has also entailed the making of a new "subject of value", one that is able to transcend the socialist past by becoming a (self-)making, Western European person (Ozoliņa-Fitzgerald 2015; Samaluk 2015). Although both Poland and Slovenia were impacted by a transition and the Europeanization process, there were also important differences between the two countries, stemming from diverse socialist histories and transition processes (Bohle and Greskovits 2012; Mencinger 2004). During transition, Poland went through a neoliberal "shock therapy" and implemented violent neoliberal reforms, and Slovenia adopted a gradualist approach, thus progressively "upgrading" its social protection system while maintaining social cohesion (Mencinger 2004; Śliwa 2009; Vaughan-Whitehead 2003). How these diverse, yet partly shared histories affects the way Polish and Slovenian workers are received in the UK and how they inform their value struggles is presented as follows.

Method and Sample

The following findings arise from 37 semistructured interviews conducted between 2008 and 2012 with Polish and Slovenian workers living and working in and around London. Interviews lasted between one and two hours and explored reasons for migration in light of the changed conditions within workers' places of origin, their experiences of migration and encounters with the normative-discursive structures in the UK. The sample consists of 16 Polish and 21 Slovenian workers, among which were 24 women and 13 men, between 23 and 42 years old; 32 held a post- or undergraduate degree, and five had vocational educations, and all arrived with good English language skills. Most of the workers were employed in the service sector.

From Socialist to Neoliberal Work Ethic

Following the EU's enlargement to include postsocialist CEE countries in 2004, UK migration policies were designed to welcome "hard-working immigrants seeking to better themselves" and to contribute taxes, while preventing them from accessing welfare benefits unless they were in registered employment for at least a year (HO 2004: 1). Since neoliberalism contractualises citizenship upon quid pro quo exchange relations, it constructs morally deserving and non-deserving citizens and legitimises the utilisation of noncitizens through their production function as commodified "assets" that are strategically utilised for undesirable jobs. In the UK, CEE workers are, on one hand, discursively "orientalised" as poor and underdeveloped and a threat to the welfare state; on the other hand, they are also constructed and utilised as desirable, hard-working labour (MacKenzie and Forde 2009; Samaluk 2014a, 2015). CEE workers are thus primarily perceived for what they are assigned to do. Due to this imposed racialized class position, one research participant felt pressured to work harder in order to prove that she is morally worthy of staying in the UK:

> Usually prejudice as well, oh Yugoslavia... Those communist countries... Like you are not the same in the same kind of category than someone, who's French or Spanish... I kind of felt like I have to work harder so they don't throw me out of the country... ("Alenka", Editorial assistant, Slovenian, 35)

Although most informants were willing to work hard to achieve their self-making projects, they also started demonstrating the expected work ethic because of the racialized class logic they encountered in the UK. Judgments of self and how to act are made from within social relations, which can include and reflect the actual or imagined judgments by others and their underpinning, normative, and at times, racist discourses (Sayer 2005). Since CEE workers are only welcome in the UK as long as they work hard and without complaint, this also pressures them to self-discipline within such normative judgments and to start acting accordingly. However, in order to fully understand migrants' agency and their subjective experiences of group-making, there is a need to take into account both vices and virtues of lay normativity (Sayer 2005). For instance, "Piotr's" example, which follows, demonstrates that migrant workers can also start using these normative judgments strategically in order to gain a competitive advantage in a transnationalised market:

> He wanted to have hard workers...I also somehow boosted, increased the strength of this feeling in him, that Polish workers are the best workers in the world ... The money wasn't compensating for the amount of work you are doing ... I took a trust credit. My father didn't want me to go and he said I would get back with debts... I promised myself... I'll come back with money. ("Piotr", Door-to-door sales representative, Polish, 30)

Piotr explains how he strategically increased employers' perceptions of the seemingly *Polish work ethic*. Research on transnational employment agencies shows that, for the purpose of the UK labour market, transnational employment agencies market CEE workers as embodying a seemingly distinctive *socialist work ethic* (Samaluk 2014a). This is a form of misrecognition because it "hides the system of inscription and classification (which work in the interests of the powerful)" (Skeggs 2004a: 4). Piotr's willingness to work hard in a low-paid job was informed by his poor material conditions and a "trust credit" that made him promise his father that he would return without debt. Although during the socialist era, work played a central role in organising social life, it also provided stability and social security, which in the process of neoliberalisation was replaced by insecure and precarious work that produced job instability, greater casualization and the emergence of the working poor (Stenning et al. 2010). In this regard "Anna" explains how working hours in Poland expanded enormously after the collapse of socialism and with the process of neoliberalisation:

> My impression of Polish working life is that there is no private life, because it's so difficult to get a job in Poland…It's very difficult to compete in the market, so people spend as much as the employer want at work. However when I was young my father used to come back from work at 4 pm and we had a dinner. So it's after the collapse of communism, when capitals kicked in and when working hours expanded indefinitely. So people work between 6 am till 10 pm, it's just to compete. So when I was in Warsaw, I knew of people…married couples, who hardly ever saw each other… Poland to me is because of competition and lack of jobs, people spend too many hours working. When I came to the UK for the first time, I worked between 6 am and 11 am and it was enough for me to make a living. ("Anna", Project manager, Polish, 30)

Anna's example demonstrates that, unlike popular perceptions, CEE workers embody a distinctive *socialist work ethic*; their hardworking "character" arises from structural conditions caused by the neoliberalisation process. The increase in unemployment and the rise in precarious work in Poland put pressure on the employed to work longer hours, either in order to keep the job or to earn a living wage (Stenning et al. 2010). These structural changes have thus resulted in an increased subordination of workers' private lives to job prospects and income (Śliwa 2009). The example shows that the seemingly distinctive *socialist CEE work ethic* has actually developed in the process of neoliberalisation that disciplined workers into *the neoliberal work ethic* and informed their migration strategies. Anna thus saw migration as a strategy not only to improve her work prospects and material situation, but also to achieve a better work-life balance. By the end of the 1990s, Poland had the largest migration potential amongst all CEE countries, and after EU-accession the country experienced the largest emigration in its recent history (Fihel and Okolski 2009; IOM 1999). Due to neoliberal restructuring in Poland and its lay normativity, the willingness to labour longer within low-paid jobs was much more prevalent with Polish rather than Slovenian workers, who embody a different history.

Since Slovenia was less impacted by the neoliberal, colonising processes during the transition, Slovenian workers found more favourable conditions in their places of origin, characterised by low levels of unemployment, the retention of employment protection legislation, a lower wage gap and maintenance and enhancement of the social protection system (Stanovnik 2004; Vodopivec 2004). This produced very different valuations of the neoliberal moral economy they encountered in the UK. Unlike Anna, who could achieve a better work-life balance by moving to the UK, Marko experienced a worse work-life balance in the UK:

I would say that this work-life balance is definitely much better in Slovenia. Already like, let's say working hours...When you look at the numbers, the numbers are really nice...But many times I think people don't see, how many hours of work this is, they just compare the salaries. In Slovenia they compare the salary which they get for 160 hours a month, with the salary you get here for 300 hours... ("Marko", Student/Unemployed, Slovenian, 28)

Most Slovenian respondents found the long working hours they encountered in the UK problematic in achieving work-life balance. There is also a much narrower gap in medium hourly earnings between Slovenia and the UK than between Poland and the UK.[1] Unlike Polish workers, wage differentials that come with working longer hours were not an incentive for Slovenian workers' emigration. Although a (self-)colonising imagination of "the West" guides both Polish and Slovenian self-making strategies among migrants to the UK (Samaluk 2015), different impositions of neoliberalisation in their places of origin also create different valuations of the neoliberal moral economy they encounter in the UK. Slovenian informants thus mainly migrated in order to get reputable qualifications, new experiences and to explore greater opportunities for career paths or professional development. This, however, started changing with the

---

[1] Eurostat: Median gross hourly earnings: http://ec.europa.eu/eurostat/statistics-explained/index.php/File:Median_gross_hourly_earnings,_all_employees_%28excluding_apprentices%29,_2010_%28%C2%B9%29_YB15.png

current economic crisis, and consequent austerity measures that led to an increase in precarious work, longer working hours (Kanjuo-Mrčela and Ignjatović 2015) and a rise in (re-)emigration that is yet to be thoroughly explored.

Despite these structural differences within Polish and Slovenian workers' places of origin, analysis uncovers that Slovenian workers also strategically performed the neoliberal work ethic once they learned about the local labour practices and institutions. "Tilen" explains how he added the work ethic to his CV, upon a friend's suggestion:

> I know everyone is hardworking, that was added... [A friend] suggested me...That the English people like hardworking people! ("Tilen", Unemployed, Slovenian, 29)

Performing the neoliberal work ethic at the entry level was especially important for low-paid and low-skilled jobs. Workers in these jobs recalled how employers were not interested in education, experience or working skills, but rather in workers' willingness to be flexible, hardworking and to work without complaint, as was explained to me by "Vesna":

> Here you just need to tell them how much of a hard-working person you are and that you are quite flexible...and able to work under pressure, which is not that important in Slovenia... I would point out this flexibility and working under pressure much earlier than in Slovenia. ("Vesna", Shift leader in a hotel, Slovenian, 26)

Performance of *the neoliberal work ethic* thus became a strategy for workers to compete for entry-level, low-skilled and low-paid jobs. In order to access these jobs, some workers also told me that they had intentionally left out their qualifications and rather emphasised their compliance with the neoliberal work ethic. While in highly-skilled and better-paid jobs workers increased their value through other means, the findings still demonstrate that they also (self)disciplined according to neoliberal morality. For instance, "Irena", a research assistant, explained to me that she had started using "*the cliché of being hardworking*" (Research assistant, Slovenian, Female, 25) once she learned about local institutions and practices. Moreover, "Katarina", an architect, speaks of the normalization of unpaid overtime in her profession:

> They don't pay overtime, so, but you work all the time overtime. So you have a year's salary and that's all the money you get…That's normal, that's normal in my profession…The contract is saying that you are not allowed to work more than 48 hours a week but if it's necessary you sign that you will and that you will not ask for any payments or anything' (Architect, Slovenian, Female, 40)

Analysis thus indicates that workers do not only adopt the neoliberal work ethic because of their poor material conditions or to gain access to entry level jobs, but also to actualise their self-making projects. Also, previous research points to the reinforcement of the work ethic over time and to the consolidation of instrumental work values among the higher qualified workers in Britain (Rose 2005). In this regard "Andrej's" example exposes the symbolic mechanisms at work that award certain privileges to those who are willing to comply with the neoliberal work ethic:

> I think London…gives you certain values that are not necessarily that present back home… it's a funny culture because it's just—banking is a very special world and people do things just so it makes them look good. And sometimes people stay late just to show their managers they're staying late. ("Andrej", Banker, Slovenian, 26)

By demonstrating the work ethic, even workers in high-skilled and better-paid jobs increase their reputation as committed and devoted workers and thus as deserving and modern citizens or citizens-to-be. Andrej's example exposes the symbolic mechanisms at work that earn certain privileges to those who are willing to comply with the neoliberal work ethic. These examples speak of the neoliberal doxa, the unwritten normative "commonsense" (Bourdieu 1990: 69), that normalises the neoliberal work ethic and acts as a (self)disciplining device for workers. This moral economy not only disciplines, but also effectively creates divisions and competition amongst the global precariat that shares a common space within increasingly diverse metropolitan centres.

Competing Morality: Division and Competition Among the Global Precariat

During the increased economic growth, CEE workers were viewed in the UK as economic assets; however, this changed as a result of the current economic crisis that further decreased living and working standards and enabled employers to recruit the local workforce for jobs previously reserved for migrant workers (McCollum and Findlay 2011). Since the economic imperative for employing migrant labour has diminished and since workers from new EU member states cannot easily be prevented from working and living in the UK, they are increasingly being scapegoated for the diminishing welfare state (Samaluk 2013). While labour migration is a product of the opening up of global markets and consequent global inequalities, migrant workers can be perceived as a threat to scarce resources and scapegoated for diminishing jobs, labour standards and the shrinking welfare state:

> I work with someone and he was unhappy about me being here, because he believed, based on The Sun and Daily Mail … that because of me being here, he has to queue longer for seeing the doctor and that we are basically taking the capacity… I also remember in the Sun or in Daily Mirror there was a picture of people I know… The picture was about Polish people queuing to vote and they took this picture and put it in the article about queuing for jobs. I thought this was awful! They slapped the picture in the article about that there is so many Polish people that there are not enough doctors, not enough schools and everyone is overwhelmed. ("Anna", Project manager, Polish, 30)

Anna's example indicates how CEE workers can be challenged at work on the basis of stereotypical images constructed in the populist press. Along with politics, the media plays a major role in spreading culturally racist discourses against CEE migrants in the UK (Fox et al. 2012). As seen from Anna's example, these discourses can be premised upon false or anecdotal evidence that diverts attention away from the distributive injustice engrained within a transnationalised economy. This is, according to Fraser (2009a), a form of representational injustice or misrepresentation, as it frames politics within a supposedly sovereign nation-state that is in fact part of a broader scale that constitutes a metapolitical frame and aims to utilise and discipline the global precariat. Moreover, these cultural politics hide the fact that the social protection of citizens is provided at the expense of economic dependence of peripheral areas and subjects (Fraser 2011). These peripheral areas and subjects are also the object of much debate and stereotypical constructions. The British working class has, in discourses of purported welfare dependency, been recast as immoral, unmodern and in need of disciplining (Haylett 2001). This cultural discourse not only increases social stratification and division among allegedly "deserving" and "undeserving" citizens, but it can also turn migrant workers against the local poor:

> I worked here ever since from the first day I came to this country, I worked, I paid my taxes, I never asked for anything back. No benefits, nothing like this. And there was a lot of people in this country that it's a third generation now of people who never worked a day in their life. And that pisses me off because, of course, I've lived here now for 7 years and of course I'm a Londoner, I live here, and because I pay for those people as well. ("Ania", Receptionist/Admin, Polish, 34)

Ania's example demonstrates that despite being affected by similar structural conditions, she judged the local poor upon the same neoliberal morality that legitimises increasing social stratification on various local and global scales. This neoliberal morality also creates divisions amongst the global precariat and disables collective resistance against distributive injustice. At this point, it is crucial to expose the resisting strategies of migrant workers who embody different values that can thus reevaluate the dominant symbolic order.

Resistance Against the Neoliberal Moral Economy

Since the neoliberal, colonising project had very different "success rates" in Poland and Slovenia, the strategies of resistance among Slovenian and Polish workers also vary. My analysis demonstrates that Slovenian workers were much more willing to resist and take risks than their Polish contemporaries, who were already badly affected by neoliberal processes in their places of origin. "Vesna", for instance, explains how she resisted the long working-hours culture in the UK, because she values her work-life balance above her career:

> I get hours back, I don't get paid for extra hours, but I get free days. I am a bit stubborn about that. I can see my colleagues are willing to stay extra hours even if they are not paid for it... My salary is, sorry, is not that big that I would be willing to stay extra hours... I appreciate my free time much more... They already know that I will not stay longer, if I am not going to get hours back, so they are not asking me that much.' ("Vesna", Shift leader in a hotel, Slovenian, 26)

Vesna perceived the neoliberal work ethic as unacceptable and therefore challenged it. In contrast to her colleagues, many of whom were from other CEE countries, she was not willing to fully comply with the neoliberal work ethic and resisted it. Also, "Aleks" explains that he decided to look for another job, because his employer expected him to sacrifice his private life for work:

> I was doing well, but I also wanted to have some life, whereas at that particular point in time I was just working... I took few holidays...and people there were like: "You are not very serious about, we want you here, we don't want you to go on weekend breaks... One thing led to another and I just had enough and after 15 months I decided to find another job. ("Aleks", Waiter/IT, Slovenian, 33)

Aleks was not prepared to indefinitely perform the neoliberal work ethic expected by his employers and thus left the job. The embodied history that Slovenian workers carried with them thus played an important role in some workers' noncompliance with neoliberalisation, despite the fact that their jobs were insecure. Moreover, neoliberal attempts to induce individual responsibility upon subjects to compete in the market did not sit well with "Lija":

> A lot of money and no time, and I don't want to be part of this... You are an individual; you don't mean anything to this city. I don't think I want to be part of a working force here in the UK, because I think they just work

and my philosophy of life is not just work... I can't see myself working here in a real job. Part time maybe, but real job no. They don't have this sense of life like we have still. ("Lija", Nanny/Student, Slovenian, 27)

Lija's critique of neoliberalisation in the UK is expressed through the forgotten *sense of life* that has been lost through an imposed neoliberal morality that attempts to subordinate people's lives to work and capital accrual. Different perspectives can thus uncover different "spatial and temporal configurations of value that are not only about extraction and accrual, but also based on relationality (time and energy with and for others)" (Skeggs 2011: 509). Lija explained that she did not want to participate in this neoliberal doxa and was planning to return to Slovenia once she finished her studies. These examples expose a critical migrant's gaze, which, through its evaluation of neoliberalisation, also brings new values to the UK. A migrants' gaze, informed by different embodied histories, points to diverse moral economies and thus challenges the seemingly "naturalised" and "ahistorical" neoliberal morality. Moreover, Slovenian workers' rejection of the neoliberal morality also had specific gender dimensions. Most Slovenian women expressed the view that they would not feel comfortable having children in the UK. As "Veronika" explains, this is not only due to long working hours, but also a lack of public childcare services and social networks:

Now that I'm single I'm willing to work that much, but in the future I hope to have a family and I don't see myself here, because I wouldn't say that it's a friendly place to raise children, but not because it's not safe, but because of the work. It's either only work and I don't want kids to be raised by their nanny, but on the other hand I don't want to be a house wife. Because in Slovenia wherever you live it takes you 30 minutes to get there, you work 8 hours and everything is taken care of, you have nursery or school. You also have people. I would really have to get a great job to stay here. ("Veronika", Translator/unemployed, Slovenian, 33)

Most Slovenian women perceived the UK as an unfriendly place to have children, due to its long working-hours culture, poor work-life balance

policies and also because they lacked social networks. Also, comparative studies expose that apart from long working hours, the UK also has
one of the highest proportion of female part-time workers, which needs
to be put also in the context of a scarcity of child-care provisions and
parental leave measures (Bishop 2004; Cousins and Tang 2004). This
is quite the opposite of Slovenia, which had, due to its socialist history,
a strong and long-standing tradition of socialisation and professionalisation of care that enabled women's participation in the labour market
and enabled equality amongst sexes (Einhorn 1993: 151; Weiner 2009).
Although the aim of such social protection was also to exercise a form of
demographic control/planning, the emancipatory potential of this socialist tradition needs to be taken into account for building a more equal
future. Slovenian work-life balance policies have further evolved toward
a more "universal caregiver model" (Fraser 2009b) and today recognise
a one-year paid parental leave that could be shared by both parents and
still offer established public child-care centres throughout the country
(UEM 2005). In the EU, Slovenia also has the lowest gender gap in pay,
hours worked and employment and as such stands in stark contrast to
the UK.[2] Due to this ongoing history of emancipatory social protection
against marketization (Fraser 2011), the ability to equally participate on
the labour market and be economically independent still presents one of
the most important values for Slovenian women and can inform their
return strategies.

Equal participation in the labour market for both women and men has
been one of the most important values in all socialist countries; however,
comparative analysis highlights that these values have considerably
changed in Poland due to the neoliberalisation process. Research comparing eight postsocialist countries finds that only Slovenia and Lithuania
create favourable conditions for women's continuous employment, while
in Poland parents are left nearly without any state support (Javornik-
Skrbinšek 2010). Moreover, this points to the importance of child-care
policies, not only for enhancing women's continuous employment,
but also for women's economic and personal autonomy. Particularly in

---

[2] Report on equality between women and men 2014: http://ec.europa.eu/justice/gender-equality/
files/annual_reports/150304_annual_report_2014_web_en.pdf

Poland, care has been subjected not only to neoliberal but also conservative agendas supported by the revived role of the Catholic Church, which encourages welfare responsibilities to be privatised within the family (Glass and Fodor 2007; Stenning et al. 2010). In this vein, "Magda" reflected on the retraditionalisation of women's roles in Polish society and poor child-care facilities:

> Not enough kindergartens, people would queue...Very patriarchal, very Catholic Church dominated politics...The political discourse is that women should have babies and you need to be all maternal and womanly and have your baby and your career can wait. ("Magda", Health care assistant, Polish, 25)

Retraditionalisation went hand in hand with the decreased role of the state in the provision of work-life balance policies. Reduction in the provision and access to public, state-funded care and the support offered to working mothers, has resulted in a privatisation and individualisation of care, reshaping constructions of motherhood and contributing to growing stratification amongst Polish mothers (Awsiukiewicz-Tomczak 2009; Stenning et al. 2010). Women's "return" to the domestic sphere was often portrayed as a "corrective" of socialist policies (Owczarzak 2009). In this regard, some feminists critique the colonising act of Western feminism that participated in the global expansion of neoliberalism, neglected local, CEE feminisms and diverted attention to micropolitics that converged with neoliberal critiques of "the nanny state" (Fraser 2009b; Miroiu 2004; Owczarzak 2009; Slovova 2006).

This points to a neocolonial, binary logic in which the "transcending of socialist past" is used to legitimise the destruction of socialist feminist values that combine both redistributive and representational justice. The post-1989 Solidarity government in Poland was openly pro-Catholic and thus targeted welfare in order to reinforce presocialist gender norms and return men to the position of breadwinner (Glass and Fodor 2007; Watson 1993). This also led to women being made redundant more quickly and more often than men and women finding it harder to find work or get well-paid work (Stenning et al. 2010). In this regard "Maria" expressed worries regarding sex discrimination in the Polish labour market:

I would be more worried if I was applying for a job in Poland. First of all I'm a woman and I might have children in the future and I think in Poland it would play a bigger role. ("Maria", Lecturer, Polish, 31)

Most young Polish women perceived Poland as a place where they would not have the same chances for achieving their career or personal aspirations. Apart from general exit strategies of many Polish "precariatised" workers toward increasing their overall value and achieving a better work-life balance, many young female informants also saw migration as emancipation from newly imposed retraditionalisation:

The main reason was that I felt that I don't fit anymore in the Polish society, that I don't find myself comfortable with all the tradition, with all the stereotypes, with all the pressure and all the rules you have to follow to be a good citizen, good daughter, wife or sister.("Joanna", Accounts assistant, Polish, Female, 27)

Joanna's example shows that retraditionalisation that went hand in hand with neoliberalisation also reevaluated Polish women's citizenship status, and often has reduced it to their domestic role. In this regard, Forrester et al. argue that Polish women had more rights under state socialism than they do now, with the state and the powerful Catholic Church using "Western" discourses to legitimise the demands that women return to their "natural" role as mothers and wives (2004: 16). The comparative perspective thus also reveals gendered dimensions of the neoliberal moral economy.

Conclusion

The aim of this chapter was to explore how Polish and Slovenian migrant workers' value struggles and strategies are informed by their embodied and ongoing histories. It exposes neocolonial relations within contemporary Europe that affect how CEE workers are perceived and utilised on the UK labour market and how they resist or strategically utilise these racialized inscriptions to compete in the transnationalised market. By focusing on CEE workers' value struggles across spatial and temporal dimensions, the chapter challenges the positive and negative morality that is assigned to CEE workers in the UK upon their embodied socialist history. The analysis shows that the seemingly *socialist work ethic* is in fact *a neoliberal work ethic* that is a product of changed (moral) economies that arose from postsocialist, neoliberal restructuring.

The chapter finds that neoliberalisation in Poland resulted in Polish workers' exit strategies, their compliance with the neoliberal work ethic and their "willingness" to take up low-paid jobs in the UK. Due to deteriorated, neocolonial conditions, Polish workers saw emigration as emancipation from unemployment, poor pay and poor work-life balance. This was, conversely, not the case for Slovenian workers whose country of origin was, up until the current economic crisis, less impacted by neoliberalisation. Wage differentials that came at the expense of a long working-hour culture were therefore neither an incentive for Slovenian workers' emigration nor for their emancipation. However, despite structural differences within Polish and Slovenian workers' places of origin, analysis uncovered that Slovenian workers also started strategically performing *the neoliberal work ethic* once they learned about the local labour practices and institutions. Although this was particularly the case for workers who were competing for entry-level, low-skilled and low-paid jobs, workers in high-skilled jobs also self-disciplined into *the neoliberal work ethic* in order to increase their reputation as committed and devoted workers, and therefore, as deserving and modern citizens (to be). The neoliberal work ethic thus acts as doxa, a moral "commonsense", an unwritten norm that powerfully informs workers' action and behaviours. This moral economy also effectively creates divisions among "deserving" and "undeserving" citizens and migrants and effectively misframes the reality of the current neocolonial, cultural-political economy.

The comparative focus also exposes different valuations and capabilities of resisting neoliberal morality. The analysis demonstrates that Slovenian workers were, due to the favourable, original conditions in which they lived, much more willing to resist and take risks than their Polish counterparts. The embodied history that Slovenian workers carried with them played an important role in some workers' noncompliance with neoliberalisation, despite the fact that their jobs were threatened. Slovenian workers' acts of resistance point to different valuations that are not only about capital accrual but also about noncommodified relations with and for others and emancipatory social protection for women. The chapter shows that the ability to equally participate in the labour market and be economically independent still presents one of the most important values for Slovenian women and can inform their return strategies. In the Polish context, however, many female informants also saw migration as emancipation from reestablished, presocialist gender norms that discursively reconstructed them as citizens and workers, reducing their rights and social protection, disabling equal participation in the labour market, and pushing them back into the domestic sphere.

Within the neo-Polanyian framework, the analysis provides empirical corroboration for Fraser's (2011) argument concerning the "triple movement", in which the conflict between marketization and social protection must be mediated by emancipation, and conflicts between protection and emancipation are mediated by marketization in order to expose negative liberty. By demonstrating how embodied histories of (post)socialism and neoliberalism operate in different places and times, the chapter offers different perspectives, retrieves memories of alternative possibilities, and points to forgotten histories erased by a purportedly ahistorical and nonideological neoliberal project. This discussion thus contributes to studies that expose the workings of the neoliberal moral economy in seemingly detaching life-worlds from the economic and political system, when in fact, neoliberalism "colonises" life-worlds, by moving away from redistributive justice and imposing "moral" self-discipline upon seemingly independent and self-reliant individuals (Fraser 2009b; Sayer 2005).

References

Anderson, B., et al. (2006). *Fair enough? Central and East European migrants in low wage employment in the UK*. Oxford: COMPAS.

Appadurai, A. (1996). *Modernity at large: Cultural dimensions of globalization*. Minneapolis: University of Minnesota Press.

Awsiukiewicz-Tomczak, A. M. (2009). *Motherhood experiences through transformations: Narratives of intergenerational continuities and changes in post-Communist Poland.* PhD thesis. Oxford: Brookes University.

Bishop, K. (2004). Working time patterns in the UK, France, Denmark and Sweden. *Labour Market Trends, 112*(3), 113–122.

Bohle, D. (2006). Neoliberal hegemony, transnational capital and the terms of the EU's eastward expansion. *Capital & Class, 30*(Spring), 57–86.

Bohle, D., & Greskovits, B. (2012). *Capitalist diversity on Europe's periphery.* Cornell: University Press.

Böröcz, J. (2001). Introduction: Empire and coloniality in the 'Eastern enlargement' of the European union. In J. Böröcz & M. Kovasc (Eds.), *Empire's new clothes: Unveiling EU enlargement* (pp. 4–51). Telford: Central Europe Review.

Bourdieu, P. (1977). *Outline of a theory of practice.* Cambridge: University press.

Bourdieu, P. (1987). What makes a social class? On the theoretical and practical existance of groups. *Berkeley Journal of Sociology, 32*(1), 1–17.

Bourdieu, P. (1990). *The logic of practice.* Cambridge: Polity.

Buchowski, M. (2006). The specter of orientalism in Europe: From exotic other to stigmatized brother. *Anthropological Quarterly, 79*(3), 463–482.

Ciupijus, Z. (2011). Mobile Central Eastern Europeans in Britain: Successful European Union citizens and disadvantaged labour migrants? *Work Employment & Society, 25*(3), 540–550.

Cousins, C. R., & Tang, N. (2004). Working time and work and family conflict in the Netherlands, Sweden and the UK. *Work Employment & Society, 18*(3), 531–549.

Einhorn, B. (1993). *Cinderella goes to market : Citizenship, gender and women's movements in East Central Europe.* London: Verso.

Fihel, A., & Okolski, M. (2009). Dimensions and effects of labour migration to EU countries: The case of Poland. In B. Galgoczi, J. Leschke, & A. Watt (Eds.), *EU labour migration since enlargement: Trends, impacts and policies* (pp. 185–210). Surrey: Ashgate.

Fleming, P., & Spicer, A. (2004). You can checkout anytime, but you can never leave: Spatial boundaries in a high commitment organization. *Human Relations, 57*(1), 75–94.

Forrester, S. E. S., Zaborowska, M. J., & Gapova, E. (2004). Introduction: Maping postsocialist cultural studies. In S. E. S. Forrester, M. J. Zaborowska, & E. Gapova (Eds.), *Over the wall/after the fall: Post-communist cultures through an East-West gaze* (pp. 1–36). Bloomington, Ind: Indiana University Press.

Fox, J. E., Moroşanu, L., & Szilassy, E. (2012). The racialization of the new European migration to the UK. *Sociology, 46*(4), 680–695.

Fraser, N. (2009a). Feminism, capitalism and the cunning of history. *New Left Review, 56*(2), 97–117.

Fraser, N. (2009b). *Scales of justice: Re-imagining political space in a globalizing world.* New York: Columbia University Press.

Fraser, N. (2011). Marketization, social protection, emancipation: Toward a neo-Polanyian conception of capitalist crisis. In C. Calhoun & G. Derluguian (Eds.), *Business as usual: The roots of the global financial meltdown* (pp. 137–158). New York: University Press.

Glass, C., & Fodor, E. (2007). From public to private maternalism? Gender and welfare in Poland and Hungary after 1989. *Social Politics: International Studies in Gender State & Society, 14*(3), 323–350.

Harvey, D. (2005). *A brief history of neoliberalism.* Oxford: Oxford University Press.

Haylett, C. (2001). Illegitimate subjects?: Abject whites, neoliberal modernisation, and middle-class multiculturalism. *Environment and PlanningD: Society and Space, 19*(3), 351–370.

HO, Home Office. (2004). *No UK benefits for EU accession countries.* http://press.homeoffice.gov.uk/pressreleases/No_Uk_Benefits_For_Eu_Accession_. Accessed 20 Dec 2009.

IOM, International Organisation for Migration (1999). *Migration potential in Central and Eastern Europe.* Geneva: International Organisation for Migration.

Javornik-Skrbinšek, J. (2010). *Exploring maternal employment in post-socialist countries: Understanding the implications of childcare policies.* PhD thesis. University of Southampton.

Kanjuo-Mrčela, A., & Ignjatović, M. (2015). Od prožnosti do prekarnosti dela: stopnjevanje negativnih sprememb na začetku 21. Stoletja. *Teorija in praksa, 52*(3), 350–381.

Kuus, M. (2004). Europe's eastern expansion and the reinscription of otherness in East-Central Europe. *Progress in Human Geography, 28*(4), 472–489.

Lewis, S. (2003). The integration of paid work and the rest of life. Is post-industrial work the new leisure? *Leisure Studies, 22*(4), 343–345.

MacKenzie, R., & Forde, C. (2009). The rhetoric of the 'good worker' versus the realities of employers' use and the experiences of migrant workers. *Work, Employment and Society, 23*(1), 142–159.

McCollum, D., & Findlay, A. (2011). *Employer and labour provider perspectives on Eastern European migration to the UK.* Southampton: Centre for Population Change.

McDowell, L. (2009a). Old and new European economic migrants: Whiteness and managed migration policies. *Journal of Ethnic and Migration Studies, 35*(1), 19–36.

McDowell, L. (2009b). *Working bodies : Interactive service employment and workplace identities.* Oxford: Wiley-Blackwell.

Mencinger, J. (2004). Transition to a national market and a market economy: A gradualist approach. In M. Mrak, M. Rojec, & C. Silva-Jauregui (Eds.), *Slovenia: From Yugoslavia to the European Union* (pp. 67–82). Washington: World Bank Publications.

Miroiu, M. (2004). State men, market women. The effects of left conservatism on gender politics in Romanian transition. *Feminismo/s, 3*(6), 207–234.

Močnik, R. (2002). The Balkans as an element in ideological mechanisms. In D. I. Bjelić (Ed.), *Balkan as metaphor* (pp. 79–116). London: MIT Press.

Owczarzak, J. (2009). Introduction: Postcolonial studies and postsocialism in Eastern Europe. *Focaal, 2009*(53), 1–17.

Ozoliṇa-Fitzgerald, L. (2015). The moral economy of post-Soviet neo-liberalism: An ethnography of a Latvian unemployment office. *Central and Eastern European employment relations in perspective: History geography and variegation.* Conference paper. London: University of Greenwich.

Peck, J. (2002). Political economies of scale: Fast policy, interscalar relations, and neoliberal workfare. *Economic Geography, 78*(3), 331–360.

Rose, M. (2005). Do rising levels of qualification alter work ethic, work orientation and organizational commitment for the worse? Evidence from the UK, 1985–2001. *Journal of Education and Work, 18*(2), 131–164.

Samaluk, B. (2013). *Unveiling the political screen discourse on immigration.* http://www.migrantvoice.org/index.php?option=com_content&view=article&id=359%3Abarbara-samaluk-unveiling-the-political-screen-discourse-on-immigration&catid=94%3Abarbara-samaluk&Itemid=5. Accessed 20 May 2014.

Samaluk, B. (2014a). Racialised 'price-tag': Commodification of migrant workers on transnational employment agencies' websites. In M. Pajnik & F. Anthias (Eds.), *Work and the challenges of belonging: Migrants in globalizing economies* (pp. 154–177). Newcastle upon Tyne: Cambridge Scholars Publishing.

Samaluk, B. (2014b). Whiteness, ethnic privilege and migration: A Bourdieuian framework. *Journal of Managerial Psychology, 29*(4), 370–388.

Samaluk, B. (2015). Migrant workers' engagement with transnational staffing agencies in Europe: Symbolic power guiding transnational exchange. *Work, Employment and Society,* online publication (September), 1–17.

Samaluk, B. (2016). Migration, consumption and work: Postcolonial perspective on post-socialist migration to the UK. *Ephemera: Theory and Politics in Organization* (forthcoming).

Sayer, A. (2000). Moral economy and political economy. *Studies in Political Economy, 61*(Spring), 79–103.

Sayer, A. (2005). *The moral significance of class.* Cambridge: Cambridge University Press.

Skeggs, B. (2004a). Exchange, value and affect: Bourdieu and 'the self'. In L. Adkins & B. Skeggs (Eds.), *Feminism after Bourdieu* (pp. 75–96). Oxford: Blackwell Publishing/The Sociological Review.

Skeggs, B. (2004b). *Class, self, culture.* London: Routledge.

Skeggs, B. (2011). Imagining personhood differently: Person value and autonomist working class value practices. *The Sociological Review, 59*(3), 496–513.

Skeggs, B., & Loveday, V. (2012). Struggles for value: Value practices, injustice, judgment, affect and the idea of class. *The British Journal of Sociology, 63*(3), 472–490.

Śliwa, M. (2009). Globalization and social change: The polish experience. In S. B. Banerjee, V. C. M. Chio, & R. Mir (Eds.), *Organizations, markets and imperial formations: Towards an anthropology of globalization* (pp. 198–216). Cheltenham, UK: Edward Elgar.

Slovova, K. (2006). Looking at Western feminisms through the double lens of Eastern Europe and the Third World. In J. Lukić, J. Regulska, & D. Zaviršek (Eds.), *Women and citizenship in Central and Eastern Europe* (pp. 245–264). Aldershot: Ashgate.

Somers, M. (2008). *Genealogies of citizenship: Markets, statelessness and the right to have rights.* Cambridge: Cambridge University Press.

Standing, G. (2011). *The precariat: The new dangerous class.* New York: Bloomsbury.

Stanovnik, T. (2004). Social sector developments. In M. Mrak, M. Rojec, & C. Silva-Jauregui (Eds.), *Slovenia: From Yugoslavia to the European Union* (pp. 315–333). Washington: World Bank Publications.

Stenning, A., & Hörschelmann, K. (2008). History, geography and difference in the post-socialist world: Or, do we still need post-socialism? *Antipode, 40*(2), 312–335.

Stenning, A., et al. (2010). *Domesticating neo-liberalism : Spaces of economic practice and social reproduction in post-socialist cities.* Oxford: Wiley-Blackwell.

UEM, Urad za enake možnosti (2005). *Podlaga za Resolucijo o nacionalnem programu za enake možnosti žensk in moških (2005–2013).* Ljubljana: UEM.

Vaughan-Whitehead, D. (2003). *EU enlargement versus social Europe? : The uncertain future of the European social model.* Cheltenham: Elgar.

Vodopivec, M. (2004). Labour market developments in the 1990's. In M. Mrak, M. Rojec, & C. Silva-Jauregui (Eds.), *Slovenia: From Yugoslavia to the European Union* (pp. 292–314). Washington: World Bank Publications.

Watson, P. (1993). The rise of masculinism in Eastern Europe. *New Left Review, I*(198), 71–82.

Weiner, E. (2009). Dirigism and Déjà Vu Logic: The gender politics and perils of EU enlargement. *European Journal of Women's Studies, 16*(3), 211–228.

Wills, J., et al. (2010). *Global cities at work: New migrant divisions of labour.* England: Pluto Press.

Treble Troubles? Marketization, Social Protection and Emancipation Considered Through the Lens of Slavery

Julia O'Connell Davidson

In the face of the contemporary global economic and political crisis, there has been a renewal of interest in Karl Polanyi's analysis of market societies as the product of a continuous process of contestation between forces pressing for the liberalization of markets, and those seeking to protect the social fabric against marketization (the "double movement"). This includes Nancy Fraser's (2013) critical appreciation of Polanyi, in which she calls for a third vector of analysis to be added to the "double movement", namely the forces of emancipation. We need to think in terms of a "three-sided conflict among proponents of marketization, adherents of social protection, and partisans of emancipation", she argues (2013: 129). However, reading Fraser's discussion of the "triple movement" through the lens of my current interest in slavery raised a number of questions that I want to pursue in this chapter. After outlining the background to Fraser's contribution, the chapter considers white European and American thinking on transatlantic slavery historically, and, more briefly, the politics of those at the forefront of today's antislavery movement. I aim to show that

J. O'Connell Davidson (✉)
University of Bristol, Bristol, UK

© The Editor(s) (if applicable) and The Author(s) 2016   **87**
C. Karner, B. Weicht (eds.), *The Commonalities of Global Crises*,
DOI 10.1057/978-1-137-50273-5_4

in the main, abolitionists were, and remain, hard to fix as proponents of *either* market freedom *or* social protection, or indeed of "emancipation" as defined by Fraser. The postabolition experience of freed slaves and their descendants in America further suggests marketization, social protection, and emancipation are not fully disarticulable political forces. Though Fraser discusses some ambiguities of the three forces she identifies, political contestations around slavery draw attention to further equivocality in relation to each that, the chapter concludes, may make the idea of the triple movement less useful for those committed to the politics of non-domination than it may initially appear.

Modernity, Market Freedom, and the Puzzle of Social Protection

In orthodox liberal and classical sociological theory, modernity is characterized by its radical distinction from the past. The basic story goes as follows. In feudal societies, material production and human reproduction were visibly united—a person's position at birth determined their role in the process of material production, and material production was arranged with a view to sustaining and reproducing both human life and the human relations that characterized society: "Under feudalism … what we … call 'society' was understood in terms of kinship or kin-like bonds of loyalty or fealty on the model of the patriarchal household" (Slater 1998: 138). The European Enlightenment witnessed a flowering of ideas that made it possible to challenge patriarchal authority, and so also possible to separate the two cycles—production and reproduction—allowing for the development of a market-based capitalist economy.

Productive activity was no longer suborned to the imperative to preserve a society organized around kin-like bonds, and status hierarchies were gradually eliminated and replaced by contractual relations between free and formally equal buyers and sellers of labour. Unlike slaves or serfs, the individuals of modern capitalist society became proprietors of their own persons and capacities. Indeed, freedom came to look "like a function of possession" as C. B. MacPherson (1962: 3) put it in his description of "the theory of possessive individualism", and society to appear as "a lot of free equal individuals related to each other as proprietors of their own capacities and of what they have acquired by their exercise. Society consists of exchange between proprietors".

Liberal and Marxist thinkers differ fundamentally on whether this separation of "economy" and "society", or economic and political life, under capitalism is real or merely an ideological fiction, and on the nature of the "freedom" it bestows upon those who possess nothing but their own capacity to labour. Nonetheless, in Marx's work too, capitalism appears as "a distinctively modern form of sociation", one that "entailed—or was—a revolution in what might... be called the elementary forms of social life: individuality, relationship and community" (Sayer 1991: 56). Famously for Marx, capitalism also set in motion dialectical processes that would ultimately lead to its destruction. Free-market capitalism was not the end of history, but the penultimate step on an evolutionary pathway to emancipation, and one taken at enormous human cost. Some interpretations of his work (sometimes described as "vulgar Marxism") assumed that history would simply unfold along this predetermined path, and that revolution was therefore to be expected in places where capitalism was most advanced.

Through the lens of both vulgar Marxism and orthodox liberal theory, political developments in twentieth-century liberal capitalist states thus represented something of a puzzle. Instead of either class war in fully developed capitalist societies, or the clean separation of markets and political life, states began to intervene more comprehensively in the market exchange processes of a capitalist economy. In particular, they intervened in labour markets, setting limits on employers' freedom to treat human labour power as they might treat any other merchandise, legislating in ways that "contributed directly to the reshaping of liberalism" (Stanley 1998: 97). In the postwar years, this reshaping extended to a system of "worker citizenship" in advanced capitalist states, with welfare regimes and Keynesian economics being deployed to provide workers and their families with "a level of insulation from total dependence on the labour market for survival", and to protect various social and cultural institutions against market mechanisms (O'Connor 1998: 188; Offe 1984; Esping-Anderson 1990).

For free marketeers like Milton Friedman (1962), these political interventions constituted a worrying step back from modernity—liberal societies were being dragged back along "the road to serfdom". They are still regarded in this light by Tea Party Americans and others in the US who consider even Barrack Obama's modest health care law to be "slavery in a way, because it is making all of us subservient to the government" (Sullivan 2013). Meanwhile, for many Marxist thinkers, the social-democratic shift of the postwar period represented an effort to preserve capitalism against its own grave-diggers by ameliorating the conditions under which proletarians lived just enough to prevent them from taking revolutionary action against the system. Nonetheless, "worker citizenship" was secured through collective political struggle by organised labour rather than simply extended by enlightened political elites, and implied very real material and political gains for (some) working-class people. Indeed, the value and significance of these gains has become painfully obvious with their growing loss.

Since the 1970s, postwar welfare capitalism has been unpicked, a trend that has both been allowed by, and has allowed for, processes of deindustrialization in the global North and the expansion of manufacturing sectors in the global South. In the neoliberal economic restructuring that has gathered pace globally since the 1990s (being further reinforced by the 2008 global economic crisis), the social protections and labour rights of worker citizens in affluent, economically developed nations have been eroded. The consequences for the mass of the people in less economically developed countries, where the model of industrial citizenship was already more weakly established and social rights necessarily more limited, have been even more brutal (Sassen 2010).

Double and Triple Movements

Karl Polanyi's work is often considered helpful in explaining the shift from liberal to welfare capitalism, and from welfare to neoliberal capitalism. Polanyi contested the orthodox history of modernity outlined herein by observing that whilst economy and society were apparently separated in the shift from premodern or nonmarket to modern market societies, in reality, society and economy are necessarily conjoined, and history therefore unfolded and continues to be made through a process of contestation between the two. Market society, or "capitalism", is the product of a double movement: on the one hand "the movement of *laissez faire*—the efforts ... to expand the scope and influence of self-regulating markets", and on the other "the movement of protection—the initiatives, again by a wide range of social actors, to insulate the fabric of social life from the destructive impact of market pressures" (Block 2008: 1).

The "double movement" is necessary and inevitable because while nature, society and humanity must be conceptually marked as commodities (refigured as land, money and labour) in capitalist societies, in reality, Polanyi argued, their commodity status is fictitious, and there can be no pure "market society" (Hart and Hann 2009: 5). *Laissez-faire* thinkers' demands for markets to be detached from political regulation and left to the invisible governance of their own logic have, at various junctures, held great political sway. But whenever this happens, it provokes social and economic crisis, for ultimately, land, money and labour cannot be entirely abandoned to market forces. Unlike other commodities, human labour is not produced for sale across a market, its "supply" cannot simply be reduced or expanded in line with the demand for it, Polanyi argued. Moreover, if employers were set free to consume and discard human labour power as they might other merchandise, all social bonds and even human reproduction would become unsustainable. "To allow the market mechanism to be sole director of the fate of human beings and their natural environment, indeed, even of the amount and use of purchasing power, would result in the demolition of society", Polanyi (2001: 73) concluded.

One way of reading the "double movement" is to imagine it as an expression of the class struggle produced by capitalism as an economic system. Those whose interests lie with capital press to extend and deregulate markets, while organized labour resists and fights for measures to preserve society against the chaos and destruction wrought by unfettered markets. Through this lens, the social-democratic political settlement of the postwar period appears as a compromise between the forces of *laissez faire* and those of social protection as regards the commodification of labour. And through this lens, the current crisis also appears sharper and more profound than any that has gone before. Fraser (2013: 125) observes that in an increasingly globalized economy, territorial states are less able to protect their citizens from market forces. And where in the past, there were left-leaning, social democratic parties representing the interests of worker citizens and resisting pressures to extend and deregulate markets, today's political elites "are explicitly or implicitly neoliberal… Committed first and foremost to protecting investors, virtually all of them—including self-professed social democrats—demand 'austerity' and 'deficit reduction', despite the threats such policies pose to economy, society and nature" (Fraser 2013: 120–121).

For Fraser, the current failure of "society" to provide an effective counterweight to "economy" is linked to political disillusionment with "the forms of social protection that were institutionalized in the welfare and developmental states of the postwar era" on the part of a wide range of critics, including antiracists, feminists, and LGBT liberationists, whose own political projects often "focused more on recognition than redistribution" (2013: 127). These were social movements that contested the exclusions implied by "protection" (for instance, married women's exclusion from labour markets), without necessarily calling for the expansion of self-regulating markets. Fraser argues that they fit neither pole of the double movement: "Championing neither marketization nor social protection, they espoused a third political project, which I shall call emancipation" (2013: 128). We need to recognize and explore "the shifting relations among [these] three sets of political forces, whose projects intersect and collide. The triple movement foregrounds the fact that each can ally, in principle, with either of the two poles against the third" (2013: 129).

Convincing as this may appear in relation to twentieth century political contestations around war, imperialism, race, gender, and sexuality, if we take struggles around transatlantic slavery as our focus, then marketization, social protection, and emancipation do not appear as neatly separable political forces.

Modernity and Slavery

Mainstream social and political theory has paid much attention to questions about why twentieth century history did not follow the course that orthodox liberal or Marxist theory predict. However, as scholars whose thinking is informed by postcolonial and critical race theory observe, there is a prior, more fundamental problem with the standard narrative in which history unfurled in staged progress from the "primitive" to the "civilized" and from feudalism into capitalism, culminating with "the modern individual" at the story's end (for example Chakrabarty 1992; Gilroy 1993; Parekh 1995; Brace 2004; Bhambra 2007; Shilliam 2012). Liberalism as a political ideology actually developed and thrived alongside the *expansion* of European colonialism and transatlantic slavery (Mills 1998). Transatlantic slavery was *modern* slavery. The slave trade was organised in the fashion of other markets, financed and insured by capitalist institutions; enslaved human beings were put to work producing raw materials and goods that were crucial to the industrial development of Britain and the free Northern states of America (Williams 1964; Rodney 1989; James 2001); and bureaucratic techniques later employed to attempt to maximize the productivity of free-wage workers were first developed as mechanisms to maximize the productivity of enslaved plantation workers.

Through twenty-first century liberal eyes, the horrible injustice of slavery and the moral superiority of the system of free-wage labour over that of chattel slavery appear self-evident. But until the nineteenth century, the immorality of slavery was by no means obvious to most white Europeans and Americans in the modern Atlantic World. In fact, the idea of slavery as an absolute and categorical moral wrong, a status that can never, in any circumstance, be justifiably given to anyone, did not even begin to be articulated until the second half of the eighteenth century. The enslavement of Africans and people of African descent under the system of transatlantic slavery was initially imagined by white Europeans and Americans as justified by natural laws, and sanctified by God. Some may have considered slavery as regrettable, and/or believed that slaveholders had a duty of care toward the enslaved, but slavery was largely perceived as an unchangeable, God-given feature of society (Haskell 1998). The question of whether or not Christian scripture permitted or outlawed slavery continued to be the subject of dispute amongst eighteenth century Europeans, even those who condemned the cruelties associated with colonial slavery (Stoddard 1995: 390).

There is no consensus amongst historians as to what actually prompted the dramatic shift in attitudes towards slavery in Western societies (for example see Bender 1992), but in dominant liberal discourse on the history of liberal societies, it is widely assumed that the emergence of a market economy was a precondition for political freedom and equality (Friedman 1962; Reisman 2002), and that antislavery thinkers were progressive champions of a world of both political and economic freedom. And yet there was, David Bryon Davis (1992: 78) notes, "no consistent or inevitable connection between antislavery doctrine and the laissez faire ideal of a competitive labor market" in the eighteenth century, and some antislavery thinkers were as keen to preserve a paternalistic and unequal social order as they were to abolish the legal institution of chattel slavery. Indeed, neither pro- nor antislavery thinking of the eighteenth and nineteenth century are easily assimilated into a model that posits a sharp division between forward-looking freemarketeers and backward-looking traditionalists, or between modern liberal egalitarians and premodern protagonists of hierarchy.

Antislavery, Pro-Hierarchy Thinking

The original antislavery thinkers did not live in societies in which all individuals were formally constructed as political equals, and their case against chattel slavery "reflected the ambivalent attitudes of a transitional age and economy" (Davis 1992: 78). In eighteenth-century Britain and in the "free" Northern states of America, people were still largely divided into two groups—those who had masters (servants, apprentices, labourers, wives, children) and those who exercised mastery (propertied white men). For poor people to be "masterless" was widely perceived as a threat to social order, including by most of those who opposed the institution of slavery. In England from the fifteenth century on, this threat had been addressed through a series of extremely coercive measures to curtail the freedom of movement of "vagabonds" and "vagrants", and by making the parish of birth responsible for assuring masterless persons the means of life, however minimal. That arrangement came under increasing pressure as both land privatisation and industrialisation advanced apace in the eighteenth century. In these conditions, the burden of poor relief on parishes became heavier, while the demand for labourers in industrial towns expanded. The question of how to secure a supply of labour for rapidly expanding industries and to ensure that workers submitted to the discipline of factory work came to be viewed as a pressing problem.

Some key figures in the antislavery movement could be described as *laissez faire* thinkers insofar as they linked the problem of labour discipline to pauperism, and considered the Poor Laws and associated system of Parish Relief as a barrier to the effective functioning of the emerging labour market: "In general it is only hunger which can spur and goad [the poor] on to labour; yet our laws have said, they shall never hunger" (Reverend Joseph Townsend quoted by Davis 1992: 78). Pitt, Burke, Bentham, and Malthus were all simultaneously vocal opponents both of slavery and of measures to protect the poor against the pull of the market's invisible hand. Yet other luminaries of the English antislavery movement, most notably William Wilberforce, were keen to preserve the old arrangements and dependencies, and took a highly paternalist stance toward the English poor.

But even here, it is difficult to neatly slot the two different approaches into what would now be understood as "free-market" versus "social-protectionist" thinking. Advocates of *laissez faire* may have argued against the social protections that in theory allowed the poor to survive without entering paid employment, but they were not necessarily calling for workers to enjoy rights to move freely within labour markets. Indeed, until the late nineteenth century in England, the system of wage labour was grafted onto a highly traditional model of dependency, legally enshrined in masters and servants legislation. Until the repeal of this legislation in 1875, industrial-wage workers also had masters to whom they were often bound, to varying degrees, by highly coercive legal as well as pecuniary pressures. The liberalization of markets in the late eighteenth and nineteenth centuries did not yield what would be adjudged free wage labour by contemporary standards (Steinfeld 2001). And the coercive and servile elements of "free" employment relations were rarely the object of British antislavery activists' political concern or condemnation. In fact, many of the movement's key figures were themselves employers with strong views on the need for servants to be industrious, diligent, sober, faithful, and respectful to their masters (Davis 1992: 62). As Davis (1992: 95) shows, "denunciation of colonial slavery... implied no taste for a freer or more equal society". This was true in relation to racial as well as class inequalities.

By the late eighteenth century, race played a central role in proslavery thinkers' defense of chattel slavery. In the West Indies and the American South, tropes of enslaved Africans and their descendants as "evasive, disguised, lazy, childlike, lying, thieving, distrustful, capricious", yet also kind and cheerful "songsters" were deployed to support the argument that people racialized as black were, by nature, unfit or unready for the exercise of freedom (Hall 2002: 102). Though some early white British critics of colonial slavery considered enslaved Africans to be fellow human beings in the sense that they too were God's creation, this often led them to argue for the Christianization of slaves, and the amelioration, as opposed to the abolition, of slavery (Stoddard 1995: 391). Indeed, many of the white figures who are today held up as icons of the antislavery movement shared proslavery thinkers' vision of black slaves as, in William Wilberforce's words, so "uninformed" and "debased" as to be "almost incapacitated for the reception of civil rights" (Festa 2010: 14).

Wilberforce's reservations about the capacity of the enslaved to exercise freedom were so great that his primary concern was to end the transatlantic slave *trade* and not slavery *per se*. His hope was that by abolishing the slave trade, "a disposition to breed instead of buying" would be produced amongst the planter class, he wrote in a diary entry in 1818, elsewhere explaining that "our object was by ameliorating regulations, and by stopping the influx of uninstructed savages, to advance slowly towards the period when these unhappy things might exchange their degraded state of slavery for that of free and industrious peasantry" (quoted in Jordan 2005: 180–181). Nor were British antislavery campaigners necessarily keen to have the slaves they sought to liberate live alongside them on British soil. It was precisely because "The large numbers of emancipated slaves taken to Britain after the American Revolution were not welcome in a white nation that had tried to deport all blacks in the late sixteenth century" that the British established "the colony of Sierra Leone in 1787 as a refuge for blacks freed during the American War of Independence" (Davis 2003b: 65). Even Granville Sharp, one of the more radical figures of the British antislavery movement, expressed concerns about "swarms of negroes" arriving in England (Blackburn 2011: 151), and is reputed to have actively sought to discourage English gentlemen from offering succour and support to destitute black people in London on grounds that "charity would blind them to their own best interest" and discourage them from agreeing to embark for Sierra Leone (Davis 1992: 100).

For the early British abolitionists, slavery was not so much an affront to the inherent dignity and equality of every human being as to the "traditional" English values and laws that constructed all individuals—whether master or servant, man or woman, adult or child, white or black—"as *subjects* of the king;... bound by the king's laws and... entitled to the king's protection" (Davis 1992: 94, original emphasis). It was the colonial slaveholder's *unrestrained* power over the slave that was understood as wrong. Slavery was an evil "not because of its inherent injustice, its inequality, or its permanent subordination of one class of men. It is an 'artificial' and 'unnatural' relation which lacks the legitimacy of tradition and which removes bother master and slave from the restraints that should control *all* men" (Davis 1992: 96). Early British antislavery thinking was thus:

> neither a traditionalist attack on a capitalist innovation, nor a capitalist attack on an archaic form of authority. In some ways it was a combination of both... the abolitionists' ideal of the plantation's future was thus a strange hybrid: a kindly, paternalistic master ministering to his grateful Negro "yeomen", both subject to the administrative agents of the king and dedicated to the commercial prosperity of the empire! (Davis 1992: 102).

It is revealing that by the mid-nineteenth century, American proslavery thinkers articulated a *defence* of slavery in which the institution was depicted as something very like this strange hybrid (without the oversight of a king, obviously).

The Moral Economies of Slavery and Wage Labour

One strand of antislavery argument from the eighteenth century to the present day concerns the wrongness of treating human beings as objects of property. In 1845, George Bourne, one of the founders of the American Anti-Slavery Society, argued that there are a variety of ways "in which mankind hold control over each other, and sometimes unjustly and oppressively", but the singular wrong of slavery is that it makes "free agents, chattels—converting *persons* into *things*—sinking immortality into *merchandize*... not exacting involuntary labor, but sinking man into an *implement* of labor... uncreating A MAN to make room for *a thing*!" (1845: 7–8). In response to such arguments, many nineteenth century proslavery thinkers "narrowed their claims to property rights in slaves to a claim to their labor, and a right to labor for the most part warranted a further right to obedience", Stephen Best (2004: 8–9) notes, quoting Francis Lieber, 1849, as follows: "Properly speaking... the slave himself is not property but his labour is... We own the labour of the slave and this cannot be done without keeping the person performing the labour, thus owned, in bondage".

To this notion that the slaveholder, like the employer of a formally free labourer, laid claim only to the labour and obedience, not the *person* of the slave, American proslavery thinkers added a blistering critique of the system of free-wage labour in Europe and the free North (Cobden 1854; Cunliffe 1979; Greenberg 1996). Their attack on what they dubbed "white" or "wage slavery" is reminiscent of Polanyi's discussion of the consequences of allowing the unfettered operation of a market in labour. It focused on the abject squalor in which wage labourers lived, hungered and died in industrial cities, depicting their "freedom" as but the liberty to starve (and contemporary scholarship estimates that mortality in most English industrial towns in the 1830s and 1840s actually was higher "than it had been at any point in the previous 100 years of their development", (Szreter 2005)).

Proslavery thinkers cast both chattel slavery and wage labour in terms of a taken-for-granted, highly unequal power relation between two classes. As proslavery activist John Calhoun put it, "in every civilized society one part of the community lived off the labor of the other part" (Bradley and Tarver 1969: 165). The moral distinction between the two systems was that chattel slaves were acknowledged as dependants (and so in this respect as persons rather than things), and according to proslavery thinkers, their masters graciously provided for them from cradle to grave. In the system of wage slavery by contrast, the labourers' dependence was denied, leaving wage slaves adrift and forcing them to fend for themselves even when too young, too sick or too old to work. As George Fitzhugh of Virginia argued in his 1857 tract, *Cannibals All!*, "Capital exercises a more perfect compulsion over free laborers than human masters over slaves, for free laborers must at all times work or starve, and slaves are supported whether they work or not". Chattel slavery, moreover, was said to prevent the overexploitation of labourers by making the private slaveholder "responsible to society for the welfare of his Slaves" (Bradley and Tarver 1969: 165). Given the heavy emphasis on sex commerce in contemporary discourse on "modern slavery", it is also worth noting that nineteenth-century American proslavery thinkers often dwelt on female prostitution as a "problem" rooted in the system of free labour (Stanley 1998: 245).

The proslavery case was obviously self-serving. Its depiction of chattel slavery as a benignly paternalistic institution conveniently enabled slaveholders to "use and exploit some members of their society without having to admit that these people [were] being ... used strictly as a means to support the ends of the dominant group" (McGary 1998: 202). Its romantic portrait of "the organic unity of the household embodied in slavery" glossed over the routine and violent sexual exploitation of enslaved women (Stanley 1998: 245). It also hinged on assertions that private slaveholders had a necessary interest in nurturing slaves in infancy and the humanity to provide for them in old age, a claim that is contradicted by a wealth of historical evidence on chattel slavery in the American South and elsewhere in the New World (Julia O'Connell Davidson 2015). And it was explicitly white supremacist, with its vision of those racialized as black as "naturally" dependent and morally feeble, so better off under the benevolent rule of a white master.

With their defence of patriarchal authority, and their emphasis on the social, as opposed to the individual, American proslavery thinkers may look "premodern". And yet they were not opposed to all markets (transatlantic slave economies were integrally linked to and dependent on industrializing capitalist economies as much as vice-versa), nor were they necessarily yearning to return to a bygone age. They viewed the system of antebellum slavery—either as it stood, or in slightly modified form—as consistent with economic progress and modernization (Stepman 2013), yet simultaneously affording society protection against the evils of a pure-market system. More importantly for men like Fitzhugh, slavery offered protection against the threat of socialism. Indeed, in his view, antislavery campaigners were actually "committed to Socialism and Communism, to the most ultra doctrines of Garrison, Goodell, Smith and Andrews—to no private property, no church, no law, no government,—to free love, free lands, free women and free churches" (Fitzhugh 1857). The abolition of slavery would open the door to a society without law or government, in which white and black, men and women, alike enjoyed these frightful freedoms.

If this was indeed the motivating vision of American abolitionists, their political project must be judged a spectacular failure.

Emancipation and the Race of Freedom

Under the Southern system of slavery, the freedom/slavery binary of liberal thought mapped onto an imagined racial binary between white and black, such that citizenship, which implied enjoyment of the "rights of Man" including mastery over self and others, was coded as white. While slavery persisted, those racialized as black were socially fixed on American soil as perpetual outsiders. Manumission was possible, but it was regulated and limited by the state, and arranged in such a way as to be an exception that in no way undermined the rules governing the associations between race, and slave or free status. Whether born to free status, or freed from slavery, "people of colour" were not citizens. The institution of slavery provided the moorings for race as much as race provided the ideological justification for slavery. What, then, would be the status and position of those racialized as black in its absence?

This question was divisive even amongst those committed to outlawing chattel slavery. Black, and some white, activists simultaneously articulated demands for an end to bondage *and* for racial equality. But as

Frederick Douglass (2003: 240) noted in his scathing comments on "the American prejudice against color", this was a prejudice from which "the abolitionists themselves were not entirely free". For those who believed in the fiction of race and white superiority, whether proponents of abolition or not, the legal abolition of slavery represented a political dilemma because it would leave uncontained and masterless millions of former slaves, imagined as unfit for freedom by virtue of their blackness. One solution to this "problem" in the post-Civil War period in the US South was provided by the sharecropping system, which remained in place until the second half of the twentieth century (Novak 1978). This functioned to bind formally free black farmers to the land, thereby simultaneously assuring white landowners a supply of labour and preserving society against social mobility on the part of those racialized as black.

That system was bolstered by the southern convict lease system which allowed people convicted of offences like vagrancy (also "mischief" and "insulting gestures") to be contracted out as labourers, and subject to brutal regimes of coerced and unpaid labour in lumber camps, brickyards, railroads, farms, plantations and other privately owned businesses (Alexander 2010: 31). It "transferred symbolically significant numbers of black people from the prison of slavery to the slavery of prison", Angela Davis (2003a: 8) observes. In essence, what vagrancy laws criminalize is not merely poverty, but masterlessness. Their extensive use to coerce freed black men and women into a condition that implied both rightlessness and severe labour exploitation in the post-emancipation U.S. South speaks to the strength of the political resistance on the part of the ruling white elite to accept people of colour as morally worthy of inclusion in civil society.

The abolition of slavery also represented a threat to the construction of race as a hereditary, castelike, social marker in the sense that, while slavery existed, powerful legal and social prohibitions against sexual relationships between white women and black men, in combination with laws that dictated that the status of children born of enslaved women followed that of their mothers, operated to fix all persons with African ancestry as slaves and so as outsiders. Emancipation made interracial marriage and "miscegenation" into an urgent political question. Behind the widespread white opposition to crossracial sexual relations, Hannah

Rosen observes, "was the specter of black economic mobility and its consolidation, through racial integration, of a world in which race had no visible significance" (Rosen 2005: 299), in other words, a world in which whiteness was eviscerated of privilege. The passage of Jim Crow laws in southern states, which segregated those racialized as black and white in public and private spaces and which were supported by extensive and brutal legal and extra-legal violence, served to ward off this spectre (Alexander 2010; Camp 2004). These laws remained in place until the 1960s.

Reflecting on this history, Kevin Bales, a man at the forefront of the contemporary social movement against what he terms "modern slavery", often describes the emancipation of slaves in the United States as "botched". He observes that the end of the American Civil War brought freedom to all slaves, "but *only* freedom, and that was a great wrong" (Bales 2005: 5, original emphasis). Slavery is theft, and American society and economy had been built upon the stolen lives and labour of slaves, yet the debt owed them was not acknowledged:

> The result of this neglect has reverberated into our own lives… Generations of African Americans were sentenced to second-class status, exploited, denied, and abused. Without education and basic resources, it has been difficult for African American families to build the economic foundation needed for full participation and well-being in American society… At the end of the American Civil War, nearly 4 million ex-slaves were dumped with little preparation into the society and economy of the United States. (Bales 2005: 6).

Aside from noting that talk of ex-slaves "dumped with little preparation" echoes Wilberforce's fears concerning the outcomes of a sudden grant of civil rights to those whose minds were "uninformed", Bales' use of the term "botched" is interesting in that it implies slave emancipation was a particular and specific job that was done badly, a task or project that was spoiled. For this to be so, "emancipation" must either be imagined as something isolable from the political order of the society and economy in which it took place, or as a project allied to another, broader movement for political transformation.

In the USA, the abolition of chattel slavery as a legal institution meant that those formerly ascribed the status of slave were no longer ascribed that status. But they still lived in a society in which rights and freedoms were differentially allocated through reference to hierarchies of race, class, gender, age and nation. Even in the North, not all free black male citizens enjoyed voting rights at the time (no women enjoyed suffrage), and various forms of racial segregation were practiced (Stewart 1998). They also lived in a society in which different types and degrees of dependency were produced through interlocking economic, political and social inequalities (Edwards 1998). Slaves became *de jure* free in societies where it was commonplace for many groups of people who were not socially or legally constructed as "slaves" to experience often extremely heavy restraints on freedom.

Conceived as a project to eradicate chattel slavery as a legal institution, slave emancipation was not "botched" in the United States, but successful. However, efforts to sustain and even strengthen race as a system of domination were equally successful. Indeed, the continuing resilience of that system in the twenty-first century is routinely demonstrated by police killings of black citizens (Davis 2014). The problem for African Americans today is not only or even that past injustices have prevented them from building "the economic foundation needed for full participation and well-being in American society" as Bales puts it, but rather that antiblack racism remains part of the living tissue of American society. African Americans live, as Saidiya Hartman (2007: 6) puts it, "in the future created by" racial slavery. Transatlantic slavery's "afterlife" is a present in which black lives continue to be devalued and imperilled and whiteness continues to be privileged.

Imagined as a project to abolish both chattel slavery *and* race as a system of domination, emancipation was certainly a "botched" job. Yet contemporary abolitionists seemingly have little interest in tackling its failures as such. The restraints on freedom today engendered by antiblackness are uncannily absent from campaigns against "modern slavery" (Stewart 2015). The millions of black victims of America's prison industrial complex, for example, are not present in the roll call of "modern slaves" that organizations like Walk Free and Free the Slaves wish to emancipate (Julia O'Connell Davidson 2015). In fact, even though campaigners like Bales seem at one moment to acknowledge that emancipation in the United States was made hollow by racism, for them as much as for most of their white eighteenth- and nineteenth-century forebears, the struggle to end slavery is distinct from the struggle for racial equality.

Antislavery Today

There are other respects in which the politics of the new brand of antislavery activism that has developed in the twenty-first century look far from "emancipatory" in Fraser's terms. The campaign against so-called "modern slavery" is characterised by the same blend of promarket and prohierarchy thinking as was often found in eighteenth- and nineteenth-century white abolitionist politics, with matters further complicated by the fact that, since slavery no longer exists anywhere as a legal status, the question of who, precisely, the new abolitionists wish to emancipate and from what is much more difficult to answer (Julia O'Connell Davidson 2015). Those described as "modern slaves" are selectively drawn from populations affected by phenomena ranging from the exploitation and abuse of irregular migrants and migrant workers, through systems of bonded labour, early and forced marriage, to children's involvement in hazardous forms of labour. Most serious academic analyses of such phenomena link them, in one way or another, to the global neoliberal economic restructuring that has gathered pace since the 1990s, leading to a sharp growth in the numbers of people now standing without either social protection or any access to the means of life. Yet those campaigning against 'modern slavery' are rarely critics of marketization.

The Walk Free Foundation, for example, was founded by mining magnate Andrew Forrest, Australia's richest man, and author of a recent government commissioned report on indigenous Australians that smacks, in many respects, of nineteenth century *laissez faire* thought on the problem of pauperism in England (Marsh 2015). But there are nonetheless traditional aspects of (European) society that Walk Free and other new abolitionist organizations are keen to protect and promote. Thus, they run campaigns against "forced marriage" but not against compulsory heterosexuality, or women's lack of access to abortion and divorce, for instance. They manage to combine calls for the emancipation of "modern slaves" with a generally positive view both of free market capitalism and of the patriarchal family form (FTS 2013a, b). Many new abolitionist organizations support legal and other interventions that indiscriminately target sex workers, whether they have been forced into prostitution or chosen it as the best earning opportunity available to them, sometimes working with police to forcibly remove them from workplaces and then confining the "rescued" in "rehabilitation" centres that often bear more than a passing resemblance to prisons or workhouses (Soderlund 2005).

All of this returns me to questions about Fraser's notion of a "three-sided conflict among proponents of marketization, adherents of social protection, and partisans of emancipation".

Multiple Ambivalences

Fraser (2013: 129) states that each of the three constituent poles of the "triple movement" are inherently ambivalent, noting that social protection can relieve communities from aspects of marketization's disintegrative effects "while simultaneously entrenching domination *within* and *among* them"; marketization can have positive as well as destructive effects; and emancipation is also ambivalent—"Even as it overcomes domination, emancipation may help dissolve the solidary ethical basis of social protection, thereby clearing a path for marketization". What she does not comment upon is that fact that marketization and social protection are not actually mutually exclusive political projects. There may be individual proponents of marketization so libertarian as to advocate virtually no limits on commodification, but in the real world, the political backers of marketization also typically hold, and have always typically held, equally vigorous political views on the kind of social and political order in which market freedom can and should be enjoyed.

Missing from Fraser's discussion is reference to the long and ongoing history of political violence associated with marketization. Marx may have reproduced elements of the orthodox transition narrative in his analysis of the newness of modern capitalist society, but he powerfully countered liberalism's celebratory reading of that narrative with a more dismal story about the "freeing up" of "free" wage labour, showing how the creation of a class of individuals dependent on wage labour was a long and bloody process. It required both dispossession and a multifaceted legal apparatus of coercion to force "free" proletarians to sell their commodified labour power. The movement to a society in which freedom came to look "like a function of possession" was accompanied and propelled by swathes of brutal legislation extending the range of activities that were defined as crimes against property (Hill 1967). The contemporary neoliberal shift is also being supported by an aggressive process of criminalization designed to preserve both economy and society against the consequences of marketization. This includes increasing criminalization of behaviours deemed "antisocial", even of homelessness (Rodger 2008), and populations racialized as black or "minority" are disproportionately affected Davis (2003a); Sudbury 2005). Those championing the expansion and deregulation of markets are also, in the main, advocates of ever-more stringent and punitive legislation on immigration, again, with a view to preserving and protecting a particular kind of "society". And again, the human cost of such legislation and the accompanying militarization of borders is vast. The IOM (2014) recently issued a report estimating that more than 40.000 migrants had died between 2000 and 2013 in the course of "irregular" movement, for example, and immigration detention is being used on an unprecedented scale (Anderson 2013).

If it is hardly unusual for political parties in liberal capitalist societies to pursue agendas that are simultaneously economically liberal and socially authoritarian, so also Fraser's discussion of ambiguities of "the forces of social protection" seems incomplete. Yes, the social protection afforded by worker citizenship in the postwar years foundered on and reproduced divisions and inequalities in terms of gender, age, race and nationality. Far from operating as a progressive force within nations, "citizenship has constructed complex and layered levels of inequalities" in terms of access to sustenance, health and educational services, justice, protection and freedom, and in combination with immigration law, it has generated a system of "global apartheid" (Sharma 2006: 142). But another ambiguity is that whilst social democratic parties pressed to establish systems that would protect "society" (and its hierarchies), they also always sought to sustain capitalist market economies. Even in the heyday of welfare capitalism, concessions to the need for state intervention into the labour market were not accompanied by a rejection of the classical liberal assumption that labour is property that can be sold away from the self (Stanley 1998). The idea of labour power as a disembodied and market-alienable "thing", which is core to the political project of marketization, was retained by social protectionist, social democratic states, even as they sought to moderate the effects of its treatment as such. The political backers of social protection in welfare capitalist states were not agitating for the wholesale rejection of markets and their replacement by command economies.

Finally, though Fraser (2013: 131) talks of "emancipation" as ambivalent in the sense that its proponents attempt to negotiate a line between "a valid critique of oppressive protection and legitimate claims for labour-market access, on the one hand, [and] an uncritical embrace of meritocratic individualism and privatized consumerism, on the other", she does not dwell on the fact that there is, sadly, no shortage of contemporary or historical examples of movements that campaign for emancipation from one form of domination whilst supporting or failing to challenge another. Again, the history of abolitionism is instructive. In the aftermath of the Civil War, opponents of slavery were often quite explicit about the fact that freed slaves must learn to suborn themselves to the dominion of employers under the system of free-wage labour, and keenly instructed the emancipated on how to abide by "the new rules of the game: the new requirements and responsibilities of contracting on the one hand, and the new compulsions of necessity and self-discipline on the other" (Berlin et al. 1986: 117). And most abolitionists worked not merely with a market logic in which emancipation would right the wrong of slavery by transforming "chattels into self-proprietors", but also a protectionist logic in which it would be formerly enslaved *men* who would enjoy "the birthright of all free men: title not only to himself but to his wife—her person, labor, and sexuality" (Stanley 1998: 28–30).

Taken together, these additional ambivalences suggest that the "double movement" is an adjustment *internal* to any and all political projects in market societies (including many emancipatory projects) that do not challenge the fundamental premise of such societies, that is, that economic and political life are separable.

Conclusion

In liberal discourse, political life—the state, the law, civil society (the realm in which human beings are constituted as "persons")—is separated from economic life—the market (the realm in which persons act to produce and exchange commodities or 'things'). But in reality, economic and political life, or market and state, are mutually imbricated, and the idea that they are separate is precisely that, an idea. As David Graeber puts it, "States created markets. Markets require states. Neither could continue without the other, at least, in anything like the forms we would recognize today" (2011: 71). This was as true of transatlantic slave markets as it is of labour and all other state-sanctioned markets, as evidenced in the "bifurcated existence" of slaves as both things and persons (Hartman 1997). Although slaves were transacted as property, they were also acknowledged "as moral, intellectual and responsible beings" in laws that deemed them criminally culpable human agents (Douglass 2003: 275). Indeed, without the state's intervention to create slaves as *persons* (of a particular, inferior, and rightless kind), slaveholders' property rights in them as *things* would have been empty, for it was the legal edifice that fixed slaves as subpersons which contained slave flight, resistance and rebellion. The power of slaveholders over slaves in the Atlantic world was underwritten by the slave states whose laws, backed by violence, gave slaves this double life as persons and things.

The abolition of laws that gave private slaveholders property rights in individual slaves was an act of emancipation. But it did not eliminate all markets that rupture the supposedly inviolable distinction between persons and things. In wage labour, specifically human attributes and capacities (skill, knowledge, the physical power to labour) are marked as commodities, yet as these attributes and capacities are indivisible from the body and person of the labourer, employers actually buy a power of command over persons, not things (Braverman 1974; Nichols 1980; Lebowitz 2003). Nor, as has been seen, did the abolition of chattel slavery eradicate all possibility of constructing legal distinctions between persons and subpersons based on the idea of race, or between rights-bearing self-proprietors and their domestic dependents (Mills 1998). In fact, as the idea that freedom and equality is posited and confirmed when self-owning individuals voluntarily contract to exchange their commodities became more firmly entrenched in liberal societies, liberalism was recast "so as to validate unprecedented state authority over both wage labor and home life, spheres once held to be self regulating" (Stanley 1998: 268).

The political agenda opened up by this reconfigured liberalism was not so much a debate on whether states should pursue policies of *either* marketization *or* social protection, but rather on different visions of the balance to be struck between marketization and social protection, and of the nature, order and values of the society that was to be protected. The basic rules of the game were agreed, and the political arguments (framed as marketization, social protection and emancipation) focused on questions as to whether or not the playing pitch needed to be leveled (should workers be guaranteed the basic resources necessary for "full participation and well-being" in society through "social rights" and if so, what kind of rights, what level of resources, and what criteria of eligibility?), and about who should be allowed to play and in what positions (those racialized as black or brown? Women? Migrants? Homosexuals? Children?).

There is no doubt that it is preferable to be included in than excluded from the game by which access to material resources and social privileges are allocated. It is better to be exploited than "counted as not worth exploiting" as Fraser (2013: 132) puts it. It is also better to be protected against disease, starvation, and ignorance by hierarchical forms of social protection than to be counted as not worth protecting at all. And I believe that some political balances between marketization, social protection and emancipation are infinitely preferable to others, and so worth fighting for. But if we are committed to overcoming domination in all its guises, I also think we have to look beyond "the triple movement", as much as beyond the "double movement".

"No private property, no church, no law, no government, free love, free lands, free women and free churches" (Fitzhugh 1857), – Fitzhugh may have been wrong to attribute these ideals to most mid-nineteenth-century abolitionists, but the fact that a proslavery thinker perceived them as a profound threat is a reminder that to pursue a world without domination, we need to keep dreaming of what he disparagingly described as "a better, but untried, form of society". We have to keep trying to imagine a borderless world, a world in which whiteness, maleness and heterosexuality are eviscerated of privilege; in which labour, nature and money are decommodified and a truly human and sustainable global economy is established, one in which productive activity is shared amongst those able to undertake it and arranged to satisfy the needs of all.

Acknowledgement I am grateful to the Leverhulme Trust (MRF-2012-085) for supporting the research on which this chapter is based.

References

Alexander, M. (2010). *The new Jim Crow*. New York: The New Press.

Anderson, B. (2013). *Us and them: The dangerous politics of immigration control*. Oxford: Oxford University Press.

Bales, K. (2005). *Understanding global slavery*. Berkeley: University of California Press.

Bender, T. (1992). *The antislavery debate*. Berkeley: University of California Press.

Berlin, I., Hahn, S., Steven, M., Reidy, J., & Rowland, L. (1986). The terrain of freedom: The struggle over the meaning of free labor in the U.S. South. *History Workshop Journal, 22*(1), 108–130.

Best, S. (2004). *The fugitive's properties: Law and the poetics of possession*. Chicago: University of Chicago Press.

Bhambra, G. (2007). *Rethinking modernity: Postcolonialism and the sociological imagination*. Basingstoke: Palgrave Macmillan.

Blackburn, R. (2011). *The American crucible: Slavery, emancipation and human rights*. London: Verso.

Block, F. (2008). Polanyi's double movement and the reconstruction of critical theory. *Interventions Economiques* 38. http://interventionseconomiques. revues.org/274. Accessed 20 Nov 2015.

Bourne, G. (1845). *A condensed anti-slavery Bible argument: By a citizen of Virginia*. New York: S. W. Benedict. http://docsouth.unc.edu/church/bourne/bourne.html. Accessed 20 Nov 2015.

Brace, L. (2004). *The politics of property*. Edinburgh: Edinburgh University Press.

Bradley, B., & Tarver, J. (1969). John C. Calhoun's argumentation in defense of slavery. *The Southern Speech Journal, 35*(2), 163–175.

Braverman, H. (1974). *Labor and monopoly capital.* New York: Monthly Review Press.

Camp, S. (2004). *Closer to freedom.* London: University of North Carolina Press.

Chakrabarty, D. (1992). Postcoloniality and the artifice of history: Who speaks for 'Indian' pasts? *Representations, 37,* 1–27.

Cobden, J. (1854). *The white slaves of England.* Auburn: Miller, Orton & Mulligan.

Cunliffe, M. (1979). *Chattel slavery and wage slavery: The Anglo-American context.* Athens: University of Georgia Press.

Davis, D. B. (1992). The problem of slavery in the age of revolution, 1770–1823. In T. Bender (Ed.), *The antislavery debate.* Berkeley: University of California Press.

Davis, A. (2003a). *Are prisons obsolete?* New York: Seven Stories Press.

Davis, D. B. (2003b). *Challenging the boundaries of slavery.* Cambridge, MA: Harvard University Press.

Davis, A. (2014). From Michael Brown to Assata Shakur, the racist state of America persists. *Guardian.* http://www.theguardian.com/commentisfree/2014/nov/01/michael-brown-assata-shakur-racist-state-of-america. Accessed 20 Nov 2015.

Douglass, F. (2003). *My bondage and my freedom.* New York: The Modern Library.

Edwards, L. (1998). The problem of dependency: African Americans, labor relations, and the law in the nineteenth-century South. *Agricultural History, 72*(2), 313–340.

Esping-Anderson, G. (1990). *The three worlds of welfare capitalism.* Cambridge: Polity.

Festa, L. (2010). Humanity without feathers. *Humanity: An International Journal of Human Rights, 1*(1), 3–27.

Fitzhugh, G. (1857). *Cannibals all!* Kindle Edition.

Fraser, N. (2013). A triple movement? Parsing the politics of crisis after Polanyi. *New Left Review, 81,* 119–132.

FTS. (2013a). Child slavery, child labor and exploitation of children in mining communities Obuasi, Ghana. Free the slaves. https://www.freetheslaves.net/document.doc?id=309.

FTS. (2013b). *Wives in slavery: Forced marriage in the Congo.* Free the slaves. http://ftsblog.net/wp-content/uploads/2013/06/FTS-ForcedMarriage-201306-V1-web.pdf-

Friedman, M. (1962). *Capitalism and freedom.* Chicago: University of Chicago Press.

Gilroy, P. (1993). *The Black Atlantic.* London: Verso.

Graeber, D. (2011). *Debt: The first 5000 years.* Brooklyn: Melville House.

Greenberg, K. (1996). *Honor and slavery*. Princeton, NJ: Princeton University Press.

Hall, C. (2002). *Civilising subjects*. Cambridge: Polity.

Hart, K., & Hann, C. (2009). Introduction: Learning from Polanyi. In C. Hann & K. Hart (Eds.), *Market and society*. Cambridge: Cambridge University Press.

Hartman, S. (1997). *Scenes of subjection: Terror, slavery and self-making in nineteenth century America*. Oxford: Oxford University Press.

Hartman, S. (2007). *Lose your mother: A journey along the Atlantic slave route*. New York: Farrar, Straus and Giroux.

Haskell, T. (1998). *Objectivity is not neutrality*. Baltimore: John Hopkins University Press.

Hill, C. (1967). *Reformation to industrial revolution*. London: Weidenfeld and Nicolson.

IOM. (2014). *Fatal journeys: Tracking lives lost during migration*. Geneva: International Organization for Migration. http://publications.iom.int/bookstore/free/FatalJourneys_CountingtheUncounted.pdf. Accessed 2 Mar 2015.

James, C. (2001). *The Black Jacobins*. London: Penguin.

Jordan, M. (2005). *The great abolition sham*. Stroud: Sutton Publishing.

Julia O'Connell Davidson, J. (2015). *Modern slavery: The margins of freedom*. London: Palgrave Macmillan.

Lebowitz, M. (2003). *Beyond capital*. London: Palgrave Macmillan.

Marsh, J. (2015). *A master plan for indigenous freedom*. Beyond trafficking and slavery, open democracy, July 1. https://www.opendemocracy.net/beyond-slavery/jillian-k-marsh/master-plan-for-indigenous-freedom. Accessed 20 Nov 2015.

McGary, H. (1998). Paternalism and slavery. In T. Lott (Ed.), *Subjugation and bondage* (pp. 187–208). New York: Rowman & Littlefield.

Macpherson, C. B. (1962). *The political theory of possessive individualism*. Oxford: Oxford University Press.

Mills, C. (1998). *The racial contract*. Ithaca: Cornell University Press.

Nichols, T. (1980). *Capital and labour*. London: Athelone Press.

Novak, D. (1978). *The wheel of servitude: Black forced labor after slavery*. Lexington: University Press of Kentucky.

O'Connor, J. (1998). Social justice, social citizenship, and the welfare state, 1965–1995: Canada in comparative context. In R. Helmes-Hayes & J. Curtis (Eds.), *The vertical mosaic revisited*. Toronto: University of Toronto Press.

Offe, C. (1984). *Contradictions of the welfare state*. London: Hutchinson.

Parekh, B. (1995). Liberalism and colonialism: A critique of Locke and Mill. In J. Nederveen & B. Parekh (Eds.), *The decolonization of imagination*. London: Zed.

Polyani, K. (2001). *The great transformation*. Boston: Beacon Press.

Reisman, G. (2002). *Some fundamental insights into the benevolent nature of capitalism*. http://www.capitalism.net/articles/Some%20Fundamental%20 Insights%20Into%20the%20Benevolent%20Nature%20of%20Capitalism. html. Accessed 14 Mar 15.

Rodger, J. (2008). *Criminalising social policy*. London: Routledge.

Rodney, W. (1989). *How Europe underdeveloped Africa*. Nairobi: Heinemann Kenya.

Rosen, H. (2005). The rhetoric of miscegenation and the reconstruction of race: Debating marriage, sex, and citizenship in postemancipation Arkansas. In P. Scully & D. Paton (Eds.), *Gender and slave emancipation in the Atlantic world*. London: Duke University Press.

Sassen, S. (2010). A savage sorting of winners and losers: Contemporary versions of primitive accumulation. *Globalizations, 7*(1), 23–50.

Sayer, D. (1991). *Capitalism and modernity: An excursus on Marx and Weber*. London: Routledge.

Sharma, N. (2006). *Home economics: Nationalism and the making of 'migrant workers' in Canada*. Toronto: University of Toronto Press.

Shilliam, R. (2012). Forget English freedom, remember Atlantic slavery: Common law, commercial law, and the significance of slavery for classical political economy. *New Political Economy, 17*(5), 591–609.

Slater, D. (1998). Public/private. In C. Jenks (Ed.), *Core sociological dichotomies* (pp. 138–150). London: Sage.

Soderlund, G. (2005). Running from the rescuers: New U.S. crusades against sex trafficking and the rhetoric of abolition. *NWSA Journal, 17*(3), 64–87.

Stanley, A. D. (1998). *From bondage to contract*. Cambridge: Cambridge University Press.

Stewart, J. B. (1998). The emergence of racial modernity and the rise of the White North. *Journal of the Early Republic, 18*, 181–217.

Stewart, J. B. (2015). 'Using history to make slavery history': The African American past and the challenge of contemporary slavery. *Social Inclusion, 3*(1), 125–135.

Steinfeld, R. (2001). *Coercion, contract and free labor in the nineteenth century*. Cambridge: Cambridge University Press.

Stepman, J. (2013). 'The very best form of socialism': The proslavery roots of the modern left'. *Breitbart*. http://www.breitbart.com/big-government/2013/08/06/ the-pro-slavery-roots-of-the-modern-left/. Accessed 20 Nov 2015.

Stoddard, E. (1995). A serious proposal for slavery reform: Sarah Scott's Sir George Ellison. *Eighteenth-Century Studies, 28*(4), 379–396.

Sudbury, J. (2005). Celling black bodies: Black women in the global prison industrial complex. *Feminist Review, 80*, 162–179.

Sullivan, S. (2013). Ben Carson: Obamacare worst thing 'since slavery'. *Washington Post.* 13 October. http://www.washingtonpost.com/blogs/post-politics/wp/2013/10/11/ben-carson-obamacare-worst-thing-since-slavery. Accessed 20 Nov 2015.

Szreter, S. (2005). 'Health and wealth'. *History & Policy.* Paper 34. http://www.historyandpolicy.org/papers/policy-paper-34.html. Accessed 25 Nov 2015.

Williams, E. (1964). *Capitalism and slavery.* Chapel Hill: University of North Carolina Press.

State, Market, or Back to the Family? Nostalgic Struggles for Proper Elder Care

Bernhard Weicht

Introduction

As human beings, our lives are not exclusively defined by periods of flourishing and growth; we rather experience various stages of needs, vulnerabilities and changing dependencies over the life course. These dependencies, reflecting thus an inherently human attribute, require care and support by others. How these needs are met, by whom and through which arrangements are questions for each individual and for society as a whole. People and countries have found different answers ranging from family-based solutions, to publicly financed institutions and the market where care receivers can buy various arrangements and services. However, all current possibilities—in Europe at least—face pressures due to both demographic and financial developments. People live longer and societies consist of more people in older age. The resulting increasing care needs are accompanied by family and labour market changes, which lead to shortages of those actors traditionally providing care services: women

B. Weicht (✉)
University of Innsbruck, Innsbruck, Austria

© The Editor(s) (if applicable) and The Author(s) 2016   **115**
C. Karner, B. Weicht (eds.), *The Commonalities of Global Crises*,
DOI 10.1057/978-1-137-50273-5_5

within families (Federici 2012). At the same time, welfare states reconsider further investments and spending in the field of social care. For both materialist and ideational reasons, many states reduce or at least refuse to increase their expenditure on long-term care, in particular in relation to institutional investments. The materialist reasoning is heavily influenced by global economic developments, of which the financial crisis is an example, that demonstrate that declining growth and fiscal income put pressures on state finances. Importantly, however, this materialist explanation needs to be accompanied by a focus on the ideological argumentation which underlies current welfare state changes. Similar to many other fields of social provision, where commodification and marketization are recurrently seen as the solution to a crisis situation, the field of care is increasingly evaluated according to an economisation strategy (Auth 2012). Economic concepts and ideals such as efficiency, privatization, outsourcing of services and consumerism install the market logic within various contexts of care.

The financial crisis that leads to pressures on both family and public spending is thus met by an ideological logic which favours market values and practices. If the family (and historically this means women within families) cannot and the state does not want to fulfil the arising care needs, is marketization the logical consequence? Are commodification and marketization of care desirable or even possible? Additionally to these empirical and moral questions, a theoretical concern arises: Taking up Joan Tronto's call for evaluating social theories according to how they make sense of care (Tronto and Weicht 2014), I want to investigate how the dominant analyses of commodification processes (most prominently Polanyi's [2001] concept of the double movement) capture these developments within the field of reproductive work.

Starting from the normative concern that commodification can cause threats to well-being (Polanyi 2001; Sayer 2004) I want to examine the various recent political changes in the field of elder care in order to identify possible logics and practices of marketization and commodification. For that I will inspect recent policy changes and programmes in the field of care in four different European countries, representing different welfare and care regimes (Da Roit and Weicht 2013). Care regimes consist of both materialist and ideational foundations and represent a complex web of institutional, regulatory, political and cultural factors which structure "the ways in which the financing and provision of care are organised" (Simonazzi 2009: 216). Starting thus from very divergent arrangements of care, I will explore how welfare states have been reacting politically and discursively to the crisis of care sketched herein. While social politics have recurrently shaped and fostered the commodification of care (see Ungerson 1997), these processes have also always been deterred by the moral associations related to these kinds of social practices; a struggle which brought forward various hybrids of care organised and provided by an interplay of the public sector, market actors and families. Whether and to what extent commodification of care is possible is thus also shaped by the moral conceptualization of the meaning of care. What care is defined to be and to represent delineates the possibility for the success of the logic of marketization. Or, in other words, commodification processes need to be based within the moral understanding of care in society (Weicht 2015b).

I start the discussion with an empirical overview of recent policy developments in the field of care in Sweden, the United Kingdom, the Netherlands and Austria. All four countries represent diverse care arrangements and, hence, the struggle to react to the care crisis plays out very differently. This is followed by an analysis of the various policy changes through Polanyi's and Fraser's concepts and discussions of commodification processes. I will propose that while in particular Polanyi's and Fraser's discussions of "fictitious commodities" are useful for the conceptualisation of care, they are missing a crucial element that defines care and other affective labour: the moral dimension. I will thus use Sayer's exploration of moral economies to capture the often nostalgically tinted search for the ideal of care. In the conclusion I try to sketch some political perspectives based on this newly adapted conceptualization of care as a fictitious commodity.

Struggling to Organise Care

Changing micro and macro structures such as the increasing employment of women in the labour market, growing family flexibility, and aging populations have caused challenges for the availability and accessibility of traditional arrangements of informal care. The resulting increasing informal care gaps are mirrored by shortages in the public care arrangements, and both gain even more significance in light of countries' attempts to reduce public spending. Societies have thus reacted to this situation by adjusting their specific mix of informal, public, institutional and private market solutions. While the organisation of care in Europe can be characterised by great diversity, the importance of markets and the market logic is rising steadily. In some countries, however, periods of increasing professionalisation and institutionalisation of elder-care services have been followed by processes of deinstitutionalisation and deprofessionalisation (Da Roit 2010). While these countries have started introducing cash-for-care schemes in order to reindividualise the responsibility for care, continental European countries have started similar cash benefit programmes in order to secure a care system based on family and private care structures (Da Roit and Le Bihan 2010) in which migrant domestic workers play an important role (Weicht 2010). Both situations must be seen as examples of intersections between the public sector, market organisations and the private sphere of the home. Since paying cash for services has widely been promoted as increasing people's choices and autonomous citizenship rights (Rummery 2009), Shutes (2012) argues that the attention to issues such as choice and control over care characterises shifting social relations between care users, care workers, families, employers and the state. In that sense, policy changes and a possible introduction of private markets are inevitably accompanied by particular discursive patterns that constitute the meaning of care (Weicht 2015b). These discursive patterns can be found in political and public discussions on care and function, as Zadoroznyi (2009) argues, as recipes for how to think and behave in relation to care. Ungerson (1999: 585), for example, explains that through the combination of political and discursive changes in the context of care "marketisation, privatisation and consumerism have been locked into a symbiotic relationship". Political decisions thus need to conform to what Glucksmann and Lyon (2006) describe as different levels of appropriateness, within the state, the market and the family. Different societies and welfare states navigate within certain social, cultural and political boundaries to encourage, restrict and organise the intrusion of markets in the context of care. The organisation of care between the various actors (mainly state, family and markets) is thus based on broader understandings of the relationship of economy vis-à-vis society, a crucial affiliation which Polanyi (2001) rightly describes as central for processes of marketization. In the following I will evaluate recent policy changes in four countries, representing different care regimes and different levels of commodification and marketization (Da Roit and Weicht 2013).

Sweden

As is the case with all Nordic care systems, Sweden's arrangements for elder care were founded on the idea of universal, state provided and— financed high-quality care for everyone in need. In the late 1990s and early 2000s, however, increasing possibilities were opened for the private for-profit sector (Erlandsson et al. 2013), culminating in the introduction of the Act on System of Choice in the Public Sector in 2009 (Andersson and Kvist 2014). By now, Erlandsson et al. (2013) show, a fifth of all care provision is secured by for-profit providers, while still mainly paid for by the local municipalities. Additionally to this groundbreaking change, new legislation offers tax deductions for privately employed carers, an initiative which rather benefits the wealthy and causes differentiations in the treatment for different income groups. Since the Swedish population is, due to the historical legacy, traditionally critical of profit making in elder care, these policy changes have been accompanied by a strong discursive focus on values such as choice and quality and the main aim is stated to be empowerment of people through choice (Szehbehely and Trydegård 2012). The public sector's role in these newly introduced, market-based provisions is focused on governance, control and monitoring. While, importantly, this legislation still ensures the right to assistance (Szehbehely and Trydegård 2012), its new options are framed with specific neoliberal, economistic reasoning, emphasising ideas of choice in particular (Andersson and Kvist 2014). However, as Szehbehely and Trydegård (2012) show, this focus changes some of the universalist foundations of the care system. At the local level, municipalities find themselves under financial pressure which forces them to introduce stricter guidelines and has raised thresholds for the financing of care services. Additionally, the possibilities of executing individual choice are not distributed evenly, but benefit those with higher education and professional networks. Likewise, the option of tax deductions for domestically employed carers favours those with higher incomes significantly.

Szehbehely and Trydegård (2012: 307) therefore argue that "[t]he increased focus on consumerism and choice in Sweden ... constitutes a challenge to universalism". Care is, on one hand, increasingly organized via markets, and, on the other hand, carried out by families on an informal basis. While these trends must both be seen as direct outcomes of the newly introduced neoliberally framed legislation, they were not all intended by policymakers:

> While re-familialisation seems to be an unintended consequence of the contraction of home care, marketisation of Swedish home-care services is more clearly intended by national policy-makers. (Szehbehely and Trydegård 2012: 307)

United Kingdom

The United Kingdom is often seen as the European forerunner in liberalization and economization processes and, consequently, it was the first European country to marketize elder-care services (Brennan et al. 2012). Care in the United Kingdom is generally organised through a mix of informal provision, a relatively small number of publically provided services, and a large number of for-profit care providers. The last decades have additionally seen a political shift to increase individual choice, in particular by providing publically financed individual budgets instead of services (Glendinning 2008). In 2014 various changes and adaptations culminated in the introduction of the new Care Act which the coalition of the Conservatives and Liberal Democrats described as the most important reform to social care in 60 years, "putting people and their carers in control of their care and support" (Lamb 2014). The main focus of this new legislation was to reduce costs, increase transparency and openness and secure the state's possibilities for control and market oversight. While the new Care Act is not intended to challenge the market-organized care system, the state's involvement tries to address several of its failures, most notably cases of abuse and financial bankruptcy on the side of care-providing companies. The public sector's role consists therefore mainly of a control of the markets to ensure the continuation of the existing system (DoH 2014). The main objective of the new sets of laws is to implement the concept of individual well-being (as formulated in the Guide to the Care Act). Norman Lamb, then social care minister, describes this aim as follows:

> Until now, we've had a one size fits all approach to care. The focus has been on what disabilities someone has, or what services local authorities can provide, rather than on the individual. That's disempowering. So for the first time the system will be built around each person—what they need, how they can best be cared for, and what they want. By providing and legislating for Personal Budgets in the Care Act we are giving people the power to spend money on tailored care that suits their individual needs as part of their support plan. (Lamb 2014)

Individual well-being can then be achieved if people are individually empowered to exercise choice in order to plan their own future. Informal carers and family members are described as experts and partners who can contribute to the functioning of the market arrangements. The key of this system is information and choice, provided by the public sector, as well as control over companies:

> As well as giving people more choice we have to give them better information in order to identify good care ... We're also getting tougher on those who deliver bad care. (Lamb 2014)

The consequences of the new legislation are that family-provided care and markets remain as the main sources of elder care in the United Kingdom. Unintended negative effects of this system (in particular maltreatment or the closing of care homes due to financial insolvency) should be limited by increasing individual information and choice and by the state's control of companies and care organisations.

Netherlands

The Dutch elder-care system has long been dominated by formal, professionalized care services, publicly financed and provided in both institutions and people's households (Da Roit 2010). Since the 1990s, however, widespread policy changes of individualization and marketization have also taken place in the field of care. While the introduced regulations resulted in a complex web of public and private provisions, they specifically "tend to foster informal care and market-related principles" (Da Roit 2010: 27). In 2013, new legislation presented substantial reforms of the Dutch long-term care system. With a focus on "active citizenship" policymakers revaluated the definition of which services count as "real care" and which people require this sort of publicly financed services. For all other people the WMO, a new social support act, redirected services and responsibilities for care, support and activation for people with disabilities or frailty to municipalities and communities. Martin van Rijn (2013), then state secretary for health, welfare and sport describes these changes to long-term care as allowing more quality of life for older people. The main starting point for the legislation is the idea that everyone wants to stay at their own home for longer and wants to remain independent as long as possible (Ministerie van VWS 2013). Those who require support or care (or, rather, as it is formulated in the legislation, those who want to receive support or care) need to find out what they and their social networks can do themselves (van Rijn 2013).

The new legislation is strongly framed with emotional advertising, focusing on what communities (which refers to families, social networks, neighbours) can do themselves. Tonkens and Duijvendak (2013) point out how these new regulations continue a process of deprofessionalization and informalization, in which many forms of elder care are neither seen as a professional service nor as a commodity, but in which care is something that is arranged and provided individually by one's own surroundings. This focus fits into neoliberalization processes in that it is specifically justified by concepts such as emancipation, self-control and the assumed (or imagined, see Weicht 2015b) wish that all people want to stay longer at home. Being in control of the care that is provided and being in charge of organising and arranging these services emphasises the responsibility of the individual. The deprofessionalization and, possibly, decommodification is thus linked to a shift of responsibility for care from the public to the private, or, in other words, from the state to the individual and his or her family.

Austria

The Austrian care system is traditionally based on care provided informally, usually within people's family settings. Roughly 80 percent of people with needs are cared for at home by close relatives, most of whom are women (Österle and Hammer 2004). Apart from the provision of a relatively small number of public institutional and home-care services, the Austrian care system mainly relies on the payment of cash benefits. This so-called "Pflegegeld", which was introduced to secure and financially support care within families, is a universal benefit of varying amounts depending entirely on the level of care needs. In recent years (see Weicht 2010) this freely usable cash payment has increasingly come to be used to finance about 40.000 live-in migrant care workers who live in the older person's household and provide 24-hour care and support. This practice came suddenly onto the public agenda in 2006, during an election campaign, requiring policymakers to find some solutions for the then-illegal employment arrangements. Starting with a legal amnesty and followed by the creation of new laws, the practice was regularised and legalised in 2008. The new legislation thus provided the background for a continuation of the Austrian elder-care system in the light of changing demographic and social structures and the related care crisis (Österle and Bauer 2012, Weicht 2015a). While the legal problems of the arrangements (employment laws, immigration laws) have been dealt with, concerns related to the employment settings in an informal domestic context remain intact (Weicht 2015a).

The new legislation was framed to ensure people's wish to stay at home and be cared for within their own surroundings. Additionally, threats to the system of widespread informal care provision could be diminished and avoided. The result is a complex form of informal, yet commodified care which relies on the fact that migrant domestic care workers are substituting the traditional informal care provided by (female) family members. Since both the discursive and political construction of these arrangements lack a conception of a proper employer-employee relationship, migrant care workers are mainly seen as supporting the families in their struggles to organise care for their lovedones (Weicht 2015a).

Liberalization, Protection, Emancipation

In the brief (and necessarily incomplete) descriptions herein I have tried to capture both the concrete changes to legal regulations and the discursive frames surrounding the new legislations in the field of elder care. Evaluating the policy changes in these four different care regimes, I want to make a few observations: First, path dependency of social policies (Pierson 2006) cannot be reduced to institutional factors, but can also be identified in the discursive frames surrounding political decisions. This means that the arguments brought forward in favour of new legislation relate to the earlier conceptualization of the care system and its discursive context. Second, there is no clear trend observable toward either commodification or public provision of care. Rather, various (often divergent) developments need to be understood as being based within the internal logic of the political and social system. Third, however, all political reforms show a strong trend toward individualization of responsibilities and the introduction (or extension) of a market logic focusing on choice, empowerment and control.

In analysing these reactions of states to crises (both financial and in terms of care provision), it becomes obvious that not only are different services created, funded or cut, but that legislation redefines responsibilities and relationships between the individual, the state and the market in the field of care. Karl Polanyi (2001) famously identified the shifts between the economy vis-à-vis society as the crucial attribute of the "great transformation". Polanyi's work (and related debates) thus offers various insights into the understanding of these shifts in times of crisis. The first insight relates to the observation that even in modern capitalism, markets are always embedded within state structures and struggles emerge between attempts to strengthen or weaken the state's control and influence over the functioning and results of markets. Polanyi thus contrasted the trends of increasing commodification with striving for stronger social protection, aptly described as the "double movement". While the empirical scenarios described herein clearly show both of these trends, it can also be observed that Polanyi missed (or ignored) the family context, the realm of reproductive work, as also argued by Nancy Fraser (2014). The struggles to organise care, in fact, relate to a distribution of responsibilities and possibilities between the market, the public sector and the family.

The second important insight Polanyi offers relates to his perception of the process of commodification which he understands in Marxist terms as a shift of the goal of production from use value to exchange value. Importantly, Polanyi argues that this commodification process also relates to labour, land and money but that they, due to their constitutive role in the fabric of social life itself, can only be commodified unsatisfactorily, and, hence, he describes them as "fictitious commodities". Filling the gap of forgetting care in his analysis, can the concept of a "fictitious commodity" be applied to attempts to subject care to market exchange? Fraser (2014) utilizes Polanyi's concept but criticises his "ontological" reading and, instead, proposes a structural conception of "fictitious commodities". Focusing on the fact that something is usually not produced for sale (like care) and that marketizing this would thus violate its nature, is, she argues, too defensive (and conservative) and would ignore the "communitarian bias", thereby overlooking "forms of domination that are not grounded in market mechanisms" (Fraser 2014: 548) but which arise from the gendered distribution of labour and the split between the public and the private realm:

> Preoccupied exclusively with the corrosive effects of commodification upon communities, it neglects injustices within communities, including injustices, such as slavery, serfdom and patriarchy, that depend on social constructions of labour, land and money precisely as non-commodities. (Fraser 2014: 544)

Fraser's structural reading, on the other hand, emphasises that a marketization of labour (or, as in our case, care) would undermine and destroy its own conditions of possibility. A complete commodification of care would thus undermine the very possibilities of markets and other commodities. The struggles and movements Polanyi describes Fraser would rather sketch as "three-sided struggles, encompassing not only neoliberals and social protectionists, but also proponents of emancipation, including those for whom exploitation represents an advance" (Fraser 2014: 551). Commodification and marketization of care could then involve simultaneous attacks on both informal caregiving and the public provision of services (Fraser and Bedford, 2008) and, likewise, emancipation for women as those responsible for care could drive a struggle in favour of marketization processes.

What do these theoretical insights provided by Polanyi and Fraser now mean for the understanding of the changes of care policies? All examples have indeed shown negotiations and struggles among the three spheres of markets, the state and the family. Additionally, Fraser's (2013) triple movement of the attempts for liberalization, social protection and emancipation all feature prominently as frames for the justification for recent policy changes. Sweden's emphasis of choice and empowerment of individuals uses the frame of emancipation to allow (and increase) the potential of markets and families beside the traditional form of social protection. In the United Kingdom, the focus on state control and oversight, which should improve individual well-being, represents attempts to reembed the markets, while leaving their existence and significance largely unchallenged. The Dutch movement toward decommodification, deinstitutionalization and deprofessionalization uses the frames of emancipation and individual control against both the influences of markets and institutional social protection. In Austria, finally, the rejection of an increasing role of the public sector in care (social protection) allows a model of informal commodification, based on the idea of family preferences and informal solutions. All four examples, however, share one crucial feature: the rise (or emphasis) of (/on) individual responsibility for the arrangement and provision of care.

Searching for the Ideal

We have so far seen that in the light of crisis these four countries have recalibrated their care systems within the market-state-family nexus. Polanyi's analysis of fictitious commodities helps us point to the possible resistance to an unrestricted marketization of care, due to its inherent nature as something being "produced" for immediate use, rather than for market exchange. Fraser's proposal of a structural reading of fictitious commodities added another perspective which allows the integration of the realm of families and communities into the parallel struggles for liberalization, protection and emancipation. In the empirical cases, the triple movement can be observed in states' attempts to navigate various interests within conditions of both financial and social crises.

However, while concepts of fictitious commodities provide insights into the complex nature of (de-)commodification processes of care, they miss a crucial aspect related to all kinds of affective and/or reproductive work: the moral dimension of concrete social practices (Sayer 2007). A moral economy perspective, then, also focuses on norms and sentiments regarding the responsibilities and rights of individuals and institutions with respect to others (Sayer 2000: 79). Sayer (2000) summarizes these norms as posing different questions: what should or should not be commodified? Who should be supported and by whom? How are responsibilities toward others allocated and how can these responsibilities be discharged to others? Importantly, all those moral questions furthermore relate to an imagined ideal situation which sketches the different notions of proper care. Care, like other affective labour, is not only embedded into structures of social protection and the local community or family but also in a particular moral framework which defines why things matter to people (Sayer 2004; 2011). Sayer (2004) importantly reminds us that the state does not represent one clearly demarcated side in the struggles mentioned herein; rather, countries try to negotiate various interests and movements representing attempts for liberalization, protection and emancipation at the same time, against the background of a morally charged, and often nostalgically recalled, ideal of care. Complete commodification, complete informalization or complete social provision of care are thus hindered by the moral framework through which care gains a particular meaning in society (Weicht 2015b). This meaning needs to focus more specifically on why care matters to people and which values are related to the production and consumption of care (Sayer 2007). A focus on the latter, Sayer (2003) argues, is often missing in the analysis of commodification processes, while it is in consumption that a process of singularising its use value takes place while the service remains a commodity. For people in need of care, this means that the nature of care consists entirely of its use value while possible production for exchange (market) value of the service becomes meaningless. An exclusive focus on the means and practices of production of care ignores this crucial dimension, as Tronto explains:

> As institutions for care emerge in the market, it has made sense to use market and public policy analyses to think about them. But to follow the logic of the market, or of policy, rather than to start from the logic of care itself, means that the basic questions about the nature and purposes of care never arise. (Tronto 2013: 9-10)

Tronto (2013) argues that a focus on commodification from within a market logic would presume the existence of a rational, independent and able consumer (see also Weicht 2011) who requests services from another actor. However, this dyadic image of care is misleading as caring practices are nested within concrete and particular relationships (Tronto 2013). Because of that, emotional connection and closeness play an important part in defining the "product" itself, the care delivered. Lewis (2007) therefore questions whether all care can potentially be commodified with the argument that care is not only a task but also an emotion. This idea describes care as being based within informal, close relationships which are characterised by mutual affection. Professional care (for example in public care homes) is positioned in opposition to this idealised notion, as Zadoroznyi illustrates:

> Most notably, informal care is *diffuse* (that is, unspecified), *based on feelings* (which might be anything from obligation to love); it is provided by 'identifiable kin and friends' on the basis of a generally *ascribed* relationship with

the person being cared for; and is oriented to a *particular* person with whom there is a relationship and affective ties. In contrast, the logic of (formal) care provided by professionals is based on *functional specificity, achievement, universalism* and being *affectively neutral.* (Zadoroznyi 2009: 271)

This dichotomy of informal, affective care on one hand, and professionalised, functional care on the other (Weicht 2015b), is based on the idea that "the social world is organized around contrasting and incompatible moral principles" (Gal 2004: 261) which structure our daily lives and public and private relationships. The dichotomous construction of these moral principles or associations means that an idea of care as a labour of love is constructed as "emotionally agaped work" with the principal goal of the well-being of the other and which can therefore not be completely commodified (Lynch 2007):

The emotional work involved in loving another person is not readily transferred to a paid other by arrangement; neither can it be exchanged. To attempt to pay someone to do a love labour task ... is to undermine the premise of care and mutuality that is at the heart of intimacy and friendship. (Lynch 2007: 565)

Care work in this understanding cannot be commodified since this would mean the commodification of inherently human traits, such as love, mutuality, commitment and feelings for others (Lynch 2007). But these moral associations not only affect the imaginations and demands of the consumer of care but also influence the provider, in particular people who provide (informal) care within their families:

Women may resist the view that their paid caring work is simply a commodity, and they may resist even more thinking of the unpaid work they do at home, caring for children out of affection and developing bonds of trust and family, merely in terms of the market value to which it would be equivalent if paid for. (Held 2002: 21)

Importantly, the moral associations with informal care are closely related to a nostalgic imagination of family provision and community life. The exclusively positive and embracing notion of community (which Fraser also criticizes in Polanyi's accounts) sketches a place of comfort free from pressures associated with current processes of commodification. Both the traditional family and the traditional community are experienced to be under threat by economic developments and are thus described as manifestations of other times or at other places. Informal care reflects a moral ideal and an image of the good society which is positioned in contrast to both the market and the state (Nisbet 1966). Dench et al. (2006: 4) in their discussion of changes of a particular London neighbourhood provide an example for the ideological link between modern "impersonal welfare provisions" and the loss of traditional "kinship support". However, as Sprigings and Allen (2005) demonstrate, many political changes which build on the idea of this community have taken for granted that community is something good. It is crucial to understand that the loss is in itself an imagination of an idealized situation, of the idealized family and the idealized community. Hence, the nostalgic construction does not necessarily refer to real events and situations. In relation to "the caring family" Beck and Beck-Gernsheim (2001: 129-30), for example, argue that "the pre-industrial family was mainly a union born of necessity and compulsion". The idealization of community, as well as the idealization of traditional family practices, acts as nostalgic sketches of counterdiscourses to trends of individualization, marketization and commodification (Weicht 2015b).

Empirically, however, as the descriptions herein have shown, the split between a nostalgically imagined understanding of informal care on one hand, and commodified and/or professional care on the other hand is misleading and does not reflect the reality of hybrids of love and instrumentality (Ungerson 2000) and contract and affect (Glucksmann and Lyon 2006). Lyon and Glucksmann (2008: 114) argue in this context that "a simple dualism … cannot readily distinguish between different kinds of commodity or non-commodity relations". Rather, markets and state arrangements do play an important role in many aspects of the organisation of informal care (Ungerson 2005) and informal provisions complement public or market-organized arrangements so that new forms and mixes, "which transcend the public/private, market/non-market and paid/unpaid distinctions, as well as the love/money/duty nexus" (Glucksmann and Lyon 2006: 7.1), have emerged. The empirical cases have perfectly illustrated this: All countries reject an uncritical embracing of both markets and public institutions but, instead, emphasise individual choice, preferences and emancipation. All countries (not least for economic reasons) place some role of care provision in the hands of families and communities while, at the same time, emphasizing the state's role in securing the rights of carers and those for whom care is provided. The indispensable moral dimension of the meaning of care thus prevents a clear decision in the struggles for or against increasing commodification. The values related to (and associated with) care create the conditions under which it is judged "where the boundaries of the market should be" (Held 2002: 31). The initial question is thus not restricted to whether or not care can or should be commodified but entails a focus on the moral dimension of the market itself and "how members of a society think about the market and its purposes" (Tronto 2013: 115). This focus on the moral dimension also brings us back to Polanyi's understanding of society vis-à-vis economy, in which he emphasizes the significance of the underlying ideals of the social institutions, rather than their simple functionality:

> The true criticism of market society is not that it was based on economics—in a sense, every and any society must be based on it—but that its economy was based on self-interest. Such an organization of economic life is entirely unnatural, in the strictly empirical sense of exceptional. (Polanyi 2001: 249)

Individual choice and control are crucial frames in all four countries under investigation. Sweden's introduction of markets should allow and increase individual choice and the United Kingdom outlines the state's role as securing individual choice in a competitive, profit-driven market. In the Netherlands, the process of decommodification and deprofessionalization is explained by allowing the execution of individual preferences; and in Austria the legalization of the employment of migrant care workers is justified with fostering and supporting families' own solutions to the care crisis. However, as Tronto (2013) remarks, the concept of choice contains very particular meanings in neoliberal society in which the individual is regarded as entirely self-dependent for every step, decision and practice. "Care", Tronto (2013: 40) argues, "becomes entirely a personal and private matter; individuals make "choices" about care for themselves and for those around them". The triangular struggle between liberalization, social protection and emancipation is thus framed upon the normative ideal of independence and choice. Responsibilities for vulnerabilities, disabilities and dependencies are considered private matters which the individual and his or her family have to deal with autonomously. This does not mean, however, that the state's role is diminished and that markets (and families) are increasingly disembedded; rather, through policies, regulations and interventions the state secures the possibilities for choice and individual solutions. It used to be illegal for Austrian families to employ migrant workers in their own households. Through state intervention this existing practice was legalized, regularized and supported both financially and ideologically. The Dutch trend to re-informalization and deinstitutionalization, which supposedly secures the eminent desire to remain at home, stems from cuts in the public provision and the careful legal orchestration to request care and support from people's informal networks. Sweden's introduction of markets into a system of universal public provision has required substantial legal and political changes challenging the Scandinavian logic of public services (Brennan et al. 2012). In the United Kingdom, finally, the state felt the need to intervene in the market-driven system and to reembed some of the markets' practices and institutions. These processes also put in question the meaning of choice and individual freedom itself, particularly for some of the most vulnerable members of society (Tronto 2013). The concepts of choice and independent decision-making institutionalize a market logic, promoted and secured by the public sector. Polanyi already pointed to this paradox which a market-driven and politically instituted idea of choice and freedom presents:

> Inescapably we reach the conclusion that the very possibility of freedom is in question. If regulation is the only means of spreading and strengthening freedom in a complex society, and yet to make use of this means is contrary to freedom per se, then such a society cannot be free. (Polanyi 2001: 257)

Recent legislative changes in the field of care have thus fostered increasing individualization of social risks. This process is intertwined with a nostalgically imagined ideal of care, represented by the concept of "being there for each other" (Weicht 2015b). Importantly, both the idea of choice and the idealisation of informal care can possibly be used to justify individualization and, hence, a market logic. But can the imagination of ideal care also be used beneficially? Or, as Tronto (2013: 159) asks, "[c]an institutions be similarly arranged so that they provide the same elements of care that the family ideally provided" (Tronto 2013: 159)? Can the nostalgic ideal be used productively (Blunt 2003) to sketch progressive arrangements of care without falling into the trap of a "communitarian bias" (Fraser 2014)?

While nostalgia has often been seen as the antithesis to a radical critique of neoliberal social arrangements, by providing ideas, images and desires it could actually function as an important part of the "radical imagination" (Bonnett 2010) for what bel hooks (1990) calls the politicization of memory which rejects the longing for times gone by in favour of a "remembering that serves to illuminate and transform the present" (hooks 1990: 147). This notion of nostalgia would relate to elements of comparison with unwanted and criticized aspects of current social conditions and is thus utopian rather than melancholic (Pickering and Keightley 2006). Boym (2001) similarly proposes a separation between restorative and reflective nostalgia, whereby the latter takes up a reconstruction of elements and monuments of the past, focusing on dreams of other times and other places as a potential for a progressive intervention in modern social and economic discourses. This element of using the past to imagine the future Boym (2001) also describes as creative nostalgia, since the focus on the past here provides ideas, imaginations, dreams and desires which help to shape the present and the future:

> One is nostalgic not for the past the way it was, but for the past the way it could have been. It is this past perfect that one strives to realize in the future. (Boym 2001: 351)

In the context of care this might mean that the yearning for informal care, one's own home and concrete, affective relationships, is based on and emerges from real social processes through which people experience a fragmented and challenging society (Bonnett 2010). The nostalgic ideal-ization of informal care can be read as a desire for alternatives to both the demands, pressures and coldness of the market, as well as the "top-down and top-heavy bureaucracy of the capitalist welfare state" (Brenner and Haaken 2000: 344). Challenging the trends to individualize social risks and care needs requires us to move beyond Fraser's (2013) triple move-ment and emphasize the moral dimension of the "fictitious commodity" of care. While liberalization, social protection and emancipation are all crucial components of the struggles for ideal care arrangements, any form of affective labour also requires a recognition of the moral connotations and associations.

Conclusion

Care, in its commodity form, a product that is bought and sold, is also discussed in Arlie Hochschild's book, *The Outsourced Self* (2012), in which she describes various fields traditionally characterised by personal, inti-mate and emotional relations and which now have increasingly become part of the market logic. The subtitle of the book, *Intimate life in market times*, not only refers to historical changes and developments in the ways in which people relate to each other but also suggests an uncomfortable dichotomy between personal intimacy and financial exchange (see also Zelizer 2005). However, Hochschild shows how, in a growing number of everyday personal situations, such as falling in love, minding children, having a baby and caring for the elderly, emotional, intimate relations are not seen as interfering with the market logic but become the very essence of the commercial transaction.

The four national cases have shown how various interests, strategies and perspectives are intertwined. It has become obvious that, indeed, markets (in whatever form) are always embedded and that states play an active role in securing the conditions for the possibilities of markets. The cases of Sweden, the United Kingdom, the Netherlands and Austria have also shown how different actors exploit the very logic of the so-called triple movement. The logic of emancipation characterizes arguments for empowerment and the freedom from domination and abuse, present for example in the explanations for market oversight in the United Kingdom and Sweden. The logic of social protection are exemplified by the emphasis on social security and the rights to receive care, apparent in the soothing justifications of new legislation in, for example, Sweden, Austria and the Netherlands. Finally, the logic of liberalization or marketization strongly articulate the concepts of efficiency and choice. Executing one's own choice has been a fundamental component of all four countries' argumentation strategies for new legislation. This also means that in all four examples an individualist, atomistic logic of the market has informed the design of policies and practical regulations.

Focusing on the internal logics and justifications of political claims and practices has allowed us to extend both Polanyi's and Fraser's conceptualizations of the crucially important relationship between the state, the market and society. Importantly, in their conceptualization of commodification both Polanyi and Fraser focus almost exclusively on the production side and thereby ignore the sphere of consumption which plays an essential role for the understanding of care and other forms of affective, reproductive labour. By including also the consumption side I have focused much more strongly on the relationships on which care labour and the "commodity" of care are based. This highlighted that beside the logic of liberalization, social protection and emancipation, inclusion of the moral dimension is essential to understand the possible commodification and decommodification processes in the context of care. These moral economies contribute to the fact that care manifests itself as a "fictitious commodity" which, in turn, also affects the production side and the ways care is organized, provided and financed. Including the moral perspective has been an attempt to tackle both the cultural and economic dimension of welfare (Fraser and Bedford 2008). For a just and supporting arrangement of care, the institutional contexts as well as the ideological framing play an important role. How people imagine care influences concrete relationships and practices. Tronto rightly points out that

> [c]aring is not only about the intimate and daily routines of hands-on care. Care also involves larger structural questions of thinking about which institutions, people and practices should be used to accomplish concrete and real caring tasks. (Tronto 2013: 139)

The examples have also shown that simplified calls for a re-embedding of markets fall necessarily short as the underlying logics are not restricted to a particular context of producing care labour and services. Likewise, the moral dimension of care does not readily translate into specific practices and arrangements. Political decision makers indeed often utilize the nostalgic conceptualization of care, as for example in the case of the regularisation of migrant care workers in Austria (Weicht 2010) which can advantage some and disadvantage others. However, the same ideal might be the starting point for many people, both as carers and care receivers to think about this practice and to define for themselves the meaning of care. In that sense Fraser raises the following important and broader question:

> Will the arrangements that re-embed markets in the post-neoliberal era be oppressive or emancipatory, hierarchical or egalitarian—and we might add, misframed or well-framed, difference-hostile or difference-friendly, bureaucratic or participatory? (Fraser 2013: 241)

As Fraser (2013) points out, liberalization, social protection and emancipation can all be beneficial for some, while detrimental for others. The same goes for the moral dimension. The political consequence of this analysis thus calls for awareness of different, sometimes contradictory effects of (changing) care regimes, with the aim of arranging care according to the different aims and dimensions without marginalising or disadvantaging some over others. An intersectional analysis (Weldon 2008) of the processes and links to moral economies is needed which takes into account the consequences for different groups, for example according to race, class, gender, nationality and age. As Fraser (2013) has shown in relation to liberalization and social protection, and this also applies in terms of the moral dimension, the protection of one can lead to the domination of others.

Starting with an ideal concept of care, based on a productive rather than regressive nostalgic sketch, the moral dimension compels us to imagine new forms of communal care that move beyond the market logic of individualization and choice. Brie (2015) for example suggests new forms of a "commoning" of care and Federici (2012), similarly, discusses new forms of free communities. Innovative forms of solidarity, resistance to the capitalist logic and new imaginations of caring for each other also point beyond the concrete arrangements for dependent people (Winker 2015). Paul Kershaw (2005) therefore suggests a redefinition of both care and citizenship and a necessary reconciliation within a new theoretical and political framework. Stopping and resisting the various trends toward individualization and privatization of care, which manifest either as commodification or as familialization or informalization, seems to be a crucial component for these political strategies.

References

Andersson, K., & Kvist, E. (2014). The neoliberal turn and the marketization of care: The transformation of eldercare in Sweden. *European Journal of Women's Studies, 22*(3), 274–287.

Auth, D. (2012). Ökonomisierung von Pflege in Großbritannien, Schweden und Deutschland. *Zeitschrift für Gerontologie und Geriatrie, 7*, 618–623.

Beck, U., & Beck-Gernsheim, E. (2001). *Individualization: Institutionalised individualism and its social and political consequences.* London: Sage.

Blunt, A. (2003). Collective memory and productive nostalgia: Anglo-Indian homemaking at McCluskieganj. *Environment and Planning D: Society and Space, 21*(6), 717–738.

Bonnett, A. (2010). *Left in the past: Radicalism and the politics of nostalgia.* New York: Continuum.

Boym, S. (2001). *The future of nostalgia.* New York: Basic Books.

Brennan, D., Cass, B., Himmelweit, S., & Szebehely, M. (2012). The marketization of care: Rationales and consequences in Nordic and liberal care regimes. *Journal of European Social Policy, 22*(4), 377–391.

Brenner, J., & Haaken, J. (2000). Utopian thought: Re-visioning gender, family and community. *Community, Work & Family, 3*(3), 333–347.

Brie, M. (2015). *Polanyi neu entdecken: Das hellblaue Bändchen zu einem möglichen Dialog von Nancy Fraser und Karl Polanyi.* Hamburg: VSA Verlag.

Da Roit, B. (2010). *Strategies of care: Changing elderly care in Italy and the Netherlands.* Amsterdam: Amsterdam University Press.

Da Roit, B., & Le Bihan, B. (2010). Similar and yet so different: Cash-for-care in six European countries' long-term care policies. *Milbank Quarterly, 88*(3), 286–309.

Da Roit, B., & Weicht, B. (2013). Migrant care work and care, migration and employment regimes: A fuzzy-set analysis. *Journal of European Social Policy,* *23*(5), 469–486.

Dench, G., Gavron, K., & Young, M. (2006). *The New East end.* London: Profile Books.

Department of Health. (2014). Factsheet 10: The Care Act—market oversight and provider failure. https://www.gov.uk/government/uploads/system/uploads/attachment_data/file/366093/Factsheet_10_-_Market_oversight_and_provider_failure.pdf. Accessed 10 June 2015.

Erlandsson, S., Storm, P., Stranz, A., Szebehely, M., & Trydegård, G.-B. (2013). Marketising trends in Swedish eldercare: Competition, choice and calls for stricter regulation. In G. Meagher & M. Szebehely (Eds.), *Marketisation in Nordic eldercare: A research report on legislation, oversight, extent and consequences.* Department of Social Work: Stockholm.

Federici, S. (2012). *Revolution at point zero: Housework, reproduction, and feminist struggle.* Oakland: PM Press.

Fraser, N. (2013). *Fortunes of feminism: From state-managed capitalism to neoliberal crisis.* London: Verso Books.

Fraser, N. (2014). Can society be commodities all the way down? Post-Polanyian reflections on capitalist crisis. *Economy and Society,* *43*(4), 541–558.

Fraser, N., & Bedford, K. (2008). Social rights and gender justice in the neoliberal moment: A conversation about welfare and transnational politics. *Feminist Theory,* *9*(2), 225–245.

Gal, S. (2004). A semiotics of the public/private distinction. In J. Scott & D. Keates (Eds.), *Going public: Feminism and the shifting boundaries of the private sphere* (pp. 261–277). Urbana: University of Illinois Press.

Glendinning, C. (2008). Increasing choice and control for older and disabled people: A critical review of new developments in England. *Social Policy & Administration,* *42*(5), 451–469.

Glucksmann, M. & Lyon, D. (2006). Configurations of care work: Paid and unpaid elder care in Italy and the Netherlands. Sociological Research Online, 11(2), http://www.socresearchonline.org.uk/11/2/glucksmann.html. Accessed 12 June 2012.

Held, V. (2002). Care and the extension of markets. *Hypatia,* *17*(2), 19–33.

Hochschild, A. (2012). *The outsourced self: Intimate life in market times.* New York: Metropolitan Books.

hooks, b. (1990). *Yearning: Race, gender, and cultural politics.* Boston: South End Press.

Kershaw, P. (2005). *Carefair: Rethinking the responsibilities and rights of citizenship*. Vancouver: UPC Press.

Lamb, N. (2014). *Care Bill becomes Care Act 2014*. https://www.gov.uk/government/speeches/care-bill-becomes-care-act-2014. Accessed 10 June 2015.

Lewis, J. (2007). Gender, ageing and the 'new social settlement': The importance of developing a holistic approach to care policies. *Current Sociology, 55*(2), 271–286.

Lynch, K. (2007). Love labour as a distinct and non-commodifiable form of care labour. *The Sociological Review, 55*(3), 550–570.

Lyon, D., & Glucksmann, M. (2008). Comparative configurations of care work across Europe. *Sociology, 42*(1), 101–118.

Ministerie van Volksgezondheid, Welzijn en Sport. (2013). Hervorming van de langdurige ondersteuning en zorg. https://www.rijksoverheid.nl/documenten/publicaties/2013/04/25/hervorming-van-de-langdurige-ondersteuning-en-zorg. Accessed 10 June 2015.

Nisbet, R. (1966). *The sociological tradition*. London: Heinemann.

Pickering, M., & Keightley, E. (2006). The modalities of nostalgia. *Current Sociology, 54*(6), 919–941.

Österle, A., & Bauer, G. (2012). Home care in Austria: The interplay of family orientation, cash-for-care and migrant care. *Health and Social Care in the Community, 20*, 265–273.

Österle, A., & Hammer, E. (2004). *Zur zukünftigen Betreuung und Pflege älterer Menschen: Rahmenbedingungen—Politikansätze—Entwicklungsperspektiven*, on behalf of Caritas Österreich. Vienna: Kardinal König Akademie.

Pierson, C. (2006). *Beyond the welfare state: The new political economy of welfare*. Cambridge: Polity Press.

Polanyi, K. (2001). *The great transformation: The political and economic origins of our time*. Boston: Beacon Press.

Rummery, K. (2009). A comparative discussion of the gendered implications of cash-for-care schemes: Markets, independence and social citizenship in crisis? *Social Policy & Administration, 43*(6), 634–648.

Sayer, A. (2000). Moral economy and political economy. *Studies in Political Economy, 61*, 79–103.

Sayer, A. (2003). (De)commodification, consumer culture, and moral economy. *Environment and Planning D: Society and Space, 21*, 341–357.

Sayer, A. (2004). *Moral economy*. Published by the Department of Sociology, Lancaster University. http://www.comp.lancs.ac.uk/sociology/papers/sayer-moral-economy.pdf. Accessed 5 May 2015.

Sayer, A. (2007). Moral economy as critique. *New Political Economy, 12*(2), 261–270.

Sayer, A. (2011). *Why things matter to people: Social science values and ethical life.* Cambridge: Cambridge University Press.

Shutes, I. (2012). The employment of migrant workers in long-term care: Dynamics of choice and control. *Journal of Social Policy, 41*(1), 43–59.

Simonazzi, A. (2009). Care regimes and national employment models. *Cambridge Journal of Economics, 33*(2), 211–232.

Sprigings, N., & Allen, C. (2005). The communities we are regaining but need to lose: A critical commentary on community building in beyond-place societies. *Community, Work & Family, 8*(4), 389–411.

Szebehely, M., & Trydegård, G.-B. (2012). Home care for older people in Sweden: A universal model in transition. *Health and Social Care in the community, 20*(3), 300–309.

Tonkens, E. & Duijvendak, J. W. (2013). Wie wil zich nu laten douchen door de buurman? *Sociale Vraagstukken.* http://www.socialevraagstukken.nl/site/2013/05/12/wie-wil-zich-nu-laten-douchen-door-de-buurman/. Accessed 10 June 2015.

Tronto, J. (2013). *Caring democracy: Markets, equality, and justice.* New York: New York University Press.

Tronto, J., & Weicht, B. (2014). 'As long as care is attached to gender, there is no justice': An interview with Joan C. Tronto. *Tijdschrift voor Genderstudies, 17*(3), 259–271.

Ungerson, C. (1997). Social politics and the commodification of care. *Social Politics, 4*(3), 362–381.

Ungerson, C. (1999). Personal assistants and disabled people: An examination of a hybrid form of work and care. *Work, Employment & Society, 13*(4), 623–643.

Ungerson, C. (2000). Thinking about the production and consumption of long-term care in Britain: Does gender still matter? *Journal of Social Policy, 29*(4), 623–643.

Ungerson, C. (2005). Care, work and feeling. *The Sociological Review, 53*(2), 188–203.

Van Rijn, M. (2013). *Hervorming langdurige zorg: naar een waardevolle toekomst.* https://www.rijksoverheid.nl/documenten/kamerstukken/2013/04/25/kamerbrief-hervorming-langdurige-zorg-naar-een-waardevolle-toekomst. Accessed 10 June 2015.

Weicht, B. (2010). Embodying the ideal carer: The Austrian discourse on migrant carers. *International Journal of Ageing and Later Life, 5*(2), 17–52.

Weicht, B. (2011). Embracing dependency: Rethinking (in)dependence in the discourse of care. *The Sociological Review, 58*(s2), 205–224.

Weicht, B. (2015a). Employment without employers? The public discourse on care during the regularisation reform in Austria. In A. Triandafyllidou & S. Marchetti (Eds.), *Employers, agencies and immigration: Paying for care* (pp. 113–130). Farnham: Ashgate.

Weicht, B. (2015b). *The meaning of care: The social construction of care for elderly people*. Basingstoke: Palgrave Macmillan.

Weldon, L. (2008). Intersectionality. In G. Goertz & A. Mazur (Eds.), *Politics, gender and concepts: Theory and methodology* (pp. 193–218). Cambridge: Cambridge University Press.

Winker, G. (2015). *Care revolution: Schritte in eine solidarische Gesellschaft*. Bielefeld: Transcript.

Zadoroznyi, M. (2009). Professionals, carers or 'strangers'? Liminality and the typification of postnatal home care workers. *Sociology, 43*(2), 268–285.

Zelizer, V. (2005). *The purchase of intimacy*. Princeton: Princeton University Press.

Moral Economy Versus Political Economy: Provincializing Polanyi

John Holmwood

This chapter was begun during a study leave in the USA, a time marked by stark oppositions.[1] It was a year of celebration of the 50th anniversary of the Mississippi Freedom Struggles and the achievement of civil and political rights for African Americans (Payne 1995). However, by 2013 the Voting Rights Act of 1965, central to the implementation of political rights, had been struck down by the Supreme Court. Almost immediately, a number of states introduced voting registration amendments that would restrict access to voting by poor and African American people.[2] In addition, a criminal justice system responsible for mass incarceration (Alexander 2010) was under increasing scrutiny, especially in light of

[1] I should like to thank the Egalitarianism seminar at the Institute for Advanced Study, Princeton, especially Danielle Allen, Gurminder K. Bhambra, Sara Edenheim, Michael Hanchard, Charles Payne, and Mara Viveros Vigolla, for discussions that facilitated the development of the arguments in this chapter, and also Robert J. Antonio for his critical comments.

[2] See the page at the American Civil Liberties Union website: https://www.aclu.org/issues/voting-rights.

J. Holmwood (✉)
University of Nottingham, Nottingham, UK

© The Editor(s) (if applicable) and The Author(s) 2016   **143**
C. Karner, B. Weicht (eds.), *The Commonalities of Global Crises*,
DOI 10.1057/978-1-137-50273-5_6

extrajudicial killings of African American men by police officers, which garnered additional media attention with the shooting of Mike Brown in Ferguson, Missouri, on August 2014, attention that was especially pronounced with the demonstrations following the failure to indict the officer responsible (Rodgers 2014). The killings continued, alongside further demonstrations and grass-roots organisations to combat them (for example, #blacklivesmatter). The academic year ended with the white supremacist killing of members of the African Methodist Episcopal church in Charleston, Virginia on 7 June 2015.

"Stop All the Clocks..."[3]

And yet it seemed for white America, and for sociology, the clocks did not stop; business went on as usual. The reality of "race" in America was not regarded as a challenge to the sociological imagination. In one sense, how could it? After all, the American Sociological Association's sections on "Racial and Ethnic Minorities" and on "Race, Gender and Class" are among the biggest and most active. The events described herein are easily assimilable to ordinary topics addressed by sociologists who identify their research with those fields. Yet, I want to suggest that, despite the significance of this work, there is an underlying problem of the discipline concerning the displacement of "race" in the way in which modernity is understood (perhaps also indicated in the elision of "race" and "ethnicity"). Essentially, I suggest that notwithstanding the continued significance of race as a "phenomenal" issue, it is displaced from the centre of sociological concern by other mechanisms seen as being more fundamental. In effect, the deeper structures of sociological thought represent race as a "residual" factor, a historical legacy that lags behind deeper social structural changes assumed to gradually remove it.

Let me explain further by reference to the "standard view" at the moment of the seeming success of the civil rights movement. According

---

[3] The line comes from the poem by W.H. Auden, but it was brought to mind by an article about riots in Baltimore following the police killing of Freddie Gray in The Atlantic magazine by Ta-Nehisi Coates (2015), "The clock didn't start with the riots".

to this view, race discrimination was broadly regarded as a "particularist" distortion of the rational "logic" of markets and bureaucracies, and, perhaps more significantly, of the universalist values of democracy itself. Indeed, in his influential account, Myrdal (1944) saw it as a limit on the values intrinsic to the "American creed" of equality, a limit that was destined to die away as the creed became more thoroughly institutionalised. The most influential US sociologist of the postwar period, Talcott Parsons, did not discuss race until the 1960s, after the successes of the civil rights movement, only to posit the "full integration of the Negro American" (Parsons 1965) and the development of a welfare state based upon (Marshallian) social rights (Parsons 1971). The latter was regarded as an expression of a "principle of equality [which] has broken through to a new level of pervasiveness and generality. A societal community as *basically* composed of equals seems to be the 'end of the line' in the long process of undermining the legitimacy of ... older, more particularistic ascriptive bases of membership" (1971: 119).[4]

Parsons's optimism was clearly misplaced. The victory of the civil rights movement seems to have inaugurated not further reform, but reaction. Rather than extend a previously segregated system of welfare and employment to include African Americans, it is as if it was preferable to US electorates to retrench it for all (Gilens 1999; see also King and Smith 2014). This is a fundamental challenge to contemporary sociology and not just in the USA. From a sociological perspective—certainly, for example, that of Parsons—a regime of social rights can be understood as a distinctive form of moral economy beyond the strict political economy of capitalism. Yet this moral economy has been dismantled by neoliberal policies that began in the 1970s. The puzzle has been to explain how this

---

[4] It might be supposed that Parsons's failure to publish his account of *American Society* (2007) in his lifetime—a project begun in the 1950s—had something to do with the intractability of racialized social problems in the light of his account of them. Tellingly, Parsons also suggested the title, "*The Action of Social Structure*", yet, given his concern to establish the distinctiveness of the USA as a "multi-ethnic society" (Alexander 2007), what seems most significant was the failure of social structure to produce its effects in the very area of racialized domination. Indeed, elsewhere his account of the "system of modern society" (1971) makes only one mention of colonialism and Empire to indicate its "transitional" character (1971:137), notwithstanding it is not a transition to modernity that he discusses, and the USA is identified as the new "lead society" with no mention of it as a colonial "settler" society and the racialized character of the processes of settlement.

dismantling could arise, with most explanations looking to imperatives of globalisation; that is to argue that, once again, political economy has triumphed over moral economy (see also Piketty 2014). "Race" as an integral aspect of the process has been neglected. It is this neglect that I want to explain as following from deep, unacknowledged structures of the sociological thought.

Political Economy Versus Moral Economy

My reference to Parsons's account of capitalist development and its transcendence of "political economy" has a polemical purpose. Few sociologists accept his account (or, perhaps, even read it) and, indeed, for his critics, nothing is more to be expected than the return of "political economy". However, it is this "naturalisation" of capitalist political economy that I want to question and to do so through reflections on the way in which Karl Polanyi's work has been used to establish this "truth" (notwithstanding its status as a truth that Polanyi himself was concerned to rebut). After all, there is a paradox in contemporary neoliberalism, where its differentiation from "classic" liberalism presupposes an intervening period of "not-classic liberalism" to establish neoliberalism as a project of return or reordering. Neoliberalism may assert the necessity of the logic of markets, but it is a necessity that must confront the reality of alternatives.

For those seeking to utilise the work of Polanyi there is, necessarily, a cyclical process. There is, once again, a conflict between democracy and the global financial order similar to that which characterised the 1920s (Streek 2011; Block and Somers 2014) and which was the impetus to Polanyi's landmark book, *The Great Transformation* (2001 [1944]). Where Polanyi analysed a "first wave" of marketization in the emergence of capitalism in the eighteenth and nineteenth century and a "second wave" in the 1920s and 1930s that was a harbinger of fascist atavistic responses, so we are to understand that there has there has been a "third wave" of marketization (against a post-1945 countermovement of welfare reforms) beginning in the 1980s (Burawoy 2013; see Piketty 2014). "Market fundamentalism" (Block and Somers 2014), it seems, is a default policy option available to global elites to address any economic crisis; and commentators have returned to Polanyi to understand how that fundamentalism is constituted in terms of an ideology of the "self-regulating" market.

Leaving aside the "Eurocentrism" of the formulations of the three waves for a moment, they hardly explain the weakness of democratic responses and their faultlines. Significantly, the political economy of capitalism invoked is usually a political economy without colonial formations and, consequently, it is a political economy in which nation-states do not have to engage with a colonial past and a postcolonial present (as will become clear, I regard race in the US and elsewhere as a colonial/postcolonial issue). For example, despite Polanyi addressing the emergence of capitalism in Britain in the eighteenth and nineteenth centuries, there is no discussion of Britain as a colonial and imperial power. Moreover, Polanyi's core conceptual apparatus—the analysis of the three fictitious commodities of land, labour and money—appears to have no place for a treatment of "race", except as a residual category of the "social" in its resistance to market incursions. Nor is there a discussion of race in the many commentaries on Polanyi and the attempts to update his work (for example Blyth 2002; Dale 2010; Block and Somers 2014).

Polanyi's object in *The Great Transformation* was the emergence of a classical political economy and the "disembedding" of economic relations from a wider nexus of social obligations in the establishment of self-regulating market relations governed by impersonal economic laws enshrined in a classical political economy. There is a clear parallel with E.P. Thompson's (1971) idea of a moral economy, although the latter does not discuss Polanyi. Thompson coined the term "moral economy", in his account of food riots in eighteenth-century England, to capture the everyday understandings of inequality, prices, and mutual (if asymmetrical) obligations that sustained economic relations prior to the emergence of the capitalist system of extended exchange relations. For Thompson, riots, and other actions by eighteenth-century crowds, sought to hold to account merchants and other intermediaries seeking to introduce a new market for corn. In doing so, they counterposed a moral economy of appropriate prices to a new political economy of market freedom that, in Thompson's phrase, "demoralised" understandings of the theory of trade, replacing "embedded" understandings with abstract ideas of the "public good" (1971: 89).

For many historians prior to Thompson, these riots were "spontaneous", "irrational" actions by an "unruly" populace, but Thompson sought to show that they had the sanction of local tradition and the regulation of prices was frequently viewed sympathetically by magistrates and other local worthies. Moreover, "riots" had specific targets, being directed at specific ends, and did not usually "spill out" beyond those, which would be expected if they had simply been instances of "collective contagion". For Thompson, the riots were an indication of a moral economy of normatively regulated exchange relations undergoing displacement by a new regime, namely that of a political economy of market exchanges. The latter was a political economy because although the idea of market exchanges was justified by the idea that it expressed natural laws of economic organisation and motivation, it required political agency to introduce the supposedly spontaneous self-regulated market system. Riots and other conflicts that were the focus of Thompson's concern were evidence of this new political agency and resistance to it, a resistance that would have to be overcome as the new regime of political economy came into being.

These arguments have been criticized on similar grounds, namely that the dichotomy between a precapitalist moral economy and a capitalist political economy is too sharply drawn. In the case of Polanyi, it is even suggested that the dichotomy is contradictory, since his critique of capitalist political economy is directed at the "fiction" of the "self-regulating market" and, thus, that he implies that all markets, even capitalist markets, must be embedded in social relations to some extent (Granovetter 1985; Swedberg 1997; for critical discussions see Krippner 2001; Machado 2011). These arguments are partly misplaced, not least because, in the case of Polanyi, his argument is directed at the classical political economy as a *discourse* of public policy, rather than as an empirical description of the reality of markets. The "revisionist" interpretation of Polanyi and Thompson misses the critical focus of their work, especially their arguments concerning the incoherence of liberal political economy. However, some revisionism is necessary, particularly one approach that addresses race, which remains absent from other revisionist approaches concerned mainly with establishing an empirical programme for a "new" economic sociology (for example Granovetter 1985; Swedberg 1997).

For Polanyi, the incoherence of political economy is established in his critique of the idea of the self-regulating market as the organizing principle of public policies necessary for the establishment and reproduction of market-exchange relations. Public policies based upon an incoherent and contradictory understanding will reproduce that incoherence in specific policy failures, notwithstanding the apparent "perfection" (or "utopia") of their theoretical construction. A similar idea is found in Durkheim's (1984 [1893], 1992 [1937]) argument of the pathological nature of a classical liberal political economy that reproduces the conditions giving rise to anomie at the same time as ostensibly promoting the individual's well-being or happiness as the utilitarian principle of welfare.

In Polanyi's case (and Durkheim's), this incoherence is the point at which the lever of criticism is entered and the possibility of social reform and alternative moral economies that looked beyond liberal capitalism and its violent transition might be developed (for example, those expressing complex freedom, moral individualism or social rights). However, I posit the necessity for an alternative revisionism directed at the neglect of race in the treatment of moral economy and the constitution of labour as a category of political economy (I have argued elsewhere [Holmwood 2000a] that the significance of money in Polanyi's account is to establish an "internal" limit on commodification in contrast to the "external" limits indicated by labour and land). This is proposed as a form of revisionism that, nonetheless, retains—and deepens—the critique of (neo-) liberal public policy as a racialized fiction and not simply as an "antisocial" fiction.

While Thompson does not address the topic directly, the contradictory nature of political economy is, in effect, the default position of his Marxist orientation and the "postponed" revolutionary alternative. Many of those who utilise Polanyi do so as a surrogate for a discredited Marxian analysis that seems overly focused on the capital-labour struggles centred on production. In this context, Polanyi is seen to add dimensions of land and money and their associated social struggles. Paradoxically, in going beyond Marx, Polanyi, and those who adopt his approach, leave the category of labour and how its commodity status is understood untransformed. Yet, at a minimum, Polanyi must be seen as providing an analysis that expresses capitalism as much more "loosely-coupled"—to use Perrow's (1984) happy phrase—than the "tightcoupling" expressed in Marxian (or neoliberal) theory. For the latter, production and distribution in a capitalist system are simply too "tightly coupled" to allow reforms in the area of "distribution" without the transformation of relations of production, and relations of production are also, themselves, tightly coupled to the "logic" of the capital-labour relations. Each part is mutually dependent upon other parts, and change of one part cannot be undertaken without a simultaneous change in other parts. From the perspective of "tight coupling", revolution is the only answer to the problem of reform.

It follows that, in the absence of a revolutionary moment, the Marxian argument is potentially fatalistic in that it encourages the perception that there is no alternative to political economy and the policies based upon it. Marx (1975) was aware of this problem, at least in his early journalistic writing for the *Rheinische Zeitung* in 1842/3 concerning the debates on the introduction of laws against the theft of wood and the plight of the Moselle wine growers. He presents those debating this as being cognisant of the wine growers' suffering and, at the same time, as declaring themselves unable to address it without the unintended consequence of deepening that suffering. "Fatalism" in the face of human problems was part of the alienated self-understanding of emergent capitalism and its system of political economy.

It is precisely an alternative conception of the loose coupling of capitalism that allows Polanyi to entertain institutionalised "countermovements", which decommodify land, labour and money, just insofar as they regulate or restrict free exchanges. The attractiveness of this account over the Marxist alternative is that it seems to allow the possibility of substantive reform within capitalism and, thus, an understanding of its varieties (for example see Esping-Andersen 2000). But this also involves a paradox. The "logic" of the self-regulating market (or the "capital-labour relation") is a theoretical construct informing public policy (or its radical critique) and not necessarily a description of the practical operation of market exchanges. Empirically, markets require implementation and implementation meets a resistance, Polanyi suggests (2001: xxx), that can come from "all corners of the compass" (meaning it can be progressive or conservative in its orientation).

Let's pause to consider how this is a radical challenge to the Marxist understanding and its implications. The Marxian account of class struggle depends upon a dialectic of formal and real subordination of labour to the capital-labour relation (Marx 1976). Labour can have manifold forms, reflecting different prior conditions, as it becomes subordinated to capital until it is transformed in its real subordination to the form of labour integral to the capital-labour relation, namely individuated and commodified labour-power. Whereas, there will be resistance to commodification or class struggles motivated by understandings that pre-exist processes of formal subordination, class struggle, proper, is constituted by the real subordination of labour within the capital-labour relation and the wage form, and, as such, becomes the object of struggle and transformation.

The implications of Polanyi's analysis are different and suggest a critique of Marx's idea of capitalism and its contradictions. For Marx, the contradictions of capitalism ultimately render it impossible to reproduce, but that impossibility, apparently, does not call into question its realisation as an approximation to its pure form. For Marx, capitalism must first be realised, in order for it to be overcome. But Polanyi seems to be suggesting something different. What if the contradictions of capitalism (that is, those intrinsic to the idea of the self-regulating market) give rise to forms of resistance that modify capitalism away from its pure form in the moment of its coming into being? In other words, this suggests that the idea of the real subordination of labour is itself a "utopia" in precisely the same sense that Polanyi attributes to the liberal idea of the self-regulating market. If the "utopia" of the self-regulating market is an error of thought (with practical consequences), so too, must be the idea of the real subordination of labour.

In other words, this must pose a question mark over the idea of labour-power as the commodity form intrinsic to capitalism and expressive of its "economic logic". This, in turn, poses a further question of how such an idea arises. I want to suggest that it is a contingent feature of the historical circumstances that are treated as exemplary for understanding the emergence of capitalism, reflecting a Eurocentrism to which Polanyi himself is not immune.

Dispossession and the Idea of Labour Power

My concern is to open the space for a consideration of race as a determining factor in the formation of capitalist modernities. So far, I have suggested that resistance to commodified labour can, in Polanyi's terms, involve "social" responses of manifold orientations. However, such a formulation is no more than suggestive of a space in which race can be conceptualised. That space, however, is vulnerable to expressions of it as opposed to the logic that is otherwise contained in the operation of "impersonal" markets or administrative systems. Indeed, I suggest it is necessary to go further and challenge Polanyi's representation of the "fictional" status of *labour power* as the commodity form intrinsic to the idea of self-regulating markets.

Polanyi's argument depends upon a separation of the human individual and his or her labour power. As with other "fictional commodities" (land and money), Polanyi argues that, "the postulate that anything that is bought and sold must have been produced for sale is emphatically untrue in regard to them" (2001: 72). He goes on, "labor is only another name for a human activity which goes with life itself, which in its turn, is not produced for sale but for entirely different reasons, nor can that activity be detached from the rest of life, be stored or mobilized" (2001: 72). Yet the emergence of capitalism shows that it coincides with chattel slavery, where *it is precisely the case that there is no separation between the human individual and his or her labour.* Under chattel slavery the individual, and not his or her labour power, is treated as a commodity and is detached from the rest of life, "stored" and "mobilised". This separation is evident in the designation "slave" which reduces (and dehumanises) the individual to their labour, in contrast to the term enslavement, which retains the separation of the individual and their labour activity in the face of the inhumanity of the practice. In other words, whereas the idea of labour power as a commodity may be a "fiction", the commodified labourer is not; for many, it is the reality of the emergence of capitalism.

We might ask: why is Polanyi insensible of this fact? Whereas Marx sees commodified labour power as the impersonal logic of political economy, the implication is that, for Polanyi, commodified labour power should be understood as a *moral economy*, moreover, one with a limited application to the specific European (British) population that is his focus. Part of the problem lies in his treatment of colonialism and the category of land. It seems obvious that the creation of a category of workers in Europe with no access to resources other than through the sale of their labour on the market is associated with their dispossession from collective rights to land and the commons through the creation of private property in land. In that sense, land and labour (and for that matter money) are not "fictional" commodities that develop separately from each other. The commodification of land displaces the rural population and makes them available for hire as wage labour. At the same time, it creates a surplus population with a potential interest in migration, just as British colonialism is opening markets. Thus, the enclosure movement in Europe that fuels migration also creates a form of colonial enclosure through settlement, displacement and destruction of indigenous populations. At the same time, colonialism provides opportunities for investment in enterprises that require a workforce—for example, sugar and cotton plantations of the American and Caribbean colonies. The paradox is that the later colonisation of Africa means that local populations are not made available for employment through dispossession, but only by kidnap and enslavement.

This can be seen in Locke, and what MacPherson (1962) has called his theory of "possessive individualism" (as expressed in his second treatise on Government, perhaps classic liberalism's foundational text). As Lebovics (1986) has pointed out, the usual interpretation sees this theory as "anticipating" capitalism, yet it is written directly in the context of settler colonialism and of the enclosure movement. Those displaced by enclosure are offered the possibility of enclosure themselves in the form of settlement elsewhere. But what is important to Locke, on this analysis, is to show that common ownership confers no rights, only private ownership does; the displacement of common rights through possession is not to be described as "dispossession". Restrictions on private property—that enough must be left for others and nothing must be left to spoil—are, in the first case, "solved" by colonial settlement and the idea that it confronts a "terra nullius", while unlimited accumulation without spoilage is resolved through money. Classic liberalism, then, asserts private property rights directly in the context of two of Polanyi's three categories, those of land and money, and through the third, labour, as the expression of self-ownership as the basis of individual rights.

In this way, complex forms of subordination of labour to capital arise—wage labour, family labour, indentured service and enslavement—and the different forms are socially constructed (and resisted) and politically regulated. The idea of "free labour" appears to emerge as a category of disadvantaged membership in a societal community, governed by cultural norms of proper treatment. Given the well-documented debates over the humanity (or otherwise) of native Americans and Africans in the context of Spanish colonialism (Rodriguez-Salgado 2009), philosophical reflections on "stages" of history (Bhambra 2007), and religious involvement in the antislavery movement (Anderson 2014), these cultural norms were religiously inflected and racially organised. It is in this sense that commodified labour power and its separation from human individuality might be understood as a "moral", rather than an "economic" category, deriving from a particular religious tradition and applied, in the first instance, only to those understood as members.

Part of the reason why these connections have not been drawn is because of a general neglect of colonialism and enslavement in sociological accounts of modernity (see Bhambra 2007, 2014). This is compounded, too, by the generalisation of employment as the dominant means of access to resources. The normalisation of the labour market has tended to reinforce the idea that it is constituted by a primary economic "logic". I want to suggest that the generalisation of employment relations does not derive from an economic logic of capitalism, but from a political process, and that process cannot be assigned to its mere functionality for capitalism. This argument is both theoretical and substantive.

The economic "logic" of capitalism, if by that we understand the operation of markets and the sale of labour, has historically given rise to many forms of labour; but when Marx wrote it, it was associated with the rise of "day labour", much closer in form to what we would now regard as "casualised labour". As I have suggested, this form of labour has historically coexisted with many other forms, including slavery, bonded or indentured labour, family labour, gang-labour and so on, suggesting that there is no particularly strong market logic undermining these other forms, even in what are regarded as strongly liberal forms of capitalism, as in Britain or the USA. This helps us to understand how capitalism can have colonialism as an integral part and that seemingly classically liberal capitalist states such as Britain can be involved in an Imperialism that involves the extension and utilization of bonded labour and slavery (Steinfeld 1991; Orren 1991). The USA, for its part, was a settler capitalist country (see Prasad 2012), with all that implies for its institutions of political and economic domination.

I contend that it is *a political* process that establishes "free" labour and undermines forms of unfree labour or conversely, maintains them, but that it does not, by that token, produce free labour as a pure economic category (the fiction of liberal theory). There are a number of processes involved, including the trades union movement, but these processes necessarily also involve the state. The generalization and normalization of labour contracts owe less to the "logic of capitalism" and more to the emergence of the "general welfare state" (Fine 1956), where the need to generate taxes also leads to the regularization of forms of payment. In this way, the generalization of employment relations is already a process of social citizenship (albeit restricted) and the incorporation of labour into ideas of (hierarchically organised) citizenship. It is not the "logic" of the market, but the state that has produced the effects usually attributed to the former. As Durkheim argued, "it is the state that has rescued the child from patriarchal domination and from family tyranny; the state that has freed the citizen from feudal groups and later from communal groups; it is the state that has liberated the craftsman and his master from guild tyranny" (1992 [1937]: 64).

But precisely because it is the state, and the state operates in relation to prevailing modes of moral economy, the organisation of labour contracts depends on forms of recognition and misrecognition that embody the racial hierarchies bequeathed by colonialism. We are used to thinking of the "general welfare state" as the nation-state, but from the eighteenth century through to the mid-twentieth century, the European nation-state was in most cases a colonial and Imperially-aspirant state. The political community of the state extended beyond national boundaries and involved a stratified, hierarchical form of citizenship—involving subjects of the Empire as well as subjects of the nation. In other words, "race" is both integral to the formation of labour as a category and to the DNA of the modern state. The "possessive individualism" (Macpherson 1962) integral to the liberal idea of the self and its expression within market exchange relations is the product of wider social relations than simply those of the capital-labour relation and, as such, it is a moral concept given "economic" form.

The Free Movement of Capital and the Free Movement of Unfree Labour

It is my contention that once the sociological conditions of the emergence of the fictional commodities of labour, land and money are placed in the context of colonialism, we are in a position to understand the present crisis somewhat differently than current conceptions of a "third wave" of marketization. We are also better able to understand the faultlines in democracy and their racialized character. I began with a discussion of the problem of race in the USA and its immediate, vivid manifestations and I am now in a position to reflect upon the significance of understanding "labour power" as a racialized category.

Paradoxically, the retrenchment of social rights more generally following desegregation in the USA has the appearance of making "class" more relevant in the explanation of the experience of African Americans than that of "race" (Wilson 1978, 2015). This is because a significant proportion of white Americans share similar experiences of disadvantage. However, what needs to be understood is that it is "race" that explains the reemergence of "class" and not class which is the underlying explanation of "race"; this is an interpretation that poses a problem for sociological class analysis, despite appearing to affirm it. Indeed, it is precisely for this reason that Wilson (2015) makes the argument that his claim is about *race* and not ethnicity, more generally (which would be the case, if a simple version of class analysis was being affirmed).

It is significant that when Myrdal (1963) returned to consider the fate of the US welfare state in the light of civil rights, he perceived something different from what Parsons supposed would be the emergence of a regime of social rights, notwithstanding Myrdal's own commitment to a welfare regime embodying institutionalised social rights. A failure to invest in productivity meant that the USA risked the creation of an "underclass", separated from opportunities and at risk of unemployment and underemployment. For Myrdal, this was a "structural" problem that was also "racialized", but it was soon to be transformed within neoliberal discourse into a "behavioural" problem (Gans 1995). In this context it became associated with increasingly punitive polices to enforce private responsibility, from which the US carceral state derives, and also involved the pathologising of African American culture. In other words, the problem was framed as not lying with socially structured inequality or with "American values", but with African Americans being purportedly outside those values.

I could just as easily have begun the chapter with the current crisis over migration and refugees in Europe. Here, the language of antislavery is now applied to deny migrants access to European welfare. Thus, politicians and EU civil servants refer to "people trafficking" and the need to challenge its "business model", either by destroying the means of transport for those fleeing suffering in their own countries or by making Europe and its constituent countries hostile environments for migrants. Disruptions at border ports, such as that of Calais, have led to descriptions of migrants as a "swarm", disrupting British holidaymakers exercising their "right to holiday" by their illegitimate pursuit of a "safe haven".[5]

Indeed, part of the British debate around migration, more generally, and especially that of migration within the European Union, is explicitly about excluding migrants from welfare benefits, including those designed to support households where members are in low-paid employment. In other words, dominant discourse applied to low pay distinguishes between "members" of the political and social community who deserve better, and those who are not "members" and, therefore, are appropriately subjected to politically enforced market strictures. Of course, such exclusions are difficult to make and potentially illegal in light of EU requirements. In this context, the easiest way to remove benefits from migrants is to remove them from everyone. This is a process of dismantling welfare

---

[5] See for example the speech by Prime Minister Cameron, available at: http://www.bbc.co.uk/news/uk-politics-33716501.

similar to that evident in the USA following the extension of civil and political rights to African Americans.

But, is it a process which is only just beginning to unfold in Europe in a manner that was foreshadowed in the USA? Once again, it would be well to recall how the USA was represented in European comparative sociology as a "laggard" welfare state, which would gradually move closer to Europe's more institutional welfare regimes. Yet recent arguments, such as Piketty's (2014), suggest that the postwar regimes in Europe that seemed to deliver a secular decline in inequality were already coming to an end at the same time that the USA was suggested to transcend its "laggard" status. In other words, Europe began to "Americanise" at just the time that America was supposed to "Europeanise" (Holmwood 2000b). The reemergence of neoliberal moral economy begins from the late 1970s.

In addition, for many commentators, the explanation is associated with declining "solidarities" within political and social communities, as the experience of wartime solidarities and exigencies fades. This is also connected by some (for example Goodhart 2013) to high rates of immigration that allegedly undermine social democratic solidarities. In these arguments, however, immigration is typically treated as an exogenous factor and not connected back to the colonial formation of European welfare states.[6] Thus, Esping-Andersen (2000) follows Polanyi in his neglect of race in the discussion of processes of commodification and decommodification. Yet it seems clear that the politics of "immigration" is strongly associated with welfare regimes and these, in turn, have different colonial histories.

For example, Esping-Andersen identifies a specific "liberal welfare regime", in which he places the USA, Australia, New Zealand, Canada, and the UK. It is striking that each country is a "settler capitalist" country that serves to constitute the agrarian interests so significant in its subsequent development, as well as providing an explanation of a lower range in the distribution of wealth and inequality for much of the nineteenth century, as documented by Prasad (2012) and Piketty (2014). Of course, Britain is not a "settler capitalist" country, but it is a coun-

---

[6] See Banting (2005) for a more nuanced discussion.

try that settled and provided settlers, thereby, creating interconnections with settler capitalist economies and shaping its own political economy through colonial encounters. Yet these interconnections and encounters have largely been neglected in comparative studies of welfare and policy regimes (Holmwood 2014). The point is not that immigration has now begun to undermine solidarities, but that solidarities were formed on a racialized politics of colonial encounters.[7]

The importance of understanding the colonial formation of current debates on welfare and immigration is evident in the emergence of a new neoliberal argument for the free movement of "unfree labour" put forward by Posner and Weyl (2014; see also Weyl 2015).[8] It is hard to understand the resurgence of "unfree labour" and its embrace by liberal theorists, except that racialized unfree labour has always been integral to liberalism (for a discussion of the wider illiberalism associated with liberalism, see King 1999). Posner and Weyl purport to address global inequality, suggesting that attempts to address inequality within nation-states do nothing to alleviate global inequality because of a perceived need to close borders to protect domestic labour from competition and welfare budgets from the claims made by the migrant poor. Yet, they argue, it is the movement of poor people from the global South to the North, together with the sending of remittances back to the global South, that will do the most to reduce global inequality (even if inequality rises within the national welfare states of the global North).

They are conscious that "open borders" need to be sold to populations and politicians in the global North. Their solution is a rigorous "othering" of migrants, to create what they explicitly describe as a caste system. Their model is Qatar, where migration by coreligionists of the majority population is discouraged in order to reduce the development of solidarities between local populations and migrant workers. "Belonging" is a privilege of local citizens; migrants are displaced from where they belong and offered no recognition in the places to which they move.

---

[7] Lebowics's conclusion is direct, but remains outside dominant sociological understandings: "[Locke] made the colonial empire a vital bond between Britain's new elite and those they governed. He thereby strengthened the nascent liberalism of British society by building into it the promise of growth, of more for all, of social peace through empire" (1986: 581).

[8] This discussion of Posner and Weyl is based upon a short article written jointly with Gurminder K Bhambra (Holmwood and Bhambra 2015).

At the same time, Posner and Weyl suggest migrants should be paid significantly lower wages than those typical of even low-paid workers in the host society (they suggest an annual income of $5000 in the USA). They must also be deprived of rights to organize and protest, and are to be delivered into strict subordination to employers as indentured labour. While the exploitation of indentured labour will be to the benefit of employers (and consumers) in the North, they claim that it will also be to the betterment of indentured labourers themselves, who are escaping worse conditions they otherwise face "at home".

The idea of their "betterment", however, depends on the idea that the global North bears no responsibility for those conditions, and that, however constrained, indentured labour represents a "choice". At what point does "indentured labour" become so constrained that it represents enslavement? In a separate piece, Weyl (2015) argues that the forced transport of enslaved Africans to the US brought about an improvement in the circumstances of African Americans, when compared to those that remained in Africa and, at the same time, describes systematic racism as the way in which this beneficial outcome was achieved.

The argument made by Posner and Weyl is presented as a simple utilitarian argument for the efficiency of free trade. It is precisely the kind of "fiction" described by Polanyi. What should be clear, however, is that, for them, freedom of trade lies on only one side of the capital/labour relation. Global capital should be allowed unregulated free movement, while free movement of labour should be severely regulated. Domestic capital should be free to exploit indentured labour, while migrant labour should be policed and prevented from claiming rights enjoyed by other citizens (though, of course, it is unlikely that local populations in the global North could be insulated from the effects of divided citizenship and merely enjoy the fruits of the indentured labour in the form of cheap services).

Like other advocates of free markets, they are doubtful that alternative models of alleviating poverty, such as foreign aid, can be effective because of the corruption of governments (though they endorse private philanthropy, as do other liberal theorists; see for example, Barry 1990). Yet, corruption is much more a product of the free movement of capital they endorse, where "payoffs" to local elites for access to land, minerals and fuels, are cheaper than compensation would be to those dispossessed by that access.

What Posner and Weyl fail to address is that the supposed efficiency gains of free trade are appropriated by a tiny minority of the world's population and, yet, are enjoined upon all as a necessity that "rational" individuals must accept. Thus, they argue strongly for free market freedoms based upon private property, but do not reflect upon how the asymmetrical possession of private property itself derives from systematic dispossession; that is, through land grabs, enclosures, displacement of local systems of subsistence, and access to mineral extraction through corrupt contracts with local elites. It is dispossession that produces the conditions of impoverishment that make indentured labour a "choice" preferable to starvation, and that "choice" that demonstrates the "freedom" of "unfree labour".

Why should public policy support the individual rights of the few over the collective rights of the many? Why should individual rights provide returns to owners of private property, but there be no compensation for the loss of collective rights they entail? Back in the eighteenth century, Thomas Paine wrote in his pamphlet on *Agrarian Justice* of the need to provide reparation for the loss of concrete and specific rights by agricultural workers following the enclosure movement that drove them off the land (in turn, for some to migrate to settle supposedly "virgin" lands and dispossess indigenous populations elsewhere). Paine's argument remains urgent in the present as an argument for global social justice. It is one that is potentially transformative in the current debate about migration.

Current EU policy toward migration seeks to establish a hostile environment to discourage migration, while the free market option is based on unfree labour. Yet it is possible to envision a different way forward that addresses the conditions from which migrants seek respite. This would involve transfers from the global North to the global South, but they are not well-described as foreign aid. In contrast, they should be described as reparations that compensate for past dispossession (through colonial appropriation and enslavement) and that ensure compensation and proper participation in decisions about current appropriation. But it would also imply recognition of migrants as citizens, in a context where European (and other) nation-states were previously colonial states in which they were subjects. As Bhambra argues (2014), migrants are as much part of the "histories" of European nation-states, as those deemed to be their "native" and historical members on their transition from colonial/imperial states to nation-states more recently.

Conclusion

I have suggested that to address current issues of race and issues of national and global inequality, we can learn from the work of Karl Polanyi, but that in order to do so, we need to "provincialise" his work. In common with other advocates of the "provincialisation" of social theory (Chakrabarty 2000), I understand this to mean being attentive to the contingent historical conditions in which specific categories emerge and come to be decontextualised as "analytical" truths. In the case of Polanyi, I have suggested that despite understanding the development of capitalism to be associated with dispossession, his understanding of the "fictional" commodities of labour, land and money remained dependent on a particular European experience which is misdescribed (or, at least, incompletely described) in such a way as to elide the centrality of race and the nature of liberalism as a racialised moral economy.

In this chapter, I have suggested that treating political economy as a form of moral economy is a positive move, but that we should retain the Polanyian idea of the internal incoherence of (neo-)liberal moral economy, while recognising that incoherence does not derive from its abstraction from social content, but its specific incorporation of a racialized content. In arguing for the importance of a "thick" conception of social rights against the "thin" neoliberal conception of individual rights, it is necessary to address the nature of access to rights and the continuation of domination for some, despite recognition of others within any prevailing form of rights. I have suggested broadening the concept of moral economy in order to understand that supposedly commodified labour power—free labour—does not derive from an economic "logic", but from a political process of inclusion, exclusion and domination. Once that analytical shift is made, we can understand that the faultline in democracy remains that of race and that the failure to extend social rights is one of the reasons why they are currently unravelling.

These are lessons being made visible in Calais, Kos and Lampedusa, on the streets of cities in the United States, and elsewhere, if we had the (sociological) imagination to see and to learn.

References

Alexander, J. C. (2007). Foreword. In T. Parsons (Ed.), *American society: A theory of the societal community.* Edited and introduced by Giuseppe Sciortino. Boulder: Paradigm Publishers.

Alexander, M. (2010). *The new Jim Crow: Mass incarceration in an age of color-blindness.* New York: New Press.

Anderson, E. (2014). Social movements, experiments in living, and moral progress: Case studies from Britain's abolition of slavery. *The Lindley lecture at the University of Kansas.* Available at: http://kuscholarworks.ku.edu/bitstream/handle/1808/14787/Anderson_Social_Movements.pdf?sequence=1. Accessed 10 Aug 2015.

Banting, K. (2005). The multicultural welfare state: International experience and North American narratives. *Social Policy and Administration, 39*(2), 98–115.

Barry, N. (1990). *Welfare.* Milton Keynes: Open University Press.

Bhambra, G. K. (2007). *Rethinking modernity: Postcolonialism and the sociological imagination.* Basingstoke: Palgrave MacMillan.

Bhambra, G. K. (2014). *Connected sociologies.* London: Bloomsbury Academic.

Block, F., & Somers, M. (2014). *The power of market fundamentalism.* Cambridge: Harvard University Press.

Blyth, M. (2002). *Great transformations: Economic ideas and institutional change in the twentieth century.* Cambridge: Cambridge University Press.

Burawoy, M. (2013). Marxism after Polanyi. In M. Williams & V. Satgar (Eds.), *Marxisms in the 21st. century.* Johannesburg: Witswatersrand University Press.

Chakrabarty, D. (2000). *Provincializing Europe: Postcolonial thought and historical difference.* Princeton: Princeton University Press.

Coates, T -N. (2015). The clock didn't start with the riots. *The Atlantic.* 30 April 2015. http://www.theatlantic.com/politics/archive/2015/04/ta-nehisi-coates-johns-hopkins-baltimore/391904/. Accessed 10 Aug 2015.

Dale, G. (2010). *Karl Polanyi: The limits of the market.* Cambridge: Polity.

Durkheim, E. (1984 [1893]). *The division of labor in society*. New York: Free Press.

Durkheim, E. (1992 [1937]). *Professional ethics and civic morals*. London: Routledge.

Esping-Andersen, G. (2000). *The three worlds of welfare capitalism*. Princeton: Princeton University Press.

Fine, S. (1956). *Laissez Faire and the general-welfare state: A study of conflict in American thought, 1865–1901*. Anne Arbor: University of Michigan Press.

Gans, H. J. (1995). *War against the poor: The underclass and antipoverty policy*. New York: Basic Books.

Gilens, M. (1999). *Why America hates welfare, race, media and the politics of antipoverty policy*. Chicago: University of Chicago Press.

Goodhart, D. (2013). *The British dream: Successes and failures of post-war immigration*. London: Atlantic Books.

Granovetter, M. (1985). Economic action and social structure: The problem of embeddedness. *American Journal of Sociology, 91*(3), 481–510.

Holmwood, J. (2000a). Three pillars of welfare state theory: T.H. Marshall, Karl Polanyi, Alva Myrdal in defence of the "national" welfare state. *European Journal of Social Theory, 3*(1), 23–50.

Holmwood, J. (2000b). Europe and the 'Americanisation' of British social policy. *European Societies, 2*(4), 453–487.

Holmwood, J. (2014). Beyond capital: The challenge for sociology in Britain. *British Journal of Sociology, 65*(4), 607–618.

Holmwood, J. & Bhambra, G. K. (2015). Capitalist dispossession and new justifications of slavery. *openDemocracy*, 3 July 2015. https://www.opendemocracy.net/beyondslavery/john-holmwood-gurminder-k-bhambra/capitalist-dispossession-and-new-justifications-of-s. Accessed 10 Aug 2015.

King, D. S. (1999). *In the name of liberalism: Illiberal social policy in the USA and Britain*. Oxford: Oxford University Press.

King, D. S., & Smith, R. (2014). 'Without regard to race': Critical ideational development in modern American racial politics. *Journal of Politics, 76*(4), 958–971.

Krippner, G. (2001). The elusive market: Embeddedness and the paradigm of economic sociology. *Theory and Society, 30*(6), 775–810.

Lebovics, H. (1986). The uses of America in Locke's Second Treatise of Government. *Journal of the History of Ideas, 47*(4), 567–581.

Machado, N. M. C. (2011). Karl Polanyi and the new economic sociology: Notes on the concept of (dis)embeddedness. *RCCS Annual Review, 3: Revista*

Crítica de Ciências Sociais. http://rccsar.revues.org/309. Accessed 10 Aug 2015.

MacPherson, C. B. (1962). *The political theory of possessive individualism: Hobbes to Locke.* Oxford: Oxford University Press.

Marx, K. (1975). *Early writings (translated by Rodney Livingstone and Gregory Benton).* Harmondsworth: Penguin Books.

Marx, K. (1976). *Capital: A critique of political economy* (Vol. 1). (translated by Ben Fowkes). Harmondsworth: Penguin Books.

Myrdal, G. (1944). *An American dilemma* (with the assistance of Richard Sterner and Arnold Rose). New York: Harper and Brothers.

Myrdal, G. (1963). *The challenge to affluence.* New York: Pantheon.

Orren, K. (1991). *Belated feudalism: Labor, the law, and liberal development in the United States.* Cambridge: Cambridge University Press.

Parsons, T. (1965). Full citizenship for the Negro American? A sociological problem. *Daedalus, 94*(4), 1009–1054.

Parsons, T. (1971). *The system of modern societies.* Englewood Cliffs, NJ: Prentice-Hall.

Parsons, T. (2007). *American society: A theory of the societal community.* Edited and introduced by Giuseppe Sciortino. Boulder: Paradigm Publishers.

Payne, C. (1995). *I've got the light of freedom: The organizing tradition and the Mississipi freedom struggle.* Berkeley and Los Angeles: University of California Press.

Perrow, C. (1984). *Normal accidents: Living with high-risk technologies.* New York: Basic Books.

Piketty, T. (2014). *Capital in the twenty-first century.* Cambridge, MA: Belknap.

Polanyi, K. (2001). *The great transformation: The political and economic origins of our time.* Boston: Beacon Press.

Posner, E. A. & Weyl, G. (2014). A radical solution to global income inequality: Make the U.S. more like Qatar. *New Republic,* 6 November 2014. http://www.newrepublic.com/article/120179/how-reduce-global-income-inequality-open-immigration-policies. Accessed 10 Aug 2015.

Prasad, M. (2012). *The land of too much: American abundance and the paradox of poverty.* Boston: Harvard University Press.

Rodgers, M. L. (2014). Special supplement: Ferguson and the tragic presence of the past. *Theory and Event, 17*(3). Supplement, http://muse.jhu.edu/journals/theory_and_event/toc/tae.17.3S.html. Accessed 10 Aug 2015.

Rodriguez-Salgado, M. (2009). How oppression thrives where truth is not allowed a voice': The Spanish polemic about the American Indians. In G. K.

Bhambra & R. Shilliam (Eds.), *Silencing human rights: Critical engagements with a contested project*. London: Palgrave.

Steinfeld, R. J. (1991). *The invention of free labor: The employment relation in English and American law and culture, 1350–1870*. Chapel Hill: University of North Carolina Press.

Streek, W. (2011). The crises of democratic capitalism. *New Left Review, 71*, 5–29.

Swedberg, R. (1997). New economic sociology: What has been accomplished, what is ahead? *Acta Sociologica, 40*, 161–182.

Thompson, E. P. (1971). The moral economy of the English crowd in the eighteenth century. *Past and Present, 50*(1), 76–146.

Weyl, G. (2015). The openness-equality trade-off in global redistribution. *Social Science Research Network*. http://papers.ssrn.com/sol3/papers.cfm?abstract_id=2509305. Accessed 10 Aug 2015.

Wilson, W. J. (1978). *The declining significance of race: Blacks and changing American institutions*. Chicago: University of Chicago Press.

Wilson, W. J. (2015). New perspectives on the declining significance of race: A rejoinder. *Ethnic & Racial Studies, 38*(8), 1278–1284.

Collective Identity Under Reconstruction: The Case of West Piraeus (Greece)

Giorgos Bithymitris

Well, dudes, life delivered us a simple, rare lesson. Every stab onto our bro's body was at the same time a stab on our selfishness, on our memories that we denied as we were sinking into our apathy and vanity.

(Speech delivered by "Low bap and hip hop brothers" in the memory of Pavlos Fyssas, murdered on 17 September 2013 in West Piraeus by neo-Nazis.)

Introduction

The murder of Pavlos Fyssas—a left-wing, low bap singer and metal worker from a Greek working class suburb—by a member of the neo-Nazi party Golden Dawn on 17 September 2013 triggered a wave of mixed sentiments among the working class: anger against the extreme right, fear of a potential spiral of violence and social misery, hopelessness against the almost total loss of social protection, sadness, guilt. None of

G. Bithymitris (✉)
Panteion University, Athens, Greece

© The Editor(s) (if applicable) and The Author(s) 2016   **167**
C. Karner, B. Weicht (eds.), *The Commonalities of Global Crises*,
DOI 10.1057/978-1-137-50273-5_7

these reactions can be understood independent of the ongoing reconstruction of collective identities among the local working class.

Working-class identities have been much debated in the context of "postindustrialist euphoria" (Spyridakis 2013: 12). Two major paradigms define this contested terrain. The first paradigm draws on seminal sociological works like Rifkin's thesis on the *End of Work* (1996), Bell's analysis of the postindustrial condition (1976), Bauman's theorization of postmodernity (1997), Beck's notions of risk society and reflexive modernity (1997), or the "farewell to the working class" articulated by Gorz (1994). Despite its internal heterogeneity this paradigm describes and at times celebrates a new era where work is no longer considered central to identity. The second paradigm, regenerated in the context of economic crises and austerity, argues that little has changed and that the economic sphere is marked more by continuity than by change. With the latter line of argument seemingly more consistent with the empirical evidence drawn from studies on employment and working conditions in countries like Greece (Kouzis 2005; Karamesini 2011), the present chapter aims to develop a more complex understanding of the narratives people develop about their working lives in crisis-stricken Greece. Our focus, in what follows, is both on individual accounts and recurring, collective narratives.

Turning to the concept of "collective identity", scholarship on social movements reveals a diversity (rather than a consensus) of definitions. For example, while Polletta and Jasper locate collective identity within the individual, defining it as: "an individual's cognitive, moral and emotional connection with a broader community, category, practice, or institution" (2001: 285), it is more frequently understood as something generated and created *between* individuals (Fominaya 2010: 394), something that we *do*—a process (Jenkins 1996). Taking as a point of reference Melucci's work (1995) on how social movements succeed or fail in constituting a collective actor, other social movement scholars (Calhoun 1991; Fantasia 1988) have focused on collective identity as something not pregiven but heavily conditioned by the contingent ability to distinguish a (collective) self from the "other" and to be recognized by those "others" (Melucci 1995: 47). Collective identity can thus be seen as a "descendant" of class consciousness destined to challenge structural understandings of what brings and keeps movement actors together (Fominaya 2010: 395).

The present study of collective identities of the workers of West Piraeus attempts to surpass the dilemma regarding the nature of collective identity (that is, whether an individual or intersubjective accomplishment) by separating the two levels of analysis before merging them into a common account of the ongoing transformations of collective identities with regard to their constitutive elements of class and the "national self". The main argument in what follows is inextricably linked to those shifts and their manifestations, which relate closely to two central notions of this volume: the *politics of nostalgia*, also closely related to Nancy Fraser's notion of social protectionism (Fraser 2012), and the *politics of solidarity* (see Karner and Weicht's introduction).

Simply put, the new collective identities currently taking shape in the area of West Piraeus within a broader national context of economic hardship, social turmoil, and deeply felt injustice (Bithymitris 2016) encompass hybrid structures of nostalgia and solidarity and are associated with an unusual variety of attitudes ranging from cynicism, exclusivism, nationalism and racism to collectivization, radicalism, militancy and solidarity. The area in question is currently witnessing a political-ideological power struggle between the agents of nostalgia (mainly the neo-Nazi party of Golden Dawn) and the agents of solidarity (mainly the Syndicate of Metalworkers of Attica and Ship-building Industry of Greece, SMAS).

This discussion begins with an outline of the national and local context and a brief presentation of the local collective actors who are currently crucial to the reshaping of working-class identity taking place. The methodological approach underpinning this chapter is discussed next: that is, analysis of data stemming from interviews conducted with workers from the area of study and of materials collected from local and national media and blogospheres. I conclude with a discussion of both sets of materials from this ongoing research.

Context

Neither collective identities nor the individual biographies of precariously positioned workers and the unemployed from West Piraeus can be adequately addressed, let alone understood, without outlining the local and national socioeconomic context of the last five years. My focus on the current context of pronounced economic hardship does not imply that the unfolding shifts at the cultural or political levels are mere byproducts of the recent economic crisis. While they need to be seen in their longer historical contexts, it is nonetheless crucially important to realize that the dynamics examined herein have been generated in particular during the currently unfolding social and economic turmoil.

The present research of individuals and collective narratives took place in an extremely turbulent socioeconomic environment. The Greek national economy went into recession in 2009 and on the onset of a so-called debt crisis, a program of austerity (the Memoranda policy framework), has been implemented. The increase in unemployment from about 8 % in 2007 to a staggering 27 % in 2013 has been an unprecedented negative "record", while almost a third of the Greek population are now at risk of poverty or social exclusion (Pouliakas 2014: 2).

The workers of West Piraeus—a metropolitan area comprising the municipalities of Keratsini-Drapetsona, Nikaia-Rentis, Perama, and Korydallos—have experienced the current economic hardship in a much harsher, at times devastating, way, as the crisis aggravated the gradual deindustrialization to which the wider Piraeus region has been subjected.

For over 30 years the ship-building activities located along the coastal line that includes Drapetsona, Keratsini, Perama and Salamina—the "Perama Zone" or simply the "zone" in the local idiom—were the biggest employment pool of West Piraeus, as the specialised workforce numbered some 8.000 workers, especially in the period of economic prosperity up to the 1980s (Vlachos 1996: 3). However, the zone's viability was critically hampered well before the big recession of 2009–2013. The contingent precrisis employment patterns have been thoroughly analysed by Spyridakis (2013) in an ethnographic study of the social space of the zone shared by local ship-building workers; Spyridakis confirms the further degradation and local labour market fragmentation which have defined the economic crisis.

Recent statistical data show that the social injuries suffered by the Greek working class have been particularly painful in this subregion. According to the census of the Hellenic Statistical Authority in 2011, the unemployment rate in the three municipalities of West Piraeus (Keratsini, Nikaia and Perama) amounted to 27.8 % while the national average at the time was 18.72 % (Elstat 2011). Extensive poverty, closed shops and empty working-class spaces (that is, local pubs) were the predominant images of the area during my data collection between 2012 and 2015. Without taking into account such far-reaching social dislocation, one can hardly contextualize the tumultuous local political and cultural struggles over both collective meanings and daily survival evident in the area. What is argued herein is that in this context, two main camps have formed in the resulting symbolic, political, cultural and eventually physical combat: on one side, the extreme-right party of Golden Dawn articulating the widespread and deepest fears of the unemployed, precariously employed workers and the lower-middle classes who are experiencing unforeseen downward social mobility. On the opposite end of the ideological spectrum, there are the labour unions of the zone, with the SMAS (seethe following section) at the forefront of an agonizing struggle against the crisis, which first and foremost has deeply affected local people's work and family lives. Let us briefly present the two organizational actors involved in this extremely contested terrain.

Golden Dawn: Articulating Fear, Envy and Hopelessness

Few, if any, scholars of the Greek political system would deny that the dramatic rise of neo-Nazism in Greece correlates with the social impact of the economic crisis (Ellinas 2013). However obvious this correlation, it does not provide a sufficient explanation of this multi-faceted and complex political phenomenon. Self-representing as an authentic anti-memorandum political force, Golden Dawn saw an impressive increase in its vote share at the 2012 elections, and notably in working-class neighbourhoods that had traditionally been linked with the communist left. Nikaia, or *Kokkinia* (a local idiom denoting the "red" and antifascist legacies of the area), Perama (one of the most characteristic Greek working-class suburbs) and to a lesser extent, Keratsini (another anti-Nazi battlefield during World War II), all helped fuel, in a rather notorious and self-defeating way, the organizational and electoral reservoirs of the extreme right.

Utilizing a strong public belief system according to which the dominant political powers governed as "agents" of foreign and primarily German interests, the neo-Nazi party combined its nationalist, racist discourse with elements of an "anti-systemic" polemic (Lialiouti and Bithymitris 2013). Espousing political rhetoric typical of the European extreme right, including a xenophobic stance and populist opposition to the "corrupt" political establishment, Golden Dawn gained an unexpected share of the vote, particularly among the working class and the lower-middle class (Davou and Demertzis 2013: 113).

The above-mentioned electoral gains indicate the effectiveness of the extreme right in shifting the blame for economic and social crises to an amalgam of political and financial elites, while offering what Nancy Fraser defines as "social protectionism as vehicle of domination" (Fraser 2012: 4). Summarizing this blame game, the purported, though heterogeneous "enemies" of the underprivileged in West Piraeus are discursively presented as:

- The financial elites, namely the bankers with their close ties to the "corrupted media and political system". Golden Dawn's readiness to protect the property of distressed households against "the bankers" (Golden Dawn 2015b), and its multifaceted critique against globalized financial capital indicates an elaborated discursive strategy against marketization effects. Moreover, the extreme right's "rebuilding of embedded markets" (Fraser 2012: 14), in this case by promoting the interests of industrial and shipping capital (Enet 2013), reflects Golden Dawn's reactionary social protectionism.
- The trade unions and the communist left who are presented as part of the "corrupted and traitorous" political system which condemned Greek people to mass unemployment and indignity. The "red"

unions of the zone are held to be almost exclusively responsible for the local decline and thus, the extreme right agues, they should be expelled from the local labour market (Lagos 2013).

- Last but not least, as stated on the party's official website, immigrants are considered enemies to be confined and deported (Golden Dawn 2015a).

At the same time, community-based activities, such as food allocation, broadened the repertoire of the party's collective actions at the local level, as a means of diverting attention from the party's most infamous aspects (for example, concerning links with the underworld or with employers and contractors who benefitted from the extreme right's upsurge as a mechanism of imposing "discipline and order" on employees) (Tsimas 2013). In a climate of profound disenchantment among workers and the lower-middle classes in West Piraeus, militant unionism, immigrants and other reservoirs of *otherness* have become scapegoats for the nationalist zeal of Golden Dawn's apparatus. Violence has become an instrument of double utility in the strategy of the organization: used as a means of confrontation with perceived enemies and as a symbol of power in order to attract members and voters (Dinas et al. 2013: 7).

These tendencies have crystallized in three major events: a) the physical attack against Egyptian fishermen at Keratsini on 12 June 2012 (one fisherman was seriously injured); b) a violent assault against unionists at Perama on 12 September 2013 (eight unionists were injured); and c) the lethal attack against the left-wing singer, worker of the zone and son of a unionist, Panayiotis Fyssas, in September 2013. It was Fyssas's murder that led to the arrest of Golden Dawn leaders on charges of conspiracy to create a criminal organization. After the initial shock led to democratic, antifascist demonstrations at Keratsini, locals in West Piraeus had to deal with a new trauma, namely their stigmatization not merely as victims of the crisis, but as victimizers too. During an interview conducted after Fyssas's assassination, Michalis Mitakides (2014), a famous local progressive musician, wondered: "how did we end up with such a mess … It will take a long time until this stain is totally removed". In this confusing and intoxicated atmosphere, emancipation as an alternative to marketization and social protectionism struggles to be "born".

Syndicate of Metalworkers of Attika and Ship-building Industry of Greece (SMAS): Community Unionism, Solidarity and Class Politics

The Union of Metalworkers of Attica and Ship-building industry of Greece (SMAS), the biggest metalworkers' union in Greece, is the successor of the Syndicate of Metalworkers of Piraeus and Islands, after the merger of the latter with smaller unions that represented the metalworkers of neighboring areas or professions such as metal welders, ship carpenters, and electricians.

The militant past of the union and its ideological affiliation with the Greek Communist Party has shaped its current attitudes, practices and politics. The majority of my informants, no matter if they were positively or negatively disposed toward SMAS, stressed that the union was a point of reference for the local workforce. Moreover, the union's ties with the working class of West Piraeus, its activisms in defending the electricity and water supply of the pauperized people of Perama and Keratsini or the food allocation among those most in need, strengthened the community-based character of the SMAS while challenging Golden Dawn's charities as merely a means of justifying nationalist hatred.

In line with Nancy Fraser's aforementioned analysis of the potential challenges against social protectionism—approached as a "vehicle of domination" (Fraser 2012: 4)—by an emancipatory countermovement, the community initiatives of SMAS can indeed also be seen as such alternative means of organizing and recruiting members, a collective response against the decollectivizing effects of capitalist crisis (for example, see McBride and Greenwood 2009). Rather than pushing an exclusivist and particularistic agenda, the strong occupational identity of SMAS's constituents centers on class solidarity as a central element. In a similar vein, the group identity of the zone's workers allowed for recognition of a shared structural location and problems held in common with other workers, the unemployed and the broader community in West Piraeus. As stressed by Karner and Weicht in the introduction, "'community' [can] reflect a moral ideal, an image of 'the good society', often constructed in opposition to the market and presumed to require altruism and mutual responsibility".

Yet, the severe dislocation of the workers' communities of West Piraeus, coupled with lasting inconsistencies of the zone's union movement, have adversely affected individuals' alignment with the union's calls for class solidarity. According to my informants, the current crisis of the local ship-building industry that began in 2010 is unprecedented, and a critical mass of skilled metalworkers have since retired, migrated or changed their jobs without newcomers replacing them.

Even if an anti-union turn reflects a broader trend within Greek society, the challenges SMAS now faces are also grounded in local conditions. The multiple, and to a certain extent, debatable controls that the union has traditionally imposed on contractors of the zone, its numerous strike actions over salaries and other work-related issues, its class enmity against the ship owners, all inscribed in a universe of shared meanings and symbolisms ranging from announcements, speeches, campaigns and memory sites, have also provided raw materials for a different, reloaded *politics of nostalgia* that has reconstituted itself mainly through a nationalist discourse, less subtle and ambivalent than class politics.

To be more specific, those who interpret the zone's economic malaise as a symptom of the nation's lost unity, tend to attribute blame to the union for allegedly helping to disintegrate "the national" and acting as agents of the corrupt political system. Such nostalgia expresses a feeling of homelessness, of insecurity and the desire for certainties and refuge (Duyvendak 2011), while *en passant* it reveals collective uneasiness with existing circumstances in the zone and Greece in general. As we saw in the introduction to this volume, nostalgia's temporal focus on the past indeed always entails a critique of social change and is therefore a criticism of the current situation (Duyvendak 2011), thereby articulating a loss of faith in the notion of progress (for example, Pickering and Keightley 2006) and in existing social institutions. At least for those feeling abandoned, and subsequently through the eyes of their opponents (that is Golden Dawn), SMAS, unions, the left in toto are at the moment perceived as an extension of existing social institutions that have failed to provide a safety net against the impersonal forces of the market. Therefore, the emancipatory character of local unionism and its effectiveness has yet to be proven.

Methods

The perceptions, stories and narrations which are analysed here were obtained between 2012 and 2015, through in-field face-to-face and group interviews, media analysis, field notes, speeches given by party and union leaders, communications released by political parties and unions engaged in local mass politics. The period of study stretched between two key points of reference for Greek mass politics in the age of austerity: the "double earthquake elections" of 2012 (May—June) and the election of 25 January 2015, which saw the defeat of the dominant postdictatorial coalitions of power and led the Radical Left (SYRIZA) to office together with the right-wing populist party of ANEL.

In terms of this study's oral histories component, I conducted 12 face-to-face, semistructured interviews with unemployed or underemployed individuals. The resulting interview material is of great relevance for our understanding of how recent socioeconomic and political shifts have impacted collective identities. This material also corroborates Doreen Massey's observation (1995: 186) that "the identity of places is very much bound up with the histories which are told of them, how those histories are told, and which history turns out to be dominant".

In order to further illuminate the local dynamics of identity (re)construction and negotiation under conditions of severe socioeconomic crisis, this oral history data was further complemented by focus groups involving two groups of employment counsellors who work with underemployed residents of the industrial zone of Piraeus in the context of a large-scale training programme. The present study adopts a common usage of the focus group method, as a follow-up that assists in interpreting (the) other (interview) data (Morgan 1996: 135).

Finally, empirical material analysed here also includes media discourse during the aforementioned period, enabling close analysis of eight daily newspapers (Rizospastis, Kathimerini, Avgi, Ethnos, Ta Nea, To Vima, Eleftherotypia and Epohi) and three information portals (Proto Thema, Skai, TVXS). Other sources of public discourse and cultural resources such as the blogosphere, documentaries and chronicles were also examined. Finally, field notes were taken based on observation of rituals in the daily life of the local communities.

Workers' and Ex-Workers' Narratives

Why should we be interested in stories? By telling a story, either as individuals or collectivities, we help establish who we are. In the present case, the cultural stock in West Piraeus, the local idioms and discursive practices of individuals and collectivities are crucially important since they underpin identities and, consequently, political attitudes. *Which stories interest the social researcher here?* The stories which need other stories in order to articulate a coherent narrative or an established plot; a sum of discursive practices that flow into thousands of daily individual and collective interactions. The term "discursive practices" captures the flexible usage of available "verbal sources" or "hermeneutic repertories" that shape notionally coherent speeches or texts (Potter and Wetherell 1987).

My twelve informants are male workers who live in West Piraeus. Nine of them either have worked or are currently working in the zone, while three of them have been employed elsewhere as workers, while at the time of the interview they were unemployed. Although the interviewed "zoners" declare themselves to be members of the union, they do not share the same attachment to it, nor the same opinions.

N.A. is 40 years old, a sheet metal worker from Korydallos. He has worked in the zone since the age of 16. Distinctive about his narrative is his deep attachment to the experience of his employment and his sector. His world leaves no space for other, alternative career pathways or ways of living. This is a tacit "golden rule" for the zone's working class, where individuals' job-seeking strategies are completely defined by their occupational identity. Local perceptions of the crisis as a metonym of the national economic downturn now see the zone as a "black hole" in the world of ship-building.

When I asked him to comment on the current crisis, N.A. kept talking about the crisis in the zone in particular. Toward the end of the interview he mentioned an incident that impressed him during a trip to China:

In China, I went to a banquet organized by a company where a friend of mine works and I see on the wall hanging a photo from Skaramanga [i.e. a Greek shipyard], a model for all countries. The Filipino engineer told me about Skaramanga, that there are many good technicians. When we were building ships, they were climbing trees. Now they have become somebody and we have become nothing.

Pride in the glorious ship-building past here coexists with acute awareness of the zone's present adversities and its dark, hazardous aspects. Despite N.A.'s son's difficulty in finding a job in his line of work, the zone offers no alternative either:

- My son is a refrigeration mechanic. He was working in summers; now nothing.
- Didn't he work in the zone?
- No, I didn't want him to come because it's a hazardous job.

G.A. is 45 years of age and lives in Keratsini. He has worked in the zone as a welder since 1990 and his life is marked by it. Instead of dwelling on the area's glorious past, he begins his narration with the dark side of the zone:

> There are things that caused me distress; yes many [things]. Especially the first accident; I was there. Various accidents that have happened in Perama have affected me. They made me concentrate more on my job and be more careful and harsher with my helpers.

Indeed, G.A. is more demanding of himself and the people around him in terms of rights and obligations and his narrative is organized around his opposition to the zone's union and its leadership. He comes back to the responsibilities of unionists for the situation in the zone, in terms of safety measures or the downturn in activity. His opposition to the pro-Communist faction within the union follows an "us" against "them" pattern:

> I hear from the KKE [Communist Party of Greece], the ship owners, this or that. I don't care what the ship owner does from the moment he brings in the ship and he meets his obligations; I must meet my obligations … I told them during a strike, what you do is not right because you strike against the client, it impacts upon the client, and everyone is gone from the zone.

The dichotomy here is clear: on one hand, the individual worker struggles as a job-hunter; on the other hand, the union and its political affiliations discourage the employers and minimize workers' chances to find new jobs. The old, traditional distinction between labour and capital (that is, ship-owners) has been blurred.

T.A. is a 55 year-old welder. He lives in Drapetsona. Since 2009 he seldom, if ever, has received a day's pay in the zone. He does not have a family; he is indebted with a loan and occasionally receives help from his younger brother, who also works in the zone, though more regularly. From the start of the interview T.A. stated that he did not feel he could explain what had happened in the zone. He reconstructs "the good old times" as follows:

> At that time there were jobs, we were active. We were making money and we didn't save... This is also our fault.

Along with a narrative of guilt about previous consumption patterns that, according to him, were rather exuberant, self-criticism is continuous here in terms of the mistakes made by zone workers individually or collectively—errors, he argues, that have to do with disregard for the community, apathy, and absence from union struggles.

> Thanks to the union we gained much, but on the other hand it is at fault, because [they] were going to strikes at the slightest opportunity, but we are at fault too because we were not participating. I've never taken part in a demonstration. We can't say it was only the union's fault.

G.T. is 57 years of age and from Keratsini. He has been unemployed for more than three years. Until 2008 he was occasionally working on oil tankers in the zone. For a long time he has excluded the zone as a potential employer, seeking occasional employment in municipal cleaning services, in bakeries, or in whatever comes up. Nonetheless, he has linked life in Piraeus with activity in the ship-building industry. Speaking about the glorious past of the zone, he speaks nostalgically of previous consumption levels:

We could afford a VCR at that time, how much, 120.000 [Drachmas], here, take it so that kids can watch cartoons. And all is dead now. You're afraid to go out at night.

His interpretations of the crisis largely ascribe responsibility to workers as a whole, to the unions, which by going to strikes scared away the ships, while wages were high:

Strikes now, with good wages, ships went to Turkey and Romania. I remember in 1989, a weekly salary was 250.000 [Drachmas], from 18:00 to 06:00. Overtime. Nice living. We were earning good money in night shifts.

His oppositional, self-critical identity is outlined unequivocally a little later in the interview:

Strike… What's this thing? You're living. Now go on strike in the zone; it is a graveyard. These things consumed us. What to go on strike for, 100 Drachmas? We were making 250.000 [Drachmas]. Strike… We had it coming.

V.B., a 50 year-old construction worker, unemployed for three years, lives in Keratsini. He has previously worked for a while in the zone for contractors. He came to Greece in 1990 from North Epirus (the southern part of Albania). Having suffered racial discrimination and having had his "Greekness" questioned, we should perhaps not be surprised by his own articulation of an ethnic nationalism:

I am Greek. I see foreigners, Pakistanis, working for 15 Euros. They pay no taxes, nor do they pay rent for a home. They live 100 in a room and the money they earn they send back home. In my mind, they all have to leave.

Despite all this, class admixtures remain noticeable. A bit later, when he refers to his wife's agony to cling to her work as a cleaner, V.B. reflected:

Today a worker and a pensioner suffer. Industrialists and ship owners have no need at all. All these things happen today for the benefit of ship owners and for nobody else. I see my wife who was making 900 Euros and today she's down to 600 for the same job. What happens? Where does all this money end up? Who gets all the money?

S.T. is 35 years old and has been unemployed for a long time. He has worked in storehouses of large commercial chains, in the clothing and food sectors. Despite the fact that he has no direct experience in the zone and the shipyards, in his description of the competitive advantages that Greece possessed, harbors and shipyards are prevalent:

Unfortunately because Greece had some very strong points, by striking against these points, such as shipping, Skaramanga and Perama, I mean harbors, I mean working people... Greece had the largest merchant fleet, the most flags. They struck one of the largest fleets in the world.

His account of workers on the lower level of the social hierarchy, in juxtaposition to the university-educated, and his description of international power struggles and divisions of labor reflect his own position and its impact on his working life:

When they [that is Germans and French] saw that our generation, at least the generation below 40, that essentially half of it has university degrees, they say this can't happen. Not everyone can have a university degree. What are we going to do? Work for the Greeks?

This narrative about the losers and winners of the crisis retains a discursive opposition between rulers and ruled, and very often this is tied to an opposition between "Europeans" and "Greeks". The opposition between workers and capital is discursively mapped onto different nation-states:

For example, France builds a perfume factory. Who is going to work? When Europe is united and I'm obliged to take [workers] from every country, who's going to work? I, France, keep the money. I can't let a Greek become the manager.

According to such a narrative, nations such as Greece signify the sub-ordinated classes whose destiny it is to be exploited. S.T. appears to be part of a mechanical, deterministic and ultimately fatalistic community of discourse of a deeply injured working class.

There is also the case of A.K, a 50 year-old, former tube worker in the zone and now truck driver for a multinational shipping agency located in Piraeus. He grew up in Keratsini, but he also has strong memories from the neighboring municipality of Perama and its economic growth during the 1990s. Like other research participants who have long work records in the zone and now are working in other places, A.K. strug-gles to narrate his life story in individual terms. His immediate social surroundings merge with the wider zone's recent history. He describes unionism as a physical condition, a symbiotic phenomenon within the working class: "The union has nothing to do with abstract things. The union is me, you, all of us." He is a member of the newly established union of his company and he is positively disposed towards it. Although he condemns partisanship within union movement, he is politicized and nostalgically narrates moments of past labour struggles against the state. Concerning his identity narrative, two things stand out: First, the kind of solidarity A.K. is in favour of is of a spontaneous and daily kind, lived through his interpersonal relations with coworkers and ex-workers of the zone. Second, he formulates a critical stance against the "oppor-tunistic employers who took advantage of the situation since 2009 and undermined the workers' rights". This class-oriented argument is inter-woven with his attribution of blame for the general condition of the Greek working class. When he accuses Europe as being responsible for the economic malaise of the Greek workers, he does not refer to it cul-turally, but politically, as a political procedure which should be under-stood in terms of a transnational power game where the winners are clearly depicted: "The shipping capital has no homeland, nor a flag. It is all about profits...".

Discourses of Loss

As has already been mentioned, workers' collective identities in West Piraeus cannot be understood outside the local context, particularly that of the antagonism between the local unions and the extreme right. Analysis of the accounts provided by my participants, mainly workers who have worked in the zone, also shed light on the subject's positions and identities ascribed to, and negotiated by, those living and working in West Piraeus.

All the interview material obtained here reflects the *deterioration of the social and financial situation* of the working class of West Piraeus: stress, disappointment, anger, fear, and even panic, define how my interviewees reflect on their current problems. G.A., who expects to earn money only by looking for a short-term shipping job abroad, says:

> I'm in a panic state, so to speak... If I can't ship out my mind starts playing games.

To support his son, a school boy, and his daughter, a university student, V.B. and his wife, a cleaner in a contracting company, rely on various "grey" jobs (mainly undeclared construction works). According to V.B.:

> We can't make our ends meet. I can make a living here and there and that with great difficulty... Now if my wife stops working, I'm toast. I have a loan from Social Housing at 400 Euros per month.

After the end of the interview V.B. suggested, with more than a hint of desperation, that if the bank came to confiscate the house, he would be waiting for them armed.

G.A, the welder, described his neighborhood as follows:

> Now you can see people in the street walking and muttering to themselves; I'm one of them... I was earning a living in Eleusis... God help us now.

Personal stories in West Piraeus are closely tied to the fate of the ship-building industry. In response to the question of whether the crisis has affected the zone, G.A. responds thus:

You can't imagine how much. Families living in the zone are barely surviving. Many people who have taken loans are losing their homes, their fortunes... Some become beggars, others can borrow money from acquaintances; they even scavenge.

A.K., the truck driver, states emphatically that "work is dignity. You lose your work, you lose your dignity." And A.A., a machinist from Perama, confirms the dire straits of the local working class: "I have seen unemployed colleagues ten kilos weaker... Unemployment brings decay." G.T. received his last day's pay in 2008. His reflections resemble many other accounts:

> From 2008 on the zone went dead; a graveyard. You can't hear a hammer. In Keratsini and Drapetsona people were employed in the zone and in construction... I remember shops full of people in Keratsini. Piraeus and Varvakeios [a market] were living off the zone.

This is not merely a nostalgic glorification of the past. Two of my informants, A.K. and A.A., argued that the hazardous and adverse working conditions and the consequent danger of the zone were acting like glue, binding together the zone's constituents as parts of a common fate; composing a *moral order* which is now undermined by the lasting and deep economic crisis. As Tim Strangleman has demonstrated with regard to rail workers in the UK: "What the older generation of workers were reflecting on ... was the erosion of a set of values and norms which had helped to humanize work, and had helped them build and sustain a working life both individually and collectively" (2012: 13).

What has demonstrably and profoundly changed in respect of local working class identities is the loss of optimism, of hope, and of self-confidence, which have been replaced by fatalism that is variously expressed with stoicism, cynicism, and self-sarcasm. Hopes and expectations have given way to recurring pessimism, expressed in assessments such as: "Greece can't change anyway now; we're going down"; or, "I see tomorrow gloom and doom"; or, "some hope?—No, don't say crazy things. We were getting worse year by year; now we say much, much worse year by year."

Of course, there is not a "one-size-fits-all" emotional structure at work here. An employment counsellor's reflections on her work with 25 metal-workers are worth quoting here:

> I was surprised by their complexity as characters. They were beyond the stereotypes that we as professionals may have built before meeting them.

My own experience of working both as an employment counsellor and as a supervisor of the counseling services confirms that there is great variety at work in the zone in terms of people's interpretive strategies, emotional states, skills, knowledge and competences. Yet, Sennett and Cobb's comments on the emotional structure of the American working class also apply to Western Piraeus: "All these people feel society has limited their freedom ... to develop powers inside themselves ... but they are not rebellious in the ordinary sense of the word; they are both angry and ambivalent about their right to be angry." (Sennett and Cobb 1993: 78–79) An understanding of the zone indeed needs to engage with local politics, personal and collective identity dynamics and such emotional complexities.

As already mentioned, a recurring motif in locals' narrations are nostalgic invocations of a purportedly *glorious past*. Interviewees offered various reflections on their own and others' responses to the crisis of the more immediate past and present. S.T. reflects widely:

> As a people we're shortsighted, we only see the present and we can't see far to the future. We've had the first stock market crash and, instead of sobering, we all bought houses. Rather than seeing what happened in the Athens Stock Exchange we frantically ran to buy houses.

G.T. reconstructs a loss of collective enjoyment:

> Remember, what you find good, you want it back. What does a man want, a job, growth, open businesses, go to Giorgos, who's my friend, to have a beer with, to get five souvlaki [national snack], to see my friends. We lost many things. We used to go to places that no longer exist. You went there

with your wife, sitting there, where are these now? You went to a place with your company. Where are these now?

T.A. seems to take up where G.T. left off:

Before [the crisis] people were going to the tavern, were buying clothes, were drinking whiskey, and were buying cigarettes, beverages; now they can't even buy whiskey.

For A.K., similarly, past prosperity used to mean that one was "OK with your liabilities", one had "the capacity to take your wife out". As Sennett and Cobb have shown in their classic study of the hidden injury of the working class, money and possessions are about more than consumption: they are also weapons to defend one's dignity (1993: 169). The zone's workers and, more particularly, those from West Piraeus interviewed, expressed a certain ambivalence toward mass consumption, which had previously, in the context of economic prosperity, provided "symbolic trophies" to also be displayed to the (upper) middle class, thereby providing the working class with a sense of dignity. In the context of deep economic hardship this has now given way to *self-blaming* (Lialiouti and Bithymitris, 2016): encouraged by the elites, former images of dignity have been reconstructed as "proof" of individual and collective guilt for the crisis.

A mode of coping with this ambivalence is the soteriological and homogenizing discourse of nationalism and its above-mentioned social protectionism. Golden Dawn's version has been most "successful", combining two elements: First, the glorification of the zone's past; and, second, the stereotyping of its political enemies. As argued by a leading executive of Golden Dawn during his visit to Perama shipyards: "in this place there were formerly ships and now thanks to the communist led unions and the Communist Party there is nothing… The zone will be set in motion again, the ships are going to return and the lackeys of the Communist Party will vanish" (Lagos 2013). What is more, Golden Dawn articulates a strongly anti-elitist nationalism, promising to include the internal "outsiders" of West Piraeus within the safe haven of the nation. Workers and the unemployed are thereby encouraged to develop and express anti-elitist, anti-systemic opposition without being isolated from the national community, with the latter being portrayed as a refuge of certainty, continuity and safety.

Once again, Fraser's (2012) notion of exclusivist social protectionism against financialization and marketization effects is extremely relevant here. Golden Dawn expresses its repulsion against the banks and financial capital which are, by definition, globalized, and juxtaposes them to the productive faction of the industrial, particularly the shipbuilding, capital. During an interview with an Australian journalist, a leading executive and MP of Golden Dawn, I. Panagiotaros, commented: "Instead of committing suicides the Greeks should kill those who are responsible for their problems... the bankers of course" (To Vima 2013). Meanwhile, the industrialists remain unscrutinized in the critique by Golden Dawn's leadership, which, on one hand, attributes blame for social dislocation to the bankers and the "subordinate" political elites (Golden Dawn 2013), and, on the other hand, promotes its own exclusive, hierarchical and authoritarian social protectionism as a protective shield for the popular strata.

Moreover, through identification with nationalist, anti-elitist discourse, once affluent and proud workers can now confront the bourgeois accusation of previous consumerist excesses without thereby excluding themselves from the national community. Instead, Golden Dawn discourse thrives on nostalgia, attributing blame to "traitorous elites" who "betrayed the nation and surrendered to the foreigners" (Michaloliakos 2012), without having to respond to the risky calls of the left and the unions for collective action against the ship owners and the contractors. Again using Fraser's analytical tools, the neoliberal assault by governments and supranational institutions like the IMF, the EU and the European Commission, is challenged by a strong social protectionist movement, which excludes those who are stigmatized as "foreigners" and "traitors" while integrating the popular strata *and* industrial capital in a corporatist, hierarchical scheme under the auspices of Golden Dawn.

This is not to suggest that these political and discursive strategies are singularly dominant across the zone or West Piraeus. Golden Dawn's failed attempt to create a nationalist labour union in the zone, and the maintenance of SMAS power despite the decollectivizing effects of the skyrocketing unemployment rates in West Piraeus, indicate that class identity and class politics still matter. This is also observable in many of my informants' narrations. N.A. for instance, stresses the problem of social injustice and class struggle, and he is not alone:

> Contractors want to squash you and for this reason the union grew and went to strikes. If they were fair all this wouldn't have happened... Contractors are sons of bitches ... They'd made lots of money, they'd developed infrastructure in Perama. They built villas, spent money in luxurious night clubs and so on. Much money, crazy money.

An emancipatory aspect of a class-oriented discourse is, arguably, in the making here: the suggestion is that local economic malaise and social dislocation could be reversed, were it not for the ship owners and their allies.

To sum up my core argument, which may apply elsewhere too: the erosion of class discourse and detachment from class politics also enable nationalist strategies for attributing blame in the local and national crisis context. Identity building is here heavily conditioned by the conception of "friends" and "foes", and the positioning toward SMAS and unionism in general is of great importance. Although it would be an oversimplification to suggest that a hostile or detached attitude toward the unions is straightforwardly associated with nationalism, I posit that *the extremeright thrives on a wider discursive shift of focus from class cleavages* (for example workers versus ship owners) *to national cleavages* (for example, foreign powers versus Greeks). In addition, "emancipatory moments" (Fraser 2012) are less and less frequent as the unemployed and underemployed workers depart from the ambivalence of class dialectics in favour of less sophisticated, one-dimensional interpretative repertoires.

Yet, as suggested in a group interview with employment counsellors on a training programme for 2.500 workers of the industrial zone of Piraeus and Thriasio, a majority of workers still consider the unions a necessity: "If we are not there (with the unions), we are nowhere," said a worker of the zone to a counsellor. Another counsellor said that he was impressed by the number of those who told him that although they would not run for a seat, they participated in their union, considered themselves as part of it in a rather "natural" fashion. A generational gap seems to be opening up, though. The younger workers of the zone were the most detached from this collectivity. Also, the long-term unemployed and former workers of the zone tend more easily to consider unionists and politicians to be part of an "antinational plot", which purportedly first assaulted the ship industry and then the whole economy. Such nationalist tendencies should not be seen as exceptional cases as they show parallels with other, previous capitalist crises, such as the Great Depression in the USA:

> The unemployed of the [19]30s were wage earners in theory of course, and thus abstractly shared an identity with those employed. But as months and sometimes years of idleness accumulated, the unemployed's class identity lost its concreteness. Refused entry to the world of production, the division between managers and workers, between "them" and "us" ... so crucial to the spread of unionism [changed] ... Excluded from critical production and consumption activities, many found no satisfactory outlet for their frustration. Some turned their anger inward and then suffered through the emotion's metamorphosis into a debilitating kind of self-blame. (Gerstle 2002: 102)

Epilogue

The present study of collective identities of the working class of West Piraeus reflects transformations that have occurred in the context of local, ongoing industrial restructuring, which has in turn coincided with a severe economic crisis. We have begun a much-needed exploration of the connections between recent, more general socioeconomic shifts and local sociocultural changes, including the rise of the extreme right. The material discussed here was collected mainly through interviews conducted with unemployed and underemployed metalworkers from West Piraeus, group interviews with employment counsellors who guide and consult metalworkers in the context of two large-scale training programmes, media materials and other representations of local identities found in articles, documentaries and the blogosphere.

Focusing on an understanding of how politics of nostalgia and social protectionism interface with the politics of solidarity, this chapter adds to Christian Karner and Bernhard Weicht's conceptual outline in the introduction to this volume. Put simply, analysis of the collected data reveals a complex interplay, in workers' accounts, of common narratives about *the past* (that is, the glorious past of ship-building), *the present* (that is, interpretations of current crisis and attributions of blame), and *the future* (for example, a loss of hope, pessimism). Golden Dawn has managed to consolidate its electoral gains at the local level and to recruit extreme-right activists, who act in militia-style organizations, by offering a comforting interpretative repertoire to its working-class constituents and a form of social protection: the loss of a "glorious past" in a ship-building zone, home to formerly relatively affluent and proud workers, is blamed not only on "foreign powers" but also on the communists and the unions who allegedly obliged ship owners and enterprises to "abandon" Greece. All along, there are also self-blaming patterns generated by elitist claims that workers had overconsumed during a now bygone age of prosperity. Golden Dawn purports to offer the (ex) workers of West Piraeus bonds with the broader community of the nation and a nostalgia free of guilt and, more importantly still, free of the obligation to reassess political strategies vis-à-vis contractors, employers, and capital in general. Corroborating Fraser's neo-Polanyian approach discussed in other chapters, Golden Dawn expresses a social protection steeply hierarchical and deeply exclusionary (Fraser 2012: 14). However appealing to many, the exclusive social protectionism of the extreme right against the marketization effects of the implemented austerity policies has not remained unchallenged and the battle for hegemony goes on. Again in Fraser's terms, a countermovement with emancipatory aspects has also been present: SMAS utilizes its own network of activists, its mobilization resources, its class solidarity, community-based initiatives and other collective actions drawn from the long experience of global working-class struggles in order to defend its positions. And at least so far, it has partially succeeded in restoring its pivotal position for the collective identities of workers in West Piraeus. The future remains highly uncertain, though, and to a large extent dependent upon broader political configurations at the national and European levels.

References

Bauman, Z. (1997). *Postmodernity and its discontents*. Cambridge: Polity.

Beck, U. (1997). *The reinvention of politics*. Cambridge: Polity.

Bell, D. (1976). *The coming of post-industrial society*. New York: Basic Books.

Bithymitris, G. (2016). Union militancy during economic hardship: The strike at the Greek steel company 'Hellenic Halyvourgia'. Employee relations (in press).

Calhoun, C. (1991). The problem of identity in collective action. In J. Huber (Ed.), *Macro-micro linkages in sociology*. London: Sage.

Davou, B., & Demertzis, N. (2013). Feeling the Greek economic crisis. In N. Demertzis (Ed.), *The affect dimension in political tension* (pp. 93–123). New York: Palgrave.

Dinas, E., Vassiliki, G., Konstantinides, I., & Rori, L. (2013). From dusk to dawn: Local party organization and party success of right-wing extremism. *Party politics* (December): 1–13.

Duyvendak, J. W. (2011). *The politics of home*. New York: Palgrave Macmillan.

Ellinas, A. (2013). The rise of Golden Dawn: The new face of the far right in Greece. *South European Society and Politics, 18*(4), 543–565.

Elstat. (2011). *Census*, http://www.statistics.gr. Last accessed 11 April 2016.

Enet. (2013). *Golden Dawn: The ship owners' voice in the parliament*. http://www.enet.gr/?i=news.el.article&id=390893. Accessed 10 Oct 2014.

Fantasia, R. (1988). *Cultures of solidarity: Consciousness, action, and contemporary American workers*. Berkeley: University of California Press.

Fominaya, C. F. (2010). Collective identity in social movements: Central concepts and debates. *Social Compass, 4*(6), 393–404.

Fraser, N. (2012). Marketization, social protection, emancipation: Toward a neo-Polanyian conception of capitalist crisis. http://sophiapol.hypotheses.org/files/2012/02/Texte-Nancy-Fraser-anglais.doc. Accessed 22 July 2013.

Gerstle, G. (2002). *Working-class Americanism: The politics of labor in a textile city, 1914–1960*. Princeton: Princeton University Press.

Golden Dawn. (2013). *Announcement on the issue of residence auctions*. http://www.newbomb.gr/politikh/news/story/337353/hrysi-avgi-i-kyvernisi-ypoheirio-ton-trapeziton-exontonei-ton-ellina. Accessed 30 July 2015.

Golden Dawn. (2015a). *Political positions*. http://www.xryshaygh.com/kinima/thesis. Accessed 28 Mar 2015.

Golden Dawn. (2015b). *Bankers hands off the Greek houses*. http://www.xry-shaygh.com/enimerosi/view/kanena-spiti-sta-cheria-trapezith. Accessed 10 July 2015.

Gorz, A. (1994). *Farewell to the working class*. London: Pluto.

Jenkins, R. (1996). *Social identity*. New York: Routledge.

Karamesini, M. (2011). The employment policy of European Union. In T. Sakellaropoulos (Ed.), *The social policy of the European Union*. Athens: Dionikos.

Kouzis, G. (2005). Employment flexibility and quality of work. In M. Karamessini & Y. Kouzis (Eds.), *Employment policy: Coupling the fields of economic and social policy*. Athens: Gutenberg.

Lagos, I. (2013). *Speech given during Golden Dawn's visit at the ship-building zone of Perama*. https://www.youtube.com/watch?v=nJW1jTn6H3w. Accessed 28 Mar 2015.

Lialiouti, Z. & Bithymitris, G. (2016). A nation under attack: Perceptions of enmity and victimhood in the context of the Greek crisis. *National Identities* (forthcoming).

Lialiouti, Z., & Bithymitris, G. (2013). The Nazis strike again: The concept of the German enemy, party strategies and mass perceptions through the prism of the Greek economic crisis. In C. Karner & B. Mertens (Eds.), *The use and abuse of memory: Interpreting World War II in contemporary European politics*. New Brunswick: Transaction.

Massey, D. (1995). Places and their past. *History Workshop Journal, 39*, 182–192.

Mitakides, M. (2014). Interview given during the broadcast *Protagonists* of Theodorakis, Stavros. https://www.youtube.com/watch?v=JC-d3EcgEkk. Accessed 20 Dec 2014.

McBride, J., & Greenwood, I. (2009). *Community unionism*. New York: Palgrave Macmillan.

Melucci, A. (1995). The process of collective identity. In H. Johnston & B. Klandermans (Eds.), *Social movements and culture* (pp. 41–63). Minneapolis: University of Minnesota Press.

Michaloliakos, N. (2012). *Press conference after the election of May 2012*. http://www.youtube.com/watch?v=Wg2wonvZhnC. Accessed 20 Dec 2014.

Morgan, D. L. (1996). Focus groups. *Annual Review of Sociology, 22*, 129–152.

Pickering, M., & Keightley, E. (2006). The modalities of nostalgia. *Current Sociology, 54*(6), 919–941.

Polletta, F., & Jasper, J. M. (2001). Collective identity and social movements. *Annual Review of Sociology, 27*, 283–305.

Potter, J., & Wetherell, M. (1987). *Discourse and social psychology.* Los Angeles: Sage.

Pouliakas, K. (2014). A balancing act at times of austerity: Matching the supply and demand for skills in the Greek labour market (pp. 1–41). Discussion paper no. 7915. *Institute for the Study of Labor* (IZA), Bonn.

Rifkin, J. (1996). *The end of work: The decline of the global labor force and the dawn of the post-market era.* New York: Putnam.

Sennett, R., & Cobb, J. (1993). *The hidden injuries of class.* New York: W.W. Norton and Company.

Spyridakis, M. (2013). *The liminal worker: An ethnography of work, unemployment and precariousness in contemporary Greece.* London: Ashgate.

Strangleman, T. (2012). Work identity in crisis? Rethinking the problem of attachment and loss at work. *Sociology, 46*(3), 1–15.

Vima, T. (2013). *Ilias Panagiotaros: 'The Greeks should kill the bankers instead of committing suicide'.* http://www.tovima.gr/politics/article/?aid=513975. Accessed 10 July 2014.

Tsimas, P. (2013). *The red zone and the black t-shirts,* a reportage in Perama and Keratsini, broadcasted by Mega Channel. https://www.youtube.com/watch?v=JC-d3EcgEkk. Accessed 18 Mar 2014.

Vlachos, G. P. (1996). *Problems and perspectives of the Greek building and repairing industry.* Athens: Stamoulis.

Austria Between "Social Protection" and "Emancipation": Negotiating Global *Flows*, Marketization and Nostalgia

Christian Karner

Writing in the Viennese weekly paper *Falter* about the state and entrepreneurial innovation, Austrian journalist Robert Misik recently invoked Karl Polanyi. Contrary to widespread presumptions that states and economic enterprise preclude one another, Misik argued that strong states have played key roles in the history of capitalist innovation; for only states can mobilize the resources and handle the risks involved in epochal technological shifts. Misik reminded readers that Polanyi (2001), considered too procapitalist by the left and too left-leaning by the right, had first formulated a "leftist liberalism" that warned against the social and environmental consequences of "self-regulating markets", insisting that the state was crucial to capitalist economies. Polanyi's contemporary relevance, Misik concluded, lies in protecting freedoms against the concentration of economic might; in counteracting growing inequalities; and in fighting for a "symbiotic" rather than "parasitic" relationship between politics and markets (Misik 2014).

C. Karner (✉)
University of Nottingham, Nottingham, UK

© The Editor(s) (if applicable) and The Author(s) 2016   **195**
C. Karner, B. Weicht (eds.), *The Commonalities of Global Crises*,
DOI 10.1057/978-1-137-50273-5_8

This provides an apt illustration of the discursive field that has shaped Austria over recent years. In a national context that until recently ranked amongst the relatively most resilient and affluent in the European Union (*Austria Today* 2012)—though current unemployment and growth figures paint a much less rosy picture (Hiptmayr et al. 2015)—perceptions of socioeconomic and political crises, many observed "elsewhere" but feared to impact locally, others generated "at home", are near-ubiquitous. The relationship between politics and markets is, as we discover below, central to most crises felt and debated in Austria today.

The "postimperial melancholia" (Gilroy 2004) afflicting contemporary Britain, yet to come to terms with her loss of international standing and economic might of bygone eras, is conceptually relevant elsewhere, too. Though historical circumstances differ, cultural nostalgia also plays a role in twenty-first century Austria. This manifests sometimes in obvious ways, including the commodification of Habsburg history for touristic purposes (Schlipphacke 2014: 2). At other times, nostalgia crystallizes subtly, as revealed by much-quoted surveys (Reiterer 1988: 118 f.; Bruckmüller 1996: 70) that have shown Austria's "scenic beauty", "historical treasures and achievements", political stability, and national food to rank amongst the most cherished symbols of national pride. What may appear a disparate list of symbols shares important common ground: a romanticising, backward glance whose foci include past figures or a (former) state of pristine natural beauty, at least implicitly threatened by social change and environmental degradation. I here build on previous work (Karner 2005, 2008, 2011) to ask what happens when such symbols of national identification are perceived to be under threat. This implies a preliminary question, namely what the threat is.

This chapter draws on Nancy Fraser's (2012a, b) neo-Polanyian framework, particularly her distinction between "marketization", "social protection" and "emancipation", to illuminate competing ideological forces shaping Austria today. Marketization, that is, multiple flows of commodities and international economic competition, impacting on Austria and—more widely—the European Union, provides the context to the contrasting politics examined in what follows. The latter, in turn, display features Fraser discusses as hallmarks of social protection and emancipation, respectively. However, this discussion delves deeper: through close analysis of a wide range of empirical materials, it pushes Fraser's paradigm further; I ask what—in addition to a preoccupation with ethnic/national boundaries in the case of social protection, and a diametrically opposed commitment, in the case of emancipation, to extending welfare and human rights to those beyond "the nation" and its safety nets—defines the discursive-political competitors examined below.

It is at this juncture that nostalgia will be shown to partly distinguish social protection from emancipation, thus illustrating how these political forces push in opposite directions. Schlipphacke (2014: 1–4) defines nostalgia as involving an "abrupt break between 'before' and 'after'", as "feelings of loss" of a past that "may never have been", and—following Boym—as the "affective mode of modernity". Such sentiments are, as we shall see, defining features of social protectionism, whilst virtually absent from the emancipatory agendas discussed here. While nostalgia furnishes a temporal dimension crucial to social protection, emancipation works within a spatial framework of reference. In the case of emancipatory movements, comparisons are not made through backward-looking glances at a purported past; instead, emancipation is informed by sideward-looking comparisons with elsewhere, in the here and now. Put differently, social protectionism is informed by diachronic (generally romanticizing) comparisons with "ourselves as we [supposedly] used to be". Conversely, emancipation emerges from synchronic comparisons with current injustices endured by "others elsewhere". Although, generally, synchronic invocations of "elsewhere" can certainly also slide into (Rousseau-ian) romanticization, there is no evidence of this in the emancipatory discourses discussed here, which critically focus on others' exclusion and suffering. As we shall see, these contrasting frames of reference—one temporal, the other spatial—underpin social protectionist moves toward hardening external boundaries in one case, and emancipatory movements of widening, cosmopolitan inclusion in the other.

Structurally, this discussion also invokes Nancy Fraser's neo-Polanyian discussion of the "triple movements" shaping contemporary socioeconomic relations. Fraser's key-categories—*marketization, social protection* and *emancipation*—therefore provide both central analytical categories and structuring devices. As we discover, reading contemporary Austria through Fraser's framework bears analytical dividends. However, as already anticipated, the point is not to merely corroborate preexisting social theory, a strategy that would risk becoming circular, but to allow data to in turn critically reinflect the conceptual paradigm in question. I begin with outlines of Austria's post-World War II history and of the methods underpinning this discussion. This is followed by three thematic sections, which examine the local/national manifestations of widening commodification/marketization and the competing politics of social protectionism and emancipation, respectively. Crucially, although this discussion is empirically focussed on Austria, its insights are of wider relevance across and beyond the (crisis-stricken) European Union. The development of the neo-Polanyian framework sketched here thereby offers new ways for thinking about today's most pressing socioeconomic shifts and political tensions.

Historical and Methodological Context

Even the most cursory summary of Austria's twentieth century must reflect (on) the profound contrast between the turmoil of the first half (that is, World War I and the disintegration of the Habsburg empire, economic hardship and political polarization during the First Republic, the descent into authoritarianism followed by the infamous *Anschluss* to Nazi Germany, World War II and the Holocaust), and the remarkable political and economic stability accomplished and enjoyed in the second. While Thomas Piketty's history of *Capital* (2014) inadvertently demonstrates that this paralleled concurrently unfolding trends seen across the industrialized world, Austrian post-1945 history also contained national particularities.

Among those were the specific form and success of Austria's neocorporatist "social partnership" in mediating between capital, labour and the state and in helping to control centrifugal political forces that had defined the interwar period (for example, Sully 1990). At the same time, the political consequences of social partnership have not always been assessed as favourably, with Robert Menasse (2005: 356), for example, arguing that it lacked democratic legitimacy and transparency. Combined with Western European standards, unusually high levels of political party membership (that is, at the time usually either with the Social Democrats, SPÖ, or the centre-right People's Party, ÖVP) and a for some time hampered civil society (for example, Bruckmüller 1996: 42f), other symptoms of postwar stability included growing affluence and high levels of "social peace" reflected in Austria's remarkably low numbers of minutes of strike per worker as late as the 1980s (Fitzmaurice 1991: 122). Other, specifically Austrian features of the postwar era were the gradual discursive dominance of a new, distinctly Austrian national self-understanding, which came to replace previously hegemonic pan-Germanic identities (for example Thaler 2001); and the fact that Austrian neutrality, legally enshrined since 1955, did not always sit too easily in "the market place", given the country's "growing interdependence with Western economies throughout the Cold War" and its "enormous dependence upon global trade flows" (Harrod 2012: 166).

In other respects, Austria's postwar socioeconomic transformations mirrored those observed elsewhere. Agricultural production underwent far-reaching shifts that entailed specialization, concentration on medium-sized farms often run alongside other employment (Hanisch 1994: 95) and the "industrialization" (Krausmann et al. 2003) of farming. At the same time, Austria has, of course, also been reshaped by wider socioeconomic and technological changes that defined the late twentieth century, including the digital revolution and the shift in economic orthodoxy from Keynesianism to neoliberalism. There is a case, however, that the latter has been contested more strongly in Austria than in other parts of (North-Western/Central) Europe (Karner 2008). What is more, the country's geographic location just on the Western side of the former Iron Curtain meant that some of the changes in the wake of the revolutions of 1989–1991 were felt (or feared) particularly strongly in the Alpine Republic. The rise of neo-nationalism (Gingrich and Banks 2006) in Austria in the 1990s can be read, at least partly, as a defensive reaction to social changes and perceived dislocations experienced since the 1980s.

All this has unfolded in a cultural context also shaped, as already hinted, by forms of collective nostalgia. One may think of the postwar popularity of the *Heimatfilm* (for example Larkey 1999: 223), cinematic narratives set in idyllic Alpine locations seemingly above and outside the social transformations of urban modernity. However, such similarly romanticizing, ahistorical depictions have found their critical counterparts: that is, negations of ideal-izing or exonerating representations of the national past that point toward harsh, violent, brutal, steeply hierarchical and at times inhumane historical realities. The most influential and best-documented form of this counter-discourse is the much-delayed process of *Vergangenheitsbewältigung* (that is, "coming to terms with the past") that was finally triggered in the aftermath of the "Waldheim affair" in 1986 and that led to a widespread, though not uni-versally embraced, critical scrutiny and deconstruction of Austria's previously dominant "myth of victimhood" during World War II and the Holocaust (for example, Uhl 2006). There are other examples of a countercultural tra-dition that subjects prominent self-understanding and idyllically reified ver-sions of the past to critical reexamination: for instance, the *Anti-Heimatroman* (Bischof 2004: 22; Daffner 2014), an Austrian literary genre that has, espe-cially since the 1970s, problematized traditional, rural structures of inequality and oppression.

This discussion needs to be read against this backdrop of (late) twentieth/ early twenty-first century social transformations and the competing cultural currents of nostalgia and critical (self-) interrogation. Methodologically, I build on my long-standing research on Austrian national identity nego-tiations (Karner 2005, 2007, 2010, 2011). More specifically, I draw on a large corpus of data collected over a period of more than a decade, which covers the country's wide-ranging media discourse: from the public broad-casting network (ORF); Austria's ideologically diverse press, national and regional, daily and weekly, broadsheet and tabloids; and readers' letters published in some of the country's most prominent and most widely read papers. I here focus particularly on more recent discussions—involving diverse sources and settings—of different facets of current, often transna-tional socioeconomic tensions, paying specific attention to their Austrian "receptions" and the boundaries of inclusion and exclusion drawn and reproduced in wide-ranging media representations and publicly articu-lated discourses. While political positions are centrally important to this analysis, so are their transmission by the "secondary definers" (Hall et al. 1978: 57–60) that are the media and their (re)appropriation or contesta-tion by so-called "ordinary social actors" employing means such as read-ers' letters to newspaper editors to participate in public debate of highly charged topics (Lynn and Lea 2003).

Similarly significant is the range of topics addressed in the materials analysed here: Austrian discussions—as comparable debates elsewhere—of current socioeconomic shifts and crises are profoundly transnational, indeed global, in their coverage and foci. What follows is a thematic analysis, theoretically underpinned by some of the conceptual scholarship outlined in the introduction to our volume, of a wide range of Austrian representations of, and positions on, political and economic issues that often take place elsewhere but are perceived to impact on the local and national contexts, too. The materials examined reveal diverse political positions and self-understanding formulated or reaffirmed in response to both internal and external issues. The actors participating in these discussions, for example politicians, public intellectuals and journalists, "ordinary citizens", are shown to direct their gaze to a wide range of issues and crises, the "epicentres" of which often lie beyond national boundaries. This adds to Arjun Appadurai's discussion (1990) of the transnational "flows" of people, finance, technology, ideologies and media images of our conflictual, globalizing era. What Appadurai terms "ethnoscapes", "financescapes" and "technoscapes" crossing international boundaries are all part of the contexts debated in the data, to which I turn next. And the transnational flows of ideas, information, ideologies and media images, subsumed by Appadurai's concepts of "ideoscapes" and "mediascapes", play an even more central role. What we encounter here are national receptions, by a wide variety of structurally and ideologically differently positioned social actors, of global issues, crises emanating elsewhere, and of the transnational connections that define our era. The levels of the nation-state, the European Union and global markets are all addressed, and sometimes merge, in the discourses analysed below.

This discussion centres on a small number of recent extracts—comprising various political, journalistic, and argumentative positions publicly articulated by less prominent, "ordinary social actors"—selected from the much larger corpus of aforementioned data. The particular materials analysed all exemplify recurring argumentative positions on what may appear, at a first glance, a disparate list of economic, social and ecological issues. Continuing Polanyi's and Fraser's trajectories, however, it is my contention that superficially unrelated concerns and topics are underpinned by a shared preoccupation with marketization and the competing political reactions it triggers. At the same time, while my examples are all representative of wider discursive currents, what follows is not a quantitative measurement of their relative salience across Austria's population. Instead, I offer a qualitative, thematic reading of mutually contesting interpretative and political positions brought to bear on various socioeconomic hallmarks of the contemporary world. My focus lies on the rhetorical dimensions, diverse manifestations, and ideological trajectories of these competing positions.

Marketization/Commodification

The structural shifts associated with our era's globalizing pressures are well-documented in Austria. By the 1990s, its aforementioned social partnership, a form of "(neo)corporatism" generally acknowledged—across Western Europe's smaller states—for helping to control unemployment and inflation in the postwar period and involving "encompassing trade unions and employers' associations" bargaining with the state, was beginning to appear "obsolete" to some, given rates of international trade, capital mobility and technological change (Kindley 1997: 6–7; 3). Yet, it was then also observed (Traxler 1997: 169–171) that Austrian corporatism continued to play a significant role, albeit a changing one, now focused on "gearing wages, skills, and working conditions to the requirements of international competitiveness". The economic changes since the 1980s have not only impacted on the institutions most immediately concerned with production and employment, but their effects are felt across a wider range of social domains.

Transformations experienced over recent decades can be described through Polanyian categories of analysis: increasingly unregulated markets; the "disembedding" of things, goods and relationships that were previously more firmly anchored in national institutions and local lifeworlds; and political counterreactions. Much of this can be summarized under "marketization". Frederic Jameson's (1991) suggestion that multinational capitalism entails the "commodification" of previously noncommodified realms (for example, nature and the unconscious) adds further specificity to the economic and cultural changes witnessed since the 1970s.

Returning from the level of conceptual generality to my particular empirical setting, both Polanyi's and Jameson's frames apply to contemporary Austria. Key concerns of recent years are precisely about increasingly disembedded markets and hyper-commodification. As I have shown elsewhere (Karner 2008), one such debate that has periodically occupied sections of the Austrian public for more than a decade focuses on water, which is widely seen as a public good, whose potential privatization—and hence commodification through businesses driven by profitmotives only—is often perceived as a threat to national watersupplies. There are several other debates that, though superficially unrelated, reveal similar anxieties about the widening reach of market forces. Marketization, in the materials examined here, is encountered through or, more accurately, already filtered by critical reflections on the processes and perceived consequences of widening commodification in a range of social domains.

The clearest recent example of this has been provided by widespread Austrian opposition to a possible free trade agreement, the Transatlantic Trade and Investment Partnership, or TTIP, between the European Union and the USA. Such opposition has emerged across significant sections of the political spectrum and has involved politicians, public figures, citizens' petitions and initiatives, and Austria's largest newspaper, the tabloid daily *Kronen Zeitung* (or *Krone*). Similar resistance against TTIP's relatively widely predicted and feared environmental and social consequences has been evident across Europe. Nor is such opposition ideologically homogenous, as was shown by anti-globalisation protests at the recent (June 2015) G7 summit in the Bavarian Alps, for instance, but a profound disquiet about global, unrestricted market forces can be observed on both ends of the ideological continuum. It is part of my intention here to sketch how defining differences between various opponents against a common "foe", that is, widening commodification, can be discerned.

In the Austrian context, some opposition against TTIP merges with the national popularity of organic, local food production and a wider critique of transnational agribusiness. This manifests in the aforementioned *Kronen Zeitung's* long-standing stance against a possible free trade agreement with the USA. Prominent in the paper's columns and readers' letters over many months, its position crystallized, for example, on 28 December 2014, when its front-page headline declared that the paper was committed to "fighting for our farmers", following this up with a picture caption juxtaposing "healthy food from our farmers and for our children" against "US-style mass production". The same national "deixis" (Billig 1995: 94), using personal pronouns and topographical frames of reference as discursive means of articulating and reproducing national identities, defined the accompanying article:

> [S]ecret negotiations about a trade agreement with the US are alarming to Lower Austria's politicians. With 40.116 farmers (more than 4.700 of them organic farmers) cultivating a total of 683.405 acres, Lower Austria is Austria's largest agricultural region ... Unrestricted markets would abandon [our farmers] to the billion-dollar industries of US agribusiness ... In US-style mass animal husbandry, quality or animal rights have no place ... An average US farmer cultivates ... 14-times as large an area as an average European farmer. Our mountain farms are smaller still ... Lower Austria is our breadbasket but it would not stand a chance against America's huge, genetically modified grains. (Perry 2014; my translation)

Its prominence in Austria's most widely-read paper should not be misread as an indication that opposition to TTIP is confined to the *Kronen Zeitung*. Such opposition is, as already mentioned, more widespread and ideologically heterogeneous (for example ORF 2015a). Noteworthy about many of the discourses involved are the rhetorical features prominent in the extract just cited, including a topos of scales, whereby the might of external actors and forces—through a recurring "David versus Goliath" trope—is juxtaposed with local agricultural production. Yet, this is not just seen as unequal economic competition, but perceived as a clash between entirely different ethical regimes: global agricultural markets are thus associated with genetically modified produce, with a lack of animal welfare and a lack of quality. Austrian farming, by contrast, is presented as green, organic, sustainable, committed to protecting local producers and animal rights. There is ample evidence of the local prominence of this discourse and of widespread distrust of global food industries and their production methods. For example, in 1997 1.2 million Austrians signed a petition against genetically modified crops; and in 2006 organic farmers cultivated 13.5 % of Austria's agriculturally used land, compared to a mere 3.4 % across the rest of the European Union (Gruber and Bohacek 2006: 11; 46). This should be seen in the context of a discursive realm that *Profil* columnist Georg Hoffmann-Ostenhof (2009) has described as Austria's "national religion" and as centred on political neutrality and on opposition to both nuclear energy and genetically modified food.

Changing thematic focus but staying within broader anxieties about marketization, on the left of the political spectrum one encounters recurring criticism of global financial markets and neoliberalism in the Viennese weekly *Falter* (amongst other discursive sites). While its objects of criticism and suggested responses of course differ profoundly from nation-centred "diagnoses" and advocated reactions typical of the right (see further below), we here also detect deep concern about the social and political impact of unregulated markets. The following *Falter* quotations illustrate this:

> This kind of politics has long forgotten about social dimensions ... Benevolent reform would require a reform of "the markets", a regulation of the financial industry ... [Conversely,] austerity politics leads to a social abyss and is economic nonsense ... [But] politics is being reformed in the markets' interests, when what we need is a reform of markets in the collective interest. For 40 years we have witnessed politics disempowering itself. (Thurnher 2015a; *my translation*)
>
> Creditors should support borrowers' economic development, thereby enabling them to repay their debt ... Europe has disregarded this fundamental truth in Greece's case ... In the midst of economic crisis ... the Troika tied loans to ... extreme austerity ... This caused the demand in goods and services to collapse ... and a dramatic social deterioration ... There is no justification for the Eurogroup finance ministers' self-righteous demeanour ... Jeroen Dijsselbloem is a neoliberal stirrer who aided the demolition of the previously exemplary Dutch welfare state and who now tries to make an example of Greece. (Marterbauer 2015; *my translation*)

The contexts for these arguments were provided by recent regional elections resulting in further swings to the nationalist-populist right and an ever-more deepening Greek crisis, implicating the entire Eurozone, respectively. What these positions share is deep anxiety about the current hegemony of neoliberal austerity politics and their social consequences.

The following, similarly germane position echoes both Thomas Piketty's history of capital(ism) and Polanyian critique:

> For more than 30 years incomes have increased less than returns on capital, while the tax burden has shifted towards employees … After 20 years of neoliberal politics Europe is in a depression … the only way out of any depression is through a more active state (for example the foundations of a welfare state in the 1880s, the New Deal and war preparations in the 1930s) … There is a backlog of problems only politics can handle (that is in the areas of education, the environment, infrastructure, poverty, care). (Schulmeister 2014a; *my translation*)

Such criticism is certainly not confined to one particular paper and its readers. Its growing salience was documented in a *Profil* article shortly after Syriza's Greek electoral victory in early 2015, which argued that "communists, the Greens and even social democrats now entertain new hopes for an alternative to the logic of the financial markets" (Brodning and Zöchling 2015, *my translation*). A profound scepticism of unregulated markets also characterizes the politically very differently positioned tabloid *Kronen Zeitung*, one of whose readers combines their opposition to a possible free trade agreement with the USA with criticism of the EU's perceived direction of travel:

> It is welcome news that [agricultural] minister Rupprechter supports the *Krone*'s campaign against TTIP, in order to protect our farmers against unscrupulous agribusiness … only the powerful will benefit from transatlantic trade … TTIP should also be rejected on environmental grounds … The term "free trade" implies that the global export of all kinds of goods should be the aim of every economy. The EU also follows this dogma … Where is this purported "progress" taking us? (*Kronen Zeitung* reader, 10 January 2015: 30f, *my translation*)

At this argumentative juncture the question may be posed as to whether some such positions are merely manifestations of Austrian anti-Americanism. The USA has indeed occupied an ambiguous space in Austrian postwar culture, in particular. On one hand, Americanization has manifested in a "consumerist social utopia"; at the same time, a partial reappropriation of the practices and registers of the "global cultural industries" (for example, the musical phenomenon of Austro-Pop and its reuse of Anglo-American musical genres with lyrics in Austrian dialect) also facilitated an "ethnicization" of Austrian identities in symbolic self-delineation from both US and German economic influence (for example Larkey 1999). Alongside, there has been a long "tradition" of anti-Americanism, stretching from nineteenth-century romantic poetry to contemporary "critiques of a globalized American 'turbo-capitalism'" (Bischof 2014: 47–48), some of which with anti-Semitic undertones. While a history of ideas undeniably helps illuminate important ideological continuities, this is not the analytical direction taken in the present chapter. Instead, I next explore whether Fraser's conceptual distinction between *social protection* and *emancipation* can help us trace and understand the competing, ideologically highly diverse counterdiscourses shaping contemporary Austria.

Social Protection and Nostalgia

Nancy Fraser's (2012a: 25) "triple movement" postulates that one way of counteracting (neoliberal) marketization is through social protectionist movements and discourses, "some savory, others unsavory", which pursue a reembedding of economic relations in (older) institutional arrangements that are, on one hand, undermined by (global) markets and, on the other, often hierarchical and exclusionary. Austrian examples reveal that social protectionism tends to operate with a distinctive temporal dimension, invoking a positively connoted past as criticism of the present. It is here that the ideological significance of nostalgia manifests. At times, though this only characterizes *some* social protectionists, this takes the form of a nationalist historiography with its typical schema (for example Hutchinson 1987) of a former "golden age", presumed "fall from grace", and anticipated (nation-centred) rejuvenation. Social protectionism is thereby presented as the key-mechanism through which a purportedly more satisfactory and just—clearly only for those included in the national "in-group"—life and order are to be reestablished. Put differently, social protection, so the argument or implicit premise goes, is key to reverting the downward historical spiral nationalist discourse detects and bemoans; things can, it is claimed, get better—for "us", and "again".

This argumentative schema is typical of Austria's controversial nationalist Freedom Party (FPÖ), whose social protectionist agenda is written into its self-stylization as a *soziale Heimatpartei* (loosely translated as "socially conscious homeland party"). Characteristically (of social protectionism), Heinz-Christian Strache, the FPÖ's head, recently advocated a response to intra-European labour migration and rising unemployment that would include closure—at least in certain industries but possibly more generally—of Austria's labour market to foreigners, potential repatriation and separate social insurance for foreign employees (*Kronen Zeitung*, 14 May 2015: 3). Regionally, in the run-up to the May 2015 provincial assembly elections in southeastern Styria (where the FPÖ has achieved very significant gains over recent years), the nostalgic tone of its social protectionism was particularly apparent. The promises on the FPÖ electoral posters included the following (*my translations*): "To stop the asylum chaos"; "Preserving homeland and values"; "New flats instead of new mosques"; "We fight for your safety"; "To make living affordable again"; and "More sensitivity for Styrians". Paradigmatically nostalgic assumptions indeed underpin these assessments and promises: first, perceptions of (social, cultural or infrastructural) decline; second, the claim that resources or privileges have been "mis-allocated" to outsiders (who are constructed as a drain or threat) and need redirecting towards the allegedly overlooked ethnic majority. In the context of another regional electoral campaign, the Upper Austrian FPÖ's current slogans (August 2015) posit that its regional head "understands us" and "strengthens us", that the party epitomizes "true and honest" patriotism, giving the "homeland a future" (*all my translations*). Framed as supporters' statements about the FPÖ, and through (subtly exclusive) deictic references to the in-group, such slogans reflect the party's constructions of its political opponents as purportedly out of touch with voters; of a present found again deeply wanting, of an allegedly rosier past—both typical of nostalgia –, and of a potentially brighter future, to which the party purports to hold the key.

With the FPÖ is considered a very possible contender to become Austria's strongest political force at the next national parliamentary elections (ORF 2015b), this discursive logic also manifested in a recent *Kronen Zeitung* interview (7 June 2015: 9) with Heinz-Christian Strache, in which the latter accused "cheap Eastern European workers" of pushing Austrians into unemployment, the Schengen agreement (that is the opening of inner-European borders) of increasing crime, and "more than 80 %" of asylum-seekers of being mere economic migrants; queried about his own suggested response to current migratory flows to Europe and Austria, Strache suggested asylum should predominantly be granted to Christians and only among the "genuinely persecuted". Once again, the nostalgic resonance of a purportedly better past—assumed to have predated the rise in unemployment, crime and current migratory flows—and the promise of a nation-centred future are the interpretative foundations on which such arguments are constructed. In other interviews Strache has described himself as living his "social responsibility" and possessing "high social intelligence" (*Profil*, 18 March 2013: 41) and, in further corroboration of his social protectionist politics, as living by the principle of "love thy neighbour, and for me that means, in the first instance, our Austrians" (ORF 2013).

The sometimes close discursive links between nostalgia and nationally framed social protectionism are also evident in an initiative for an EU-exit, whose national petition was signed by 261.159 people, four percent of the electorate, in late June 2015 (ORF 2015c). Its assessment of the past, present and promised future manifests in its central claims; Austria's purported "liberation" [sic!] from the European Union would allegedly achieve the following: a "regaining of freedom and sovereignty"; a departure from the EU's "democratic deficit"; an end to EU membership contributions and to having to support other Eurozone countries; a reduction of currently rising unemployment; successful defence against "ruinous" free-trade agreements; a "rebuilding of a national economy in citizens' interest"; a return to Austria's "politics of peace and neutrality"; a rebuilding of "healthy" agriculture, and support for "environmental-, health- and animal protection instead of GM and nuclear power" (http://www.volksbegehren-eu-austritt.at, my translations). Invoking an allegedly preferable pre-EU-accession era, all of this promises a return to a nostalgically reified *status quo ante*.

While the FPÖ's and other nation-centred politics of nostalgia revolve around the promised reestablishment of a purportedly more just and more secure social "order", premised on refortified national boundaries, there can little be doubt that comparable perceptions of present decline contrasted to a positively evaluated past possess considerably wider social currency. This often manifests in the trope of an "island of the blessed", or *Insel der Seligen* (see Liessmann 2005), applied in nostalgic recollections of Austria between the 1960s and 1980s. Importantly, this is not an Austrian particularity, as Thomas Piketty (2014: 96) shows:

> Continental Europe … ha[s] entertained considerable nostalgia for … the thirty years from the late 1940s to the late 1970s during which economic growth was unusually rapid. People still do not understand what evil spirit condemned them to such low rate of growth beginning in the late 1970s … [V]iewed in historical perspective, the thirty postwar years were … exceptional.

This was preempted in Kindley's observation (1997: 3) that rapid technological and economic change were widely seen "through the most pessimistic of lenses" offering "nostalgic [views of] the social and political institutions of the postwar period as symbols of stability".

Not all nostalgia becomes nationalist, of course, nor is social protectionism inevitably nostalgic. Yet, the question arises as to how other social protectionisms guard the ideological demarcation from nationalist identity politics. Therein lies a plausible reading of the contemporary dilemma facing social democracy in and beyond Austria. The commitment to providing social protection in the face of marketization constitutes political terrain now also claimed by the populist–far right. As shown by Aichholzer et al. (2014: 113), while FPÖ voters have "distinct views on … immigration, European integration and dissatisfaction with the political system", the party has succeeded in structurally "undermin[ing] the Social Democrats' support base". And while the FPÖ's singular commitment to nationals is clear, it should be remembered that although the SPÖ pushed for Austria's EU accession in 1995, in the years prior some of its party members also expressed fears of the "home labour market being swamped by cheap labour" and a consequent deflation of Austrians' wages (Bushell 2013: 231). More recently, SPÖ social affairs minister Rudolf Hundstorfer decided not to ease asylum-seekers' access to the labour market, which would have constituted an example of emancipatory politics (see below), when a report suggested that such a decision would further increase national unemployment figures (ORF 2015d).

Social democrats' dilemmas have been the subject of much debate. Amongst the most sophisticated Austrian assessments has been the charge that the SPÖ has failed to stem the neoliberal tide of marketization (for example Thurnher 2014). There are other issues illuminated by an application of Fraser's neo-Polanyian model. The shift from a "double" to a "triple movement" can also be read as reflecting historical changes: from an earlier, solid modernity (Bauman 2000), premised on class-based lifeworlds and identifications, to the long-overdue recognition and politicisation of multiple structures of power, inequality and exclusion (Brah 1996). The latter, combined with our era's transnational flows and interconnections, sharpen the (potential) differences between social protectionism and emancipation. Social democracy, in its protectionist, class-based orientation, is now forced to compete with nationalist forces for the local/national working class. Meanwhile, subaltern identity politics and struggles for empowerment have created a wider, richer political field—including green parties, lively civil societies and so on—in which social democracy can at best compete for, but certainly not monopolise, emancipatory forces. Engulfed in political competition on several fronts, the SPÖ has recently made some widely criticized choices (for example Klenk 2015; Bauer and Linsinger 2015), including the formation of a regional coalition with the FPÖ in Austria's eastern-most province of Burgenland.

Elsewhere, one occasionally encounters an alternative, left-leaning nostalgia outside party politics and far removed from any entanglements with "unsavoury" (Fraser 2012a) nationalist social protectionism. For instance, in his reflections on the SPÖ's current dilemmas, *Falter* editor Armin Thurnher (2014) has suggested that those include the party's previous glory period, under Bruno Kreisky's "democratization of all areas of life" in the 1970s, which now acts as an unreproducible and thus inadvertently demoralizing model. Writing in the same paper, economic journalist Ulrike Herrmann (2015) recently argued for what may be described as a form of transnational social protectionism: strongly criticizing Germany's "radical economic nationalism" that has achieved its export surplus by lowering labour-/production costs domestically, Herrmann called on Austria to lead an alliance with France, Belgium and Italy and other Eurozone countries disadvantaged by German neoliberal policies; to prevent Europe's further/future impoverishment and to counter Germany's growing isolation, Herrmann argued, German workers' wages need to be substantially increased.

Social protectionism, nostalgia and nationalism constitute separate, distinctive, but partly overlapping phenomena. Those overlaps themselves assume different forms in different ideological constellations. All along, we ought to remember that the divergences between nostalgic narratives of the past and romanticising invocations of a purportedly idyllic, often rural, harmonious, and unalienated way of life (Blickle 2002) on one hand, and actual historical and social realities, on the other, are many and long-established (Ward Crowe 1981). The question arises which alternative, inclusive, non-nostalgic responses to today's crises and flows are also evident in Austria.

Emancipation

Thus we turn to calls for "emancipation" for groups and individuals who experience exclusion *either* in the realm of the market *or* within the social structures upheld by protectionists (Fraser 2012a: 25). As we have seen, the latter often articulate opposition to marketization through nostalgic registers, contrasting a particular version of particular past to a present found uncertain, unjust and unsatisfactory. By contrast, the emancipatory voices that follow work through a synchronically focused axiological frame informed by ethical opposition to current local and global inequalities and exclusions. Strictly speaking, what we encounter here are not "subaltern counterpublics" (Fraser 1992), which would be "parallel discursive arenas" created and utilized by the (historically) oppressed only. Instead, we discern *emancipatory counter-publics* shared by structurally very differently positioned actors and organisations—for example Austrian/European citizens showing solidarity with asylum-seekers—and premised on a consciousness of contemporary oppression and disenfranchisement.

Unlike in the case of social protectionism, diachronic comparisons with oneself in a recent, nostalgically filtered past play little role here. Instead, emancipatory frameworks work through comparisons acutely aware of inequalities and injustices presently suffered by others. Analytically, two questions arise. The first concerns the structural effectiveness of any one emancipatory discourse. For instance, in relation to the aforementioned Austrian *Anti-Heimatroman* and its focus on rural oppression (Hanisch 1994: 481; Zeyringer 1996: 170), Catriona Firth (2011: 570) argues that well-known exemplars of this literary genre, their emancipatory intentions notwithstanding, are articulated through the registers of existing power relations, thereby "subjugating rather than enfranchising the rural subject". Nancy Fraser herself has shown that emancipatory movements can be subject to ideological repositioning over time: she makes this argument in relation to second-wave feminism, *the* paradigmatic emancipatory force, suggesting that some of its current crystallizations are complicit with neoliberal individualism (Fraser 2014). Assessing the impact, or their possible discursive contradictions, of the following examples goes beyond the scope of the present contribution and must await further examination elsewhere. But importantly, Firth's and Fraser's remarks inadvertently remind us that, particularly in a globalizing world of "triple movements", power operates on several scales and along different axes (Brah 1996), making a singular and permanent binary between power and emancipation insufficient.

While multidirectional power struggles are part of the backdrop to this chapter, the second analytical question structures the remainder of this discussion, namely *which power relations a given emancipatory discourse subjects to criticism.* The first group of examples speaks and acts on behalf of the most adversely affected by social protectionist politics upholding exclusionary structures. In the first half of 2015 the number of asylum-seekers arriving on European shores increased by 83 % compared to 2014, the vast majority of whom—according to the UN high commissioner for refugees—certainly not "economic migrants" (as Heinz-Christian Strache would have it) (ORF 2015e). The structural and discursive exclusion of asylum-seekers in and beyond Austria is now well researched (for example, Franz 2003). Recent scholarship shows that EU directives on "minimum reception standards" are implemented unevenly across Austria's nine provinces and sometimes "translate into minimum welfare and restricted ... personal freedom" (Rosenberger and König 2011: 537), and that a "reemergence of colonial thought" is discernible in the far right's anti-asylum-seekers discourse (Hipfl and Gronold 2011). In the context of intra-European wrangling over the possible distribution of asylum-seekers within the EU, and Austria experiencing serious infrastructural challenges in handling the increase in arrivals and asylum-claims (ORF 2015f), the FPÖ's recent electoral gains in provincial assembly elections have been explained with reference to its tough anti-asylum stance (and growing unemployment) (ORF 2015g). There are, however, notable counter-discourses, including, as I have shown elsewhere, local media and street magazines in Austria's main cities, and civil society organisations with a record of providing asylum-seekers with a voice and rare employment opportunities in the face of chronic uncertainty, exclusion and everyday racism. Particularly noteworthy are civil society organisations providing support structures for asylum-seekers, recording racist attacks, establishing connections between refugees and local Austrians, or sharing asylum-seekers' life stories with a wider audience (Karner 2007). Similar emancipatory counter-discourses and organisational efforts have surfaced in the context of recent tragedies of hundreds of asylum-seekers drowning in the Mediterranean. The reactions in Austria's quality press included strong criticisms of a lack of empathy and responsibility shown by European politicians preoccupied with continental/national fortification at the expense of human rights and dignity (Gächter 2015; Thurnher 2015b). Also, informed by investigative journalism on the Italian island of Lampedusa and of particular asylum-seekers' migratory stories, Anna Giulia Fink et al. (2015) pose the searching question as to how ethical responsibility for "the other" could be assumed locally, regionally, nationally and on European level, instead of perpetuating the current stalemate, where the far right insists on further restrictions and exclusions, and the left is paralysed by fear of losing more political ground. The fact that emancipatory alternatives are possible is reflected, for instance, in local initiatives working, often against considerable obstacles (for example Pölsler 2015; Schaffer 2014), to house and successfully integrate asylum-seekers in private accommodations (http://www.fluechtlinge-willkommen.at/).

Not only debates surrounding asylum, but also wider political tensions over multiculturalism reflect the differences between social protection and emancipation. The SPÖ again appears simultaneously pulled in opposite directions, partly by the criticisms levelled against it. In 2010, the FPÖ's Heinz-Christian Strache, bizarrely, called the SPÖ an "islamist party" (*Islamistenpartei*), insinuating that Austrian social democracy had forfeited its social protectionist, working-class politics (ORF Wien 2010). Conversely, *Profil* columnist Georg Hoffmann-Ostenhof (2015) has argued that part of the SPÖ's dilemma lies in its reluctance to pay more attention to migrants and their descendants; in Fraser's terminology, that social democracy could be salvaged by a shift from social protectionist to emancipatory agendas. Occasionally, the forces of social protectionism and emancipation clash more directly and physically, as in June 2015 when in the Viennese district of Favoriten (ORF Wien 2015) a demonstration by the right-wing movement "die Identitären"—bemoaning, in social protectionist fashion, that migratory flows and demographic changes will turn "us" into "a minority in our country soon"—came face to face with "antifascist", left-wing counterdemonstrations.

My final examples differ in terms of their trajectory of criticism within today's "triple movements", for they speak on behalf of others currently, most immediately affected by hyper-marketization and neoliberal politics. Reporting from Athens and reflecting on Greece's highest unemployment rates in the EU, her rapidly declining birthrates and dramatic increase in suicides, a *Falter* article summarizes as follows:

> The crisis has emptied shops like a tropical storm, economic destruction is everywhere ... [This] is not about dry politics, it's about a country, her people and their suffering ... Greece can hardly bear further cuts, the country is already bleeding dry. (Narodoslawky 2015, *my translation*)

A perhaps unexpected, surprisingly similar argument appeared in a *Kronen Zeitung* article before Syriza's January 2015 triumph at the Greek elections, formulating what may be read as a transnationally emancipatory, critical engagement with current power relations in the EU:

> The German government declares that a Syriza victory and end of the austerity programme would make Greece's exit from the Euro-zone "unavoidable" ... The Austrian government is much more diplomatic ... This is sensible, since many Greeks, understandably, perceive such German claims to be attempts to apply pressure from the outside ... which could in turn help Tsipras ... Besides, many, many Greeks are suffering very severely under austerity (mass redundancies in the public sector, massive wage- and pension cuts), thus justifying some of Tsipras' demands. And many economists agree that a new "hair cut" of Greek debt will be required. (Hauenstein 2015: 2–3, *my translation*)

Six months on, in a poll taken the day after the referendum reflecting Greeks' resounding rejection of more austerity, 91 % of *Krone* readers declared (*Krone* poll 2015) that Greece should receive no more bailouts. The emancipatory thrust of the just-quoted article(s) is clearly part of public debate in Austria today, but—equally clearly—it cannot be assumed to represent majority opinion.

Concluding Reflections

Socioeconomic crises are ubiquitous today. Arguably a defining characteristic of current crises is that they are increasingly seen to be unmanageable within existing parameters of thought and systems of action. In the empirical context examined here, such assessments have manifested, for instance, in an interview with Naomi Klein declaring capitalism to be a "crisis-generating machine" and the connections between austerity and environmental disaster to be apparent (*Profil*, 3 April 2015: 64), in journalistic admissions of the impossibility of permanent economic growth (Lingens 2015), or in calls for a neo-Keynesian turn and regulation of the financial markets, for example, through a financial transaction tax (Schulmeister 2014b).

This chapter has examined manifestations of Nancy Fraser's "triple movement"—involving *marketization, social protection,* and *emancipation*—in early-twenty-first century Austria, which inescapably implicates wider European dimensions and transnational flows and connections. This discussion needs to be read in its European context, where academic voices of both national (Schachner-Blazizek and Hauser 2015) and transnational reach (e.g Heise 2014; Piketty 2014) convincingly criticize the ineffectiveness of neoliberal, austerity politics in the Eurozone, their exacerbation of social inequalities, and a concurrent renationalization of political discourse, but are yet to persuade key decision makers that current trajectories provide reasons for deep concern and little hope.

As emphasized from the start, my intention has not been to measure the relative prominence across Austria of the competing political responses to global flows and the forces of marketization. This remains the object of important future work, which I can only hope to have helped encourage. Such more quantitative measurements will have to do more than read social protection and emancipation off election results. As I have suggested in parts of this discussion, ideological opponents sometimes share common political ground, as shown in the disparate makeup of the resistance to TTIP, for instance. An understanding of the structural shifts of our era and the competing politics of nostalgia and (global) solidarity to which they give rise, thus needs a more nuanced and detailed tracing of what exactly is being claimed and offered in any political position. This challenge is, as we have begun to see here, more complex than a simple projection of arguments onto the classical left-right spectrum may lead us to believe. Fraser's neo-Polanyian model, further enriched by the distinction between temporal- (that is, the ideological uses of nostalgia) and geographical-cosmopolitan interpretative orientations outlined here, provides a much-needed step in precisely this direction of acknowledging the internal complexity, mutual contestability, but also the occasional overlaps and partial entanglements of the competing politics shaping the early twenty-first century, in Austria as elsewhere.

Acknowledgements This chapter builds on research I conducted in the winter/spring of 2015 as a Research Associate in the Center for Austrian Studies at the University of Minnesota. I would like to thank the Center and its staff for their hospitality and support.

References

Aichholzer, J., Kritzinger, S., Wagner, M., & Zeglovits, E. (2014). How has radical right support transformed established political conflicts? The case of Austria. *West European Politics, 37*(1), 113–137.

Appadurai, A. (1990). Disjuncture and difference in the global cultural economy. In M. Featherstone (Ed.), *Global culture*. London: Sage.

Austria Today. (2012). Austrian regional unemployment lowest in the EU, July 4.

Bauman, Z. (2000). *Liquid modernity.* Cambridge: Polity.

Bauer, G., & Linsinger, E. (2015). Ohnmachthaber. *Profil, 8*, 15–21.

Billig, M. (1995). *Banal nationalism.* London: Sage.

Bischof, G. (2004). Victims? Perpetrators? "Punching bags" of European historical memory? The Austrians and their world war II legacies. *German Studies Review, 27*(1), 17–32.

Bischof, G. (2014). *Relationships/Beziehungsgeschichten: Austria and the United States in the twentieth century.* Vienna: Studienverlag.

Blickle, P. (2002). *Heimat: A critical theory of the German idea of homeland.* Rochester: Camden.

Brah, A. (1996). *Cartographies of diaspora.* London: Routledge.

Brodning, I., & Zöchling, C. (2015). Radikal chic. *Profil*, 23 February, 14–20.

Bruckmüller, E. (1996). *Nation Österreich.* Vienna: Böhlau.

Bushell, A. (2013). *Polemical Austria.* Cardiff: University of Wales Press.

Daffner, C. (2014). Through romanticism's looking glass: Nostalgia, taboos, and cinematic exorcisms in Josef Winkler's *The Cinemascreenwalker. Journal of Austrian Studies, 47*(3), 1–17.

Fink, A. G., Gepp, J., Linsinger, E., Meinhart, E. & Treichler, R. (2015). Wir müssen etwas tun. Aber was? *Profil*, 27 April, 14–23.

Firth, C. (2011). Silencing the provincial other: Focalization, identification and power in Franz Innerhofer's Schöne Tage. *German Life and Letters, 64*(4), 570–587.

Fitzmaurice, J. (1991). *Austrian politics and society today.* London: Macmillan.

Franz, B. (2003). Bosnian refugee women in (re)settlement. *Feminist Review, 73*, 86–103.

Fraser, N. (1992). Rethinking the public sphere. In C. Calhoun (Ed.), *Habermas and the public sphere*. Cambridge: MIT Press.

Fraser, N. (2012a). *Marketization, social protection, emancipation: Toward a Neopolanyian conception of capitalist crisis*. http://sophiapol.hypotheses.org/files/2012/02/Texte-Nancy-Fraser-anglais.doc. Accessed 22 July 2013.

Fraser, N. (2012b). *Can society be commodities all the way down?*. Working papers series, Fondation Maison des sciences de l'homme. http://halshs.archives-ouvertes.fr/docs/00/72/50/60/PDF/FMSH-WP-2012-18_Fraser2.pdf. Accessed 22 July 2013.

Fraser, N. (2014). Neoliberalismus und Feminismus: eine gefährliche Liaison. *Falter, 50a*, 52–54.

Gächter, S. (2015). SOS Unmensch. *Profil* 27 April, 13.

Gilroy, P. (2004). *After empire*. Abingdon: Routledge.

Gingrich, A., & Banks, M. (2006). *Neo-nationalism in Europe and beyond*. New York: Berghahn.

Gruber, A., & Bohacek, H. (2006). *Lebensmittel heute*. Graz: Kammer für Arbeiter und Angestellte für Steiermark.

Hall, S., Critcher, C., Jefferson, T., Clarke, J., & Roberts, B. (1978). *Policing the crisis*. Basingstoke: Macmillan.

Hanisch, E. (1994). *Der lange Schatten des Staates*. Vienna: Ueberreuter.

Harrod, A. (2012). Hidden hands and cross-purposes: Austria and the irreconcilable conflict between neutrality and market laws. *Austrian History Yearbook, 43*, 165–188.

Hauenstein, C. (2015). Athen: Linke fordern Schuldenerlass. *Kronen Zeitung*, 2 January, 2–3.

Heise, A. (2014). Zwangsjacke Euro: Die Fehlkonstruktion des Europäischen Economic Governance Systems. *Wirtschaft und Gesellschaft, 40*(1), 17–31.

Herrmann, U. (2015). Österreicher, stoppt die Deutschen, oder ihr verarmt! *Falter, 24*, 16–18.

Hipfl, B., & Gronold, D. (2011). Asylum seekers as Austria's other: The re-emergence of Austria's colonial past in a state-of-exception. *Social Identities, 17*(1), 27–40.

Hiptmayr, C., Linsinger, E., Nikbaksh, M. (2015). Land der Hemmer. *Profil*, 22 May, 34–38.

Hoffmann-Ostenhof, G. (2009). Unsere Nationalreligion. *Profil*, 9 March, 73.

Hoffmann-Ostenhof, G. (2015). Verbaute Zukunft. *Profil*, 5 January, 64.

Krone poll. (2015). http://mobil.krone.at/phone/kmm__1/app__CORE/sendung_id__28/voting_id__5183/voting.phtml. Accessed 6 July 2015.

Hutchinson, J. (1987). *The dynamics of cultural nationalism*. London: Allen + Unwin.

Jameson, F. (1991). *Postmodernism, or, the cultural logic of late capitalism*. London: Verso.

Karner, C. (2005). National doxa, crises and ideological contestation in contemporary Austria. *Nationalism and Ethnic Politics, 11*(2), 221–263.

Karner, C. (2007). Austrian counter-hegemony: critiquing ethnic exclusion and globalization. *Ethnicities, 7*(1), 82–115.

Karner, C. (2008). The market and the nation: Austrian (dis)agreements. *Social Identities, 14*(2), 161–187.

Karner, C. (2010). The uses of the past and European integration. *Identities, 17*(4), 387–410.

Karner, C. (2011). *Negotiating national identities*. Farnham: Ashgate.

Kindley, R. (1997). Small European states and the challenge of globalization. In D. Good & R. Kindley (Eds.), *The challenge of globalization and institution building*. Westview: Boulder.

Klenk, F. (2015). Ein Plädoyer für die Ausgrenzung. *Falter, 24*, 6–7.

Krausmann, F., Haberl, H., Schulz, N., Erb, K.-H., Darge, E., & Gaube, V. (2003). Land-use change and socio-economic metabolism in Austria—part I: Driving forces of land-use change: 1950–1995. *Land Use Policy, 20*, 1–20.

Kronen Zeitung, various dates and page numbers as given in text.

Larkey, E. (1999). Americanization, cultural change and Austrian identity. In D. Good & R. Wodak (Eds.), *From world war to Waldheim: Culture and politics in Austria and the United States*. Berghahn: New York/Oxford.

Liessmann, K. P. (2005). *Die Insel der Seligen*. Innsbruck: Studienverlag.

Lingens, P. M. (2015). Droge Wirtschaftswachstum. *Profil*, 3 April, 96.

Lynn, N., & Lea, S. (2003). A phantom menace and the new apartheid. *Discourse & Society, 14*(4), 425–452.

Marterbauer, M. (2015). Rettet die Griechen vor der Destroika. *Falter, 10*, 6–7.

Menasse, R. (2005). *Das war Österreich*. Frankfurt: Suhrkamp.

Misik, R. (2014). Der gute Staat. *Falter, 51*, 14–15.

Narodoslawky, B. (2015). Ein Land blutet aus. *Falter, 18*, 20–21.

ORF (2013). *Strache im Gespräch: Wo steht die FPÖ konkret?* http://orf.at/stories/2197973/2197974. Accessed 12 Sept 2013.

ORF. (2015a). *Proteste in 45 Ländern weltweit*. http://orf.at/stories/2274072/2274073. Accessed 18 May 2015.

ORF. (2015b). *Meinungsforscher: FPÖ könnte im Bund Erste werden.* http://orf. at/stories/2281417. Accessed 3 June 2015.

ORF. (2015c). *261,159 unterschrieben EU-Austritt-Volksbegehren.* http://www. orf.at/stories/2287503/. Accessed 2 July 2015.

ORF. (2015d). *Sozialministerium: Mehr Arbeitslose durch Asylwerber.* http:// www.orf.at/stories/2287256/. Accessed 1 July 2015.

ORF. (2015e). *83 Prozent mehr Flüchtlinge seit Jahresbeginn.* http://orf.at/stories/2287117/. Accessed 1 July 2015.

ORF. (2015f). *Weiter Streit um Flüchtlingsunterbringung.* http://orf.at/stories/2281528. Accessed 3 June 2015.

ORF. (2015g). *FPÖ braucht Verhandlungserfolg.* http://orf.at/stories/2281438/2281423. Accessed 3 June 2015.

ORF Wien. (2010). *Strache bezeichnet SPÖ als 'Islamistenpartei'.* http://wien.orf. at/stories/463929/. Accessed 19 Aug 2010.

ORF Wien. (2015). *Proteste gegen Identitären-Aufmarsch.* http://wien.orf.at/ news/stories/2714824/. Accessed 10 June 2015.

http://www.fluechtlinge-willkommen.at/. Accessed 10 June 2015.

http://www.volksbegehren-eu-austritt.at, "Warum EU-Austritt? So kann es nicht weitergehen!". Accessed 11 May 2015.

Perry, M. (2014, December 28). 'Krone' kämpft um Sicherung der Existenz unserer Bauern. *Kronen Zeitung, 5.*

Piketty, T. (2014). *Capital in the twenty-first century.* Belknap: Cambridge, MA.

Pölsler, G. (2015). Ein Dorf steht auf. *Falter, 1–3,* 44–45.

Polanyi, K. (2001). *The great transformation.* Boston: Beacon Press.

Profil, various dates and page numbers as given in text.

Reiterer, A. (Ed.) (1988). *Nation und Nationalbewußtsein in Österreich.* Vienna: VWGÖ.

Rosenberger, S., & König, A. (2011). Welcoming the unwelcome: The politics of minimum reception standards for asylum seekers in Austria. *Journal of Refugee Studies, 25*(4), 537–554.

Schachner-Blazizek, P., & Hauser, W. (2015). *EU-Topia.* Vienna: NWV.

Schaffer, T. (2014). Mi casa es tu casa? *Falter, 48,* 52–53.

Schlipphacke, H. (2014). The temporalities of Habsburg nostalgia. *Journal of Austrian Studies, 47*(2), 1–16.

Schulmeister, S. (2014a). Der rote Irrweg. *Falter, 48,* 18.

Schulmeister, S. (2014b). Die vernünftigste Steuer in diesen Zeiten. *Le Monde diplomatique, 12,* 1/10–1/11.

Sully, M. (1990). *A contemporary history of Austria.* London: Routledge.

Thaler, P. (2001). *The ambivalence of identity*. West Lafayette: Purdue University Press.

Thurnher, A. (2014). Vor dem SPÖ-Parteitag: der Fluch des Pragmatismus. *Falter, 48*, 5.

Thurnher, A. (2015a). Nach den Wahlen, vor den Wahlen: Angst, Ohnmacht, Reformpartnerschaft. *Falter, 23*, 5.

Thurnher, A. (2015b). Unsere Menschenwürde? Gerade im Mittelmeer ertrunken. *Falter, 17*, 5.

Traxler, F. (1997). European transformation and institution building in east and west. In R. Kindley & D. Good (Eds.), *The challenge of globalization and institution building*. Westview: Boulder.

Uhl, H. (2006). From victim myth to co-responsibility thesis. In R. N. Lebow, W. Kansteiner, & C. Fogu (Eds.), *The politics of memory in postwar Europe*. Durham: Duke University Press.

Ward Crowe, P. (1981). Community size and social relationships: A comparison of urban and rural social patterns in Tirol. *Anthropological Quarterly, 54*(4), 210–229.

Zeyringer, K. (1996). Kultur-Differenzen und 'Prozesse literarischen Handelns': (Deutscher) Kanon und österreichische Literatur. *Die Unterrichtspraxis, 29*(2), 165–173.

Disembedding the Embedded/ Disembedded Opposition

José Julián López

Introduction

Crises have the potential to problematize the taken-for-granted notions underpinning the flow of everyday life, enabling a broader array of interpretive tools to be brought to bear on the question of why things are as they are, or, how they might be different. After all, crisis etymologically derives from the Greek *krissis*, meaning decision. The horizons opened up in such critical moments, given the right social conditions, may be conducive to important social transformations. Indeed, underpinning the Polanyian notion of the "double movement" as developed in *The Great Transformation*, is precisely a societal reflex or "countermovement" that he argued constituted a response to the crisis of nineteenth-century liberalism.

This research was made possible by a grant from the Social Sciences and Humanities Research Council of Canada, ultimately funded by Canadian taxpayers, for which I am enormously thankful.

J.J. López (✉)
The University of Ottawa, Ottawa, Canada

© The Editor(s) (if applicable) and The Author(s) 2016   **223**
C. Karner, B. Weicht (eds.), *The Commonalities of Global Crises*,
DOI 10.1057/978-1-137-50273-5_9

Crises, however, do not, as a matter of course, bear progressive fruit. This much is clear from twentieth-century fascism (Polanyi 1957: 134).

The parallels between the crisis of nineteenth-century market society and that of twenty-first century market liberalism as condensed dramatically in the 2008 financial crisis, have led many commentators to a Polanyian reading of the current predicament (Dale 2012; Block 2007: 3). Writing in 2009, Gareth Dale noted, "The prescriptions of free market liberalism are revealed as recipes for chaos". This, he added, was also the world that Karl Polanyi contemplated in the 1930s (2010a: 1). Yet the relative ease with which what was heralded as the beginning of the demise of neoliberalism has been transmuted into a programme of punishing austerity should give us pause for thought (Seymour 2014; Mirowski 2013). Even though the financial crisis "challenged in a very public way many of the core ideas of efficient markets" (Blyth 2013: 54), what ensued, in a little over twelve months, was "the greatest bait and switch in modern history" whereby "what was essentially private sector debt problems were rechristened as 'the Debt' generated by 'out-of-control' public spending" (Blyth 2013: 73). So stunning was this reversal that, in the words of Philip Mirowski, "It took a rare degree of self-confidence or fortitude not to gasp dumbfounded at a roaring resurgence of the right so soon after the most dramatic catastrophic global economic collapse after the Great Depression of the 1930s" (2013: 2). Given the prominence of Polanyian-inspired frameworks for thinking about the crisis and its aftermath, it is important to investigate if such efforts are properly tooled for this task.

For many progressives, the lesson to be drawn from the current economic crisis is that market liberalism has gone too far, "markets need to be re-embedded!" (Dale 2010a: 207). What this means both conceptually and practically is not straightforward. Nor is it clear which is the ethos that might do the work of re-embedding, though human rights are frequently invoked (Blau and Moncada 2005; Burawoy 2006; Sjoberg et al. 2001; Somers 2008; Turner 2006). In this chapter I begin by surveying some of the current debates on the meaning of "embeddedness", which are organised as a seemingly enduring cleavage between embeddedness understood as the enmeshment of all markets in social and institutional figurations, and market society as an institutional arrangement that disembeds the economy from society. I try to demonstrate that it is not only possible, but also desirable to overcome this cleavage—to disembed the embedded/disembedded opposition.

Equally I show that a potential shortcoming of the embedded markets scholarship is that rather surprisingly it threatens to make markets disappears from the analysis. This, I argue, is to be avoided to preserve the conceptual and practical insights associated with Polanyi's work. Following this, I draw heuristically on David Lockwood's social/system integration model (Lockwood 1964) to summarise the arguments developed throughout the chapter. I then move on to briefly discuss human rights, suggesting that Polanyian-inspired social scientists, and others for that matter, who champion them, need to critically consider the social technologies and arrangements through which human rights as a normative ideal is or might be embedded.

The Embeddedness of the Embedded/ Disembedded Opposition

It is challenging to diagnose the current health and vitality of protective countermovements. This is largely due to the capaciousness of the term countermovement:

> a sprawling smorgasbord of policies, movements and institutions [come together] under the rubric of "protective response", with some cheering the alterglobalization movement for attempting to reassert social control over the market economy while others applaud its adversaries—imperialist states, capitalist corporations and stockbrokers—on exactly the same grounds. (Dale 2010a: 219)

"Countermovement"'s referential breadth is linked to the ambiguity of its cognate term "embeddedness". In a number of contributions (2010a; 2010b; 2011; 2012), Dale has shown that there are fundamentally two competing conceptions of embeddedness. In the first, economic actions and processes are conceived as inherently being enmeshed in noneconomic institutions; "the economy" is thereby conceptualised "as a subsystem 'embedded in' a social system" (Dale 2011: 1). In the second, the market economy is posited as generating a logic that actually disembeds the "economy" from "society". In this second instance, "society's" ability to govern and regulate the "economy" is eroded and the relationship between the two is inverted insofar as the "economy" is understood to increasingly fashion "society" in its own image. In the earlier case of embeddedness, that is, denoting the economy as a social subsystem, the operation of the market does not threaten its social basis, and it is possible, given the right conditions, to align the market with the social good. This is not the situation with its nemesis because the market economy is impervious to social tethering.

This conceptual schism is in turn aligned with two interpretations of "countermovements or protective movements" that hinge on whether a "hard" or "soft" Polanyi is invoked (Szelényi cited in Dale 2010b: 370). In the case of the former, Polanyi is understood as standing for "a socialist mixed economy dominated by redistributive mechanisms" and as embracing a radical socialist option in which "the market could not remain and should never be the dominant mechanism of economic coordination" (Dale 2010b: 370). In this scenario, countermovements or protective movements refer to social movements or political processes that aim to markedly curtail the steering power of the market economy, defending society while encouraging a context conducive to a transition to socialism. However, enter on stage the persona of the soft Polanyi. The market's centrality as a steering mechanism is not disputed; it is merely supplemented by redistributive mechanisms that prophylactically protect society by tempering the inevitable inequalities produced by the operation of the market. The countermovement or protective movement then becomes identified with "the social democratic mainstream for which the only goal that is both realistic and desirable is a regulated form of capitalism" (Dale 2010b: 270). Given the range of possibilities between these two positions, Polanyian notions of embeddedness and countermovement or protective movements indeed offer a conceptual smorgasbord capable of feeding the most diverse of appetites!

An attempt to move beyond the ambiguity associated with the notion of embeddedness has been proposed by Fred Block (2003). He argues that the writing of *The Great Transformation* is structured by the antagonism between two theoretical conceptions of the economy: a Marxist one and a nascent notion of "the always embedded market" (2003: 298). He claims the latter as Polanyi's most significant legacy, upon which Block subsequently builds (2007; Somers and Block 2005; Block and Somers 2014). It is true, Block concedes, that despite discovering the idea of the "always embedded market economy", Polanyi is not able to name his discovery (2003: 298). All the same, Block maintains, in a manner reminiscent of Althusser's thesis of the break between the young Hegelian and the later scientific Marx (Althusser 1969), that *The Great Transformation* represents a decisive conceptual and epistemological break from the assumptions of both market liberals and Marxists. Both of those were, says Block, ensnared by a conception of the economy as an "analytically autonomous [sphere] subject to its own internal logic" (2003: 282). Block contends that Polanyi's decisive contribution is the realisation that "even in market societies, ways have to be found to embed labor, land and money in social relations" (2003: 282).

Dale, conversely, argues that Block overstates the novelty of the "always embedded economy" thesis: after all, both the Scottish and German Historical Schools had formulated kindred notions from which Polanyi himself drew (2010b: 383). Equally, Dale maintains that Block's dismissal of Marx's sophisticated understanding of the relationship between social and economic processes is unconvincing (2010b: 383). Perhaps more significant, however, is Block's failure to account for another key influence on Polanyi's thought, whose central concepts were subject to the same type of undecidability: Ferdinand Tönnies and his seminal opposition between *Gemeinschaft* and *Gesellschaft* (Dale 2010b: 384). The former refers to a configuration of social existence characterized by small-scale, face-to-face relationships in which individuals "oriented to the purposes of their group, make its ends their own" (Dale 2011: 309). In contrast, the latter captures a social organisation whose elementary fact "is the act of exchange ... performed by individuals who are alien to each other, have nothing in common with each other" (Tönnies 1971: 76–77).

Dale's contention is not only that Polanyi's embedded/disembedded distinction is inherited from the *Gemeinschaft/Gesellschaft* couplet. He adds that the distinction, in Tönnies and in Polanyi, is ambiguous insofar as it can be understood in a descriptive sense capturing an empirical reality (communal society versus market society), or as an ideal type (the relative weight of one or the other in a given society) (2010b, 2011). Confusingly, both authors invoke one or the other, seemingly oblivious to the slippage between the two.

Dale unravels the different lineages of embeddedness by placing them in the intellectual context of their development and the manner in which they have been rewoven into new patterns. This is illuminating, as is his thoughtful consideration of the evidence for and against the "soft" and "hard" Polanyi (Dale 2010a, b). Dale sharpens our understanding of what the real world referents of the notion of protective movements might be. Finally, acknowledging that Polanyi's Marxist roots weakened as his work progressed, he shows that for all that, Polanyi remained a radical socialist, "committed to the replacement of capitalism by a socialist order" (2010b: 390; Block and Somers 2014: 221). This said, in limiting himself to the sources upon which Polanyi drew in developing the concept of embeddedness and cataloguing current uses (Dale 2011: 333–334), he puts aside the decisive issue of what to do with the contending understandings of "embeddedness".

Frozen or Liquid Embeddedness?

Drawing on other commentators, Dale notes (2011: 311) that a disembedded economy cannot reasonably be understood as referring to the chimera of an economic sphere that is not instituted by and through social relations, or to use the term Block borrowed from Polanyi, "a stark utopia" (Block 2003: 8). This much Polanyi would have learnt from the German Historical School and, despite Block's protestations, from Marx as well. Instead, "disembedded" should be grasped as a mode of embeddedness, particular to market societies, that paradoxically ejects individuals from a shared moral community. This, following Dale, would bring to the fore Polanyi's preoccupation with the conditions of ethical life in market societies and his intellectual debt to Tönnies. If following Zygmunt Bauman (1993), we take individual responsibility for the Other as the hallmark of morality, then disembedding can be linked to the realisation that "[n]either modern organization or modern business promotes morality; if anything, they make a life of a stubbornly moral person tough and unrewarding" (Bauman 1994: 10). In other words, it is the enmeshment of individuals in modern social relations and institutions, embeddedness in Block's sense of the term, that dislodges them from their social responsibility for others, thwarting a sense of shared collective life.

For Polanyi the question is how society's social institutions can be shaped so that individuals embedded within them can be free, indeed, encouraged to live moral lives:

> *How can we be free, in spite of the fact of society?* And not *in our imagination only*, not by abstracting ourselves from society, denying the fact of our being interwoven with the lives of others … but in reality, by aiming at making society as transparent as a family's life is, so that I may achieve a state of things in which I have done my duty towards *all men*, and so be *free* again, in decency, with good consciousness (Polanyi cited in Dale 2010a: 31, emphasis in original).

As Dale shows, one of the ways in which Polanyi sought to work out this contextualised ethical question took the form of his active participation in the early twentieth-century socialist accounting debates against the Austrian School. Polanyi argued for the desirability of social mechanisms that would allow individuals to put themselves in the situation of others, "empathising with their needs and *Arbeitsleid* [hardship of labour]" (Polanyi in Dale 2010a: 23). This was becoming increasingly impossible within the institutional confines of market society, as it existed then. Additionally, glossing Tönnies, Polanyi thought possible "a restoration of community" (Polanyi cited in Dale 2010a: 33), not as a return to a romantic past through the rejection of social and technological progress, an idea often erroneously also attributed to Tönnies (Cahnman and Heberle 1971: xiv), but "as a kind of cooperative phase of civilization that would retain the advantages of technological progress and individual freedom while restoring the wholeness of life" (Polanyi in Dale 2010a: 33). Subsequently, the question of the conditions for a socially instituted ethical life took a different form. At the time of writing *The Great Transformation*, following the defeat of fascism, it was the Soviet Union, Clement Attlee's Britain and the American New Deal, harbingers of a generalised transition to socialism, that seemed to provide the seeds from which new forms of community would emerge and modes of ethical life blossom (Dale 2010b: 386).

This aspect of embeddedness seems inaudible in a conceptual register that refers to the generic manner in which economic activities unfold and that Block's account of Polanyi employs, when he writes that:

even when there have been the most determined ideological efforts to build an economy based on self-regulating markets, economic activity continues to be embedded in legal, cultural, and political frameworks that are critically necessary for economic activity to continue. (Block 2007: 5)

There is a normative timbre missing here, one that Margaret Somers, Blocks' sometimes coauthor on matters Polanyian (Block and Somers 1984; Somers and Block 2005; Block and Somers 2014), captures in her Polanyian-inspired Arendtian reading of the Marshallian conception of citizenship as the "right to human personhood—recognition as a moral equal, that is—endowed by full inclusion in a social and political body" (2008: 25), which I return to, as follows. As a consequence of Block's commitment to the notion that Polanyi's great conceptual contribution is that of "the always embedded market", he argues that there can be no such thing as a disembedded market (Block 2007).

However, in arguing thus, Block silences another vital dimension of disembeddedness, namely as social processes and practices through which members of a society are denied the recognition that enables them to participate in that society as full members and as moral agents in their own right—embedded markets can be disembedding. This, as Dale establishes, is also a critical dimension of Polanyian thought. Suggestively, as already remarked, this mode of thinking about embeddedness emerges in the work of Margaret Somers, as a return of the repressed, but under a different guise.

Disembeddedness need not be opposed to embeddedness; it can, instead, be conceptualised as being nestled within it. The tendency to oppose embeddedness to disembeddedness not only encourages the choice of one or the other, inhibiting explorations of how the two can be intertwined, it also seems to foreclose its conceptual development. Embeddedness' theoretical importance appears to rest in its ability to act as a placeholder in the opposition, keeping at bay all species of market essentialism. Consequently, the need to theoretically "drill down" into embeddedness to explore the network of analytic concepts it might command, and the range of phenomena to which they might be applied, is obviated. Embeddedness remains frozen in place; were it to take liquid form, it would irrigate a larger theoretical landscape. Indeed, Block recognises this when he insists on the necessity of "moving beyond this strategic deployment of [Polanyi's] eloquence" (2007: 4).

Embedding Markets Until They Disappear

Given that embeddedness's *raison d'être* is to offer a more complex understanding of market societies than is available from market liberals and Marxists, allegedly both market essentialists in their own ways, it is worth accentuating that often its deployment, in truth, may actually evacuate markets from the analysis. This is because the notion of the social embeddedness of markets frequently congeals in an intuitive, taken-for-granted form (Krippner in Dale 2010a: 198). Even when there is an effort to make the embedded market the object of analysis, the "marketness" of the embedded market has a way of receding from view, as illustrated by Block's Neo-Polanyian analysis of American market society (Block 2007), to which I now turn.

In exploring the divergence between the trajectory of American and Western European market societies, Block argues that in contrast to the latter, where support for the welfare state has been maintained, in the USA it has been decimated, as a result of social and political realignments provoked by responses to events in the 1970s. Block explores the significant structuring of, and intervention in, the market by the American state. More notably he shows how business elites' allegiance for Keynesianism and the welfare state was politically and institutionally held in place in the postwar period and subsequently abraded over time due to post-seventy alliances with market fundamentalists and the religious right (Block 2007). As in any situation of hegemony, naturally this did not mean that in the pre-seventies era, business class resistance was entirely absent (Phillips-Fein 2010). The neo-Polanyian pedigree of the analysis is established through four theses: 1) "Market Economies are Always and Everywhere Embedded" (Block 2007: 5), 2) "Market Societies and the Contemporary World Economy Have Been Shaped by an Ongoing Double Movement" (Block 2007: 6), 3) "The Interests of Employers Vary over Time and Space, but they Play a Critical Role in Shaping the Development of Market Societies" (Block 2007: 8), and 4) "Competition among Nations within the World Economy Tends to Produce New Variations in the Structuring of Economic Institutions" (Block 2007: 8).

Published a year before the 2008 financial crisis, Block was not in a position to appreciate the ease with which European business elites and governments would abandon their welfare state commitments, and the religious fervour with which they would flagellate their populations with austerity in the name of market fundamentalism (Blyth 2013). Admittedly Block explicitly omits the European component of the analysis. Had he not, perhaps it might have been possible to identify the stress points that have given way to the seemingly implacable austerian wave buffeting the continent.

Underpinning Block's analysis are two components. The first is that the struggle to embed the market takes place on the terrain of the state between business, most often the elite sector, and society. The interaction is conceptualised via the heuristic of the double movement. As market liberals push to reorganise society around the idea of the self-regulating market, protective countermovements push back "to protect society from the consequences of market liberal policies" (Block 2007: 7). Countermovements are varied and rooted in differing cultural formations, historicities and scales. Their success and scope are contingent and they need not be progressive, for example, Fascism. The strength and path of the pendular swing between movement and countermovement crystallises the different social and political alignments and the institutional frameworks that embed markets, explaining their tendency to diverge. The second component is one that is implicit in the analysis, but that Somers and Block developed in a brilliant illustration of comparative historical methodology (Somers and Block 2005), and have recently expanded further (Block and Somers 2014), namely the causal force of ideas. It is worth exploring this in more detail because it is crucial for understanding the significance of Block and Somers' contribution to the debates on the embeddedness of the market.

Taking two different historically situated cases of welfare revolutions, The *1996 Personal Responsibility and Work Opportunities Reconciliation Act* in the USA and England's *Poor Law Amendment Act of 1834*, they argue that despite significant variance between the two, both eventuated in sweeping welfare reform (the dependent variable) and can be accounted for by the ideational causal power of market fundamentalism (the independent variable). Somers and Block position themselves as sympathetically critiquing economic sociologists who, to date, have limited their "institutionalist imagination to the standard legal, political and organizational structures of embeddedness" (2005: 264). Pushing beyond this, they propose the notion of "ideational embeddedness", broadening the notion of embeddedness to encompass "the ideas, public narratives, and explanatory systems by which states, societies and political cultures construct, transform, explain and normalize market processes" (2005: 264). Shifting explanatory weight to ideational causality does not, however, entail a commitment to the causal efficacy of all knowledge regimes: "Ideas matter. But equally important is that all ideas are not created equal. Only some ideas can exercise the causal power to undermine, dislodge, and replace a previously dominant ideational regime" (Somers and Block 2005: 265).

Somers and Block contend that market fundamentalism is an ideational species that has displayed remarkable vigour and thrived in what might have been characterised as inhospitable habitats, demonstrating a schizophrenic adeptness at both claiming scientificity while scorning empirical evidence of its inadequacy. In Somers and Block's terminology it has acquired an "epistemic privilege"; truth claims are internal to its knowledge production practices. The question remains, what is the epistemological make up of this astonishingly adaptive ideational species? Three features are identified: social naturalism, theoretical realism, and a conversion narrative. The first posits the efficacy of natural laws in human society. This results in a depoliticisation of the economy (2005: 271). The second refers to an antiscopic epistemological regime that asserts that reality is better grasped by reference to unobservable entities that exist as theoretical postulates apprehended deductively, for example, laws of human nature (2005: 272). Finally, the third points to a narratively based, highly normative mode of persuasion that discredits existing ideational regimes. Removing the "veil" that occludes the "true causes" of misery or poverty, the narrative reveals the "one and only truth" (2005: 274). Somers and Block's claim is not that market fundamentalism's social efficacy derives solely from its ideational make up. Rather, they understand it to supplement scholarship dealing with "the role of partisanship, economic resources and political institutions in shaping outcomes" (2005: 282 fn18).

Returning to the disappearance of "marketness", Block's analysis of the specificity of the USA's post-seventies trajectory (Block 2007) takes as given the epistemic privilege of market fundamentalism to explore the historical context and the political and cultural alignments that market fundamentalism enable, and with which market fundamentalism becomes entangled. This is, without a doubt, an important contribution to our understanding of the agents and historical circumstances that have given market fundamentalism social and political traction. However, in putting such overwhelming emphasis on embeddedness, the very notion of marketness is drained of significance.

To be clear, I wholeheartedly endorse Somers and Block's emphasis on the causal efficacy of ideas, the significance of political, social and cultural figurations, as well as their diversity and mutability, as necessary components in the analysis of market activities.[1] However, this glosses over the specificity of markets as patterned modes of social interaction and the manner in which marketness articulates with modes of embeddedness. This is not a question of the autonomy of the market. Ontologically, empirically, and historically we are always invariably confronting the always embedded market, in Somers and Block's sense of the term. This is not in dispute. Analytically, however, it should be possible to pull out the relational material practices that loosely couple, to use the expression Block deploys (2007: 7), with the processes that embed them, both at the level of the organisation and patterning of everyday interactions, and at the larger scale of institutional structures. For example, we can all agree that education and markets are both embedded. What makes patterned social activity educational versus market activity? The fact that this question may be rapidly approaching its expiry date makes the question even more urgent.

Ignoring the specificity of the economy as a set of changing and contradictory material relations leads to a flat and impoverished social ontology.

---

[1] That said I prefer the more comprehensive and analytically more fecund term of economic rather than market activities.

Block and Somers make fundamental contributions to our understanding of the macroembeddedness of markets, as recent developments in science studies (Callon 1998; Callon and Muniesa 2005; MacKenzie et al. 2007) and governmentality (Dean 2010; Rose and Miller 1992; Waters 1999) draw our attention to the practices, performances and mentalities through which the microembeddedness of markets is secured. Such scholarship usefully moves us away from reified and naturalised conceptions of the economy and its categories. However, as Bob Jessop and Stijn Oosterlynck argue, they can lead to "a soft economic sociology that focuses on the similarities between economic and other socio-cultural activities at the expense of the specificity of the economic" (2006: 1155). This is another way of saying that the marketness of embedded markets disappears or is ousted from the analysis.

Invoking material relations raises the spectre that one is shackled with some species of economic determinism or essentialism. Here it is difficult not to agree with Dale when he argues that Block, for instance, relies on a perfunctory dismissal of Marx as an economic essentialist (Dale 2010b: 383). This attitude is regrettably well-established and unreflexively reproduced in the social sciences. It exceeds the scope of this chapter to address this issue, but it is worth noting that a careful reading of volume one of Marx's *Capital* yields numerous conceptual tools for thinking both about the macro and micro-embedding of economic practices, while providing relational tools for understanding their contradictory relationship. In doing so, it not only draws our attention to how capitalist markets are embedded differently compared to previous market figurations but also, and significantly, it attempts to identify the specificity of the material relations that make up capitalism, without simplistically requiring that all capitalist markets converge. Read analytically, it is not the site of a determinist reading of the economy; it can provide a far-reaching understanding of the corestructure of capitalism, as demonstrated by the path-breaking work of Moishe Postone (1993).

Moreover, as Bob Jessop and his colleagues have shown through their work on Cultural Political Economy (Jessop 2013), it is possible to seriously contemplate the causal efficacy of ideas and social institutions while remaining open to the prospect of relationally attaching them to the material practices that give economic activity or markets their specificity. For Jessop, the economy is not a predetermined homogenous entity, but rather a heterogeneous, uneven and frequently contradictory amalgam of material and semiotic practices. "Economic imaginaries" seek to define economic phenomena, inevitably excluding some economic activities, in order to make the economy an effective object of calculation, management and governance (2013: 236). The object that economic imaginaries attempt to govern is made up of varied economic relations (Jessop 2013: 236).

The decisive point with respect to our discussion of Block and Somers, and the expulsion of marketness from the analysis of embeddedness more generally, is that one can accommodate loose coupling, contingency, narrativity, ideational causality, variation, and so on without reneging on the challenge of linking such phenomena to the relational interaction of the ideational and material that is specific to economic activities. As Jessop argues, if economic imaginaries "are to prove more than 'arbitrary, rationalistic, and willed' [they] must have some significant, albeit necessarily partial, fit with real material interdependencies in the actually existing economy and/or in the relations among economic and extra-economic activities" (Jessop 2013: 236). Thus, in the loose coupling that happens in the market, in addition to the epistemic privilege, economic resources, partisanship and political institutions one must certainly also take account of material relations. This is indispensable to preserve the marketness of the embedded market as an analytical feature. In other words, attention needs to be paid to what is being embedded. What is its specificity, what is its range and mode of variation? Absent these questions, then marketness risks becoming a timeless and infinitely plastic feature of social organisation, which is surely not the desired outcome of the theoretical and empirical turn towards embedded markets.

Return of the Repressed

In the previous section I argued that Block's commitment to the idea that Polanyi's great contribution is the discovery of the always embedded market has led him to regard the notion of disembeddedness in relation to the market as a *non sequitur*. Consequently, an alternative conceptual declension of embeddedness whose archaeology Dale has traced is not available to Block, namely embeddedness as the social processes and institutions through which individuals are recognised and incorporated as full-fledged members in a social and moral community. In this second declension of embeddedness, the always embedded market can in fact lead to disembedding, as Margaret Somers compellingly illustrates, but without recourse to the Polanyian vernacular. Somers shares Block's aversion to the idea of aligning the notion of the market with the prospect of disembedding (Somers and Block 2005: 280; Block and Somers 2014: 219). Be that as it may, her account, and defence, of citizenship, despite or perhaps because of its Arendtian and Marshallian tonalities, resonates with Polanyi's concern with identifying the social processes and institutions that embed individuals by interweaving their lives with those of the members of their political and social community, enabling recognition and establishing the grounds for social reciprocity (Polanyi cited in Dale 2010a: 31).

Somers characterises citizenship as "the life-blood of social solidarity in civil society and political communities comprised of noncontractual membership rights, relationships, and reciprocal responsibilities" (Somers 2008: 79). Successful citizenship whose practices are located in civil society requires that the latter's power be carefully calibrated vis-à-vis the state and market (2008: 2). In addition, the civil sphere itself is no assurance of inclusion: "Because it is comprised of inclusive democratic structures *and* repressive vilifications, of practices of solidarity as well of those of exclusion, the civil sphere is where citizenship, solidarity, and justice are possible, but by no means inevitable" (2008: 30 emphasis in original). As many scholars have shown, the relational structure of citizenship can be such that modes of inclusion generate their opposites (Bosniak 2006; Brown 1993; Fraser and Gordon 1992; Fraser 2012; Young 1989). Consequently, though "citizenship is the language of civil society, it is a language built as much on the dark side of exclusion and even dehumanization at it is on inclusion and solidarity" (Somers 2008: 69).

In a brilliant analysis of "the left behind" (Somers 2008: 99) in New Orleans in the wake of Katrina—though their status as the left behind

preceded Katrina and was merely dramatized by the event (2008: 67)—
Somers reworks Bosniak's conception of the "alien" as citizen (2006) to
show that individuals who are formally citizens can confront an internal border that leads to their exclusion. Moreover, whereas in the aftermath of Katrina, Michael Ignatieff had claimed, not without shock and
disbelief, that "When the levees broke, the contract of American citizenship failed" (Ignatieff cited in Somers 2008: 66), Somers argues that
it is precisely the injection of the language of contract into the ethos
of citizenship that produces the unequivocal exclusion made visible by
Katrina in New Orleans: "Contract is the problem, not the solution"
(Somers 2008: 71).

Developing a subtle and penetrating analysis that cannot be adequately
conveyed here, Somers shows how the contractualisation of citizenship
dramatically inflects the ethos of citizenship through the privatisation of
basic needs such as health care and retirement (2008: 80). Marketization
becomes the lens through which all manner of social phenomena are
framed and organised, culminating in the metamorphosis of the citizen into a container of human capital (2008: 108), while retrenchment
comes hand in hand with increasingly punitive disciplinary regimes
(2008: 111). The consequences of the colonisation of citizenship by contractualisation are enormous:

> In a non-contractual relationship, as long as a citizen meets the required
> obligations, she is presumed an equal member of equal worth regardless of
> the market value attached to her citizenly responsibilities. But when citi-
> zenship has been contractualized, failing to provide a good or service of
> equivalent market value in exchange for what is now the *privilege* of citizen-
> ship results in a reduction of the moral worth of the citizen. And depend-
> ing on the degree and frequency and quality of such failures to meet
> contractual criteria, there will be an increasing refusal to recognize the
> citizen as deserving of membership altogether in the political and social
> community. (Somers 2008: 89, emphasis in original)

Here we have an illustration of how a particular modality of market
embeddedness (market fundamentalism) produces social processes and
dynamics (contractual citizenship) that in effect disembed individuals

from a political and social community, depriving them in, the Arendtian formulation, of the "right to have rights" (Somers 2008: 5). Embeddedness and disembeddedness are not mutually exclusive conceptual terms; used in tandem, the explanatory focus of embeddedness is magnified.

Somers does not set out to reconcile the two conceptual declensions of embeddedness introduced by Polanyi, but the fact that, on my reading, she does is highly suggestive. Because she is working in the conceptual terrain opened up by her Polanyian muse (Somers 2008: 50), the appearance of embeddedness through the mediation of citizenship, as the socially instituted processes and institutions enabling an individual's inclusion in a social and political community, resonates with Dale's persuasive recovery of this second declension of embeddedness. If this is the case, Polanyi's contribution is not restricted to the discovery of the "always embedded market" but to the more profound and complex realisation, illustrated by Somers, that modes of embedding markets can lead to the disembedding or ejection of individuals from their social and political communities, depriving them of their right to have rights.

Embedding Embeddedness: Human Rights as an "Instituted Process"

The contemporary popularity of Polanyi's work as a mode of understanding the rise of market liberalism, in the last 40 years, has eventuated, as seenherein, in the fairly ubiquitous, though polysemic, prescription that markets need to be re-embedded. Currently it is the ethos of human rights that is frequently invoked to re-embed and tame the market liberalism of global capitalism (Armaline, Glasberg & Purkayastha 2015; Blau and Moncada 2005; Burawoy 2006; Sjoberg et al. 2001; Turner 2006). Thus far, I have attempted to demonstrate that unpacking the ambiguity attached to embeddedness requires disembedding the term from the embedded/disembedded opposition, in which it appears frozen, to explore its multiple declensions. In this section, I draw on a model proposed by the late David Lockwood, that is, social/system integration

(Lockwood 1964), to first summarise the chapter's arguments but also to generate analytical and political questions that the championing of human rights, to my mind, should raise.

Although the terms "system" and "integration", for many contemporary social scientists, have a theoretical ring of a bygone era, the analytical space they stake out usefully accommodates the two declensions of embeddedness and their interrelations explored in this chapter. This is perhaps not surprising, a student of T.H. Marshall at the LSE, Lockwood sought to overcome the unproductive debate between Parsonians and Conflict theorists—that is Ralf Dahrendorf and Jon Rex (Lockwood 1964), and to wed together the insights of Marx, Weber and Durkheim to understand the interplay between citizenship and the status system (Lockwood 1992).

By social integration, Lockwood understands the "orderly or conflictual" processes and institutions through which individuals are related to one another in society, while system integration refers to the "orderly or conflictual" relationships between the "parts" of society or the social system (Lockwood 1964: 245). Lockwood wanted to draw attention to the fact that so-called consensus and conflict theorists were arguing about two different analytical conceptions of integration (or conflict) as if they were just one. I think something similar is structuring the embedded-disembedded cleavage. Embeddedness of markets is understood as the enmeshment of markets in institutional and organisational structures; Block and Somers' always-embedded markets refers to a "systems" view of embeddedness. The second declension of embeddedness, meanwhile, draws attention to *processes and institutions through which individuals are incorporated into social and political communities.* My intent here is not suggest that we must reclaim the conceptual vocabulary of the social/system integration couplet, but that it is a good heuristic for understanding how we might disembed the seemingly irreconcilable embedded/disembedded opposition, and start thinking about their articulation.

Another insight provided by Lockwood's framework is that it draws attention to the need to embed embeddedness both at the broad level of institutional and organisational structure, but also at the level of the incorporation/nonincorporation of individuals as full members of a social and political community. Although Lockwood had some sympathy with the Parsonian analytical focus at the level of the system, he contended that the normative bias was unsustainable due to its exclusion of Marxist contributions as well as its overwhelmingly normative reading of Weber. No Marxist, Lockwood nonetheless asserted the importance of thinking about the material relations and famously provided a material reading of Weber's analysis of patrimonial bureaucracy (Lockwood 1964). The material reading took account of both institutional patterning and its relationship to the everyday lived experience or ethos.

As I have suggested, the importance of the contributions made by scholarship on embedded markets would be appreciably debilitated were it to bring about the disappearance of the marketness of the embedded market. Thus it is important to leave conceptual and empirical space to embed the embeddedness of the market in material relations. The fruitfulness of such an approach can be appreciated in the pioneering work of cultural political economy (Jessop 2009). The need to embed embeddedness, however, equally holds for the second declension of the latter—that is, integration of individuals in social and political communities.

Somers argues that citizenship (the second declension of embeddedness in terms of my analysis) must be understood as an "instituted process" because it is "at heart a matrix of institutional relationships, technologies, political idioms and rights-claiming practices that are always dynamic and contingent" (2008: 35). An empirical analysis of what this involves is provided in what is, to my mind, one of the most significant yet not sufficiently appreciated contributions to citizenship studies, Somers' 1994 *Rights, Relationality and Membership: Rethinking the Making and Meaning of Citizenship*. There is no doubt that citizenship, or other modalities for the embedding of individuals in social and political communities, relies on a strong normative element. However, it is important to analyse the social, cultural, and political relations and processes that provide certain normativities with their social traction and efficacy—something that Somers does admirably in the just mentioned article. What kind of normative life is enabled or obstructed? In other words, what are the features of a specific instituted process underwriting its normative privilege?

Inspired by Somers' notion of citizenship as an instituted process, in my work on human rights generally and the historical emergence of the human right to food more specifically, I attempt to develop a sociological conception of human rights that sees them not as a moral ideal, a global ethic, or an emerging international legal standard but as an instituted Political Imaginary (López 2015; 2016). This is partly a reaction to the widespread invocation of a normative turn toward human rights in the social sciences (Armaline, Glasberg & Purkayastha 2015; Blau and Moncada 2005; Burawoy 2006; Sjoberg et al. 2001; Somers 2008; Stammers 2009; Turner 2006), to which I am not opposed on normative or political grounds but which, on my reading, does not devote sufficient sociological attention to the historical processes through which human rights have become embedded as the powerful normative ethos of our times.

Social science scholars who champion human rights frequently do so because they understand that under the right political conditions these can be made legally binding and socially efficacious (Mittal and Rosset 1999; Blau and Moncada 2005; Blau and Frezzo 2012; Shafir and Brysk 2006; Turner 2006; Woodiwiss 2005). Others see in the struggle to realise human rights the most recent manifestations of historically ongoing struggles for justice, equality and dignity (Armaline, Glasberg & Purkayastha; Stammers 2009). In yet other instances, the emphasis is on the normative or moral power of human rights (Friesen 2015; Elliot 2007; Somers 2008; Turner 2006). While I do not discount the potential effectiveness of human rights' legal forms nor their indisputable normative persuasiveness, I would suggest that, for the most part, social scientists who champion human rights have not given sufficient attention to the processes that underpin their modern genesis, legal utility or their normative privilege.[2] Said differently, perhaps drawn in by the moral persuasiveness of human rights, they are not sufficiently concerned with conceptually understanding how they are embedded and the type of embedding that they enable.

To return to Lockwood's model, at the level of systems integration, human rights' aptness to embed individuals in meaningful social and political communities, thereby counteracting the disembedding produced by contemporary capitalist forms of market embeddedness, is going to depend on human rights' ability to dislodge the epistemic privilege of market fundamentalism and its associated institutional frameworks. However, with-

---

[2] I do, however, question the wisdom of looking for the precursors of human rights in earlier historical struggles for justice because as I argue elsewhere, we fail to analytically capture the historical and social specificity of human rights (López 2015).

out understanding the specificity of the material relations that constitute the economic it is difficult to judge whether human rights will be able to establish the "partial fit" necessary to successfully embed economic practices. Normative and legal high ground will not suffice. Indeed, the broad smorgasbord of possible Polanyian countermovements and their inherent normativities, notedherein, is related to competing understandings of the material relations that constitute the market or the economy. Part of the reason why "not all ideas are created equal", is because not all ideas can successfully pattern and mould material relations, of the economy in this context, and command the necessary institutional resources. Understanding the "marketness" of contemporary economic relations is crucial for gauging the success of human rights' ability to embed them.

Seen from the perspectives of social integration, indubitably, normative appeal and the force of the law are crucial for the integration of individuals in political and social communities. However, the social efficacy of normative and legal persuasion depends on the existence of representations, social technologies, modes of agency and subjectivity and concrete organisational forms, what I elsewhere call a political imaginary (López 2015; 2016). To use the language developed in this chapter: how are human rights embedded and what type of embedding do they enable?

My own research on the emergence of the human right to food (López 2015) leads me to argue that that human rights are most socially efficacious and command moral commitment when situations of injustice can be schematically, pragmatically, and prescriptively rendered as "violations". Obligations are known, duties defined, and remedies are available. Actors are unequivocally assigned to the categories of victims, witnesses, or perpetrators with the irrefutable obligations of claiming their human rights, advocating for human rights, and introducing appropriate remedies respectively. Despite the contemporary readings of the human right to food that trace it back to the relevant articles of the Universal Declaration of Human Rights and The Covenant on Economics, Social and Cultural Rights, the historical reality is that it was not until the mid-1990s that it became possible to talk about hunger as a human rights violation. This was not so much due to the post-ColdWar thaw as much as the collapse of the two post-World War II political imaginaries that had defined hunger through developmentalism and humanitarianism (López 2015).

Human rights are more powerful when they can be positioned as being above politics (through factual modes of recording violations, an unambiguous distinction between perpetrator and victim, and clear and measureable remedies). In their take-off period in the late 1960s and early 1970s, as Samuel Moyn has compellingly argued, this was achieved by framing human rights as new form of "antipolitics—a politics in a moral register that apparently transcended politics for which Amnesty International was the exemplar (Moyn 2010). Whether human rights can maintain their efficacy as they become entangled with politics and be bent to the arc of a broader and more substantive community is an open question, but its answer must surely pass through an understanding of human rights as an instituted process, or in my terms as a political imaginary. Echoing the Polanyi quotation introduced above, in the context of human rights this might mean posing the question of how human rights might enable us to be free not just in our social "imagination" but in our social "reality" as well.

Conclusion

I would like to conclude by moderating the apparent pessimism with which I started this chapter, and then draw out what I believe is the key substantive conceptual and political conclusion to be drawn from my discussion. It will be recalled, that in the introduction, I noted that a number of contributors had been dismayed at the manner in which the most significant economic crisis since the 1930s not only did not undermine "neoliberalism" but in fact contributed to strengthening its hand.

One should not move too quickly to trumpet the burial of the progressive transformative opportunities associated with the 2008 economic crisis and the pathologies of capitalism more generally. To be sure, a volume such as this one is premised on the hope, even if gingerly held, that transformative opportunities have not entirely been foreclosed.[3]

---

[3] We might take note of the rise to power of Syriza in Greece, the emergence of Podemos in Spain, the election of Jeremy Corbyn as leader of the Labour Party in Britain, and the waves being created by Bernie Sanders in the US Democratic Primaries, and perhaps more importantly the many examples from the Global South, specifically South America (Stahler-Sholk, Vanden and Kuecker 2007).

What might movements trying to make good on these opportunities draw from Polanyi's notion of embeddedness? To my mind, it is the following. The challenge is not merely to embed markets, but to embed them in such a way that they simultaneously reinforce the embedding of individuals in social and political communities. Analytically and politically, these tasks are considerably more challenging but potentially more fruitful and equitable respectively.

References

Althusser, L. (1969). *For Marx*. London: Allen Lane Penguin.
Armaline, W. T., Glasbergm, D. S., & Purkayastha (2015). *The human rights enterprise*. Cambridge: Polity.
Bauman, Z. (1993). *Postmodern ethics*. Oxford: Wiley-Blackwell.
Bauman, Z. (1994). *Alone again: Ethics after uncertainty*. London: Demos.
Blau, J., & Moncada, A. (2005). *Human rights: Beyond the liberal vision*. Lanham: Rowan and Littlefield.
Blau, J., & Frezzo, M. (2012). *Sociology and human rights*. Los Angeles and London: Sage.
Block, F. (2003). Karl Polanyi and the writing of The Great Transformation. *Theory and Society, 32*, 275–306.
Block, F. (2007). Understanding the diverging trajectories of the United States and Western Europe: A neo-polanyian analysis. *Politics and Society, 35*(1), 3–33.
Block, F., & Somers, M. (1984). Beyond the economistic fallacy: The holistic social science of Karl Polanyi. In T. Skockpol (Ed.), *Vision and method in historical sociology* (pp. 47–84). Cambridge: Cambridge University Press.
Block, F., & Somers, M. (2014). *The power of market fundamentalism: Karl Polanyi's critique*. Cambridge: Harvard University Press.
Blyth, M. (2013). *Austerity: A history of a dangerous idea*. Oxford: Oxford University Press.
Bosniak, L. (2006). *The citizenship and the alien: Dilemmas of contemporary citizenship*. Princeton: Princeton University Press.
Brown, W. (1993). Wounded attachments. *Political Theory, 21*(3), 390–410.
Burawoy, M. (2006). Introduction: A public sociology for human rights. In J. Blau & K. Smith (Eds.), *Public sociologies reader* (pp. 1–18). Lanham: Rowan and Littlefield.
Callon, M. (1998). *The laws of the markets*. Oxford: Blackwell.
Callon, M. (2005). Economic markets as calculative collective devices. *Organization Studies, 26*(8), 1229–1250.

Cahnman, W. J., & Heberle, R. (1971). Introduction. In F. Tönnies (Ed.), *On sociology: Pure, applied and empirical* (pp. vii–xxii). Chicago: University of Chicago Press.

Dale, G. (2010a). *Karl Polanyi*. Cambridge: Polity.

Dale, G. (2010b). Social democracy, embeddedness and decommodification: On the conceptual innovations and intellectual affiliations of Karl Polanyi. *New Political Economy, 15*(30), 369–393.

Dale, G. (2011). Lineages of embeddedness: On the antecedents and successors of a Polanyian concept. *American Journal of Economics and Sociology, 70*(2), 306–339.

Dale, G. (2012). Double movements and pendular forces: Polanyian perspectives on the neoliberal age. *Current Sociology, 60*(1), 3–27.

Dean, M. (2010). *Governmentality: Power and rule in modern society*. London: Sage.

Fraser, N. (2012). Marketization, social protection, emancipation: Toward a Neo-polanyian conception of capitalist crisis. http://sophiapol.hypotheses. org/files/2012/02/Texte-Nancy-Fraser-anglais.doc. Accessed 15 Apr 2015.

Fraser, N., & Gordon, L. (1992). Contract vs. Charity: Why is there no social citizenship in the United States? *Socialist Review, 22*, 45–78.

Friesen, B. K. (2015). *Moral systems and the evolution of human rights*. Dordrecht: Springer.

Jessop, B. (2009). Cultural political economy and critical policy studies. *Critical Policy Studies, 3*(3–4), 336–356.

Jessop, B. (2013). Recovered imaginaries, imagined recoveries: A cultural political economy of crisis construals and crisis management in the North Atlantic financial crisis. In M. Benner (Ed.), *Before and beyond the global economic crisis: Economics, politics and settlement* (pp. 234–254). Cheltenham: Edward Elgar Publishing.

Jessop, B., & Oosterlynck, S. (2006). Cultural political economy: On making the cultural turn without falling into soft economic sociology. *Geoforum, 39*, 1155–1169.

Lockwood, D. (1964). Social integration and system integration. In G. K. Zollschan & W. Hirsh (Eds.), *Social change: Explorations, diagnoses and conjectures* (pp. 244–257). New York and London: John Wiley and Sons.

Lockwood, D. (1992). *Solidarity and schism: The problem of disorder in Durkheimian and Marxist sociology*. Oxford: Clarendon.

López, J. J. (2015). The human right to food as political imaginary. *Journal of Historical Sociology*. doi:10.1111/johs.12098.

López, J. J. (2016). Human rights as political imaginary, Palgrave (forthcoming).

McKenzie, D., Muniesa, F., & Siu, L. (2007). *Do economists make markets? On the performativity of economics*. Princeton: Princeton University Press.

Elliott, M. A. (2007). Human rights and the triumph of the individual in world culture. *Cultural Sociology, 1*(3), 343–363.

Mirowski, P. (2013). *Never let a serious crisis go to waste.* London: Verso.

Mittal, A., & Rosset, P. (1999). *America needs human rights.* Oakland: Food First Books.

Moyn, S. (2010). *The last utopia.* Cambridge: Belknap/ Harvard University Press.

Phillips-Fein, K. (2010). *Invisible hands: The businessmen's crusade against the new deal.* New York: W.W. Norton.

Polanyi, K. (1957). *The great transformation.* Beacon Hill, Boston: Beacon Press.

Postone, M. (1993). *Time, labor, and social domination.* Cambridge: Cambridge University Press.

Rose, N., & Miller, P. (1992). Political power beyond the state: Problematics of government. *British Journal of Sociology, 43*(2), 271–303.

Seymour, R. (2014). *Against austerity.* London: Pluto.

Shafir, G., & Brysk, A. (2006). The globalization of rights: From citizenship to human rights. *Citizenship Studies, 10*(3), 275–287.

Sjoberg, G., Williams, N., & Gill, E. A. (2001). A sociology of human rights. *Social Problems, 48*(1), 11–47.

Somers, M. R. (1994). Rights, relationality, and membership: Rethinking the making and meaning of citizenship. *Law and Social Inquiry, 19*(1), 63–112.

Somers, M. R. (2008). *Genealogies of citizenship.* Cambridge: Cambridge University Press.

Somers, M. R., & Block, F. (2005). From poverty to perversity: Ideas, markets, and institutions over 200 years of welfare debate. *American Sociological Review, 70,* 260–287.

Stammers, N. (2009). *Human rights and social movements.* London: Pluto Press.

Stahler-Sholk, R., Vanden, E. H., & Kuecker, G. D. (2007). Introduction: The politics of social movements in Latin America. *Latin American Perspectives, 34*(2), 5–16.

Tönnies, F. (1971). *On sociology: Pure, applied and empirical.* Chicago: University of Chicago Press.

Turner, B. S. (2006). *Vulnerability and human rights.* University Park: Pennsylvanian State University Press.

Waters, W. (1999). Decentering the economy. *Economy and Society, 28*(2), 312–323.

Woodiwiss, A. (2005). *Human rights.* Oxford/New York: Routledge.

Young, I. M. (1989). Polity and group difference: A critique of the ideal of universal citizenship. *Ethics, 99*(2), 250–274.

The Politics of Nostalgia in Urban Redevelopment Projects: The Case of Antwerp-Dam

Bruno Meeus, Tim Devos, and Seppe De Blust

Introduction

In academic writing, nostalgia, the sense of loss in the face of change and a related yearning for the past, has mostly been cast as regressive and generating conservative emotions instead of forward-looking solutions (Bonnett 2010). In the analysis of urban redevelopment programmes and the deep transformations they often intend in deindustrialized (or deindustrializing) and ethnically diverse urban areas, attention to proliferating nostalgic sentiments has mostly been blamed of further endorsing exclusionary urbanisms. Scholars, for instance, point out that nostalgic emotions support regressive ethnocentric and xenophobic political agendas. White working-class urban residents often express narratives of loss of local community, of neglect and of general neighbourhood decline (Blokland 2009; Schuermans et al. 2015). The exploitation of these nostalgic emotions by ethnocentric political fractions "trap people in the past" (Watson and Wells 2005). They offer them the false promise of

B. Meeus (✉) • T. Devos • S. De Blust
Vrije Universiteit Brussel, Brussels, Belgium

© The Editor(s) (if applicable) and The Author(s) 2016   **249**
C. Karner, B. Weicht (eds.), *The Commonalities of Global Crises*,
DOI 10.1057/978-1-137-50273-5_10

a return to a mythical national and white past (Amin 2002; De Decker et al. 2005).

In addition, Third Way, and similar urban policy programmes advocating "social cohesion" in socioeconomically and ethnic-culturally diverse neighbourhoods have been criticized based on their naive "romance for local community". They neglect the broader processes that generate inequality and produce a new governmentality of "eliminating bad community and replacing it with good community" that will automatically regenerate itself (Amin 2005: 5). Local community is a nostalgic fiction, Amin argues: "The distinctive feature of mixed neighbourhoods is that they are communities without community, each marked by multiple and hybrid affiliations of varying geographical reach and each intersecting momentarily (or not) with another for common local resources and amenities. They are not homogeneous or primarily place-based communities … Mixed neighbourhoods need to be accepted as the spatially open, culturally heterogeneous, and socially variegated spaces they are, not imagined as future cohesive or integrated communities." (Amin 2002: 16) Moreover, the nostalgic search for an "authentic local community" gives political leverage to particular resident groups who receive the status of a legitimate, authentic community. In that respect, Blokland (2009: 1608) has pointed out that the claims of these resident groups seen as authentic often undermine the material interests of many other residents who actually depend most on the neighbourhood.

Finally, along with the rise of middle-class subcultures of urban living, nostalgia for "urban authenticity" has been blamed for being one of the main cultural drivers of gentrification. For "bohemians" and hipsters arriving in a little-known and "funky" area, colourful local characters, the cultural diversity in the area, the old-fashioned "watering hole" in a local pub can all be used as a badge to demonstrate the proletarian or multicultural authenticity of the area, and hence reinforce their bohemian credentials (Kasinitz and Hillyard 1995; May 1996; Douglas 2012). In a next step, the commodification of the "authentic urban neighbourhood" offers a larger group of "urban consumers a safe and comfortable place to 'perform' difference from mainstream norms. These spaces fabricate an aura of authenticity based on the history of the area or the back story of their products, and capitalize on the tastes of their young, alternative clientele" (Zukin 2008: 724), leaving bohemians nostalgic for the earlier times of urban grittiness (Ocejo

2011) and encouraging the hipsters to move the gentrification frontier further to unexplored and "authentic" terrain (Smith 1996; Douglas 2012).

However, for some years now, nostalgia is undergoing a general reappraisal in academic literature, including this book. Different authors are developing more nuanced arguments around the general statement that nostalgia is not, by definition, a conservative and regressive tendency but instead an "inevitable emotion in an era of rapid and enforced change" (Bonnett 2010: 2365). Because of its discursive power, nostalgia also offers the potential to criticize particular forms of change and imagine different futures. As a result, some authors have started to discern between different political forms of nostalgia. Boym (2001), for instance, contrasts between more conservative "restorative" forms of nostalgia that attempt to reconstruct a lost home, and more progressive, "reflective" forms of nostalgia that are ironic, inclusive and fragmentary. Legg (2005), on the other hand, distinguishes between "rooted" nostalgia for a particular imagined home and "unrooted" nostalgia as a more free-floating sense of loss. However, according to Bonnett and Alexander (2013), categorising nostalgic emotions seems a hopeless endeavour since, in practice, nostalgia generates complicated, varied and contradictory pasts, not one clear "Golden Age", nor one "Golden Future". The pasts invoked by everyday nostalgic narratives of their respondents "interrupt each other, creating a dialogue of memories and attachments that is both 'simple' and 'reflexive', sentimental and personal, but also restless and forward-looking" (Bonnett and Alexander 2013: 399). Moreover, "What is 'simple' or 'restorative' can inspire what is critical and reflective, and vice versa", therefore they claim that "it may be more useful and accurate to acknowledge that these tendencies are woven together in the nostalgic imagination" (Bonnett and Alexander 2013: 393–4).

We elaborate on these insights to examine in more detail some of the other functions nostalgic narratives have in current urban redevelopment processes. We use the case of the inner-urban neighbourhood Dam in the Belgian city of Antwerp, a medium-sized port city with around 500.000 inhabitants, to document our argument. The Dam is one of Antwerp's poorest neighbourhoods and is currently more or less split in two parts because of a largely abandoned slaughterhouse site in the middle of the neighbourhood. While the neighbourhood transformed slowly but continuously throughout the past decades, Antwerp's government change in 2013, which brought the conservative N-VA (New Flemish Alliance) to power, and their announcement of a public-private redevelopment of the slaughterhouse site planned for the near future created a new context for nostalgic emotions to proliferate and play an important role in the politics of the redevelopment process.

The Context of the Research

In contrast to other northwestern European countries, where project-driven inner-city renewal has been high up on the urban policy agenda since the 1970s, it was not until the late 1990s that Flanders started adopting a similar entrepreneurial approach (Loopmans 2007). Faced with a weak fiscal base and backed by a broad consensus that generating "a more healthy social mix" in poor urban areas would solve a range of problems (Loopmans et al. 2010), urban governments in Flanders started to focus explicitly on urban projects in disadvantaged areas to attract the middle class by means of public-private partnerships and city marketing (De Decker et al. 2012). The city of Antwerp took the lead in Flanders and pursued an active urban renewal agenda in which strategic developments played a central role (Van den Broeck 2009).

During the past decade, this urban renewal agenda has come to define investments in the nineteenth-century working class belt of Antwerp, triggering several large-scale urban redevelopment projects (such as the development of the Eilandje, the conversion of a former railway yard into the Park Spoor Noord and the implementation of several strategic projects in the deprived northern neighbourhood of Antwerp). However, due to its isolation from the rest of the city, surrounded by many large-scale infrastructures such as the ring road around the city and the railway line, the neighbourhood Dam remained to a large extent out of the reach of these developments and of large-scale gentrification. Arguably, its "grey" (post)industrial character contributed to this effect: "Dammers don't have to be scared of social displacement. ... Because there will always be a slaughterhouse with all the buzz and industries related to it", such was the argument of a project developer in an Antwerp newspaper at the end of the 1990s, just before the new owner of the slaughterhouse went bankrupt (Gazet van Antwerpen, n.d.).

Today the neighbourhood finds itself at the start of fundamental changes. The impact of the redevelopment of the slaughterhouse site on the small neighbourhood will be enormous, roughly doubling it in size and population. The neighbourhood has therefore reached an important tipping point, as the redevelopment can, generally speaking, unfold in two possible scenarios. In the first scenario, a middle-class agenda will be superimposed. This could then result in a commodification of the history of the neighbourhood and the consumption of its working-class identity by new affluent groups (Jarvis and Bonnett 2013). This would result in a reorientation of the neighbourhood infrastructure to these groups' needs (Barnes et al. 2006). In another scenario, the redevelopment of the neighbourhood and its increasing number of inhabitants could create a critical mass of less-affluent residents needed to sustain a more socially just infrastructure of basic services and affordable housing (Amin 2013; Blommaert 2014), one which can be consumed by both Flemish "old-timers", the newly arriving middle classes and the current and future "superdiverse" population (Vertovec 2007) of the neighbourhood in its entirety.

The Damcomité, a local residents' organisation of which one of the authors is a member, asked "ndvr" in July 2013 to assist, advise and support them in trying to have an impact on the redevelopment, getting a variety of local organizations involved and organizing an inclusive participatory process regarding the development of a masterplan. *Ndvr* is an enterprise working in the field of sociospatial research and participatory process guidance, cofounded by two of the three authors of this chapter. Throughout this process, ndvr assumed an independent and exploratory role, while also working in close cooperation with the city administration on one hand, and with neighbourhood organizations on the other. As such, it gradually profiled itself as a third-party actor. Ndvr executed this work pro bono, and as a part of two of the authors' doctoral research.

The process took over two years of action-oriented research. The executed fieldwork throughout this research relied mainly on mapping local social-spatial realities, organizing participatory workshops, and continuously negotiating the expanding participation process and cooperation between the different parties. This approach started from the ambition to survey and map the use of space, the daily experiences and characteristic phenomena of the neighbourhood and to translate these findings into "spatial terms", which could be useful for the master-planning competition without reducing the complexity of the local needs and context. Moreover, ndvr aimed to use this input as a means to trigger a productive dialogue about the future of the neighbourhood, which was shaped by a number of participatory workshops.

Nostalgia and Authentic Community

> [N]ostalgia can provide the grounds for fatalism, [but] it can also become a resource with which actors claim authenticity and the right to define "the community" in the future. (Kasinitz and Hillyard 1995: 162)

All over the world, local governments struggle with the demand of residents to be involved in urban redevelopment processes. Residents typically demand from the local government to be involved from the start and to go beyond standardized procedures of participation—stagnated practices as referred to by De Bie et al. (2012)—which often do not go beyond "informing" (see Arnstein 1969). In Antwerp, many of these residents form neighbourhood organizations which are increasingly professionalizing: they propose their own spatial imaginaries, support them with examples from cities elsewhere, have access to the local press and do not hesitate to raise their voice against particular urban developments. In our case study, the neighbourhood organisation "Damcomité" succeeded in becoming a partner in the redevelopment process of the slaughterhouse site from early on in the process. In this section, we investigate the role of nostalgic narratives in the establishment of this partnership against the background of a shift in political regime, as the local Antwerp coalition that reigned for decades changed in 2013.

Important for our case study, Purdue (2001) argues that "community leaders", acting as key points of contact, derive legitimacy to conduct their intermediary role from two forms of what Purdue calls "perceived social capital", that is, the social networks they are perceived to have access to. In order to gain legitimacy, a community leader should be perceived by governmental actors to have access to the relevant resident groups in the neighbourhood. At the same time, the leader should be perceived by neighbourhood residents to have access to the relevant governmental actors. The question hence becomes to what extent the Damcomité succeeds in accumulating these two forms of "perceived social capital". In at least two ways, nostalgic narratives appear to have played an important role in the creation of perceived social capital: (1) shared nostalgic narratives were the basis for two resident groups in the neighbourhood to form the Damcomité and (2) shared nostalgic narratives endorsed the legitimacy of the Damcomité to act as an intermediary in the neighbourhood.

Constructing a Sense of Local Community

The construction of the local "old-timer" identity in the Dam is interlaced with nostalgic narratives and particular meaningful sociospatial practices. "Real people from the Dam" are white and working class, they visit particular pubs, and those who moved away get together at the yearly "reunion of the Dam". Old-timers frame the redevelopment of the nearby Park Spoor Noord as "not for them" and are eager to share the rich history of the neighbourhood with anyone showing interest: the tight social networks (one big family), the Dam as a "village" in the city, and the slow decay of parochial life and the social networks in the neighbourhood over the past decades. The old-timers hence create a closed imagined community. The analysis of Red Hook old-timers by Kasinitz and Hillyard (1995) two decades ago shows profound parallels:

> To be considered a real old-timer, one generally has had to have also experienced the old days—roughly the middle decades of the twentieth century when waterfront jobs were plentiful and Whites were the majority in the neighbourhood. To some extent, however, old-timer status is inheritable: the children of old-timers who grew up in the neighbourhood are more or less considered to be part of the group, as are those who have moved out of the area but who have stayed in close contact with local networks and social groups ... [T]o be an old-timer means to be White and working class. (Kasinitz and Hillyard 1995: 146)

Just like in the case of Red Hook and other communities (May 1996), the old-timers' voice in the Dam is a voice of frustration, of staying behind in a quickly diversifying and marginalizing neighbourhood. What remains is the identity of "being the authentic neighbourhood resident". In the open meetings of the Damcomité, old-timers repeatedly ask who really is "from the Dam". During these meetings, the old-timers, however, recognize and appeal to the organizational resources provided by the middle-class newcomers.

The new middle-class residents that have entered the neighbourhood in the past decade, mainly as a result of the relative ease of buying houses in the neighbourhood, have shown to be sensitive to the nostalgic narratives of the "old-timers". Arriving in a neighbourhood with a bad reputation (or no reputation at all, as the neighbourhood is mostly unknown to other people in Antwerp, besides its meat restaurants), the old-timers' stories of the "good old days" help the middle-class newcomers to identify with the narrative of an authentic (but white) lively neighbourhood, projecting the hopeful image that the neighbourhood could be full of bustle again. The social networks connecting middle-class newcomers and working-class old-timers are the result of particular "go-betweens" in the neighbourhood: middle-class newcomers whose grandparents are "old-timers" from the Dam, pedigreed old-timers with middle-class lifestyles, and so on.

Through the go-betweens, the middle-class newcomers have adopted the narrative of a village in the city and the idea of a big family. While most of the neighbourhood shops have disappeared over the years, together with most of the slaughter- and meat-industry activities, the former slaughter halls are in the middle of the neighbourhood and the streets around the slaughterhouse still host a few renowned meat restaurants as well as some small meat-oriented enterprises. It comes as no surprise then that a new "mnemonic community", an imagined community based on nostalgic narratives and practices (Zerubavel 1996), has been constructed around the living memory of the meat industry to which both the old-timers and the newcomers seem to relate. In 2012 one of the middle-class newcomers painted a public utility box in the neighbourhood in the squared pattern of the wrapping paper often used by Belgian butchers, together with a cow saying "welcome". When the petition for participation was presented to the press in June 2013, middle-class newcomers and old-timers posed together in front of this new artefact that illustrated the newly developing mnemonic community.

Constructing the Damcomité as a Legitimate Intermediary

While a number of neighbourhood organisations have succeeded in building up perceived social capital in the former social-democratic government coalitions in Antwerp, the current conservative local government has proven to be critical of these residents and their organisations (Nieuwsblad 2013), claiming they represent a "cultural left-wing" support base of the former government. In other words, they are perceived to represent the "wrong" social capital. In 2010 already, the current mayor of Antwerp (and chairman of the Flemish conservative party N-VA) launched the pejorative concept of "bakfietsvlaming", referring to Flemish urbanites who use a carrier cycle or "bakfiets", to describe the cultural urban middle classes who support the former socialist mayor and "talk progressive but act regressive in their everyday life" and use the carrier cycle as a cultural marker (De Standaard 2010). The concept of "bakfietsvlaming" was widely taken up in the press, became the symbol of an imaginary "social group" (De Standaard 2011), and was nominated as word of the year in 2011 (Het Laatste Nieuws 2011). The essentially derogatory concept proved extremely efficient in undermining the voice of those who could be identified in some way or another as belonging to the "cultural left wing" (Blommaert 2011). Different action committees, resident groups and other political activists have, as a result, lost their legitimate voice or potential to become partners from the start, as they could easily be framed as inauthentic "bakfietsvlamingen".

It is all the more remarkable then, that the Damcomité, in which white "cultural" middle-class residents undeniably play an important role, has somehow avoided being classified under this "cultural left-wing" connotation. A crucial aspect here is that the Damcomité's perceived social capital extends to the old-timers of the neighbourhood. The main perception problem of the "cultural" middle class who are seen as only recent urban residents (and gentrifiers) is their perceived inauthenticity as compared to the older Flemish working-class urban residents. While not a deliberate political strategy, the Damcomité has succeeded in being perceived as at least partly representing the "authentic residents" of the neighbourhood Dam.

Already at the first meeting with the alderman, in the period when a petition for participation first gained traction, it turned out the alderman himself made use of the nostalgic narrative "the meat must stay". During these and subsequent meetings, the alderman stated that the soul of the Dam has to be maintained. Besides "the meat must stay", the alderman used the expression "the Dam has a 'dikke ziel' or 'thick soul'", an important play on words since "dikke ziel" refers to a particular kind of rump steak served in some local meat restaurants. Hence, for the alderman the authenticity of the neighbourhood can be found in the history of meat. The new mnemonic community in the neighbourhood was constructed around the history of meat. Allying working-class old-timers and middle-class newcomers could then easily allow newcomers to present themselves as authentic representatives based on this shared narrative. As a result, and again in the words of Kasinitz and Hillyard, the old-timers give the middle-class newcomers an effective political tool: "With their superior organizational resources and their willingness to minimize the most blatantly racist aspects of the old-timers' narratives, these Johnny-come-latelies make better use of the good old days than the old-timers ever could" (Kasinitz and Hillyard 1995: 162). In other words, it is as a result of the support of the "authentic" old-timers that the Damcomité could increase its perceived social capital and its legitimacy to act as "community leader".

Inspiring Nostalgia

In the previous section we argued that nostalgic narratives about the authentic community of the Dam played an important role in the creation of a legitimate intermediary in the neighbourhood Dam. However, the fact that only one group of residents—the new mnemonic community in the Dam—is seen as the legitimate partner for the redevelopment projects allows for potential exclusionary claims against the stakes of the other residents in the neighbourhood (Brown-Saracino 2007). Moreover, as mentioned in the introduction, nostalgic narratives about "authentic urban villages" in urban planning have often acted, alongside neotraditional new urbanism ideas, as a vehicle to facilitate the gentrification of poorer neighbourhoods in different cities throughout the world (and hence to "solve" the social problems in these areas by displacing the poor). This process has been documented, for instance, by Barnes et al. (2006), Zukin (2010) and Jarvis and Bonnett (2013). Wealthier newcomers, out of a sense of nostalgia for authentic urban places and authentic urban experiences, consume the commodified and kitsch authenticity of a neighbourhood (Atkinson 2007). In this section, we demonstrate how the Damcomité made use of its budding legitimacy as an intermediary to formulate a preferred redevelopment scenario that could potentially block the further gentrification of the neighbourhood and the crucial role of nostalgic narratives in the construction of this advice, a role that was twofold. We noticed that nostalgic narratives, and particularly the living memory of the meat history, were crucial (1) in opening up the deeply institutionalized planning process in which participation would effectively be limited to communication and information, and (2) in offering a meaningful narrative through which substantive arguments about the needs of various groups in the neighbourhood could be related to the proposals of the urban department without directly challenging them.

The Urban Planning Repertoire Versus the Nostalgic Repertoire

In response to repeated queries by the Damcomité and ndvr for more information about the status of the project definition, the urban planning department organised an informative meeting in the local parish hall (an important old-timers' place) on the 4th of June, 2014, in which the key ambitions in the project definition were briefly explained and debates with residents were facilitated.

Before the presentation, the alderman gave a short speech in which he repeated the importance of maintaining the "thick soul" of the neighbourhood Dam. The presentation made clear that the planning department had not constructed a singular "selling image". Rather, the PowerPoint slides listed, besides statements about the general port identity, eight ambitions:

1) re-establishing the historical connection with the water of the nearby "Lobroekdock" and the potential of the quay for the development of a high- quality public space;

2) a new "qualitative front" at "Lobroekdock" to establish the identity of the neighbourhood in that direction;

3) strengthening open and green space (5000 m²)

4) a new central and lively square in the Dam to connect old and new;

5) housing as main allocation: a balanced mix of housing including young and old, small and large, different types, complementary to the existing stock; affordable, innovative housing forms, subsidized ownership (social housing);

6) extending the "supply" of public services: schools, child care, youth clubs, a small sport hall;

7) room for a mix of economy and housing: no "annoying activities", searching for an interweaving of activities, promoting the creative economy, strengthening local retail, room for entrepreneurs and local initiatives; continuing the historical presence of meat-processing businesses;

8) mobility: enabling infrastructural access but awareness of the perils of trans-local traffic, "secret routes" and parking problems.

Clearly, the information offered to the audience was extremely concise. Moreover, what we see here is not a ready-made blueprint one can, for instance, find in the "authentic urban village" promo-talk described by Barnes et al. (2006) but rather a "makeshift" planning proposal, an assemblage of at least three different "repertoires": (1) vague urban planning concepts such as the "creative economy", "a balanced mix", and an "interweaving [of] activities", "establishing an identity" and even "affordable housing"; (2) concrete proposals such as "at least 5000 m² of open green space"; and (3) nostalgic narratives such as references to "the historical presence of meat processing" and to "back to the water". We focus in particular on the different political effects of the "urban planning repertoire" compared to the nostalgic repertoire.

Many of the hollow concepts we find in the list of ambitions can be seen as part of a policy in which gentrification is, if not facilitated, at least not blocked. One of the most recent, vague planning concepts that have appeared in Flemish urban planning literature, *the creative economy*, can be seen as part of a globally circulating gentrification-facilitation discourse in which the creative class is brought into poorer neighbourhoods (Novy and Colomb 2013). When asked about the meaning of this creative economy, the presenter referred to attracting cultural entrepreneurs working in architecture, arts, and so on whose arrival will give the neighbourhood "a boost", thereby clearly referring to the creative-class narrative. Challenging this discourse, even in the participatory setting on offer, appeared difficult, since most residents were not aware of the particular policy strategies underpinning these vague concepts. As a result, during the debates that followed the presentations, many of these formal urban planning concepts were neglected. Ideas such as "attracting the creative economy" or "the need for a balanced mix of housing" were never explicitly challenged. During the discussions, the need for work opportunities for local people, however, turned out to be very important. Even more overwhelming was the support for local shops and services (ATMs, post offices, supermarkets, and so on) often accompanied by nostalgic narratives about the number of shops that used to be in the neighbourhood (see also Kasinitz and Hilyard [1995] for a similar situation). Similarly, the vague idea of a "balanced mix of housing" was not challenged, but at the same time many residents worried about rising house prices in the neighbourhood and criticized the increasing number of student-oriented new constructions.

In short, most of the debates did not engage directly with the repertoire of formal planning concepts—most of them being too vague to be challenged or even to be understood. As a result, the potential gentrification scenario that resides in the vague concepts remained unchallenged, although various issues of direct relevance for the audience present, and often incompatible with a gentrification scenario, were discussed in a more substantive language.

The nostalgic repertoire, by contrast, had very different effects. An important starting point is that the nostalgic narrative in the presentation did not construct a clearly delineated and singular past. Instead, the port and meat history were both taken into account. So far there is no singular identity, no pastiche, no kitsch involved. There is, however, a choice to not include a myriad of other histories such as, for instance, the history of the Dam having been a fiscal island outside the citywalls, the history of social innovation in the neighbourhood, the history of very different social housing developments, the history of an isolated urban village, the histories of Moroccan, African and Asian immigration in the neighbourhood, and the more recent diversification and gentrification of the neighbourhood, to name but a few.

In the presentation, however, the nostalgic narratives interacted with particular planning concepts and not with others. The narrative of "back to the water" was articulated with reference to the potential of the quay for the development of a high-quality public space; the narrative of meat-processing with the still existing bustle of small meat-processing companies, restaurants and pubs around the former slaughterhouse site. They were not, however, connected to the need for an identity, to the balanced mix of housing, or the proposal for 5000 m² open and green space.

It comes as no surprise that the nostalgic narratives in the planning departments' presentation were not contested by the audience. The audience itself consisted mainly of a combination of old-timers and middle-class newcomers who had been constructing a mnemonic community based on, among other things, the area's meat-history, as we explained earlier. The crucial role of the nostalgic narratives in the presentation was that they communicated the particularity and the authenticity of the neighbourhood to the audience. Through the use of particular nostalgic narratives, the planning department showed that it had the ambition to deviate from homogenizing and standardized planning practices. It showed that the local identity and the local histories of the neighbourhood somehow mattered to them. At the very least, it created a sense of involvement. Not surprisingly, then, the nostalgic repertoire resonated much more with the audience than the formal planning repertoire.

Challenging Gentrification Through a Nostalgic Detour

In August 2014, as a result of further delay in compiling the "project definition" by the urban planning department, disappointment about the lack of real debate and a general lack of clarity about the possibilities for further participation, the Damcomité decided to write a document detailing the neighbourhood residents' view of the future of the slaughterhouse site and of the neighbourhood at large. The general feeling among the members was that there had been enough "generic participation" moments and that enough material had been collected by the Damcomité, by ndvr and at the 4th of June debate. It was decided that a document containing the most important substantial demands that had been uttered during the preceding years would be prepared.

In compiling this document, the Damcomité chose to remain as close as possible to the ambitions put forward by the urban planning department (UPD). Yet, while the UPD mainly proposed hollow concepts— concepts that could fit a gentrification scenario—the Damcomité started to fill these "hollow concepts" with substantial suggestions. Of crucial importance was the discursive merging of "rational" substantive arguments and "nostalgic" sentiments in filling hollow concepts. Table 10.1 summarizes the discourse of both repertoires in four of the ambitions. Unrooted, rooted, restorative and reflexive nostalgia all turned out to articulate with particular substantive arguments. What becomes clear is that the Damcomité strategically amplified the nostalgic narratives that were introduced by the alderman, in the presentation of the UPD and by its members (that is *the meat must stay, the "thick soul" of the Dam*). Legitimacy, to speak in the name of an (imaginary) authentic community, was then used to argue against potential gentrification with a nostalgic discourse, without directly challenging vague concepts. As a result, no clear "counter-image" was produced that could be challenged by the UPD or the alderman.

Conclusion

This chapter and its examination of the politics of redevelopment in a disenfranchised urban area resonates with the Polanyi-inspired concept of an "always embedded economy" (Block 2003; Fraser 2013). The question which manifests as part of this framework is how exactly new capital injections become embedded in particular neighbourhoods. At first sight, this question boils down to the degree in which existing neighbourhood residents are allowed to participate in the actual decision-making processes.

Table 10.1 The articulation of substantive arguments with nostalgic sentiments in the advice of the Damcomité to counter the gentrification threat

Planning concepts proposed by planning department	Gentrification threat	Substantive arguments of Damcomité	Nostalgic sentiments put forward by Damcomité
High-quality public space	Development of high-quality public space to attract higher-income households	Current residents do not have private gardens and need local and safe public spaces, so invest in small local public places and more housing without private gardens instead of in houses with private gardens	Living memory of street conviviality meets free-floating nostalgia for neighbourhood life and social cohesion
Affordable housing	Discourse of affordable housing limited to subsidized home-ownership	Most of the current residents pay rent of more than a third of their income, only investing in long-term affordable housing can benefit them	To keep the authentic "thick soul" of the Dam, the poorer old-timers and their children should have the option to stay in the neighbourhood
Creative economy & interweaving different functions	Prioritizing commercial space for a particular "creative class"	Unemployment is high, cheap spaces for local talents are needed most	Craftsmanship and combination of commercial and residential activities is part of the history of the neighbourhood and inscribed in the architecture of the Dam
Basic services	Predominantly middle-class oriented services such as higher-end supermarkets	Only when the critical mass of local-oriented consumers with limited budgets increases, local services accessible to everyone can survive	Old-timers remember the range of services and local shops that disappeared over the years

Indeed, if various local needs and existing embedded economies are not taken into account, a "new" economy risks being embedded solely in the lifestyles, moral frameworks and production and consumption patterns of a future affluent group of residents, favoured by the "facilitation of gentrification"-scenario that urban governments in different parts of the world have been applying for some time now. However, all over the world, urban governments are confronted with the demand of increasingly professionalizing neighbourhood associations to have a say in the decisions surrounding these capital injections, recognizing that early participation of local partners is important if only to avoid later resistance. Their often-competing claims raise the question as to which voices in a neighbourhood will be heard, which resident groups eventually become partners in the redevelopment process and what potentially emancipatory moments this new capital investment produces for some and not for others. When we endorse Amin's (2005) claim that urban neighbourhoods do not consist of one community, but instead, of a diversity of translocal and overlapping communities, questions about the local "embeddedness" of the economy indeed immediately become very complicated to resolve.

In line with a main theme of this book, this chapter focused specifically on the role of nostalgia in this complex process. In urban studies literature, the legitimation of local nostalgic voices by urban governments has often been criticized for resulting in the amplification of the ethnocentric or nationalist feelings of disenfranchised white communities, in supporting naive social cohesion policies and in enabling the commodification and gentrification of former working-class neighbourhoods. However, through our work in the neighbourhood Dam, we realized the need to analyze in more detail some of the other work nostalgia does.

Our analysis of Dam in the Belgian city of Antwerp suggests that nostalgia has played a role in at least the following politics of embedding future investments in the neighbourhood: (1) nostalgia has triggered the development of a light and unstable sense of community (Blommaert and Varis 2015) in the neighbourhood, of which the organisation Damcomité did become a representative. More particularly, shared nostalgic narratives about the living memory of the meat industry and its embeddedness in the neighbourhood infrastructure have united working-class old-timers and middle-class newcomers in a local coalition. (2) While the new conservative Antwerp government discursively constructs more established neighbourhood organizations and action committees in the city as supporters of the former social-democratic government, a strategy which undermines their role as intermediaries in urban redevelopment processes, the government appears to be sensitive to the nostalgic narratives mobilized by this local neighbourhood coalition. This has helped the Damcomité to gain legitimacy in representing the neighbourhood. (3) Nostalgic narratives about, among other things, the meat history of the neighbourhood have found their way to the formal list of ambitions presented by the urban planning department. The presence of this "nostalgic repertoire" effectively generated a sense of involvement for (a particular group of) neighbourhood residents and legitimated the use of nostalgia as a strategic discourse in discussions about the future of the neighbourhood. (4) When the Damcomité advised investment in the neighbourhood infrastructure that would support a future socioeconomically and ethnic-culturally diverse population, nostalgic narratives—reproducing the living memory of the meat industry—acted as strategic discourses to defend these claims.

Our case study shows that the different tendencies in the nostalgic imagination (Bonnett and Alexander 2013) indeed continuously fueled and inspired political debate and that they did not necessarily generate regressive and exclusionary suggestions. The concrete or vague sense of loss appears to be a powerful sentiment urban planners should reckon with, particularly in the case of disadvantaged urban neighbourhoods. Nostalgic discourses can form a backdrop for urban planners to engage with local stakeholders and can in turn be mobilized by local coalitions as a means to put local values on the urban redevelopment agenda.

References

Amin, A. (2002). Ethnicity and the multicultural city: Living with Diversity. *Environment and Planning A, 34*(6), 959–980.

Amin, A. (2005). Local community on trial. *Economy and Society, 34*(4), 612–633.

Amin, A. (2013). Telescopic urbanism and the poor. *City, 17*(4), 476–492.

Arnstein, S. R. (1969). A ladder of citizen participation. *Journal of the American Institute of Planners, 35*(4), 216–224.

Atkinson, D. (2007). Kitsch geographies and the everyday spaces of social memory. *Environment and Planning A, 39*(3), 521–540.

Barnes, K., Waitt, G. R., Gill, N. J., & Gibson, C. R. (2006). Community and nostalgia in urban revitalisation: A critique of urban village and creative class strategies as remedies for social 'problems'. *Australian Geographer, 37*(3), 335–354.

Block, F. (2003). Karl Polanyi and the writing of 'The Great Transformation'. *Theory and Society, 32*(3), 275–306.

Blokland, T. (2009). Celebrating local histories and defining neighbourhood communities: Place making in a gentrified neighbourhood. *Urban Studies, 46*(8), 1593–1610.

Blommaert, J. (2011). *Interview Jan Blommaert*. In De Standaard 16 April 2011.

Blommaert, J. (2014). Infrastructures of superdiversity: Conviviality and language in an Antwerp neighborhood. *European Journal of Cultural Studies, 17*(4), 431–451.

Blommaert, J. & Varis, P. (2015). Enoughness, accent and light communities: Essays on contemporary identities. *Tilburg Papers in Culture Studies,* paper 139.

Bonnett, A. (2010). Radicalism, antiracism, and nostalgia: The burden of loss in the search for convivial culture. *Environment and Planning A, 42*(10), 2351–2369.

Bonnett, A., & Alexander, C. (2013). Mobile nostalgias: Connecting visions of the urban past, present and future amongst ex-residents. *Transactions of the Institute of British Geographers, 38*(3), 391–402.

Boym, S. (2001). *The future of nostalgia*. London: Basic Books.

Brown-Saracino, J. (2007). Virtuous marginality: Social preservationists and the selection of the old timer. *Theory and Society, 36*(5), 437–468.

De Bie, M., Oosterlynck, S., & De Blust, S. (2012). Participatie, ontwerp en toe-eigening in een democratische stadsvernieuwing. In E. Vervloesem, B. D. Meulder, & A. Loeckx (Eds.), *Stadsvernieuwingsprojecten in Vlaanderen 2002–2011. Een eigenzinnige praktijk in Europees perspectief* (pp. 29–33). ASP Editions: Brussels.

De Decker, P., Kesteloot, C., De Maesschalck, F., & Vranken, J. (2005). Revitalizing the city in an anti-urban context: Extreme right and the rise of urban policies in Flanders, Belgium. *International Journal of Urban and Regional Research, 29*(1), 152–171.

De Decker, P., Van den Broeck, P., & Loopmans, M. (2012). Van bewonersgerichte stadsvernieuwing naar stadsontwikkeling: 30 jaar beleid voor de stad. In D. Holemans (Ed.), *Mensen maken de stad* (pp. 37–47). Antwerpen: EPO.

De Standaard. (2010, May 8). *Een mens die niet verandert is een saai mens.* http://www.standaard.be/cnt/6c2pu6pi. Accessed 24 Nov 2015.

De Standaard. (2011, March 5). *Zoektocht naar sociologisch fenomeen 'bakfietsouder'*. http://www.standaard.be/cnt/l2375hm6?word=bakfiets. Accessed 24 Nov 2015.

Douglas, G. C. C. (2012). The edge of the island. Cultural ideology and neighbourhood identity at the gentrification frontier. *Urban Studies, 49*(16), 3579–3594.

Fraser, N. (2013). A triple movement? Parsing the politics of crisis after Polanyi. *New Left Review, 81*, 119–132.

Gazet van Antwerpen. (n.d.). Dossier wijken: Den Dam

Het Laatste Nieuws. (2011, November 29). *Bakfietsvlaming, frietrevolutie en vlinderakkoord strijden om 'Woord van het jaar 2011'*. http://www.hln.be/hln/nl/957/Binnenland/article/detail/1355244/2011/11/29/Bakfietsvlaming-frietrevolutie-en-vlinderakkoord-strijden-om-Woord-van-het-jaar-2011.dhtml. Accessed 24 Nov 2015.

Het Nieuwsblad. (2013, March 12). *NV-A-schepen haalt uit naar actiecomités*. http://www.nieuwsblad.be/cnt/dmf20130311_00500290. Accessed 24 Nov 2015.

Jarvis, H., & Bonnett, A. (2013). Progressive Nostalgia in novel living arrangements: A counterpoint to neo-traditional New Urbanism? *Urban Studies, 50*(11), 2349–2370.

Kasinitz, P., & Hillyard, D. (1995). The old-timers' tale. The politics of nostalgia on the waterfront. *Journal of Contemporary Ethnography, 24*(2), 139–164.

Legg, S. (2005). Contesting and surviving memory: Space, nation, and nostalgia in Les Lieux de Mémoire. *Environment and Planning D: Society and Space, 23*(4), 481–504.

Loopmans, M. (2007). From SIF to city fund: A new direction for urban policy in Flanders, Belgium. *Journal of Housing and the Built Environment, 22*(2), 215–225.

Loopmans, M., De Decker, P., & Kesteloot, C. (2010). Social mix and passive revolution. A neo-Gramscian analysis of the social mix rhetoric in Flanders. *Belgium. Housing Studies, 25*(2), 181–200.

May, J. (1996). Globalization and the politics of place: Place and identity in an Inner London Neighbourhood. *Transactions of the Institute of British Geographers, 21*(1), 194–215.

Novy, J., & Colomb, C. (2013). Struggling for the right to the (creative) city in Berlin and Hamburg: New urban social movements, new 'spaces of hope'? *International Journal of Urban and Regional Research, 37*(5), 1816–1838.

Ocejo, R. E. (2011). The early gentrifier: Weaving a nostalgia narrative on the lower east side. *City & Community, 10*(3), 285–310.

Purdue, D. (2001). Neighbourhood governance: Leadership, trust and social capital. *Urban Studies, 38*(12), 2211–2224.

Schuermans, N., Meeus, B., & De Decker, P. (2015). Geographies of whiteness and wealth: White, middle class discourses on segregation and social mix in Flanders, Belgium. *Journal of Urban Affairs, 37*(4), 478–495.

Smith, N. (1996). *The new urban frontier: Gentrification and the revanchist city*. London: Routledge.

Van den Broeck, J. (2009). The structure plan: Traditional cooking or nouvel cuisine? In B. Secchi & P. Vigano (Eds.), *Antwerp, territory of a new modernity* (pp. 233–241). Amsterdam: SUN.

Vertovec, S. (2007). Super-diversity and its implications. *Ethnic and Racial Studies, 30*(6), 1024–1054.

Watson, S., & Wells, K. (2005). Spaces of nostalgia: the hollowing out of a London market. *Social & Cultural Geography, 6*(1), 17–30.

Zerubavel, E. (1996). Social memories: Steps to a sociology of the past. *Qualitative Sociology, 19*(3), 283–299.

Zukin, S. (2008). Consuming authenticity. From outposts of difference to means of exclusion. *Cultural Studies, 22*(5), 724–748.

Zukin, S. (2010). *Naked City. The death and life of authentic urban places*. Oxford: Oxford University Press.

Longing for Communal Purity: Countryside, (Far-Right) Nationalism and the (Im)possibility of Progressive Politics of Nostalgia

Bernhard Forchtner

Introduction[1]

When Karl Polanyi (2001: 44), in *The Great Transformation*, noted that the self-regulated market economy was turning land into a profane commodity, he was fully aware that this aspect of dismbedding markets from society "threatened his ["man's"] natural habitat with annihilation". Much more, Polanyi was aware that expansion of the market prompted calls for community and protectionism from, among others, fascists and national socialists all over Europe. Indeed, the fact that far-right nationalist revolts, past and present, have referred to the destruction of the land is not surprising. After all, it is a sacred matter in nationalist imaginaries. Though its significance is not restricted to nationalists, classical national-

[1] The research leading to these results has received funding from the People Programme (Marie Curie Action) of the European Union's Seventh Framework Programme (FP7/2007–2013) under REA grant agreement no. 327,595. I am grateful to the editors as well as to Raimundo Frei for comments on an earlier version of this article.

B. Forchtner (✉)
University of Leicester, Leicester, UK

C. Karner, B. Weicht (eds.), *The Commonalities of Global Crises*,
DOI 10.1057/978-1-137-50273-5_11

ist metaphors such as father- and mother*land* indicate an intimate relation, a relation perhaps most forceful at the level of the countryside and landscape. In fact, Anthony D. Smith (2009: 50) has convincingly argued that nationalist communities have their "'ethno-scapes' in which a people and its homeland become increasingly symbiotic". As such, nationalist identities are invested with feelings of belonging to such spaces—but as markets put continuous pressure on the natural environment, fields, hedges and other iconic objects representing these "ethno-scapes" are threatened. This regularly feeds into feelings of nostalgia which, as in the case of (far-right) nationalists, facilitate a longing for pure community associated with an imagined countryside.

Given that the far-right, ranging from "moderate" to radical actors, is experiencing continuous growth across Europe, and given also that local and global environmental destruction shows little sign of slowing down, this chapter asks, first: how does a paradigmatic far-right, nationalist actor, the *British National Party* (BNP), narrate the effects of market forces on the countryside? Or, more specifically: what boundary work and (nostalgic) longing for communal purity do these actors perform when talking about the countryside? The significance of this paper thus lies in taking the BNP as a case through which relevant representations of the countryside can be carved out.

Second, and taking up a concern raised in the introduction to this volume, this chapter goes beyond a case study by asking: based on what criteria can the politics of nostalgia, whether limited to protests against perceived and real destruction of the countryside (as in this chapter), or not, be evaluated? Given that the countryside is not only a point of reference for nationalist nostalgia, to do with community and purity, I take the BNP as a starting point to explore different ways in which nostalgia can be part of various types of narratives. The significance of such an endeavour lies in constructing a model through which varieties of nostalgic stories can be evaluated—opening up the possibility to speak of *progressive* politics of nostalgia in the first place. Indeed, nostalgia can be part of very different types of stories, and can thus facilitate very different sentiments and identities: stories which feature nostalgia might facilitate exclusion—but they might also enable more open and egalitarian symbolic boundaries. I will propose a Habermasian-inspired notion of collective learning processes as a framework in order to evaluate the "progressiveness" of stories featuring nostalgia. Here, collective learning processes are understood as nonlinear processes of societal self-production which enable more or less open and egalitarian symbolic boundaries, openness to ambiguity, doubt and self-criticism, as well as the reciprocal inclusion of each other in and through the stories actors tell each other.

I start by looking at the relation between nationalism, the (British) countryside, nostalgia and the BNP, including the corpus of texts on which this chapter is based. Subsequently, I analyse the BNP's discourse on the countryside along the dimensions of purity and pollution. The section "From Nostalgia to Collective Learning?" takes up these findings, viewing the BNP's position on the countryside as only one type of nostalgic story. By drawing on narrative theory, I outline alternative forms in which nostalgia can be present in stories we live by, not only backward-looking and regressive stories, as illustrated by the BNP. By drawing on a Habermasian-inspired theory of collective learning, I propose how to evaluate these varieties. I close by emphasising the need for recognising the significance of the environment in the self-production of societies.

From Nationalism and the (British) Countryside to Nostalgia and the BNP

While Polanyi pointed out violent reactions to disembedding markets from society in the twentieth century, capital-driven industrialisation had already led to nationalist reactions much earlier: emerging as an ideology among the intelligentsia and the middle classes in Western urban centres during the eighteenth and nineteenth centuries, this carrier group idealized "rural folkways as the embodiment of purity and truth", vis-à-vis the alienating individualism and materialism of their existence (Smith 1983: 190). The city became the manifestation of modernity and those disenchanted with the latter consequently identified the countryside as harbouring what had been lost but should be reclaimed. The dichotomy of country and city seems to offer intuitive meaning, demarcating imagined purity from modern ambivalence, and has even found its way into classic analytical separations such as the one suggested by Ferdinand Tönnies (2002: 35) of community (*Gemeinschaft*: lifewordly, familiar, a living organism) and society (*Gesellschaft*: artificial, alien, mechanical; for critical view, see Urry 1995: 8–11).[2]

In Britain in particular, this significance of the countryside has a long tradition due to the early beginnings of industrialisation (Ditt 1996: 2ff). Much more, in and through this process, it was linked early on to the nation. There is indeed almost endless material on the connection between Englishness, national identity and the countryside, on the symbolic significance of, for examples, hedges and fields, small forests and thatched cottages (Williams 1973; Lowenthal 1991; Daniels 1993; Matless 1998; Darby 2000; Agyeman and Neal 2006; Chakraborti and Garland 2011). In fact, one of the most famous English poems, William Blake's *And did those feet in ancient time*, voiced a dislike of the industrial revolution ("these dark Satanic Mills"), while simultaneously speaking of the English countryside as a "green and pleasant land".[3] In addition, the idea of safety and fullness emerged with force when, in the context of an expanding capitalist worldeconomy (Wallerstein 2011), the "global reach of English imperialism, into alien lands, was accompanied by a countervailing sentiment for cosy home scenery, for thatched cottages and gardens in countervailing sentiment in pastoral countryside" (Daniels 1993: 6). In other words, the countryside turns into something particularly significant, as an imagined security (at home) becomes threatened by "alien" elements (abroad). This countryside is the principal symbolic landscape which represents national harmony; it is "Britain's imaginative heartland" (Hewison in: Urry 2000: 200).

Key nationalist assumptions about the natural environment (in Britain and beyond) have long spread to other political camps, but it is in far-right thought that authenticity and purity remain most systematically linked to the countryside. At its core, these assumptions concern both an aesthetic as well as symbolic dimensions (Forchtner and Kølvraa 2015: 204–6):

---

[2] The dichotomy was not without relevance for the emerging working class either. Peter Gould (1988) illustrates that 'lower classes' too associated nature with community and brotherhood—while also being involved in class-related conflicts over access to property/land.

[3] This phrase was taken up by the BNP in its 2009 *Manifesto for the European Elections* (BNP 2009: 8). Furthermore, Polanyi (2001: 102) has an entire section, captioned 'Satanic Mill', which uses the phrase at various points as a cipher for the effects of capitalist industrialisation, and refers to Blake explicitly.

aesthetically, the natural environment is considered in terms of national beauty and enjoyment, while the symbolic dimensions concern thinking about the environment in terms of historical continuity, demarcation and the sovereignty of 'the people' over a certain piece of land (Anderson 2006: 6). Consequently, the (British) countryside and landscape suggest "not simply scenery and *genres de vie*, but quintessential national virtues" (Lowenthal 1991: 213). Enjoying the countryside, this emblematic site of the nation, enables the flourishing of what Michael Billig (1995: 6) calls "banal nationalism". The latter describes mundane assumptions and habits associated with the experience of, for example, fields and forests as British spaces. That is, Billig points to banal processes through which subjects are constituted as national ones—even on such profane occasions as a walk through the countryside. In such contexts, hiking through green fields does not simply give pleasure through experiencing nature's beauty, but turns into experiencing that which is supposed to be quintessentially British. Unsurprisingly, the English shires—green, orderly fields separated by hedgerows, and so on—are thus visible in almost every relevant publication from the BNP and are prominently displayed on the party's website under the section *Environment*.

Viewing the countryside as a space of community and purity points to the significance of nostalgia. Indeed, a feeling of loss, a lack of home and its security, characterises nostalgia. In nationalism, nostalgia is linked to notions of a mythical Golden Age, a point in time when the nation allegedly experienced unity and glory, fullness and greatness. The feeling of nostalgia is described by Svetlana Boym (2001: 8) as "a mourning for the impossibility of mythical return, for the loss of an enchanted world with clear borders and values; it could be a secular expression of a spiritual longing, a nostalgia for an absolute, a home that is both physical and spiritual."

Bryan Turner (1987: 150f) has provided another conceptualisation of nostalgia, emphasising four dimensions. The first dimension is about a feeling of decline and loss, while the second concerns a perception of the present as being in cultural crisis and, consequently, a longing for unity. It is here that Turner points to the countryside (and the work of Polanyi) in identifying "the emergence of markets, capitalist relations and urban cultures" in opposition to rural naivety as a prominent nostalgic theme.

Third, Turner speaks of "a sense of loss of individual freedom and autonomy" characterising nostalgia, and reminds the reader of Weber's iron cage and Marx's notion of alienation. The fourth dimension of nostalgia concerns the "idea of a loss of simplicity, personal authenticity and emotional spontaneity", of *unspoiled* spontaneity. Having already indicated the BNP's nostalgic desire for communal purity, let me now, finally, introduce this actor.

Since the demise of the British Empire began after World War I, the far-right in Britain has been represented by several parties, of which the BNP has certainly been one of the most successful (Copsey 2008; Goodwin 2011; Richardson 2013). Via its founder, John Tyndall, the BNP is linked to the (re-)emergence of the British far-right, continuing in the tradition of the *League of Empire Loyalists* and the *British Union of Fascists*. Interestingly, the latter had an agricultural policy whose author, Jorian Jenks, argued for a net of independent, family-run and self-sufficient farmers, as well as a strengthening of the organic links between land and (rural) people, while rejecting "urban-based plutocrats" (Moore-Colyer 2004). Thus, the countryside played (and plays) a key role in imagining national autarky and securing the heritage of the people vis-à-vis capital, especially in the form of multinational companies.

Founded in 1982, the BNP, during the 2000s, celebrated local election victories and, most importantly, a breakthrough in the 2009 European election (6.2 %, resulting in two MEPs). Furthermore, membership increased from a couple of hundred in 1982 to a high of around 14.000 in 2010 (Goodwin 2011: 124f).[4] This success has led to some academic interest in the party which, however, rarely focuses on the party's "green" agenda. Currently, (academic) interest in the BNP in general has withered away due to the sharp decline in the party's fortunes. Still, during the 2000s, the BNP provided an illuminating example of a far-right nationalist actor. I therefore draw on data taken from the BNP, first and foremost on articles taken from the party's *Identity* magazine, published between 2000 and 2010, which feature the countryside as a "primary topic" (van Dijk 1991). This is supplemented by relevant sections from manifestos and the party's website. In the context of this study, a focus

---

[4] The latest figure I am aware of puts the number of BNP members at 500 (Ramsey 2015).

on the party's magazine as an inward-looking, ideology-driven genre (Mudde 2000: 20ff) provides much better insights into the link between ideology and countryside than simply looking at a party's polished, outward-looking manifestos (in fact, no substantial differences in content were found, though the magazine offers more colourful, deeper insights into the role played by the countryside). The next section introduces the analysis of this material.

Analysing Far-Right Discontent: Purity and Pollution in the Countryside

Like other contributions to this volume, I am interested in the nexus of market forces and nostalgia, the longing for an imagined community, pure and united. Against this background, this section analyses the construction of the countryside by starting with a few general remarks on the role of market forces in the BNP's discourse on the countryside before looking at two specific dimensions: first, the longing for in-group purity, paradigmatically represented by children situated in the countryside. Second, I point to ways in which this supposedly pure space is in danger of pollution through the influx of (human) migrants.

While the effect of market forces on social relations is certainly not the only cause of nostalgic feelings, market forces are central in far-right discourses on the countryside, and the natural environment at large is visible in many of the collected articles. In issue 23 of the BNP's *Identity*, Lee Barnes (2002: 12) states that "we are faced with environmental catastrophe brought about by rampant consumerism and greed for profit", while Anthony Holroyd (2002: 23) claims that it is capitalism which "ruins the surrounding environment in order to satisfy the need for continuously increasing output". Importantly, this anticapitalism does not talk about class and property relations, but global actors and "international big business" (Barnes 2002: 12). It is, however, already in such comments that the countryside is assigned a sacred status.

It is in this context that the late Emile Durkheim's (2008) assumption about identities and orders as acceptable due to their constructed, *sacred* core is helpful. In other words, the BNP, in its celebration of the country-side, views the latter as a symbol of the nation, and thus the countryside is turned into a sacred "ethno-scape". Sometimes, this is as explicit as in the following contribution to *Identity* (2002a: 11) in which "global forces" are held responsible for pollution: "the BNP is pledged more strongly than at any stage in its history to fight the despoliation of our sacred homeland". The pollution of the sacred (for more on the social dynamics of symbolic purification and pollution, see Douglas 1966) is similarly visible in Barnes' (2004a: 14) comment: "Our countryside—and with it our heritage—destroyed." Interventions like these share a stark rejection of the profane commodification of the land; the dominance of market forces over what is sacred.

And although such statements foreground the destruction of the coun-tryside, the rejection of the city is in no way missing in such pieces. The city is viewed as lost, something opposed to the purity of the country. In line with this, Ian Buckley (2002: 22) claims that "outside the decayed urban parts of Britain you can still find a few places that are still as our land should be". Reawakening cannot take place in cities characterised by commerce and movement, only where potentially unspoiled, pure, 'natural' spaces exist: in the countryside.

The BNP's Pure Countryside

Against this general background of marked forces polluting *our* scared coun-tryside, I focus, first, on how that which is considered to be pure is symbol-ised. This, however, does not imply that purity can be understood without a view on market forces. For example, Phil Reddal (2008: 93), in a piece on *Spiritual nationalism*, claims that "Nationalism is the polar opposite of neo-liberalism, and where Nationalism promotes the workings of Nature; neo-liberals fear it and try to halt its progress." The important point here is the justification for why these two should be viewed as opposing each other: those best positioned to "fully grasp the ethos of nationalism"—Reddal mentions foresters, gardeners, rangers and fisherman—recognise nature's "eternal Laws". Of course, there is more to nature and its allegedly "eternal Laws" than just the countryside. After all, the latter includes a great deal of cultivation; but Reddal clearly conceptually locates the countryside within "nature" when stressing the significance of "the land" and "all things that grow" for nationalists (going as far as including "naturalistic sporting pursuits such as fishing"). Enjoying the countryside, truly indulging in it, is thereby also linked to acknowledging ultimate order. In contrast, market forces are deaf when it comes to "the workings of Nature", their proposals are artificial and superficial.

Let me sketch out some typical representations of the pure, of what is apparently natural, in opposition to that which appears to be artificial, by returning to one of the aforementioned inventions by Barnes (2004b: 11). The latter gives meaning to the pollution of sacred spaces by claiming that "torn pages of pornographic magazines pollute the woods where I once gathered bluebells for my mother. (...) Only by destroying nature and making everything equally ugly, can the memory of our natural beauty and ancient greatness be extirpated."

This extract is particularly telling in its juxtaposition of purity and innocence (the woods, collecting flowers, mother) with ultimate profanity, indeed dirt: not only is nature destroyed (due to construction work), but this place, which gave the author's mother much innocent joy, is now polluted by "pornographic magazines". Although, memories of greatness have not yet entirely vanished, they are clearly endangered as economic and cultural forces threaten the countryside, leading to the destruction of history, culture and the traditions of a people.

As artificial (societal) rules are seen in opposition to nature and its timeless laws, the only hope for a sustained existence of the national body is to grow with and out of its land. Only thus is the nation invested with authenticity, purity and innocence—and able to reject the artificial, corrupted and impure associated with the city. It is in the city that self and society get lost—and it is in the countryside that innocence is rooted. Thus it comes as no surprise that many images of *our* countryside include not only archetypical features such as hedges and old, traditional buildings (for example an ancient cathedral), but also symbols of innocence, such as happy families, mothers and children.

Against this background, one can better understand the reason behind putting a possibly 6-year-old (blond) girl on the first front cover of the BNP's magazine *Identity*. In fact, what the reader sees is not only a child, but a child standing half on a rock sticking out of some grass in front of a few trees. This connection of childhood and nature, I argue, paradigmatically summarises the relation between nationalism and country. Surely, for the BNP, there can hardly be anything more innocent than a blond, white girl, and nothing less contrived than a stone sticking out of the nation's soil. As both children and nature are innocent and pure, they are ideal referents for nostalgic longing.

This image confirms Raymond Williams' (1973: 139) observation that fusing nature, the past and childhood can be a powerful move in (amongst others) Western societies. Here, the countryside is positioned as the place for the unalienated *birth* of community and its promising future. Similarly, Denis Cosgrove (1988: 234) reminds us that the romantics viewed children as fulfilling "full communion with nature". Innocent, authentic joy and spontaneous fun are situated in the countryside, both understood as time and space now under threat from market forces. The observation by Williams and Cosgrove are regularly confirmed in the BNP's *Identity* in which the commodification of land is viewed as threatening *our* memories. This is clearly present in contributions like those of Barnes above and that of Diana Brit (2009: 24) who states: "As a child, growing up in the countryside, I remember roaming across fields and climbing trees. (…) My memories of childhood are being destroyed by multinational businesses, with the destruction of our environment." This final extract neatly brings together the various strands this article investigates: a nostalgic look back at the past coupled with a rejection of the market forces which are destroying this past.

The BNP's Fear of Polluting Others

Indeed, where there is purity, there is a danger of pollution. Thus, I now turn from a focus on how purity is conveyed to particular agents of pollution, defined by Douglas (1966: 41) simply as "matter out of place", an uncleanliness which opposes a certain order. Besides market forces in general, this draws our attention to how migration is viewed.

In some cases, this is more or less subtly linked to the issue of invasive species and (implicit) links between the latter and the human world.

This argument by nationalists, in particular from the farright, claims that nations are (eco)systems which—if too many alien elements enter—lose their natural equilibrium and collapse. One article, for example, is entitled '*Emblem of Hope*' as *Britain's red squirrels fight back against invaders* (Identity 2002b: 10) and describes the species' survival in the face of a "relentless invasion of imported American grey squirrels". Kenneth Olwig (2003: 72) has argued that linking "alien species" with "alien races" and cultures feeds into an understanding of flora and fauna as being (in) authentic and based on the "cartographic–pictographic episteme" which combines a notion of hard-edged boundaries with pictorial images of nature as having given birth to "natives". In most cases, however, the link between pollution and "aliens" is less subtle, pointing explicitly to human migrants. Indeed, the latter are paramount in the BNP's manifestos but also on its website where stopping immigration is proposed as a solution to relieving the pressures on the countryside.

In an article by Darren James (2002: 18, *italics* added), then coordinator of the BNP's *Land and People* rural affairs circle, migration is related extensively to the future of the countryside, including the following passage: "[g]reat swaths of lush pastureland and precious wildlife habitats are succumbing to floods of development to house 'white-flight' *refugees* fleeing the folly of enforced multiculturalism". The evil of immigration and its result, multiculturalism, are linked to the countryside, a countryside which will only survive if an end is put to immigration. Here again, the issue of pollution of sacred spaces is at the heart of the matter and, in this case, constructed through the victimisation of 'indigenous' (white) British who have supposedly become "'white flight' *refugees*" (the latter describes the movement of 'whites' from 'ethnically' mixed inner-city districts to more affluent, 'ethnically' homogeneous suburban or exurban regions).

The idyll of living in the countryside, and the dangers this idyll faces, is similarly visible in a short story by Bea Kaye (2009). In it, a small Scottish village is taken over, step by step, by Muslims, leading to, among other things, the theft of sheep and chickens (and special offers at the newly opened halal butcher). But the indigenous inhabitants stand together, and so community prevails and the newcomers are, ultimately, driven out. This story radicalises the aforementioned threat to the countryside ("white flight") by laying out a concrete scenario of alien invasion.

Such stories demonstrate clearly that the countryside, as a space of pure community, is a space of true unity. While traditional understandings of the countryside and *Gemeinschaft* have stressed such unity, something reproduced by the BNP, there is no acknowledgement of the many conflicts occurring in local communities, for example, concerning status and access to the land (Urry 1995: 10).

In addition, it is the sheer number of people migrating into Britain which serves as an important point of intervention. Clive Wakley (2010) discusses the recurrent topic of overpopulation in great detail and relates it to various dimensions, from traffic congestion to energy generation, landfill and water provision, including the wider effects on the countryside. Such articles offer room to elaborate on apocalyptic scenarios, including the collapse of *our* entire civilization as too many of *them* cause too much pollution. Wakely (ibid.: 52f) formulates this decisively when describing the impact of immigration in terms of "colonialisation" and talking about "the dispossession of our children and grandchildren of their homeland".

We have now come full circle, in that, here we return to childhood and its symbolic relation to *our* land. This has hopefully clarified, first, the significance attached to (global) markets as a predatory force destroying the countryside; second, the fact that the BNP and nationalists at large view this space as pure and sacred, as the natural and innocent birthplace of a national community; and, third, the significance of migrants in the process of polluting this space, and thus the possibility of sovereign, national conduct. All this points to the idea of an organic social order linked to the countryside, and thus imagined organic relations to the land must be defended against threats from market forces in general and migrants in particular.

From Nostalgia to Collective Learning?

The previous section responded to the first question raised in the introduction and was concerned with how a paradigmatic far-right, nationalist actor narrates the effect of market forces on the countryside. My second aim is to use this case as a starting point to think about different *forms* in which nostalgia can feature in stories. Not limiting myself to the actual content of stories (as I have done so far), I will outline three modes of emploting narratives—romance, tragedy and (post-heroic) irony—in order to provide an understanding of (the politics of) nostalgia. The BNP, for example, tells romantic stories about clashes between good and evil, black and white (or rather: white and black), thereby offering certainty and a positive self-image. Other forms, however, convey different senti-ments, other ways of being emotively positioned—and depending on these, progressive politics of nostalgia may be possible or not.

I start by taking a look at how nostalgia has been conceptualised as more or less progressive before I, second, introduce the concept of nar-rative and its archetypical forms. These are, third, connected to nostal-gia, thereby outlining three types of stories based on nostalgic sentiments which position the audience differently. Finally, these storytypes are viewed as social mechanisms which, drawing on Habermasian ideas, enable the blocking or unblocking of collective learning processes.

Nostalgia?

It is a widely shared assumption that nostalgia is a regressive way of situating oneself in time—an assumption which appears not to be without basis. In fact, explicit cases of nationalist nostalgia can easily be found in my data, such as when one author in *Identity* (Kaye 2008: 27) states that "nostalgia for how we once were becomes inseparable from nationalism". Boym (2001: 41–55) views such a dimension of nostalgia (what she calls "restorative nostalgia") as a relation to the past in which the latter shines bright and should be restored in the present. Here, the longing for the "restoration of origins" is of a serious, uncompromising nature, and it is this type of nostalgia which is paradigmatically present in the BNP's discourse on the countryside. For example, Barnes imagines woods free of pollution and Brit idealises a countryside free of commercialisation, like states which apparently existed in the past and need to be restored.

However, Boym also points to another dimension of nostalgia, "reflective nostalgia", which is characterised by an awareness of the imperfect ways in which the past can become present and an ability to open up multiple ways of belonging (for a similar point, see Turner 1987). More recently, Michael Pickering and Emily Keightley (2006: 921) have argued for a separation of retreat versus retrieval: while the former denotes a "desire to return to an earlier state or idealized past", the latter "recognize[s] aspects of the past as the basis for renewal and satisfaction in the future".

In fact, and returning to the case of the countryside, a similar differentiation can be found in the work of David Matless (1998: 120f) which includes an instructive comparison between the views of organicist England (represented, for example, by the *British Union of Fascists*, a forerunner of the BNP), which juxtaposes country and city, with the preservationist movement of the 1920s and later, which attempted to preserve the country through planning. Emerging at a time when planning was seen as a way to avoid political and economic crises, these preservationists represent a particular type of modernism that allied progress with preservation—something in opposition to organicist imaginaries and their "nostalgia for how we once were".

Considering Boym, Pickering and Keightley, as well as others, provide us with an idea of how a "reflective" variety of nostalgia—in contrast to what we have gotten to know from the BNP—might look like. In order to add further substance to this theorising and enable a better understanding of the character of "renewal and satisfaction in the future", let us start by turning to a discussion of Polanyi by Nancy Fraser (2012). Her (not explicit) critique of varieties of nostalgia centres on the concept of *double transformation*, which she attempts to transform into a *triple transformation*. Being aware of oppressive aspects of social protectionism, she points to emancipation and the idea of "participatory parity" in the public sphere of civil society as a third element to be considered. While claiming that each crisis must not simply be seen as an objective breakdown but a truly "intersubjective process", reactions to such crises, for example, in and through nostalgic imaginaries, should be evaluated by drawing on her progressive ideal.

Recognising the need for a theoretically informed differentiation of nostalgia, I propose to start not by considering a concrete ideal but the formal nature of the "intersubjective process" that Fraser mentions. The argument I will develop in the next section is that subjects do not simply float through the public sphere or interact via 'rational' argumentation.

Instead, the public sphere consists of stories participants tell about themselves and others. Neonationalist groups tell stories, as do their centrist and left-wing opponents, and their analysis and evaluation are important because they affect the symbolic self-production of the group in question. My proposal does, however, not include an evaluation of particular content or claims of stories—a task I do not consider meaningful in a (post)modern context in which beliefs and values are differentiated and have pluralised. Instead, I focus on formal properties of stories by identifying types of narratives which might facilitate "reflective" nostalgia (or not). It is this characteristic of stories to which I now turn.

Emploting Narratives

In order to understand types of narratives, I draw on the concept of narrative archetypes developed by Northrop Frye (1957) and taken up by, for example, Hayden White (1973) under the notion of "modes of emplotment". Modes of emplotment denote the framing and perception of narratives on a fundamental level. The focus is therefore not on the content of specific narratives, what I have considered in section three, but on their formal properties and the way the latter positions audiences differently and mobilises different sentiments (as we will seeherein, not all nostalgic stories are emploted romantically, as in the case of the BNP).

Narratives are not simply about the chronological reporting of events; they connect past and present through selectively constructing coherence between a beginning, a middle, and an end. Indeed, and most fundamentally, it is through narratives that human beings comprehend temporality (Ricoeur 1988: 241). Those who narrate a story do so by arranging events via different culturally available plot structures or modes—and it is through these structures (besides the particularities of the actual story) that time is experienced. As such, I am interested in nostalgia as a mood, a way of experiencing time, as a primarily affective dimension which characterises the stories people tell about themselves and which underlies their identities. The effect of plot structures is thus in no way neutral. By suggesting a certain development of the story, the audience is positioned in a certain way, opening up possibilities to interpret some events, while downplaying others. That is, the different modes in which events can be arranged facilitate different relations between *our* past, present and future in terms of the openness or closure toward doubt and self-criticism.

The aforementioned work by Frye offers a theory of four modes which serve as archetypes of Western storytelling, facilitating doubt and self-criticism to various degrees. These are the modes of romance, tragedy, irony/satire and comedy. Before linking them to the theme of nostalgia, let me introduce them briefly: *romance* structures traditional stories of idealised heroes who face evil, clearly demarcated others. Setbacks might occur, but they are part of the hero's development and rarely touch his character. This is a struggle between light and darkness and thus "subtlety and complexity are not too much favoured" (Frye 1957: 195).[5] In contrast, *tragedy* makes the audience identify with a subject who did not triumph, but was defeated. The audience is thus left with a catastrophe, and as such a happy ending is constantly prevented. Although this does not necessarily end in despair, tragedies certainly carry the possibility of radical retreat (see Jacobs 2001 and Frei in this volume for illustrative cases). *Irony's* key characteristic is an attitude of detachment, a feeling of distance. Irony is not a distinct narrative genre but sits parasitically on other types—especially romance and its attitude of certainty. As it is subversive, antinaive and able to take different perspectives into account, there cannot be a happy ending. But as actors cannot be entirely detached and fragmented, a more precise notion might be that of postheroic irony in which ambiguity and even fragmentation are central aspects but which do not imply a total distancing from every value.

Emploting Nostalgic Nostalgia

Drawing on these three different ways of making sense of time, nostalgia can, ideally andtypically, be part of stories about *us* and *them* in three different ways (Table 1). Nostalgia can give rise to feelings of (a) utopian zeal and the strict attachment to an imagined past (romantic mode),

---

[5] While comedy is more flexible than romance, in that oppositions are ultimately overcome without crushing the opponent, it resembles romance in featuring a happy ending. For matters of practicality, I thus only focus on the modes of romance, tragedy and irony.

Table 1 Nostalgia and its modes

Past	Present	Mode
Something longed for	Restoration of a loss	Romance
	Retreat in the face of this loss	Tragedy
	Facing loss	Irony

(b) depression and hopelessness in the light of an imagined past (tragic mode) and (c) ambiguity and distance from the cosiness of an imagined past without dropping the longing for this past (ironic mode).

The first way of embedding nostalgia in narratives connects a feeling of loss in the past with a present-day rejection of this loss, rejection not only of loss itself but also rejection of problematizing the loss. The loss is to be restored within a Manichean frame whereby the mythical nature and effects this imagined past has in the present are not questioned. Instead, the imagined past is simply rearticulated: *we* need to find *our* voice (again) and change the current state of affairs. Such an exercise of voice is closest to the narrative genre of romance. Frye (1957: 186) himself characterised romance as "marked by its extraordinarily persistent nostalgia" for a golden age, and Frederic Jameson (1983: 91) speaks of "a reconquest (...) of some feeling for a salvational future". Such stories are highly mobilising and usually carry (away) newly formed social movements or nations. Stories by the BNP are emploted in such a mode and, indeed, Kaye's aforementioned story about a small Scottish village is a paradigmatic example: it departs from a golden age (the organic order of a small, rural village), introduces danger to this state as the villain (immigrants) arrives, and closes with the victory of the people, the reconquest of what had initially been: a countryside apparently pure and natural, lacking any "polluting" elements.

Opposite to such a rejection of loss is a retreat. By speaking of retreat, I think of retreat from the public sphere, a silence in the face of what is perceived as an utterly profane present (and future). Due to a loss, everything appears shattered and grey, and thus these stories facilitate exit from the public sphere (or even life). The despair characterising such nostalgic, tragic stories contradicts collective action. One possible example of such stories might be told by disillusioned countryside activists who remember (or imagine) the past beauty of their greenbelt, but have seen their protests against its destruction defeated time and again. As a consequence, they have retreated from activism, restricting their protests to the private sphere. While far-right nationalists like the BNP stage a fight between light and darkness, those who live by a tragic narrative do not intervene any longer—they might still nurture their own garden, but have given up hope and optimism which would fuel collective action beyond their garden fence.

The third type is one in which the longing for a past is linked to a present in which this loss is more or less faced; the past is not 'closed' (either as an ideal or as something which cannot be realised anymore in any meaningful sense) but linked to a present-day awareness of the inappropriateness of this past in the present. The commitment to the past, a nostalgic longing, is therefore not without limits or based on excess. Rather, it is characterised by what might be called postheroic irony, an irony able to uphold longing, to uphold multiple ways of continuing one's story, while acknowledging ambivalence and contingency. Such a sentiment prevents a heroic, coherent subjectivity and self-righteous happy endings—and although it is certainly a demanding form of intersubjectivity, it can enable collective engagement. An example of such a narrative is found in a recent foreword to a collection of poems published by the National Trust, an organization responsible for the protection of what is viewed as Britain's cultural heritage and historic landscapes. In it, the author (Bell 2010: 8) articulates a desire to escape from daily anxieties and enjoy a "broader and fresher life" by "indulging in a little harmless nostalgia, *for a world that never was*" (italics added). While the countryside and its lost beauties are nostalgically called to mind, a simple, backward looking nostalgia is prevented as the dream of a Golden Age is explicitly rejected.

I have introduced three types of telling nostalgic stories. The point was not to evaluate the particular content of these stories: for example, whether or not the BNP is correct in imagining porn-free woods, previous greenbelt activists rightly considering their activism without effect, or visiting the countryside helps us to cope with "daily anxieties". Instead, I stressed structures of experience, affective dimensions of story types—ranging from rigid black:white dichotomies to despair and feelings of ambiguity. It is this dimension which, I suggest, offers a way to evaluate nostalgia and identify what might be called progressive in certain politics of nostalgia.

Collective Learning Processes and Varieties of Nostalgia

As groups reproduce themselves (at least symbolically) through the stories they tell, the ways in which nostalgic stories are emploted is of great significance. In this final section, I suggest understanding the aforementioned story types as social mechanisms through which more open and egalitarian symbolic boundaries emerge (or do not). Drawing on the work of Jürgen Habermas (1984, 2008) and its development by others (Strydom 1992; Eder 1999; Miller 2006), I view such processes of boundary development as collective learning processes which may well be blocked. My claim is that those favouring progressive politics of nostalgia must not tell predominantly romantic stories but aim for complex ones which, nevertheless, enable narrative networks.

The aforementioned concept of collective learning is grounded in Habermas's reconstruction of the deep structures of intersubjectivity, the pragmatic, weak but unavoidable features of communication (inclusiveness, equal communicative rights, sincerity and freedom from repression and manipulation) that anybody tacitly presupposes, once she or he seriously enters into argumentation in order to check a problematic validity claim (recently, Habermas 2008). Instead of reducing this notion of learning to an aggregation of individual knowledge or a rationalism oriented toward an exchange of arguments (for example Habermas 1984: 22, 2008: 53), I suggest that collective learning is primarily about prediscursive forms, through which time is experienced, and the way they structure communication within and between groups (Forchtner and Eder 2016). In other words: these prediscursive forms are narrative modes of emplotment and, in particular, the sentiments they facilitate: romantic certainty, tragic despair and ironic ambivalence.

For example, romantic stories foster strong ties and enable collective action. Yet, they tend to hamper collective learning processes as these stories leave little room for ambivalence, for truths other than that which is supposed to constitute the subject. The BNP is a prime example of how to tell such stories. In turn, full-blown tragic stories based on nostalgia also tend to prevent collective learning. After all, if relations are established in this type of narrative, they are private ones which do not enable action beyond the actor's garden fence. Finally, stories with a post-heroic spin are able to avoid this while remaining fuzzy and "breaking the spell" of romantic stories. As they offer multiple ways to connect, rather than just binaries, the subject positions in these stories remain fragmented but, at the same time, open to change. As a matter of fact, while this story type enables societal learning, the continuous flow of narratives across boundaries, it is also by far the most demanding. The argument in favour of irony as a mode of emplotment is, however, reminiscent of a proposal made by Ronald Jacobs and Philip Smith (1997), who suggested balancing romantic and ironic narratives in order to warrant solidary without (nationalist) excess. By understanding the three modes as mechanisms within a Habermasian-inspired framework, Jacobs and Smith's outline is further developed by grounding its evaluation. How such a combination of modes might look is an empirical question—though this contribution has hopefully succeeded in illustrating that the stories from the BNP do not manage to do so.

Conclusion

In this article, I have, first, illustrated how members of the farright construct the countryside as a nexus of nostalgia for a lost communal purity in the face of market forces. Recalling Turner's four dimensions of nostalgia, the BNP views cultural crises as being endemic in today's world, a world from which homogeneity and unity, imagined to have characterised the nation and its customs in the past, are vanishing. Turner further points to the freedom and alienation which are present in the BNP, most forcefully when the latter proclaims the virtues of the countryside vis-à-vis the city and that true freedom can only be experienced within the old order. Finally, truly being is only, or primarily, possible in the countryside. Ordinary, child-like play, polluted by neither commercialisation nor migrants, requires this haven of authenticity and simplicity. It is against this background that the aesthetics of the national countryside are often intertwined with symbolic claims central to a nationalist ideology. It is this "symbolic aesthetic" which can be seen as a central finding, explaining the significance of the nostalgia for the loss of countryside in (far-right) nationalism.

Second, this analysis of stories becomes a springboard for developing a model of various nostalgic, narrative structures and their evaluation. By conceptualizing three different relations between past and present—romantic, tragic and ironic ones—the article carves out three different preargumentative relations to a lost past. Indeed, the way groups construct their relation to, for example, the natural environment (past and present) impinges on the stories they tell about themselves. The narrative perspective proposed here is, however, a formal one which does not assess the truth value of the factual content of such stories. As I have illustrated, the BNP's discourse on the countryside does not facilitate a collective learning process and cannot be viewed as "progressive"—not simply because of the particular claims made by the party but due to their Manichaean form. But all too often, centrist and even leftist actors will show similar attitudes when being critical of invasive species or the power of multinational companies. In a (post)modernity characterised by pluralism and a lack of truth, one might sympathise with, for example, a social movement and the particular claims and content it disseminates. Not only might our favoured political actors err, they might also shield themselves from criticism and doubt when telling their stories in a romantic mode (and not ironically subverted), thereby blocking their evolution, the influx of new ideas and positions.

For the politics of nostalgia to be progressive, nostalgic stories need to remain open to ambiguity and discomfort instead of cosiness and self-righteousness. This is also true when it comes to the countryside and the natural environment in general, which is not only relevant as a space which keeps us healthy. Much more, and as the persistent investment by individuals and social movements shows, the countryside remains a deeply sacred space, a place for dreaming of other worlds, of utopias which have never been.

References

Agyeman, J., & Neal, S. (2006). *The new countryside? Ethnicity, nation and exclusion in contemporary rural Britain*. Bristol: Policy Press.
Anderson, B. (2006). *Imagined communities*. London: Verso.

Barnes, L. (2002). Stop the bandwagon of destruction. *Identity*, *23*, 12–13.

Barnes, L. (2004a). Deculturalisation and the awakening of the Albion. *Identity*, *44*, 13–15.

Barnes, L. (2004b). Deculturalisation and the awakening of the Albion—conclusion. *Identity*, *45*, 11.

Bell, J. (2010). Foreword. In S. Carr (Ed.), *Ode to the countryside. Poems to celebrate the British landscape* (pp. 8–9). London: National Trust.

Billig, M. (1995). *Banal nationalism*. London: Sage.

BNP (2009). *Manifesto for the European elections 2009*. London: BNP.

Boym, S. (2001). *The future of nostalgia*. New York: Basic Books.

Brit, D. (2009). Support British culture & maintain our traditions. *Identity*, *102*, 24–25.

Buckley, I. (2002). Happy memories in the Ribble Valley. *Identity*, *27*, 22.

Chakraborti, N., & Garland, J. (2011). *Rural racism*. Oxon: Routledge.

Copsey, N. (2008). *Contemporary British fascism: The British national party and the quest for legitimacy*. Basingstoke: Palgrave.

Cosgrove, D. (1988). *Social formation and symbolic landscape*. Madison: University of Wisconsin Press.

Daniels, S. (1993). *Fields of vision. Landscape imagery and national identity in England and the United States*. London: Polity.

Darby, W. J. (2000). *Landscape and identity. Geographies of nation and class in England*. Oxford: Berg.

Darren, J. (2002). Our land & our people. *Identity*, *22*, 18.

Ditt, K. (1996). Nature conservation in England and Germany 1900–70: Forerunner of environmental protection. *Contemporary European History*, *5*(1), 1–28.

Douglas, M. (1966). *Purity and danger*. London: Routledge.

Durkheim, E. (2008). *Elementary forms of religious life*. Oxford: Oxford University Press.

Eder, K. (1999). Societies learn and yet the world is hard to change. *European Journal of Social Theory*, *2*(2), 195–215.

Forchtner, B., & Eder, K. (2016). Europa erzählen: Strukturen Europäischer Identität. In H- W. Platzer & G. Hentges (Eds.), *Europäische Identität in der Krise?* Wiesbaden: VS (forthcoming).

Forchtner, B., & Kølvraa, C. (2015). The nature of nationalism: Populist radical right parties on countryside and climate. *Nature & Culture*, *10*(2), 199–224.

Fraser, N. (2012). *Marketization, social protection, emancipation: Toward a neopolanyian conception of capitalist crisis*. http://sophiapol.hypotheses.org/files/2012/02/Texte-Nancy-Fraser-anglais.doc. Accessed 10 June 2015.

Frye, N. (1957). *Anatomy of criticism: Four essays*. Princeton: Princeton University Press.

Goodwin, M. (2011). *New British fascism: Rise of the British ational party*. London: Routledge.

Gould, P. (1988). *Early green politics. Back to nature, back to land, and socialism in Britain, 1880–1900*. Brighton: Harvester Press.

Habermas, J. (1984). *The theory of communicative action Volume I. Reason and the rationalization of society*. Boston: Beacon Press.

Habermas, J. (2008). Communicative action and the detranscendentalized 'use of reason'. In *Between naturalism and religion: Philosophical essays* (pp. 24–76). Cambridge: Polity Press.

Holroyd, A. (2002). Humanising British housing in the 21st century. *Identity, 26*, 22–23.

Identity. (2002a). The last stand to save King Arthur's court. *Identity, 24*, 11.

Identity. (2002b). 'Emblem of hope' as Britain's red squirrels fight back against invaders. *Identity, 26*, 10.

Jacobs, R. (2001). The problem with tragic narratives: Lessons from the Los Angeles uprising. *Qualitative Sociology, 24*(2), 221–243.

Jacobs, R., & Smith, P. (1997). Romance, irony, and solidarity. *Sociological Theory, 15*(1), 60–80.

Jameson, F. (1983). *The political unconscious. Narrative as a socially symbolic act*. London: Routledge.

Kaye, B. (2008). Nationalism & nostalgia. *Identity, 88*, 27.

Kaye, B. (2009). The outpost. *Identity, 99*, 20–21.

Lowenthal, D. (1991). British national identity and the English landscape. *Rural History, 2*(2), 205–230.

Matless, D. (1998). *Landscape and englishness*. London: Reaktion Books.

Miller, M. (2006). *Dissens*. Bielefeld: transcript.

Moore-Colyer, R. (2004). Towards 'Mother earth': Jorian Jenks, organicism, the right and the British union of fascists. *Journal of Contemporary History, 39*(3), 353–371.

Mudde, C. (2000). *The ideology of the extreme right*. Manchester: Manchester University Press.

Olwig, K. (2003). Natives and aliens in the national landscape. *Landscape Research, 28*(1), 61–74.

Pickering, M., & Keightley, E. (2006). The modalities of nostalgia. *Current Sociology, 54*(6), 919–941.

Polanyi, K. (2001). *The great transformation: The political and economic origins of our time*. Boston: Beacon Press.

Ramsay, A. (2015). *Another note on party memberships in the UK.* https://www. opendemocracy.net/ourkingdom/adam-ramsay/another-note-on-party-memberships-in-uk. Accessed 16 Aug 2015.

Reddal, P. (2008). Spiritual nationalism. *Identity, 93*, 10–11.

Richardson, J. (2013). Ploughing the same furrow? Continuity and change on Britain's extreme-right fringe. In R. Wodak, M. KhosraviNik, & B. Mral (Eds.), *Right-wing populism in Europe* (pp. 105–119). London: Bloomsbury.

Ricoeur, P. (1988). *Time and narrative* (Vol. 3). Chicago: University of Chicago Press.

Smith, A. D. (1983). *The ethnic origins of nations.* Malden: Wiley-Blackwell.

Smith, A. D. (2009). *Ethno-symbolism and nationalism. A cultural approach.* London: Routledge.

Strydom, P. (1992). The ontogenetic fallacy: The immanent critique of Habermas's developmental logical theory of evolution. *Theory, Culture and Society, 9*(3), 65–93.

Tönnies, F. (2002). *Community and society.* New York: Dover Publications.

Turner, B. (1987). A note on nostalgia. *Theory, Culture & Society, 4*(1), 147–156.

Urry, J. (1995). *Consuming places.* London: Routledge.

Urry, J. (2000). *Sociology beyond societies.* London: Routledge.

van Dijk, T. (1991). *Racism and the press.* London: Routledge.

Wakley, C. (2010). The curse of overpopulation. *Identity, 103*, 52–57.

Wallerstein, I. (2011). *The modern world system IV. Centrist liberalism triumphant, 1789–1914.* Berkeley: University of California Press.

White, H. (1973). *Metahistory. The historical imagination in nineteenth-century Europe.* Baltimore: John Hopkins University Press.

Williams, R. (1973). *The country and the city.* Oxford: Oxford University Press.

"Varieties of Nostalgia" in Argentinean and Chilean Generations

Raimundo Frei

Argentinean and Chilean contexts are fertile terrains for varieties of collective nostalgia. Over the last four decades, neoliberal reforms have been implemented, resulting in several economic crises, and social malaise, as well as the idealization of lost social rights. In addition, leftist political groups yearn for political engagement which was boosted during the sixties and seventies, and also for networks of solidarity which grew during right-wing dictatorial periods (in Argentina, 1976–83; in Chile, 1973–90), yet both later diminished with the return of democracy. However, during the last decade, various state and civil society initiatives have reacted against neoliberalism and there has been a broad process of (re)politicization (Roberts 2012). This countercycle of "Polanyian re-embedding" can be observed across Southern Cone political milieus, making them suitable "case studies" for linking nostalgia with processes of commodification, neoliberal orders and their conflicting politics.

R. Frei (✉)
United Nations Development Programme, Santiago, Chile

© The Editor(s) (if applicable) and The Author(s) 2016   **295**
C. Karner, B. Weicht (eds.), *The Commonalities of Global Crises*,
DOI 10.1057/978-1-137-50273-5_12

In terms of the sociology of nostalgia, my approach attempts to go beyond a bipolar understanding of collective nostalgia. That is to say, contemporary theories about nostalgia (for example, Boym 2001, Pickering and Keightley 2006) repeatedly move from a negative 'feeling of loss' (melancholic-restorative) to a positive yearning for the past (utopian-reflective). I suggest that it is necessary to discard such a polar division. Instead, I illustrate the existence of a variety of nostalgic narratives and, thereby, offer an understanding of different intersections between cultural structures and social formations.

To do so, I propose thinking about collective nostalgia from the perspective of the 'content of the *future*', instead of exclusively from the 'content of the *past*'. That is, when reflecting on nostalgia, it is crucial to examine images of the future embedded in nostalgic narratives, instead of exclusively fixing on past circumstances and present feelings of mourning. This emerges from empirical findings: by analysing memories of ordinary Argentineans and Chileans, I found that symbolic processes of longing for past periods normally depend on collective images of the future.

Actually, Boym (2001: xvi) appears to work under a similar assumption when stating that "[N]ostalgia is not always about the past; it can be retrospective but also prospective". The past and its content do, however, seem to be characterised here by a significantly stronger effect than in my model; there is something visible, for example, in her statement that "fantasies of the past determined by needs of the present have a direct impact on realities of the future" (idem). My suggestion is thus to invert Boym's rationale by examining how 'fantasies of the future', influenced by present feelings of loss, might have an impact on our understanding of the past.

In the following, I will briefly outline modern Argentinean and Chilean historical contexts. Secondly, I will discuss the field of research into nostalgia. Here, I provide theoretical reasons for taking a narrative (structural) perspective. I argue that via narrative analysis it is possible to look at the intersection between feelings of past experiences and images of the future, thus finding different narrative trajectories (Zerubavel 2003). Finally, I present four varieties of nostalgia by carving out generational stories with different 'senses of endings'.

Argentina and Chile: Neoliberal Experiments and Post-Neoliberal Eras

Even if there were attempts to implement neoliberal policies during the Argentinean dictatorship (1976–83), there was no consensus amongst the military forces to go through with them. The oil crisis of the 1980s provided a reason to opponents (within the military regime) to go against the neoliberal reforms. The dictatorship ended after Argentina lost the Falklands War. But still, the new democratic government—Alfonsín's presidency—was unable to offer economic stability. Consequently, Argentina suffered major hyperinflation in 1989. The new government—supported by the World Bank and the International Monetary Fund's (IMF's) guidelines—promised a renewal of the economy through liberalization and free markets. With this new promise, president Menem carried out multiple privatizations of public firms, as well as fostering a policy of monetary 'convertibility' whereby the Argentinean currency was converted into dollars by the government to halt inflation (Novaro 2009).

This new promise of renewal again failed during the crisis of 2001 when almost half of the population fell into poverty. This crisis revealed a large clientelistic, corrupt network (many public enterprises that were sold eventually favoured politicians and union leaders). In 2003, new illusion and promises brought Néstor Kirchner to presidency. Kirchner promoted strong reactions against Menem's and the IMF's neoliberal shifts, appealing for a 'national and popular government'. The narrative force of his government was so eloquent that this period in Argentinean history has been labelled a 'postneoliberal era' (for example, Segura 2015).

On the other side, Chile was one of the first countries worldwide in which strong neoliberal policies were adopted. After the failed project of Salvador Allende's socialist revolution—ended by a coup d'état in 1973—a military junta led by Augusto Pinochet adopted economic measures of (neo)liberalization. These measures reacted against a long process of collective mobilization and national industrialization by several governments since the 1930s. The dictatorship engaged not only in crimes against human rights and torture, but also structural shifts in economic and social terms. Understood as a 'developmental dictatorship' (Huneeus 2000), the military worked with a group of economists ('the Chicago boys') influenced by Milton Friedman (he coined the term '*the miracle of Chile*') and Friederich Hayek (Undurraga 2014). This so-called 'neoliberal experiment' included shrinking the state by selling off public firms, and privatizing the pension system and parts of the health sector and education system.

In 1989, when the dictatorship ended following a contesting plebiscite (46 % of the population voted for continuity of the military regime in this national referendum), the new centre-left government decided to augment the public budget for social policies—via tax reforms—but did not 're-embed' the market into society (in Polanyi's terms). Given good economic performance and growth rates, poverty diminished and consumerism flourished. Nevertheless, over the last fifteen years, in particular since students' and subcontracted miners' protests in 2006, dissatisfaction has emerged about pensions, health and education systems, and social inequalities.

In both contexts, nostalgic narratives have emerged in recent years: in Argentina, some groups long for a mythical national past of "splendour" while others yearn for a period of political compromise. In Chile, nostalgia for a time of collective solidarity during harsh dictatorial conditions has grown alongside a yearning for social rights nullified by the right-wing dictatorship. In order to explain these variations sociologically, I will clarify which groups support such narratives and what they expect from the future. I first provide a theoretical justification for looking simultaneously to the past and to the future to understand collective nostalgia.

Looking Beyond the 'Polar Constellation' Within the Field of Research into Nostalgia

Research into nostalgia can be divided into three areas. First, a myriad of research has investigated nostalgia at the psychological level. Understood as either a defensive mechanism or a necessary and positive idealization of the past, nostalgia is here seen as an unconscious, cognitive experience.[1] Second, sociocultural theory—particularly in the field of memory studies—views nostalgia as a symbolic artefact of (post)modernity (for example Boym 2001; Radstone 2007), focusing on macrocultural structures, often with little empirical input, or based mostly on examinations of cultural representations (for example, literary oeuvres and films).

A third group of research—more empirically oriented—focuses on the political and symbolic meanings of nostalgia circulating in different social formations and embedded in social practices (for example, Bonnett 2010). I locate myself in this third group, as I attempt to connect empirical research based on 'ordinary people's experiences' with wider reflections on time. Hence, my research offers contextual insights that are often only conceptually discussed in theories of nostalgia.

Also aligned to the latter group of research, Pickering and Keightley (2006) draw attention to different 'modalities of nostalgia', defining the phenomenon as a 'feeling of loss, lack, and longing' (2006: 921). Pickering and Keightley argue that 'feeling[s] of loss' might be melancholic or utopian, claiming: "we should perhaps reconfigure [nostalgia] in terms of a distinction between the desire to return to an earlier state or idealized past, and the desire not to return but to recognize aspects of the past as the basis for renewal and satisfaction in the future" (2006: 921).

Similar to Boym's restorative and reflective nostalgia (2001: 41–55), Pickering and Keightley explore two polar modes of nostalgia. However, from an empirical point of view, it is unclear why one should restrict oneself to two poles. Do we always move between these two poles? Is this contingent on *how* the past is idealized or yearned for?

In order to take a step forward within the field of nostalgia research, it is necessary to broaden those modalities and find criteria for doing so. I next look for 'varieties of nostalgia', suggesting three cultural domains (though there may be more) wherein social scientists might observe such criteria: feelings, and iconic and narrative structures.

---

[1] Sixty years ago, Fodor already spoke of 'varieties of nostalgia' in the context of psychoanalysis. He understood nostalgia as "yearning for our prenatal home" (1950: 30), that is longing for the mother's womb.

Following, Raymond Williams's (1977) *structures of feeling* concerns "meanings and values as they are actively lived and felt" (1977: 162), which imbue whole periods. This has attracted much research attention. For example, by defining nostalgia as an 'experience of loss', as Pickering and Keightley do, idealizations of the past might be shown to impinge upon a group's sense of belonging and collective identity. Yet, when understood as *feelings* of loss, modalities of nostalgia have been precisely shrunk to just two of them: (negative) melancholic mourning or (positive) utopian desire to recover past experiences.

Iconic structures (Alexander 2010; Bartmansky 2011) offer a conceptual broadening. The mediatisation of past images as well as an increasing focus on media devices for remembering (photographs, films, serials, spaces and so on) have nourished a close relationship between media icons and nostalgia. I argue, however, that the variability gained here is not produced by the mediated object itself, but by different feelings or, crucially, by diverse narratives attached to those objects.

Indeed, *narrative structures* are most crucial to understanding the variability of nostalgia and help us go beyond a simple, polar evaluation of nostalgic feelings. Narratives are indeed temporal sequences produced by recounting past events (Toolan 2001). Through narratives, past events are reported. They are elaborated on from present points of view and put in motion different horizons of expectation. As a result, past-present-future elements are not detached from each other, but are observed as moving together. "Varieties of nostalgia" might thus be found when looking at the intersection between different images of past periods, present evaluations (containing 'feelings of loss'), and future horizons.

Moreover, narratives are part of social contexts and social practices. Storytellers are embedded in networks of relationships, in which those stories circulate (Somers 1992, 1994). For narrative theory, identities are products of stories circulating in social spaces. My claim is that by examining narrative structures (that is, how past, present and future are linked in stories circulating in specific social contexts) one can scrutinize feelings of loss attached to different horizons of expectation in specific social formations. I emphasize the 'sense of ending' (Kermode 2000) of nostalgic narratives, pointing out that critical assessments of present social circumstances are not only linked to nostalgic feeling of loss, but also related to how these narratives construct a sense of the future. Therefore, a 'sense of ending'—how stories end for the storyteller—conveys a key criterion for broadening narrative trajectories (for example, declining, progressive, circular forms; see Zerubavel 2003). Consequently, variations in nostalgia emerge from different images of the future.

Varieties of Nostalgia in Generational Stories

The following analysis is based on 60 narrative interviews conducted between October 2012 and January 2013 in Buenos Aires and Santiago de Chile.[2] I focused on two 'generational sites' (Mannheim 1952). I collected life stories of, first, adults born between 1965 and 1974 and, second, young people born between 1986 and 1994. These generational locations are marked by the return to democracy in both countries, symbolically framed by different attempts to settle accounts with crimes against human rights, and by a period of boom in consumerism and neoliberal orders, as well as economic crises during the nineties, and, last but not least, recent youth activism. The central aim of my research was to look at the intersection between biographical and historical time in these two "postauthoritarian" generations.

For present purposes, I scrutinize these generational stories for varieties of nostalgia. Interestingly, in an early contribution to the sociology of nostalgia, Davis (1979) illuminated connections between generational and nostalgic experiences:

> I would point to two aspects of nostalgic experience (...) essential for any proper understanding of its relationship to society at large. These are: its sources in the perceived threats of identity discontinuity and its role in engendering collective identities among people generally, but most especially among members of "the same generation". (Davis 1979: 100)

---

[2] The sample included 30 "ordinary people" from each national capital and was balanced in terms of gender and class.

Approaching generational experiences sociologically, I define them as narrative constructions about 'having [one's] own (historical) time' (Corsten 2001). More precisely, taking experiences of social change or disruptive collective events (traumatic or triumphant ones), people born during a similar period hear/recount/tell stories about their circumstances, thereby sharing memories of past experiences and projecting 'horizons of expectation' (Koselleck 1979). Generational narratives draw 'temporal boundaries' (our time/their time; Frei 2015) and connect biography with history (Alwin and McCammon 2007).

The following narratives stem from these generational contexts, yet they also illuminate different intersections between national, class and gendered memories within these 'time' locations. As a result, I carve out four 'varieties of nostalgia' by drawing on what people recounted and the narratives circulating in these national, generational and class settings.

As we will see, these varieties entail four "senses of endings", connected to struggles between 'market[s], state[s] and societ[ies]' (in Polanyi's terms): (*I*) '*Future as decadence*' responds to new governmental forces (for example Kirchner's) which partly modified the neoliberalism of the 1990s. Clientilistic 're-embedding' has brought about a counterreaction by the upper-middle class claiming a deep sense of insecurity. (*II*) '*Future as resignation*' reflects disillusionment with political promises of 're-embedding' and the dissolution of networks of solidarity within lower-middle and working classes. The former element (re-embedding) was indeed part of the democratic promise after the Chilean dictatorship. Many people now feel detached from current political projects and yearn for the old days of solidarity. (*III*) '*Future as repetition*' reflects a coalescence between Argentinean state and civil society youth groups in a 'spirit' of rediscovering the seventies (as a generational 'structure of feeling' of engagement and solidarity) and projects of re-embedding. (*IV*) '*Future as utopia*' involves young, middle-class Chileans and civil-society actors who struggle for 're-embedding' education—organized under private principles—within state control (public and free education).

Sense of Ending (1): Future as Decadence

The first variety of nostalgia comprises *a* past 'lost forever' and *a* future of inexorable decadence, portraying a trajectory from a positive and mythical past to a tragic and corrupted present-future.

"Claudia", born in 1966 and growing up in an upper-middle class sector of Buenos Aires, started her life story with the following statement: "When thinking about the past, people often say that 'all the good times are gone'. As the years go by, I'm starting to feel that way too. And to be honest, in this world—and especially in Argentina, where we are lacking many, many things these days!—I feel that way: all the good times are gone."

In terms of Labov's sociolinguistic categorization, Claudia's first assertion might be regarded as an evaluation of her story, that is "the means used by the narrator to indicate the point of the narrative, its raison d'être: why it was told, and what the narrator is getting at" (Labov 1972: 366). Indeed, Claudia told her story to show me what was happening in Argentina at that time: a country submerged in decadence.

The future here is grey and hopeless. For Claudia, there is no hope in Argentina. Her future lies in living abroad, in a safe place where her children—all of them studying in private universities—can pursue professional careers. For those from the upper-middle class, and usually from the right-wing political sectors, this evaluation is linked to "the *corrupt* Kirchners" and to feelings of fear and insecurity, which contrasts with the image of a peaceful childhood. Upper-middle class Argentine respondents drew a distinction between their childhoods, when they could—for instance—ride bicycles without fear, and nowadays, when their children cannot.

As a matter of fact, crime rates have risen in Buenos Aires since the 1990s and they increased further after the 2001 economic crisis. Simultaneously, an industry of private security (alarms, walls, cameras and so forth) has developed and the popular media have focused on a daily life of crime, kidnapping and murders (Kessler 2009). The private-security industry stands for a widespread 'commodification of security' (Loader 1999) in both Argentina and Chile.

Connected to this, during the 1990s, parts of Buenos Aires's upper-middle class began moving to private areas—gated communities—in which walls and private security created a strong in-out boundary (Svampa 2001). Private neighbourhoods shifted an old culture of middle-class urban life, bringing about a new sociability characterized by a process of isolation and homogenization. For the upper-middle class, the outer world began to be seen as a space of risk, insecurity and crime.

This social group lives surrounded by strong measures for security and control, in protected private neighbourhoods, avoiding public spaces. Family table conversations are often marked by media news about crimes (hearing about horror from a safe *distance*). Their position differs from the experience of those living in conditions of poverty, who, in daily life experience drug trafficking and the highest rates of crime in their neighbourhoods. The incapacity of the state to offer control and security affects mainly those living in conditions of poverty. All my interviewees (especially women) in poor neighbourhoods recounted experiences of brutal violence and widespread feelings of fear. The atmosphere of violence experienced by those on the outskirts and on the streets is replicated in the home (domestic violence).

Nevertheless, a similar narrative sequence is discernible among parts of the lower- and upper-middle classes: there was a time (a mythical beginning) when we could feel safe on the streets (memories of taking the bus or walking home at night). Such a period coincides with childhood and adolescence, yet the political context is omitted. This omission is crucial due to the impossibility of denoting the last dictatorship as a safe place. According to Kessler (2009: 102), such a transformation (omitting dictatorship) only took place after the wave of transitional justice as state policy during the last decade (since Nestor Kirchner's government which began in 2003). By denoting the period of dictatorship as a traumatic tragedy for the nation as a whole, President Kirchner blocks any representation of the dictatorship as a time of 'good' social order. Consequently, upper-middle class stories cannot easily represent their childhoods' 'quiet good times'. When they do, they have to conceal the historical context, or show some sort of bewilderment when their "quiet time" meets the dominant national discourse of hideous times.

While the dictatorship is recognized as a time of crimes against human rights, some respondents longed instead for a period of 'triumphant' *Menemism*. After the hyperinflation of 1989, Carlos Menem's government enforced a monetary policy of convertibility (one dollar became one Argentine peso). The upper-middle class benefited from this new economic stance: travelling abroad, some degree of 'Americanization' (symbolized by food deliveries) and a period of conspicuous consumption (for example, by those who could afford better cars or bigger houses) were recounted as a model for *their* Argentina. Claudia, who described these changes extensively, affirmed: "I belong to the generation of change, the one that left behind the old ways of spending your vacations—with our parents along the Argentinian coast—for trips to the Caribbean, Miami, Orlando (…) Europe etc."

However, even this 'glorious past' of travelling and purchasing power was 'polluted' after the crisis of 2001. Menem's period symbolizes corruption, waste and a failed state. In the public sphere, this time is not seen as 'triumphant' but revealed as a time of 'neoliberalism and privatization'. This negativity is some form of *narrative hyperbolization* triggered by new governments (Novaro 2004). In order to intensify the sensation of political renewal (*the postneoliberal era*), the nineties have to appear as strongly dominated by harsh individualism and privatization.

Consequently, neither the dictatorship nor the neoliberal era of the 1990s can be entirely recovered nostalgically. The idealized past is, rather, located in a mythical golden age of Argentina's history. The upper-middle class thus invokes a remote past, prior to the emergence of *Peronism* in the forties,[3] as a time of 'national prosperity'. Given its enduring anti-Peronist orientation (Carassai 2014), the upper-middle class thereby demarcates themselves.

Linked to fear/insecurity, the present is recounted as traumatic in relation to a nostalgically distant past. This story of decadence has a long tradition in Argentina (Semán and Merenson 2007: 251–74), being frequently told by an array of public actors: we had everything to become a great country, but the political caste corrupted the "natural order". It is a Latin American version of Spengler's (1923) '*Untergang des Abendlandes*'. An ideal type of narrative of decline, this nostalgic emplotment endows the past with positive features,

---

[3] Since 1940, when Colonel Peron became minister of labour and later assumed his first presidency, Peronism has dominated the Argentine political spectrum (Ostiguy 2009). Peronism ranges from a historical working-class party with strong influence on trade unions to, nowadays, clientelistic networks entangled in poor districts (Levitsky and Murillo 2008). Moreover, Peronism has switched from left to right several times. Presidents Menem and Kirchner, for example, both belong to while representing antagonistic positions.

while the present and the future are viewed as being in decay and decadent. As Zerubavel states, "this unmistakably backward-clinging historical stance typically includes an inevitably tragic vision of some glorious past, that, unfortunately, is lost forever" (2003: 16). The key point is that such a past is irrecoverable. Here, primordial codes (Giesen 1999: 32) create 'strong temporal boundaries'. The old time of social respect for order is acutely confronted by present (moral) chaos in schools, on the streets and in speech (manners). The more the present time is polluted, the more the past is mythologized. The magnitude of 'evil forces' foretells an inexorable future tragedy.

Sense of Ending (2): Future as Resignation

The second variety of nostalgia involves being resigned to recovering a defining past experience while longing for it. The past only reappears as a lure of memory.

For those who opposed the Chilean dictatorship (1973–89), the 1980s have become a nostalgic site of memory. Nostalgic feelings are visible in relation to the struggle against dictatorship—in particular among working-class respondents who experienced the rise and fall of powerful networks of solidarity. Memories of those born in the seventies are filled with stories of that time.

People remember the severe economic crash of 1982, the first financial crisis of the 'neoliberal experiment' when several banks saw interventions and the rate of unemployment rose acutely. People lost their jobs and suffered severe poverty during those years. Additionally, several floods (in 1982, 1984, 1986) and the 1985 earthquake are remembered by those who lived in the worst material conditions.

"Yani", born in 1969, lived in a poor shantytown at that time. She remembered in her interview how her mother organized soup kitchens with neighbours in order to offer minimal nourishment to the poorest. For Yani, this is a key symbol that harks back to a time of strong solidarity between neighbours, which contrasts with today's 'individualistic' society.

A decisive consequence of the economic crash was public mobilizations. After ten years of dictatorship, the public arena began to see groups arguing for the end of the military regime. Later, a group of centre-left politicians successfully pushed to end the military regime within the existing legal framework: via a plebiscite (Garretón 1988: 17). Regarding this referendum in October 1988, my interviewees recounted the public excitement in the run-up. Those weeks and the day of the plebiscite itself are remembered as a public feast as well as a glorious triumph by those rejecting the dictatorship. An innovative television campaign promoted a positive future and was crucial in modifying a more tragic template of despair and fear focused on military repression and its victims (Stern 2006: 363–70). The aim was to increase the electoral participation in a context in which electoral fraud was a real possibility. Finally, 92 % of the electorate voted, the greatest turnout in the history of Chile. The campaign used a very clear cultural code: vote for joy and a future (the anthem was: Chile, *joy is coming*).

Respondents had vivid memories of the campaign, and its hope for a new, promising future that would leave behind a difficult past. However, after 20 years, by 2011–12 (the years of my fieldwork), their stories were full of disillusionment. There are different layers and forms of such 'disappointment', associated either with the commodification of the education system, the situation in the health system or social inequality. In a more diachronic sequence, people remembered first feeling disappointed in the middle of the 1990s. Consider Yani's account of this temporal location:

> During the '90s, the economic situation of my family improved. What is sad is that families were increasingly more distant from each other, since we all improved our material welfare. Families started to have their own worlds. I think when we were desperate and in need we all looked to each other. When the situation improved, particularly during 1994 and 1995, households became independent, and that is sad.

For a decade, Yani's mother had organized the 'common pot' in her shantytown. Yani experienced both how networks of solidarity emerged in times of 'necessity and despair' and, from the 1990s onward, how most of those networks faded away as the economy grew. Her story did, in fact, link three aspects: the deactivation of solidarity, economic growth, and processes of social individualization.

With regard to the decline in solidarity, public mobilization decreased abruptly during the nineties (Oxhorn 1994). The new centre-left coalition promoted 'labour' and mitigated, or directly hampered, civil-society organizations. Further, many nongovernmental organizations disappeared when international foundations stopped offering financial support. In addition, magazines and newspapers most critical of the dictatorship collapsed due to a lack of external support (Stern 2010: 223). The epic struggle was over. Yani's account expresses part of this widespread deactivation. Particularly in the poor shantytowns, extensive networks of solidarity and support diminished. A consequence of this fading was a nostalgia for a world of communality and social support. As Stern points out, poor women, especially, voice such nostalgic feelings: "under dictatorship *we were better* at valuing moral solidarity" (2010: 189).

Concerning Yani's impression that her neighbourhood is improving economically, she is referring to the 'transitional success story'. Between 1990 and 2006 the percentage of people living in poverty dropped. Compared to other South American countries, indexes of social development (with the exception of inequality rates) strongly improved (Drake and Jacksic 1999). The public budget grew and new programmes of subsidy emerged.

Yani's account of the improving economy also parallels the story of the 'consumer boom' during the 1990s. The middle classes experienced a great transformation in terms of the accessibility of new products during those years (for example, technological devices). This was also the time of building commercial centres, as new settings for the 'consumption story'. A new economy based on credit has evolved during the last 30 years, allowing families unparalleled access to consume products while simultaneously going into ever-greater debt.

Disillusionment with the postdictatorship period grew partly because growing debt became a social concern. The Asian crisis of 1997 disclosed unpaid debts. Nevertheless, there is a stark difference from the Argentine story: there was no radical economic collapse in Chile, as happened in Argentina during 2001. Therefore, there was no image of the 'evil neoliberal 1990s', as in the Buenos Aires stories. This is crucial, as no story opposing consumption is apparent.

Finally, Yani's representation of 'families having their own worlds' is also part of the repertoire of those times. Political deactivation, indifference toward collective projects, stories about an increasingly private world and consumption run in parallel. Different scholars have insisted on the ambivalence of such a 'new world': positive feelings of self-expression and individualized biographies evolve together with a sense of hyperindividualism (for example, Beck et al. 1994).

Approaching the present time, intense irritation was expressed in relation to the health system and abusive forms of private payment. In addition, the burden of responsibility increases as their children come of age. Yani was worried about her offspring's education. For the majority, education and health as 'businesses' aroused anger and discontent. In spite of these circumstances, neither a final tragic evaluation emerged nor was the current state of affairs harshly criticised. Rather, all of their accounts reveal deep levels of ambiguity regarding the present. One metaphoric setting for such ambiguity is the appraisal of technological advances. People demonstrated an enormous fascination with the latter by using and consuming new devices, while simultaneously expressing fear over their effects on the new generation (the loss of 'communication', 'creativity', 'real enjoyment').

In such a context, there are individualized versions of resignation: 'Eventually, you are on your own.' Or, additionally, there is a more fatalistic version expressed by some respondents: hopefully things will get better—but probably they will not.

Among these respondents, the weight and force of democracy emerged after living an entire childhood and youth under dictatorship. The 'joy is coming'—the slogan of the campaign against the military regime—fostered a sense of a radical turning point. The plebiscite was remembered as a mythical episode, burdened with promises of progress, justice and social mobility. The ensuing disenchantment did not completely break the lure of this 'turning point'. Meanwhile, the present and its circumstances resisted a 'happy ending'. Henceforth, their families, their children and their private stories became their consolation. In Santiago de Chile, for this adult cohort, the story of being 'on your own' prevails. All in all, the future remains private and strongly ambivalent, as present circumstances have become fragile, under constant threat from the commodification of health, education and pensions. The *future* is revealed as ambiguous, lacking 'great expectations'.

Sense of Ending (3): Future as Repetition

The third variety of nostalgia is an attempt to recover an idealized past. The future should coalesce with the 'spirit' of this past.

The end of the crisis of 2001 is often narrated by Argentine young people as the beginning of Nestor Kirchner's government. Kirchner managed to mend the economy after the meltdown. He broke the 'Washington consensus' when, together with other leftist Latin American leaders (for example Chavez in Venezuela, Lula in Brazil), he rejected the ALCA (in English: FTAA, the Free Trade Area of the Americas) and did not adhere to the IMF's guidelines, thereby enhancing national pride and connecting Argentina to the Latin American community.

Kirchner aimed to leave behind an era of corruption. His campaign slogan was 'Argentina, a serious country', promoting a renewal of politics. The interest in Nestor Kirchner's government, however, lies here in two turning points of Argentine collective memory. Beyond their policies or economic management (see Levitsky and Murillo 2008), the narrative and symbolic impact of his government comes from two 'recoveries': recollections of the last dictatorship as an indisputable tragedy, and the revitalization of classical Peronism—the dominant political constellation in Argentina (see endnote three)—as a triumphal memory.

Kirchner transformed the memory frame by canonizing the tragedy of the victims as a universal trauma and simultaneously canonizing the generation of the seventies as a heroic victim group.[4] As president of the state, he proclaimed the victims as indisputable figures of national trauma and remarked on the sacrifice of those heroic victims who fell struggling for the ideal of social justice. Soledad Cattogio observes in Kirchner's discourse some resonance with the religious figure of martyrdom, "which made it possible to reconcile the apparently mutually exclusive figures of the hero and the victim in commemoration activities" (Cattogio 2013: 696). Hence, I suggest that the heroic victims became a 'canonical generation' (Ben-Ze'ev and Lomsky-Feder 2009): their stories must not only be handed down as a tragedy, but also serve as a model for future political action (in particular, for youth organizations).

---

[4] Kirchner's narrative turn has ample precedents in previous decades, in particular, in the second generation of human-rights activists.

It was in this context that "Marianela"—born in 1986 and daughter of middle-class public servants—became interested in politics and social concerns. As part of this 'social awakening', she enrolled in a school theatre group with which she visited a 'home of memory'. When I asked her age at that time, she was astonished to realize the intersection of that period with Kirchner's coming into office. Indeed, reflecting upon such a coincidence, she stated:

> I was 16 (…) we are talking about 2002, 2003 (…) it must have been 2003 because I was 17, 18 (…) 2003, 2004 (…) what a coincidence!
> *RF: What is a coincidence?*
> The change of government. I mean, all of that. Néstor Kirchner took office (…) at that time that didn't mean much but now, to us, to the young people, to my dad, to all of those who are committed somehow to politics, this was a very important government change, irrespective of the criticisms one may have (…) In 2003, 2004, especially 2004, emerges a (…) a hope for change, right, in the country. That was also the year (…) I had never thought about it, the fact that that was the year I became interested in politics, there must be some connection.

The 'return' of memories of the dictatorship sprang up in family discussions, schools, universities, the media and on the streets. At the 2006 commemoration of the 30th anniversary of the coup d'état, Kirchner had already promulgated this day as national holiday for remembering. The commemoration left a special 'time mark' for young people.

The majority of young respondents became members of or created civil organizations around 2006: student councils, university groups, sports clubs, musical bands, religious communities or solidarity as well youth political associations. This strong activism in civil society groups is visible in their life courses and is considered key to characterizing this young Argentine cohort (Natansón 2012). As many respondents suggested, this new engagement started with Kirchnerism. This context is not only framed by memories of the dictatorship, but also impinges on the *revival* of Peronism.

In my respondents' stories there are two visible experiences of such a revival. First, there is the re-emergence of (left) Peronist youth organizations within school councils or university political organizations. Marianela remembered people from the 'Evita' movement arriving at her university in 2006. For "Julián"—my youngest respondent, born in 1994—it was surprising that the organization 'Arturo Jauretche' was chosen to lead the student council at his school (The National School). For "Camilo", the emblematic organization 'La Cámpora'—the most powerful youth organization during Kirchner's rule—dominated 'the songs' of every public commemoration. With a group of friends and ex-schoolmates, Camilo and Luna set up a young organization called 'John William Cooke'.

For the non-Argentinean reader, all these names probably make no sense. Yet, these names are a key piece of the story. Evita, Campora, Jauretche and William Coke were all mythical figures in leftist Peronism. To the best of my knowledge, there is no case in Latin American history where dozens of youth organizations used mythical figures to label their units. Occasionally a 'new left', 'new socialist youth' or 'Catholic youth' appears, but youth organizations usually attempt to mark a certain distance or cause some disruption. Hence, as 'new generational units' (Mannheim 1952), they barely caused a generational rupture, rather, they mobilized a desire to recover mythical figures.

The second defining circumstance was the 'farm crisis' under Cristina Fernández's government (Néstor Kirchner's wife), a national conflict between government and the agro-export sector over taxes. The agro-industry had expanded astonishingly after 2003 due to previous modifications to agricultural land (especially the cultivation of soybeans) as well as the rise in food prices in world markets. Hence, the government attempted to raise taxes, thereby unleashing enormous mobilization by the agricultural sector over several months. Beyond the technical details of the political and economic conflict, the dispute was fiercely framed as a division between 'us' (the people, the government) and 'them' (oligarchic landowners). Such a division not only reproduced the classical emotional structure of Peronism (Svampa 2006: 395), but also stimulated young people to locate themselves within this historical polarization. Consider Marianela's account of this 'turning point':

> They (the government) wanted to introduce a tax on the withholding of big landowners' exports, and so there was in general a great social opposition; and well, at that moment, it was not achieved. And well, and it (...) It was then when it somehow began (...) It started (...) People started taking sides. At that moment I was not a Kirchnerism follower—I came more

from Marxism (…) And in that moment, when the farm crisis took place, I said no—the place that one must be is here and, I mean, the "other" (…) I am not going to be with Rural Society, no way! (RF: Rural Society: the most important association of the right-conservative agricultural sector).

The reemergence of political Peronist organizations in schools and universities and the acrimonious farm crisis were conjunctures in which polarizing memories of previous decades crystallized. Those years (2003–9) were framed by Kirchner's heroic narrative in which Argentina was taken out of its critical economic situation, thus recovering (that is, canonizing) the spirit of the "70s-generation" as a symbol of commitment to social justice. Around those years my young Argentine interviewees started becoming involved in civil organizations and remembering together the 'bitter past' of the dictatorship in schools and family-table discussions. Later, Argentinean political discussion was polarized by 'the farm war', revitalizing the emotive dichotomy of Peronist discourse. The number of youth 'Peronist' organizations grew (or the numbers of their members did), as did political polarization. Crucially, those who engaged in civil organizations narrated the return of youth activism as a continuity of the precursors of social change. This "epic of return" (Frye 1957: 317) also narrowed down feelings of generational identification (and rupture) and instead stimulated the figure of intergenerational legacies worth reviving.

Therefore, the future, as seen here, involves a spirit of 'recovering' a worthy experience of commitment. When I asked my young respondents about the future, for one group (pro-Kichners), it appeared as a hope of continuing to be committed to social justice. The intergenerational connection is fostered by linking political projects from the forties (classical Peronism), seventies (youth militancy) or eighties (the recovery of democracy) with their own civil or political engagement.

Sense of Ending (4): Future as Utopia

The last variety of nostalgia consists of reconfiguring a mythical golden age in the present-future. This is a romantic plot, characteristic of progressive and utopian narratives.

"Miguel", from a middle-class background, remembered a feeling of disgust with regard to the amount of time spent in secondary school. Indeed, as a turning point in his early adolescence, he recalled the implementation of the 'full school day'. This public reform was announced in 1996 and gradually enacted in subsequent years. Although it was already common for upper-class students, it represented a significant change for middle- and working-class students: they began to spend the entire day at school.

The augmenting of time within schools ran parallel to another important life-course modification. As a political goal of the first democratic governments, there was increasing enrolment in secondary schools, reaching 93.7 % of the young Chilean cohort in 2003 (Cox 2006: 7). This, along with large numbers of students finishing secondary school, put greater pressure on middle-class students to enter university. This pressure was very clear when remembering parents' wishes for their future. Miguel invoked his mother's desire as follows: "My mother's dream was always that I would go to university, probably because nobody in the family had attended university before."

This middle-class template implies a progressive narrative, to use Koselleck's terms (1979). That is, the past must no longer guide the future and the latter is open to new possibilities. In the context of the Chilean educational promise, the parents' space of experience must not constrain their sons and daughters' horizons of expectation (that is, university). As a result, schools and the university system were burdened with the future expectations unleashed by that narrative. The failure of the promise—or consciousness of its impossibility—would create a critical conjecture.

It is within a highly class-structured educational system that Chilean citizens have viewed the student protests of recent years. The first great massive protest took place in 2006. These protests were coined the 'penguin student movement' or 'penguin revolution' due to the resemblance of the student uniforms to seabirds (see Donoso 2013a, b). For my interviewees, this first student uprising involved a demand for 'better education' (that is, better quality). This goal crystallised the progressive narrative in which a high level of education (a university degree) represents a key resource in order to achieve a fairer society (as well as upward mobility). Through sit-ins and street protests, secondary students opposed those who wanted to maintain a private market system and privileged access to university establishments.

Years later, a great number of my respondents enrolled in a private university or entered tertiary or technical institutions (yet, many of them could not afford even one year of study). This choice matches a new state policy concerning financial access to university. During those years, a new form of state credit (*Crédito con Aval del Estado*) was implemented. Through this, students gained access to loans not only for public universities (as used to be the case), but the entire university system, including private institutions. The formula to augment student participation was achieved by modifying the sources of credit: instead of the state, the financial system would provide sufficient resources for middle-class families. As a result, many of my interviewees not only entered private universities, but also became burdened with debt. Around 2011—when the first cohort taking up this credit left university—the process of indebtedness was quite visible to families and students. The progressive narrative of the first generation studying thus faltered. Indeed, what was promulgated as a progressive public policy (augmented coverage via the financial system) would become a symbol of neoliberal policy.

In addition, many respondents started getting involved in civil organizations (related to university or otherwise). The time after the protests of 2006 was an intense period of civil engagement and networking. The organizations involved are multiple. Miguel, for instance, became president of the student council at his private university. However, political parties are conspicuously absent. Compared to previous generations, this absence is noteworthy. This contrasts not only with Chilean canonical forms of politics (see Hite 2000: 16), but also with the Argentine revival of the Peronist tradition under Kirchner's left-wing government.

The second wave of massive protests took place in 2011, and for my respondents this conveyed a strong feeling of 'being there, doing history'. The marches were remembered as being massive. The crowd and (national) effervescence were central. A focus was put on the large number of artistic innovations at every demonstration, with bodypainting, diverse artistic happenings, and flash mobs.

Through the marches, the desire for 'public, free, and high-quality education' (or 'fairer access to public education') gained support. As various respondents mentioned, the attention to 'free and public' was connected to a demand for the 'end of profit' as well as for the state being the guarantor of social rights (that is, Polanyi's re-embedding). Increasingly, this demand coalesced with a wider collective desire for managing other previously privatized sectors (especially health and social security).

The most visible demand—resonating with life-course paths and family conversations—concerns the mounting of indebtedness. The student movement revealed unsustainable levels of debt within the financial system, thereby contradicting the promise of the progressive narrative (a better future through the possibility of social mobility). The construction of a more egalitarian society contrasts with high levels of inequality reproduced by educational differences.

Over the cycle of protests, a revival of the past was visible at the aesthetic level. Songs, melodies and catchwords evoked the atmosphere of the late 1960s left-wing protests. The signposts reproduced the form of the letters of former protests. What is more, a new generation of young musicians (for example Manuel García, Chinoy) who supported the student movement recovered the tonality of previous decades (new folk songs). In contrast to previous student protesters, in which the creation of cultural distance was achieved through musical traditions such as hip-hop or punk (Donoso 2013b: 9), the 'tonality' recovered in 2011 echoed what Boym calls "reflective nostalgia": "re-flection suggests new flexibility, not the reestablishment of stasis. The focus here is not on recovery of what is perceived to be an absolute truth but on the meditation on history and passage of time" (2001: 49). For the student movement, the recovery concerns not the *truth* of the canonical generation of the 1960s, it is rather the impulse to recover a mythical past of public education, and to finish with 'profit', as a utopian, romantic stance.

The occurrence of two cycles of protests in 2006 and 2011 bestowed a primary sense on a *romantic* quest (that is the emergence of conflict and struggle). This aspect is regularly encapsulated in the catchphrase '*we are the generation without fear*'. This sentence, or similar ones ('we don't fear any longer'), functions as a temporal and moral boundary: it draws a double distinction between a before and an after (fear provoked by the dictatorship versus the current social protests), and between those paralyzed by fear (older cohorts) and them. Such a generational story is enmeshed in the student movement as a romantic progression. The hero-subject gained consciousness of his mission, and the villain was more clearly entangled in polluted networks (dictatorship, neoliberalism, profit). The societal model (private versus public) was at stake (Salinas and Fraser 2012). Structurally, the romantic plot takes the form of a utopian stance, the plot "can unite persons in the pursuit of this utopian future" (Jacobs and Smith 1997: 68).

Romantic modes of emplotment normally feature a theme of ascent. Even if a 'romantic saga' contains rises and falls—the struggle of a hero or heroine—"its overall trajectory is clear enough and unidirectionally progressive" (Knutsen 2002: 121). Yet, the image of the future in romantic plots is, however, not entirely evolutionary. As Jameson maintains, romantic emplotment is a "re-expression of utopian longings" (1981: 91) whereby a mythical golden age is recovered to illuminate near futures. In a similar vein, Frye (1957) affirms: "the perennially child-like quality of romance is marked by its extraordinarily persistent nostalgia, its search for some kind of imaginative golden age in time or space".[5] All in all, here, the mythical golden age is not lost forever but allocated to the present/future.

Conclusion

This chapter has looked at four varieties of nostalgia in Argentina and Chile against a background of neoliberal and transitional (from dictatorship to democracy) orders. In the first variety, the future is forecast as a tragedy, since society follows a path of decadence. The golden age is lost forever for the old Argentinean upper-middle class. By contrast, in the fourth variety, the future is open to a utopian stance ('free of profit'), since progressive forces (the Chilean student movement) struggle against evil forces. Hence, my first conclusion corroborates that, as a narrative structure, Boym's and Pickering and Keightley's polar distinctions are also present in my material.

Yet, I offer two more varieties of nostalgia. The second variety offers a more ambiguous position, as the past is viewed as an experience of solidarity, while the present (and near future) merely reaffirms individualistic

---

[5] I thank Bernhard Forchtner for pointing out this aspect of Frye's work to me.

values. The past is not lost forever, since it remains as a deposit of experiences for the Chilean lower-middle class. The third variety represents a cyclical form of recovering 'worthy' values and experiences, which offer Argentine youth symbols of commitment. It is not an entirely utopian narrative, it is also an experience of recovering old generational repertories to project political futures. I argue that by analysing whole narrative sequences—past-present-future structures—I have been able to open up this dichotomy prevailing in the 'field'. More research on varieties of nostalgia might be useful to further develop this strategy.

Argentinean and Chilean countercycles of 're-embedding' after decades of market liberalization provide fertile terrain for various nostalgias. These varieties stand not only for conflicts between civil society groups and governmental policies, but also for how processes of commodification affect daily lives. This is crucial since all generational stories are affected by being in a historical time which, simultaneously, embraces political and economic practices. The boost in consumption, for instance, is part and parcel of the Argentinean and Chilean history of the 1990s. In some cases, the inability to see a different future (resignation) is linked to ambiguous feelings toward the markets (that is, consumption appeal). Here, nostalgia for solidarity is just an aesthetic move without willingness to invest in the recovery of this lost past.

This is why all these narratives are intersected by class positions; 'memory of the economy' also affects perceptions of being in time. Within highly unequal socioeconomic structures—as in the Southern Cone societies—varieties of nostalgia are affected by generations (being in historical times) and classes (being in historical markets). Gender is also revealed as a significant category when recounting intergenerational links (mother-daughter), as sources of yearning (for example, the soup kitchens run by women in Chile), or as impinged upon by domestic violence.

A further conclusion is that young generations can stimulate recovery and romantic utopias in (post)modern societies. It is noteworthy that these Chilean and Argentinean examples eventually translated into youth involvement in classical political issues (that is, occupying state positions and parliamentary seats). This contrasts with some views about young social movements (for example, the occupy movement) as postmodern 'reticular' performances without ambitions of political power.

References

Alexander, J. (2010). Iconic consciousness: The material feeling of meaning. *Thesis Eleven, 103*(1), 10–25.

Alwin, D., & McCammon, R. (2007). Rethinking generations. *Research in Human Development, 4*(3–4), 219–237.

Bartmanski, D. (2011). Successful icons of failed time: Rethinking post-communist nostalgia. *Acta Sociologica, 54*(3), 213–231.

Beck, U., Giddens, A., & Lash, S. (1994). *Reflexive modernization: Politics, tradition and aesthetics in the modern social order.* California: Stanford University Press.

Ben-Ze'ev, E., & Lomsky-Feder, E. (2009). The canonical generation: Trapped between personal and national memories. *Sociology, 43*(6), 1047–1065.

Bonnett, A. (2010). *Left in the past. Radicalism and the politics of nostalgia.* New York: Continuum.

Boym, S. (2001). *The future of nostalgia.* New York: Basic Books.

Carassai, S. (2014). *The argentine silent majority.* Durham and London: Duke University Press.

Catoggio, M. S. (2013). The consecration of political suffering: Martyrs, heroes and victims in Argentine political culture. *Journal of Latin American Studies, 45*(4), 695–719.

Corsten, M. (2001). "Biographie, Lebensverlauf und das "Problem der Generation", Bios: Zeitschrift Für Biographieforschung. *Oral History Und Lebensverlaufsanalysen, 14*(2), 32–59.

Cox, C. (2006). Policy formation and implementation in secondary education reform: The case of Chile at the turn of the century (No. 3), Washington.

Davis, F. (1979). *Yearning for yesterday: A sociology of nostalgia.* New York: Free Press.

Donoso, S. (2013a). Dynamics of change in Chile: Explaining the emergence of the 2006 Pingüino movement. *Journal of Latin American Studies, 45*(1), 1–29.

Donoso, S. (2013b). *Repoliticising education policies and the politics behind them: Tracing the evolvement of the Chilean student movement's collective action frame.* Washington D.C.: Washington D.CLASA Conference.

Drake, P., & Jaksic, I. (Eds.) (1999). *El modelo chileno: democracia y desarrollo en los noventa.* Santiago de Chile: LOM.

Fodor, N. (1950). Varieties of nostalgia. *Psychoanalytic Review, 37*(1), 25–38.

Frei, R. (2015). The living bond of generations. The narrative construction of post-dictatorial memories in Argentina and Chile. Unpublished dissertation at the Humboldt Universität zu Berlin.

Frye, N. (1957). *Anatomy of criticism: Four essays*. New Jersey: Princeton University Press.

Garretón, M. A. (1988). Popular mobilization and the military regime in Chile: The complexities of the invisible transition (No. 103), Notre Dame.

Giesen, B. (1999). Kollektive Identität. In *Die Intellektuele und die Nation 2*. Frankfurt am Main: Suhrkamp.

Hite, K. (2000). *When the romance ended*. New York: Columbia University Press.

Huneeus, C. (2000). *El régimen de Pinochet*. Santiago de Chile: Sudamericana.

Jacobs, R., & Smith, P. (1997). Romance, irony, and solidarity. *Sociological Theory, 15*(March), 60–80.

Jameson, F. (1981). *The political unconscious. Narrative as a socially symbolic act*. London/New York: Routledge.

Kermode, F. (2000). *The sense of an ending*. Oxford: Oxford University Press.

Kessler, G. (2009). *El sentimiento de Inseguridad. Sociología del temor al delito*. Buenos Aires: Siglo XXI.

Knutsen, T. (2002). Twentieth-century stories. *Journal of Peace Research, 39*(1), 119–127.

Koselleck, R. (1979). *Vergangene Zukunft*. Suhrkamp: Frankfurt am Main.

Labov, W. (1972). *Language in the inner city: Studies in the Black English vernacular*. Philadelphia: University of Pennsylvania Press.

Levitsky, S., & Murillo, M. V. (2008). Argentina: From Kirchner to Kirchner. *Journal of Democracy, 19*(2), 16–30.

Loader, I. (1999). Consumer culture and the commodification of policing and security. *Sociology, 33*(2), 373–392.

Mannheim, K. (1952). The problem of generations. In P. Kecskemeti (Ed.), *Essays on the sociology of knowledge* (pp. 286–320). London: Routledge.

Natanson, J. (2012). *¿Por qué los jóvenes están volviendo a la política? De los indignados a la Cámpora*. Buenos Aires: Random House.

Novaro, M. (2004). Menemismo, pragmatismo y romanticismo. In M. Novaro & V. Palermo (Eds.), *La historia reciente. Argentina en democracia* (pp. 199–221). Edhasa: Buenos Aires.

Novaro, M. (2009). *Argentina en el fin de siglo. Democracia, Mercado y Nación (1983–2001)*. Buenos Aires: Paidos.

Ostiguy, P. (2009). Argentina's double political spectrum: Party system, political identities, and strategies, 1944–2007 (No. 361, Vol. 80), Washington, DC.

Oxhorn, P. (1994). Where did all the protesters go?: Popular mobilization and the transition to democracy in Chile. *Latin American Perspectives, 21*(3), 49–68.

Pickering, M., & Keightley, E. (2006). The modalities of nostalgia. *Current Sociology, 54*(6), 919–941.

Radstone, S. (2007). *The sexual politics of time. Confession, nostalgia, memory.* London, New York: Routledge.

Roberts, K. (2012). The politics of inequality and redistribution in Latin America's post-adjustment era. Working paper no, 2012/08, United Nations University. New York: World Institute for Development Economics Research.

Salinas, D., & Fraser, P. (2012). Educational opportunity and contentious politics: The 2011 Chilean student movement. *Berkeley Review of Education, 3*(1), 17–47.

Semán, P., & Merenson, S. (2007). Percepción de la historia, sentimientos e implicación nacional en Argentina y Brasil. In G. Alejandro (Ed.), *Pasiones Nacionales. Política y Cultura en Brasil y Argentina* (pp. 249–298). Edhasa: Buenos Aires.

Segura, R. (2015). Legitimación de desigualdades socioespaciales en la Argentina posneoliberal. Límites y estigmas en la experiencia urbana de sectores populares de la Región Metropolitana de Buenos Aires. In M. Castillo Gallardo & C. Maldonado (Eds.), *Desigualdades. Tolerancia, legitimación y conflicto en las sociedades latinoamericanas* (pp. 471–495). RiL Editores: Santiago.

Somers, M. (1992). Narrativity, identity, and social action: Rethinking English formation. *Social Science History, 16*(4), 591–630.

Somers, M. (1994). The narrative constitution of identity: A relational and network approach. *Theory and Society, 23*(5), 605–649.

Stern, S. (2006). *Battling for hearts and minds: Memory struggles in Pinochet's Chile, 1973–1988.* Durham: Duke University Press.

Stern, S. (2010). *Reckoning with Pinochet: The memory question in Democratic Chile, 1989–2006.* Durham: Duke University Press.

Svampa, M. (2001). *Los que ganaron. La vida en los countries y barrios privados.* Editorial Biblos: Buenos Aires.

Svampa, M. (2006). *El dilema argentino. Civilización o Barbarie.* Buenos Aires: Taurus.

Spengler, O. (1923). *Der Untergang des Abendlandes. Umirisse einer Morphologie der Weltgeschichte.* München: C.H. Beck.

Toolan, M. (2001). *Narrative. A critical linguistic introduction (Second).* New York: Routledge.

Undurraga, T. (2014). *Divergencias. Trayectorias del neoliberalismo en Argentina y Chile.* Santiago de Chile: Ediciones Universidad Diego Portales.

Williams, R. (1977). *Marxism and literature.* New York: Oxford University Press.

Zerubavel, E. (2003). *Time maps. Collective memory and the social shape of the past.* Chicago and London: University of Chicago Press.

The Egyptian Economic Crisis: Insecurity, Affect, Nostalgia

Amal Treacher Kabesh

"Bread, Freedom and Social Justice"

Egypt has been marked by corruption and chronic exploitation, and the Egyptian people have suffered inexorably as a consequence of a fraudulent and persistent economic system. Islamic movements, especially the Salafi movement, purport to provide a counterpoint to corruption and argue for an economic system based on Islamic principles and a return to Islamic financial principles set out by the Prophet Muhammad. While the discourse of Islamic financial practice may appear as mere nostalgia, it claims to provide an alternative framework within which to think about a different moral order based on fairness and a discourse that counteracts the economic practices and exploitations that exist in Egypt today. Moreover, these fiscal principles are presented as a counterpoint to local and global inequalities. For many of the Egyptian population, this economic discourse, based on a particular moral practice, was appealing (approximately 25 % of those who voted in the election held in 2013 cast

A.T. Kabesh (✉)
University of Nottingham, Nottingham, UK

© The Editor(s) (if applicable) and The Author(s) 2016   **323**
C. Karner, B. Weicht (eds.), *The Commonalities of Global Crises*,
DOI 10.1057/978-1-137-50273-5_13

their vote for the Salafi movement). This chapter will explore the appeal of Islamic finance for many Egyptian people and will elucidate how living with insecurity, exploitation and corruption are corrosive of any hope of living a life based on security and decency.

Interwoven with an account of the appeal of the Islamic movement in relation to a different moral economy, I explore the responses of some who can be broadly defined as identifying with the centre-left in Egypt. I explore how this broad spectrum of people (people like me) is attached to a neoliberal ideology, despite declarations to the contrary. While fastened to diverse ideologies, both factions share common fantasies of repair and restoration for the individual and the nation. As I am engaged with illuminating the effects of living with persistent insecurity, I draw on autoethnography to tease out the consequences, emotional and social, of economic uncertainty on ordinary people. There is, in any case, a dearth of accurate statistics in relation to poverty, unemployment and health in Egypt, as governments have frequently concealed the dire economic conditions of many of the Egyptian population and there is little engagement with the consequences of poverty.

"Bread, freedom and social justice" was the rallying call during the January 2011 Revolution. This slogan, which dominated the demonstrations, encapsulates the failure of successive Egyptian governments (led by Gamal Nasser from 1954 to 1970, Anwar Sadat from 1970 to 1981, and Hosni Mubarak from 1981 to 2011) to build a society based on social justice and equality. These political, social and economic failures led, understandably, to profound disaffection and disappointment. "Bread, freedom and social justice" summed up the demands from Midan Tahrir in Cairo and across Egypt during the protests in January 2011. Many Egyptian people filled city centres, shouting out their demands for a better life. Drained by years of corruption, exploitation and unemployment, and struggling to survive, the majority of the Egyptian populace had reached a breaking point. These words, "bread, freedom and social justice", sum up pithily what is required to repair the damage of socio-politico-economic corruption and bad governance. "Bread, freedom and social justice"—though it has to be pointed out that "dignity" was used interchangeably with "social justice"—these three demands express an interlinked chain that are the basic requirements for a good life. Dignity/social justice is not possible without bread and material stability, while freedom is not available without an infrastructure based on social justice.

Egypt is an important country both geographically and politically, especially given its proximity to both Europe and the oil reserves in the Gulf. Egypt controls the Suez Canal which, along with the Panama Canal, is one of the world's most important trade routes. It continues to play a pivotal role in the Arab/Israeli conflict and reconciliation. In addition, as Osman (2010: 5) points out, it is the birthplace and centre of a number of trends and ideas, including Arab nationalism. Egypt, though, has a long history of being colonized and invaded, from the later Islamic empires to Napoleon's France and colonial Britain. Geography and nature have been generous, but history has been harsh (Osman 2010: 15). Egypt has frequently fallen to invaders and, throughout its long history, its inhabitants have been second-class citizens.

Egypt under Nasser managed to overthrow some vestiges of its colonial past, but there was a profound failure to create and consolidate a society based on social justice at the level of internal politics. Gamal Abdel Nasser was the first Egyptian to rule the country for centuries, and the excitement and hope this raised cannot be overestimated. In 1952, the military government took power and began to implement changes, attempting to build a fairer society. As Osman points out, the economic underpinning of the Nasserite transformation was twofold: reform of landownership and of the public sector (2010: 45). Land reform—a fairer distribution of land away from the landowners and toward the *fellaheen* (peasantry)—was popular and had immense social effects. The Nasserite economic revolution also created a new public sector and a new class of state-owned factories, companies and enterprises. In addition, almost all of Egypt's sizable businesses were nationalized in an attempt to remodel the structure of wealth by transferring ownership from a narrow capitalist class to millions of ordinary employees, poor labourers and struggling workers. Nasser's project was given an inclusive national appeal by its emphasis on civic notions such as social equality, identification with the poor and Egypt's role as the leader of the Arab world free of an Islamic dimension (Osman 2010: 51). However, as Julian Go points out, decolonization promised independence from the past and "a blessed future—a future whereby colonial exploitation would be replaced with economic 'development' and social 'progress'" (Go 2013: 5). The project of decolonization was based on a belief in modernity and on faith that the future was there for the making. Liberation from the past would ensure a blessed and prosperous future. Many, if not most, Egyptian people are still waiting, with scant hope, for this prosperous future to arrive.

In the subsequent political era, Anwar Sadat enabled a more open-door financial system based on the free market, and this is perceived as either progressive or not, dependent on the political views held in relation to the benefits of global capitalism. Introducing a more liberal capitalist system for the economy, usually described as *al-infitah* (opening up), Sadat's economic policy was in direct contradiction to Nasser's fiscal strategies. Sadat's main driving strategy was designed to open Egypt up to foreign trade, investment and market economics. The success or not of Sadat's opening Egypt up to foreign intervention is dependent, as always, on whether the person concerned is a beneficiary or not, and Sadat's economic policies are seen as either fat years for a minority or lean years for the majority, for whom the cutting of subsidies by 50 % for necessary food items such as rice, flour and sugar led to millions of people taking to the streets in violent protest. The demonstrations were squashed, speedily and with force, by the military. Sadat embedded Egypt's economy in a system based on global capitalism. This economic project—which "overturned markets embedded in social institutions and subject to moral and ethical norms"—led to "morals and ethics [being] subordinated to, even modeled on, markets" (Fraser 2012: 4).

Sadat was assassinated in 1981 because, according to one of his critics, he "accepted an end to the military conflict between the Arabs and Israel ... which depreciated Egypt's regional weight" (Kandil 2014: 173). Following this assassination, Hosni Mubarak became President of Egypt and inherited, with inexorable effect, Sadat's fiscal policies. Mubarak blamed ordinary people for a growing economic crisis—and especially the growth of the population—which, for Mubarak, was *the* cause of Egypt's profound difficulties. A conference convened by Mubarak to discuss the crisis, however, disagreed with his claim that it was due to population growth. Kandil reports that Egypt's top economists "agreed that opportunist capitalism had tilted the economy toward foreign trade and finance, and away from productive sectors" (2014: 202). The consequence of this is that Egypt shifted from being a net exporter of food to being a net importer so that, by the 1980s, Egypt was importing 60 % of its food. Significantly, the demand for imported goods amongst the Egyptian upper classes rose considerably. Alongside this grim economic situation, corruption greatly increased, especially amongst civil servants whose standard of living meant that they could, or would, not turn back. A vast patronage network was firmly in place. A period of grace was enjoyed by Mubarak due to the oil boom and the revenue raised by the Suez Canal. However, the oil crisis of the 1980s was a catastrophe for Egypt: inflation rocketed and unemployment increased. The crisis was deepened by the decision of the USA to suspend its aid package of $265 million dollars unless Egypt submitted to the demands of the International Monetary Fund (IMF). The IMF package was accepted in 1991.

Mubarak's regime lacked vision: instead of a programme of financial initiatives that would have aided Egypt's population—most of whom live in poverty—a society based on corruption and exploitation prevailed. The political system descended to frightening, worrying and staggering levels of corruption, coercion, oppression and cruelty under Hosni Mubarak's rule. Two examples, one structural, the other auto-ethnographic, provide a sense of the scale and extent of the corruption. First, valuable land continually was sold to business enterprises so cheaply that it cost "the same as a bowl of *fuul*", a brown bean—a staple of the Egyptian diet, especially for the poor, 20 pence of which would feed a family of four (July 2015). Providing evidence for specific examples is impossible as, needless to say, corruption was cleverly hidden, but the following may illustrate the extent of the corruption: in May 2015, Hosni Mubarak and his two sons were imprisoned for embezzlement of 9.3 million pounds sterling, money which was earmarked for renovation of presidential palaces (BBC News, 15 May 2015). Second, the streets were usually filled with farmers selling fruit and vegetables but, one day—moving on to the autoethnographic—when driving around trying to buy fruit, I found that the streets had suddenly been emptied of the vendors. I then discovered that they had all been arrested, as they did not have a license to sell their produce. It can very safely be assumed that they had not paid the police the fee demanded and that this led to their arrest.

At the beginning of his presidency, Mubarak was perceived as a leader who would bring balance to Egypt.

[His] speeches, his choice of words, the way he described himself and his vision for the country's future suggested a man who was concerned less with his legacy or with how he was viewed as a leader and more with his capacity to deliver. Mubarak seemed pragmatic, wholly concerned with Egypt's immediate economic problems, the inheritance of *al-infitah*. (Osman 2010: 167)

As mentionedherein, there is a lack of information on social policy in Egypt. Past government reports have skimmed over the extreme problems of health, poverty and education, and it is unclear whether more accurate statistics will be provided under the present regime, led by Fattah Al-Sisi (who was previously a military General). This has resulted in a wide chasm between the actual state of profound difficulties and the false image provided by government agencies. It is difficult to provide adequate statistics for Egypt, as these are largely massaged to provide a better image than is actually the case. According to a United Nations report published in 2014, Egypt is ranked 110th in relation to the human development index and has dropped two places from the previous year (United Nations 2014). Education, healthcare and transportation provisions have deteriorated. Public hospitals are slum buildings and there are many photographs taken by doctors that are available on the internet that reflect filthy conditions. There are over 60 children per class in state schools (all middle-class parents send their children to private schools) and transportation is poor and dangerous, as bus drivers, frequently high on drugs, drive without caution. Crushing socioeconomic conditions, exploitation and corruption mark Egypt. Official statistics, which probably underestimate the extent of poverty, suggest that 40 % of the Egyptian population live on two dollars a day and, while reliable figures are not available, some live on just one dollar a day (Abdou and Zaazou 2013: 103). At present (July 2015) there is little hope: inflation is rocketing, food—including staples such as bread and sugar (meat for many is out of the question)—has become extremely expensive and unemployment is severe. Indeed, unemployment is the norm, especially for young men under 35 and, while gaining employment has always entailed drawing upon social networks and past favours, the economic crisis demands the skills of manipulation, careful negotiation and utilizing family and social relationships with proficient dexterity.

Material conditions affect men and women equally, but with different consequences. Women have to carry the burden of feeding and caring for the family; frequently, poor working-class women undertake household tasks for middle-class families, tasks which include cleaning, washing, cooking and child care and for which—frequently, alas—the women are paid little. Within Egyptian society it is incumbent for men to provide materially and failure to do so is perceived and experienced as shameful (Treacher Kabesh 2013). In middle-class families it had been common-place for women not to contribute to household expenditures, but this is now changing, as a dual income is becoming more necessary even for middle-class families.

For men, employment provides crucial social membership and is tied into esteem, respect and honour. The 2011 January Revolution did not arise out of nowhere, as there had been much political and union activity prior to this iconic date, even if this had mixed results. Asef Bayat describes the complex situation of the various activities that had taken place, frequently with mixed results. For example, a human-rights organisation reported 70 strikes against large companies during 1998, and in 1999, and it was reported by the Egyptian press that at least five strikes and sit-ins were occurring each week (Bayat 2009: 71). At times, wages were increased by this, at the expense of the self-employed poor and the unemployed. The gains are often problematic because, while new labour laws are contested, they can often strip workers of job security. In 1994, for example, the labour unions compelled government and business to accept "the right to strike for the right to fire" (Bayat 2009: 72).

Alongside political unrest and persistent activism there is, inevitably, much anxiety that socio-politico-economic conditions will not improve. I am writing as an Egyptian citizen here—in Cairo it is all we talk about, in an endless circular fashion: we have much to be anxious about, and this is linked to previous historical failures. There were many driving motivations that led to the 2011 Revolution in Egypt, including the absence of proper political participation, the high cost of living, ever-increasing inflation, corruption and a dire lack of employment prospects, especially for young men. In short, the protests expressed the profound necessity for social justice and a political fury at the complete lack of equal opportunities for all. The following section seeks to understand the powerful appeal of the Muslim Brotherhood and the Salafi movement during the 2011 Revolution and the elections that took place in 2013. The Salafi (which means a "return to the past") and the Muslim Brotherhood constitute the Islamist movement. There was an immense swell of support for these Islamic movements—they won 70 % of the vote—and at the presidential election won by Muhammad Morsi, but this has since collapsed. While this chapter focuses on the various reasons for the initial support for Islamic movements, it must be pointed out that the subsequent collapse was due to an "alarming deterioration of Egypt's economic prospects" while the Muslim Brotherhood was in power (Butter 2013). Also—and of special note for this volume—there was much tension, disappointment and anger due to the dire financial mismanagement and lack of attention to fiscal matters by the Muslim Brotherhood during their one-year rule.

The Appeal of a Moral Economic Order

The principles of Islamic finance are based on the Shari'a system, which refers to the commands, guidance and prohibitions under Islam and guides believers in all aspects of life—actions, behaviour, morals, emotions and thought. Islamic finance claims to be based on honesty in all dealings, timeliness in payment (whether debt or asset) and bargaining to be undertaken with honesty and tolerance. Shari'a principles forbid the payment of interest and the buying or selling of goods that are unlawful—for example, pork and alcohol. In short, Islamic finance is based on moral principles that are drawn from the Shari'a system and claims to be fair and honourable. The guiding principles, it is argued, will lead to purity. The discourses of Islamic finance have resonances with those of Islamic feminism, which argues that Islam as a faith, belief system and practice is the only foundation that provides true liberation for women. Western women, it is argued, are oppressed due to their burden of work and household responsibilities, their oppression by having to be sexual objects, the requirement to be a consumer and so on.

Egypt is a deeply religious society and everyday language is replete with references to God and to spirituality. Islam as a practice is deeply embedded in Egyptian subjectivity and everyday life. For example, the call for prayer, which takes place five times a day, fills the soundscape and is a reminder of the existence of God and the importance of prayer. The arguments asserting the goodness and morality of Islamic finance speak to an existing spirituality and the wish for a different moral order. Religion is a resource that both comforts and sustains people as they struggle with severe economic conditions. Just as importantly, religion operates as an explanation and people will often, for example, declare that God "made me like this" and/or God "ordered it like this". Small everyday incidents, such as being stuck in a traffic jam, are often explained that they are God's will and, more importantly, that God is protecting the individual. Everyday discourse focuses on God as a protector and as merciful. To provide just one example, people will often say that they are poor or have little money because God wants to protect them from being greedy, ruthless or exploitative. God is perceived as sympathetic and will ensure that the person will survive. Gratitude is commonplace and prevalent, and the normal response to any situation is to thank God. This customary gratitude, as I understand it, hinders resentment (at least consciously) and enables a sense of dignity. These religious discourses based on faith and trust can, however, obscure an understanding of structural economic forces that ensure that exploitation and inequality endure.

Alongside, or perhaps interwoven with, this profound religious belief system, Egyptian subjectivity is forged from relationality and interdependence. Subjectivity, whatever gender, is formed from social connection and belonging; moral value is not accorded to autonomy and neither is individuality valued. Persons are understood as nodes in systems of relationships and are constituted by those relationships. Belonging is crucially important and involves being part of a family and a social network. In short, *being* someone also implies *belonging* to someone, as Ferguson puts it (2013: 228). Dependence, in contradiction to Western values, is not seen as bondage or restraint but, rather, as important the "glue" in a social system which provides for the existence of possibilities for affiliation. These affiliations are hierarchical but, nonetheless, provide bonds and a way of being that are based on belonging (Ferguson 2013: 226).

This description is, perhaps, rather blunt, as Egyptian subjectivity is of course complex and contradictory. While autonomy is not valued, people are still required to be self-possessed and to fulfill their obligations. There is no state support for the poor and/or unemployed and, by necessity, there is much reliance on the family for financial support. But—and this is a crucial "but"—this is accepted as an aspect of the social and familial network as long as the person concerned is perceived to be trying their best to find work and to "carry their responsibility" (to draw on a commonplace Egyptian expression). Let me further elaborate on this through an anecdote: an acquaintance, a young man aged 34, was at risk of becoming one of the chronically unemployed and he was subjected to much family criticism manifest in two questions repeatedly put to him (during 2014–15): first, "Are you not embarrassed to take money from your father?"; and, second, "Can you not do more to take responsibility?" These questions were quite apposite as the father concerned had been very ill. There is, I am suggesting, a contradictory ideology at work which focuses on both personal responsibility and interdependency. Maturity is based on being able to look after and respond to others while, simultaneously, material dependency that requires excessive demands on other human beings is frowned upon. It is men's responsibility to meet these material obligations and demands. Belonging necessarily involves obligation and responsibilities.

Belonging and social membership are important values in their own right and it should also be recognized that these aspects of moral personhood have arisen within and are constituted by a society that had been colonized for centuries and in which exploitation has been a persisting reality. The need for a different moral order arises from a number of various and interlinked matters: chronic insecurity, enduring exploitative and corrupt economic practices and the inheritance of colonialism. Egypt is a society marked by loss, insecurity and precariousness and its culture is "constituted around and marked by an unworked-through loss" (Lloyd 2003: 215). Furthermore, Lloyd writes, in Egypt—as in other societies that have been colonized—insecurity and coercive violence are a constant presence (2003: 216). Insecurity and violence form a chronic condition.

Violence occurs because colonization is about the perceived necessity of bringing the colonized to the point "where they can become political subjects in a modern sense, capable of self-submission to the *regular-*

ity of law and of attachment to abstract principles rather than affective ties" (Lloyd 2003: 212). In short, colonization is about the discipline of the political economy of neoliberalism. Contemporary political economy requires a new set of psychic and ethical dispositions and a new social body that is forged out of neoliberal subjectivity. In one way, the arguments from the Islamic movements can be seen as a refusal to be dominated and coerced into global capitalism. Drawing inspiration from the *hadith* and *Sunnah* (the collected sayings and habits of the Prophet Muhammad), the Islamic movements argue for the moral system taught and adhered to by the Prophet Muhammad. During his lifetime, Prophet Muhammad argued against the rampant accumulation of wealth by the businessmen who lived and ruled Mecca. As Karen Armstrong has argued, the Prophet Muhammad's life was a ceaseless struggle "against greed, injustice, and arrogance" (2006: 19). His lifelong *jihad* (here I am using *jihad* in its original and still pertinent sense—struggle) was against the injustice of material exploitation and greed and established the Islamic principle that "strictly forbade usury, which it interpreted to mean any arrangement in which money or a commodity was lent at interest, for any purpose whatsoever" (Graeber 2011: 275). The ideological turn to the era of the Prophet Muhammad can be understood as comprising two different attempts to heal the violence of colonialism. First, it is the rebuttal of the demands of global neoliberalism and, second, it is an attempt to heal the violence that has gone before, through which Egyptian subjects were told repeatedly, either explicitly or implicitly, that they were lacking the required attributes to be a successful subject. Mary Evans writes that the neoliberal account of the ideal citizen is of a person who is "not hampered by social or personal ties" (2015: 148) but is, rather, tied into the accumulation of wealth; however, as Suad Joseph argues (in corroboration of my earlier observations), Middle Eastern subjectivity is tied into relationships with others, and being mobile and detachable are not valued attributes (1999). Moreover, Lloyd argues that the colonized culture is "denied any orientation to the future other than one dictated by a colonial modernity that must annihilate not only the complex tissues of its actuality but even its very potentialities" (2003: 217). The Islamic movements refuse the persistent orientation toward a particular version of modernity and, excluded from the future, they looked to the past for potential, respect, power and a mode of being that provides full subjectivity.

I posit here that the arguments arising from the Islamic movements, especially the Salafis, for a different economic order had positive pulling power because they appealed profoundly to many desires for liberation. These desires capture the need to be released from the daily struggle to survive and the ongoing exertion needed to provide adequately for the family. Above all, there may be a wish to be released from the corrosive effects of anxiety, humiliation and shame. An ethnographic example may help to illustrate the material conditions of the poor: the porter in our apartment building is on call 24 hours a day; he takes care of and cleans the building, washes the cars of the inhabitants daily (this is essential due to the sand and dust) and earns just 60 lb sterling a month. He is a gracious man who, despite his considerable efforts, barely earns enough to sustain his family. Interwoven with the wish to be liberated from the daily struggle, there is also the desire to be emancipated from the corrosive effects of exploitation. Our porter's family could not survive if his wife did not work—she cleans the homes of the middle classes, who pay little and can verge on the rude (if not abusive); she has to tolerate this rudeness and exploitation and her husband has to witness this offensive behaviour. They have no alternative but to accept these conditions—the acceptance of which does not, necessarily, entail apathy.

Affect, Nostalgia and Fantasy

Nostalgia attaches itself to many periods of Egyptian history which may or may not coalesce. I have traced through the following four periods, in particular, as providing nostalgic fantasy and emotion. They are the Pharaonic era, the time of Prophet Muhammad, leaping forward to the time of King Farouq and, more recently, the Nasserite period due to his intransigent critique of colonialism. In their discursive evocations, these diverse periods are given the following characteristics and readings:

- *the Pharaonic* era: when Egypt was a great civilization with many scientific, medical and philosophical achievements and, above all, a period in which Egyptians ruled Egypt;
- *the time of Prophet Muhammad*: this is perceived as a time of purity and faith, when God revealed himself to human beings. While, it was a struggle for Islam to be accepted as a religion and Muslims faced massive challenges, it is perceived as a time when Islam was respected. Crucially, the period of Prophet Muhammad is celebrated as a time free of colonization and when exploitation and the accumulation of wealth for its own sake were being challenged;
- leaping ahead, *the era of King Farouq* (1936–52) is perceived as a time of material prosperity, stability and comfort, even though Britain ruled Egypt. The country's economy was stable as illustrated by the exchange rate at the time—then, two Egyptian pounds bought one pound sterling while, today the exchange rate is one pound sterling for 12 Egyptian pounds;
- finally, favourable comparisons are made with reference to *Gamal Nasser and Abdel Fattah el-Sisi* and both are represented and perceived as strong and powerful leaders capable of leading Egypt as Egyptians.

The reasons for nostalgia are multiple and overdetermined. Importantly, nostalgia can be seen as progressive or retrogressive—for example, the Salafis' demands for moral economic structures and institutions present themselves as progressive. Simultaneously, the views upheld and propagated about women—that women should not be seen in public, should not work and should receive only limited education—are profoundly problematic. Nostalgic discourses are selective, for the Salafis draw upon certain beliefs that were held by the Prophet Muhammad while ignoring and bypassing his views on women as equal citizens who should have equal material rights to men. Uncertainty and insecurity, as Michael Pickering and Emily Keightley posit, "create fertile ground for a sentimental longing for the past, or for a past fondly reconstructed out of selectively idealised features" (2006: 925). Longing to return to the past, nostalgia can point toward what has been and is no more.

The Salafis argue that Egypt should not import food or goods, but should become self-sufficient (again). This argument is based on a belief that food should be uncontaminated and should not be touched by those who consume alcohol. For example, they oppose the import of wheat from Russia because alcohol is available in Russia. This arguably also needs to be read in relation to the history of Egypt's agricultural industry. As already mentioned, for example, in 1970 Egypt used to *export* 65 % of its sugar production but, by the early 1980s, it was *importing* 35 % of its sugar requirements (Kandil 2014: 202). Yet, to disentangle different forms of nostalgia further, Pickering and Keightley (2006) point out that we need to distinguish the desire to fully return to a wrongly idealized past, on one hand, from a recognition of select aspects of the past that may provide a basis for renewal, on the other. The Salafi ideology advocates a complete return to the past, while for others (for example, the Nasserite political party), the material stability of the past serves as a poignant contrast to the deterioration of material conditions endured in the present. Such more selective, nuanced nostalgia may, indeed, help identify more beneficial ways of living.

The vexed material conditions of poverty, the decline in living standards, and the corrosion of stability can lead to shame, humiliation, anxiety and the weakening of social bonds. Egypt's informal welfare structure has fallen apart and has impacted wider family and neighbourly relations. Families can barely support themselves, and this has led to the serious erosion of connections. The despair can be overwhelming and can lead to envy and a lack of compassion toward others, characteristics based on fantasies of who inhabits a life of material comfort. An Egyptian idiom—"the hand in the water cannot feel the hand in the fire"—is frequently drawn upon as an explanation for, and criticism of, feelings of envy, indifference and insensitivity. Perhaps there is also the understandable need to disavow the humiliating consequences of not being able to provide, the effects of inhabiting a society that is impoverished and dependent on global aid (Egypt is a recipient of aid from the European Union of about five billion Euros annually and, from the USA, 1.3 billion dollars in military aid).

The effects of cumulative loss are complex. Loss entails embodied experiences and responses to the past. For example, Egyptian TV channels repeat plays, comedies and television shows from the 1960s and 1970s and they remain extremely popular. This includes one channel that repeatedly broadcasts a concert of Umm Kulthum who was known as the voice of Egypt and was legendary in her lifetime and beyond. The televised concerts broadcast her singing well known songs, the camera panning the audience, many of whom were smoking, dressed elegantly and having fun. We tell family stories of listening to her when we were growing up—in my case this includes stories of an uncle who adored her voice and would rip open his shirt in ecstasy while listening to her— and, while my father loved to listen to Umm Kulthum, my stepmother could not abide her voice. As Boym (2001) points out, none of us are immune to nostalgia, we reminisce with enjoyment and, arguably, we yearn for a time of hope and security; for some of us who come from middle-class and professional families, this meant a time when Cairo was cosmopolitan. It was an era when Egyptians truly believed that the future was there for the taking. Nostalgia is the composite "feeling of loss, lack and longing" (Pickering and Keightley 2006: 921). Nostalgia, as Boym (2001: xiv) points out, provides continuity with the past and, I would add, it can make available a feeling of being-there-and-then. Walking into a department store recently I was overwhelmed with the smell, sight and sound of the department stores of my childhood, I was filled with a visceral sense in which the past and the present had melded into one temporality. Loss and absence are laden with affect, fantasy and longing, which is embodied as the body yearns for "home, to be at home, to be at home in one's land, a land conquered, impoverished and plundered for its raw materials" (Walkerdine and Jimenez 2012: 2). Crucially, the long-ing is for living in, and being attached to, a country that has not been plundered and impoverished.

Loss, and that which has never been, affect human beings psychically, physically and morally and the consequences break the human spirit. The effect on bodies is problematic as it can lead to "affective responses of which we may not be aware: bodily dispositions, chronic illnesses, ways of being and defending against the anxiety, hurt and pain of what is experienced" (Walkerdine and Jimenez 2012: 9). The effect of perpetual stress, financial insecurity and precariousness corrode human beings and the experience of, and witnessing, vulnerability is frequently rendered absent and silenced. This does not mean, however, that these conse-quences are not transmitted from one generation to the next, rather the transmissions occur often silently because the experiences of the parent generation are so painful that they cannot bear to talk about them. These intergenerational dynamics can be very effective because they operate in psychosocial ways as a kind of affective and collective continuum, in the sense that a continuous series of events can blend into each other gradually and seamlessly, making it hard to say where one ends and the next begins (Walkerdine and Jimenez 2012: 10).

There are many responses to being corroded—insecurity and vulnerability from sanguine acceptance, anger, resentment and contempt toward the other who holds different values and beliefs. One response that those of us on the centre-left of the Egyptian political spectrum have indulged in is that we mocked with cruel dismissal the ideology of the Salafi movement. We ridiculed their profound belief that God would provide whatever was required for Egypt to become prosperous, we scorned their wish to return to a time of Islamic purity and we derided their refusal to accept globalization. We were unkind and dismissive. What threatened us? A partial answer may be that we could not (cannot) bear to know our attachment to neoliberal subjectivity and global capital, no matter our declarations to the contrary. We had (have) to stringently disavow the meanings, for ourselves and for others, of an alliance with a transnational capitalism "who's rapacious, brutal, and destructive past is continually reproduced in the present" (Ferguson 2013: 219). Different hauntings, different narratives, different memories, different psychic processes all coalesce and exist simultaneously. We need to bear in mind.

> the awareness of everyone's vulnerability to the workings of time and decay, the quiet suffering that attends our ordinary condition of mortality, and for which perhaps the only compensation is our tenderness for each other's vulnerabilities, for what Adam Zagajewski (2001) calls "the mutilated world" (Hoffman 2010: 414).

What is lost when we become "good" subjects by being complicit with the dominant economic order?

The aforementioned is one reason; the other explanation, I would argue, is that we could not bear the vulnerability of other human beings or indeed ourselves. Vulnerability and precariousness are part of the human condition, which frequently provokes contempt, disavowal and distance rather than concern for the other human being. Cairo is full of examples of vulnerabilities and insecurities, as poverty is everywhere—rural and urban merge, the poor inhabit affluent areas, female refugees from Syria sell baked goods from rickety tables on the street. Poverty is inescapable and is in the air we breathe; it touches us at our very core, no matter what we declare to the contrary. Instead, alas, of reaching out with concern and thought toward alternative modes of thinking about inequality and social justice, we closed down on thinking. This is not to say that we would have to agree with the Islamic movements, as much of their thought is profoundly problematic; they are deeply hierarchical and patriarchal, but rather, we could have risked opening up a another register of thought, imagination and judgement.

James Ferguson argues that in thinking about the social world of extreme inequality which we inhabit, "dealing with (rather than denouncing) this reality means going beyond pious wishing for equality to ask how *in*equalities are socially institutionalized, and whether such modes of institutionalization are politically or ethically preferable to others" (2013: 232). Thinking within this framework would require facing up to our complicities, problematic attachments, contempt and fear. Above all, it would require a stringent confrontation—as Ferguson argues persuasively, that for all of us, "subjection is preferable to abjection" (2013: 231). Those who are perilously insecure will accept subordination in exchange for social membership and a state of belonging; conversely, feeling abject is to be avoided at all costs. In short, for those who are "abjected, *sub*jection can only appear as a step up" (Ferguson 2013: 231). It is not belonging, the severing of social and human bonds and above all, falling into the social void that is terrifying and to be defended against at all cost. Materially comfortable the middle class may be, but, in a different way, it has remained attached to what we knew and valued. We gave ourselves over to a system based on corruption, neoliberal capital and exploitation. Our fear of poverty, alienation and exploitation led us to be contemptuous. From our different subject position and class location we, too, would rather be subjected than abjected. The need to belong can lead to compassion and identification with other human beings or, as I am describing here, to disidentification leading to contempt and derision.

In her book *Cruel Optimism*, Lauren Berlant poignantly argues that all attachments are optimistic and, rather worryingly, that "cruel optimism is the condition of maintaining an attachment to a significantly problematic object" (2011: 23–4). For Berlant, all optimism is cruel "because the experience of loss of the conditions of its reproduction can be so breathtakingly bad, just as the threat of the loss of *x* in the scope of one's attachment drives can feel like a threat to living itself" (2011: 24); we therefore make "affective bargains about the costliness of one's attachments, usually unconscious ones, most of which keep one in proximity to the scene of desire/attrition" (Berlant 2011: 25). Desire, identification, attachment and the need for security and belonging lead many of us who inhabit insecure societies to be fearful, complicit, compliant, thoughtless and cruel. We wish it to be otherwise, but that desire should not obfuscate our precarious understanding.

There Can Be No Conclusion at Present

This chapter has undertaken an exploration of the psychic effects of inhabiting a corrupt system and of the complicities involved in corruption that are profound and taint all involved. The lack of an adequate material structure, of a welfare system that includes benefits for the sick, the disabled and the unemployed, of an adequate education system and so on and so forth leads to poor physical and mental health. Living with perpetual insecurity impacts profoundly on lived experience and eats away at people's resources, along with their moral, physical and emotional well-being. The use of the word "perpetual" is deliberate, as insecure material conditions have always existed for the poor and material insecurity is currently increasing for the middle classes, as there is at least one unemployed person in most Egyptian families. The middle classes are nostalgic for a time of security that did exist, while the poor yearn for a time of material security they may never have known. Pickering and Keightley (2006: 920) write—and it is worth taking heed of their argument—that.

> [I]n longing for what is lacking in a changed present, nostalgia for a lost time clearly involves yearning for what is now not attainable, simply because of the irreversibility of time; but to condemn nostalgia solely to

this position leaves unattended not only more general feelings of regret for what time has brought, but also more general questions for how the past may actively engage with the present and future.

The current military regime in Egypt, led by Abdul Fattah al-Sisi, has instituted important attempts at economic renewal. A new Suez Canal has been built in order to enable two-way traffic and cut down the waiting time for ships passing through the canal, and the old Suez Canal has been deepened, which will facilitate larger ships using it. It is envisaged that this will increase the revenue from the canal to 100 billion dollars over the next decade. While some commentators (for example, Galal Amin) doubt that the revenue will increase substantially and it is unclear whether the new project will be able to provide the projected increase in employment, it remains an important and significant project for the following reason: for the first time in living memory, money is being invested in Egypt, as opposed to the corruption—or, more frankly, theft—that took place under the previous regime. Alongside this project, Fattah al-Sisi has instituted significant road-building projects linking agricultural areas to Cairo, the old roads have required repair for years. In addition, money is now being spent on providing adequate infrastructure in very poor areas. The building of the new Suez Canal is an attempt to repair the past and the damage caused by colonization, as many lives (120.000 men died) were lost in the building of the first Suez Canal in the nineteenth century. Gamal Nasser nationalized the Suez Canal in 1956, which led to the Tripartite Aggression—Egypt was attacked by Britain, France and Israel—and these three powers had to withdraw. In contemporary Egyptian history, 1956 remains a high point and marks a short period of hope, optimism and release from colonization; this new Suez Canal can be understood as a symbolic project that will restore Egypt's faith in itself, as the project was financed by the Egyptian people and does not, as yet, involve foreign finance or investment.

Corruption has been a way of life in Egypt over successive generations and it is difficult to gauge whether it will be overcome by the present military regime. Al-Sisi set up a fund—*Supporting Egypt*—and contributed a large amount of his own personal money. He encouraged rich people to do the same, which some did, along with many middle-class people. Egypt in 2015 is marked by tension, fear and oppression alongside the fervent hope that the country has embarked on a material revitalization that will lead to economic stability. Most people, across lines of class and gender, support al-Sisi and openly state their love for him. They declare freely that "Egypt is not ready for democracy", that "Egyptians need a strong dictator" and, perhaps the most heartfelt of all, that "Democracy cannot feed our children". The visceral need for material security means that democracy and freedom are not priorities. Hope as a state of mind overcomes and suppresses any doubt about the current military regime and people are, on the whole, silenced by loyalty and visceral need. "What issues from the empty mouth?", asks Lloyd pertinently; due to a persistent and damaging colonial legacy "we"—that is, many of the Egyptian people—have become too "deeply embedded (in the) habit of disavowing the personal and cultural damage that is in part the legacy of our colonial past" (Lloyd 2003: 205).

Hope can be cruel, as it can lead to profound disappointment, and yet hope always points to the precariousness of being and living. Hope, along with nostalgia—perhaps hope can be perceived as nostalgia—lets us know that our moral, physical, spiritual and emotional lives are awry and depleted. This may lead to melancholia, which can be recalcitrant and, as Freud (1917) pointed out, is shameless as it leads to resignation and passivity. Nostalgia is an attempt to compensate for the loss of hope and possibility of optimism, for the loss of what has been destroyed due to colonial rule and the absence of what has never occurred because of persistent exploitation and corrosion of any likelihood for social justice. Nostalgia can bind people together and, as Nira Yuval-Davis (2006) asserts, belonging has become a crucial aspect of political agendas. I am not arguing for a romantic embrace of nostalgia—rather that the content of nostalgic fantasies and narratives needs to be reflected upon and understood. Boym explores the value of thinking about reflective nostalgia, which she argues "dwells on the ambivalences of human longing and belonging and does not shy away from the contradictions of modernity" (2001: xviii). Egypt has extensive and profound challenges ahead and these will require stringent confrontation, not just with the dire material realities, but also with the psychosocial effects of inheriting and inhabiting a society that has been impoverished and depleted for generations.

References

Abdou, D., & Zaazou, Z. (2013). The Egyptian revolution and post socio-economic impact. *Topics in Middle Eastern and African Economics, 15*(1), 92–113.

Armstrong, K. (2006). *Muhammad: Prophet for our time*. London: Harper Perennial.

Bayat, A. (2009). *Life as politics: How ordinary people change the middle east*. Cairo: The American University in Cairo Press.

Berlant, L. (2011). *Cruel optimism*. Durham and London: Duke University Press.

Boym, S. (2001). *The future of nostalgia*. New York: Basic Books.

Butter, D. (2013). *Egypt in search of economic direction*. London: Chatham House.

Evans, M. (2015). Feminism and the implications of austerity. *Feminist Review, 109*, 146–155.

Ferguson, J. (2013). Declarations of dependence: Labour, personhood, and welfare in South Africa. *Journal of the Royal Anthropological Institute, 19*(2), 223–242.

Fraser, N. (2012). *Can society be commodities all the way down? Polanyian reflections on capitalist crisis*. FMSH-WP-2012-18, <halshs-00725060>.

Freud, S. (1917). *Mourning and Melancholia*. London: Hogarth Press.

Go, J. (2013). *Postcolonial sociology*. Emerald: Bingley.

Graeber, D. (2011). *Debt: The first 5,000 years*. Brooklyn and London: Melville House.

Hoffman, E. (2010). The long afterlife of loss. In S. Radstone & B. Schwarz (Eds.), *Memory: Histories, theories and debates*. New York: Fordham University Press.

Joseph, S. (1999). *Intimate selving in Arab families: Gender, self and identity*. Syracuse: Syracuse University Press.

Kandil, H. (2014). *Soldiers, spies, and statesman: Egypt's road to revolt*. London: Verso.

Lloyd, D. (2003). The memory of hunger. In D. L. Eng & D. Kazanjian (Eds.), *Loss: The politics of mourning*. Berkley and Los Angeles: University of California Press.

Osman, T. (2010). *Egypt on the brink: From Nasser to Mubarak*. New Haven, CT and London: Yale University Press.

Pickering, M., & Keightley, E. (2006). The modalities of nostalgia. *Current Sociology, 54*(6), 919–941.

Treacher Kabesh, A. (2013). *Postcolonial masculinities: Emotions, histories and ethics*. Farnham: Ashgate.

United Nations (2014). *Sustaining human progress: Reducing vulnerabilities and building resilience*. New York: United Nations.

Walkerdine, V., & Jimenez, L. (2012). *Gender, work and community after de-industrialisation: A psychosocial approach to affect*. London: Palgrave Macmillan.

Yuval-Davis, N. (2006). Belonging and the politics of belonging. *Patterns of Prejudice, 40*(3), 197–214.

Zagajewski, A. (2001). Try to praise the mutilated world. (trans: Cavanagh, C.). *The New Yorker*, September 24.

Epilogue

Christian Karner and Bernhard Weicht

Our era's crises are ubiquitous and systemic. As we are writing these lines, new polarizations—or arguably merely revamped versions of older, albeit partly forgotten or conveniently overlooked schisms—are apparent across Europe and beyond. Questions concerning national sovereignty (such as in the case of the Russian annexation of Crimea) or the limits of trans national and international solidarity (such as in the European reactions to the increased numbers of refugees and asylum seekers) are reminiscent of the national struggles of the late nineteenth and early twentieth century, which provided the historical starting point to Polanyi's analyses. One recent conflict in particular symbolizes the ongoing friction between the state and the market, between local, political "communities" and international, economic interests. In the summer of 2015, the most recent "chapter" of the long-standing Greek debt and austerity crisis, which also crystallizes structural flaws implicating the Eurozone in its entirety (for example Heise 2014), saw an escalation of the clash between neoliberal austerity and left-wing politics that left no space for socio economically meaningful and mutually face-saving compromises. Greece, it seems, is given no choice but to implement additional, further impoverishing "reforms", if the country is to avoid complete socio

© The Editor(s) (if applicable) and The Author(s) 2016   **345**
C. Karner, B. Weicht (eds.), *The Commonalities of Global Crises*,
DOI 10.1057/978-1-137-50273-5

economic implosion. The capital controls forced onto Greek citizens in the context of their government's stand-off with its international creditors left little doubt about how bad things had become, and how much worse they might yet get. Greeks' ongoing nightmare can very plausibly be read as an example of the timeliness of (neo-)Polanyian categories: *dis-embedding marketization*, essentially what externally imposed austerity programmes and purported reforms have amounted to, clashing with "counter-moves" promising to socially re-embed economic relations—and hence, ultimately, people. Given that the far left *and* the far right have responded strongly to the Greek crisis, we undoubtedly here encounter corroboration of Polanyi's (2001) "double movement" implicating socialist and fascist counter-reactions to supposedly "self-regulating markets" and their social and human costs. Yet more accurately, and like several other contexts examined in this book, Greece today, in her ongoing struggles with transnational market forces and her internal ideological tensions, conforms to Nancy Fraser's depiction (2012) of a "triple movement" positing the mutually contradictory reactions of *social protection* and *emancipation* against ever-widening marketization.

In recent years, in both the academic realm and broader public discussion, the revived interest in Polanyi's theoretically groundbreaking work coincided with the publication of two other major works that take a particular interest in the historically non-linear development of economic and social structures: Thomas Piketty's (2014) seminal history of income and wealth inequality since the eighteenth century, and David Graeber's (2012) *Debt*, whose *longue durée* perspective stretches even further to cover 5000 years of history. Their different disciplinary locations notwithstanding (that is, economics and economic history in Piketty's case, and social anthropology in Graeber's), these greats of contemporary social science share more than an unusual willingness and ability to research across vast stretches of time and geographical space. Both Piketty's *Capital* and Graeber's *Debt* reveal social histories defined by ruptures and discontinuities. In Piketty's case, this manifests in his central thesis, illustrated through a wealth of statistical data, that the post-war period was, particularly in Western Europe, a historically unusual epoch of declining social inequalities (and a "golden age of growth"), in part due to the continent's recovery from the mass destruction of the preceding World Wars, and partly the outcome of some redistribution of wealth achieved by welfare states and progressive taxes. On either side of this historical anomaly Piketty documents the workings of a "patrimonial capitalism" defined by growing inequalities and a concentration of wealth, reflecting situations in which the "rate of return on capital remains significantly above the [economic] growth rate for an extended period of time" ($r > g$) (Piketty 2014: 25).

David Graeber (2012: 211ff) reveals yet larger "cycles of history", in which the social dominance of "coinage" and "credit" alternate and broadly correspond to the institutionalization of exchange, war and slavery in the first case, and of trust in the second. Graeber maps these monumental alternations onto the "axial age" (that is 800 BC–600 AD); the Middle Ages—when "virtual credit money returned ... and slavery largely disappeared" (Graeber 2012: 251; 297); the "age of the great capitalist empires" (1450–1971), or the "age of exploration" that saw a return from "credit economies" to, albeit in new forms, "gold and silver ... vast empires and professional armies, massive predatory warfare ... [and] chattel slavery" (2012: 308). Finally, Graeber detects the recent "beginning of something yet to be determined", the contemporary era in which he observes that "neoliberalism", meaning the market and capitalism, have become "the organizing principle of almost everything" (2012: 376). Yet, at this present historical juncture Graeber concludes—in a vein pertinent to our volume—by arguing that our "giant debt machine" is now running into its "social and ecological limits", leading him to propose the following:

> [W]e are long overdue for [a] Biblical-style Jubilee: one that would affect both international debt and consumer debt ... not just because it would relieve so much genuine human suffering, but also because it would be our way of reminding ourselves that money is not ineffable, that paying one's debts is not the essence of morality, that all these things are human arrangements and that if democracy is to mean anything, it is the ability to all agree to arrange things in a different way. (Graeber 2012: 390)

In light of the most recent crises these comments have become even more topical since the publication of Graeber's book. There is, however, also an obvious "problem" in this conclusion: the undeniable fact remains that not "all agree", or are likely to, on this course of action. Far from it, and as demonstrated by several of our chapters, reactions to contemporary crises are varied and hotly contested, revealing—in corroboration with Bourdieu's argument (1977) outlined in our introduction—that far-reaching, consciousness-raising social transformations pit "the dominant" against "the dominated" in the resulting discursive, political struggles. Once again turning to Nancy Fraser, her distinction between social protection and emancipation points toward yet more nuanced fault lines cutting across the category of "the dominated".

Let us reiterate the crucial common denominator shared by two otherwise very differently oriented *magni opi* in the social sciences of the early twenty-first century: where much political and everyday discourse assumes timeless economic laws or linear "progress", Piketty and Graeber instead detect the peaks and troughs of economic history. Put more simply, and to state the historically obvious, socioeconomic relations and institutions have often shifted and been transformed profoundly, and in ways that cannot be described as unidirectional. It surely takes an embarrassing amount of ideological amnesia, self-interest or arrogance not to acknowledge this. What is more, some of the available prognoses of the likely consequences and limits of our current trajectories indeed make for grim reading. More than 40 years after Ernst Friedrich Schumacher (2010 [1973]) first argued that *small* was *beautiful*, growing numbers of people are articulating concern about the (feared un)sustainability of our socioeconomic status quo. This also manifests in academic circles, such as the M.A.U.S.S movement (*Mouvement Anti-Utilitariste dans les Sciences Sociales*) around Alain Caillé and the recently published "convivial manifesto" formulated by a group of mainly French intellectuals: this counters what it presents as our era's defining and purportedly self-destructive characteristics—the "primacy of utilitarian self-interest" and (quasi-religious) "belief in the desirability and benevolence of economic growth"—with an alternative vision premised on convivial sociability, ecological sustainability, and the "paradigm of the gift" (Adloff 2014: 9, 16; *our translation*). Echoing some of the conceptual strands summarised in our introduction, the *convivial manifesto* considers the "subordination of all human activities under commercial norms" and reactionary ideologies that respond to growing "social, ecological and public insecurity" to be amongst today's most pressing threats (Les Convivialistes 2014: 41; 53; *our translations*). Regardless of whether or not one wishes to endorse this particular assessment, we here again come "face to face" with some of our central concerns: with the general commodification of (almost) all aspects of life, with forms of collective unease in the light of increasing marketization, and with the often romantically backward-looking reactions to a world of insecurity and uncertainty.

While we have refrained from making predictions, the question needs to be raised as to whether current crises are indeed catapulting us toward humanity's next major change of directions. Are we, in specifically Polanyian terms, yet again discovering that allowing largely unregulated markets to turn labour, land and money into "fictitious commodities" will trigger "countermovements", aiming for society's "self-protection", albeit perhaps in ways more varied and unpredictable than Polanyi himself saw?

It is in the interface of these different, classical and current contributions to social theory and political discourse that our volume finds itself and has sought to offer its insights. Our contributions reveal the importance of relating to our conceptual points of reference as bodies of scholarship that need to be subject to continuous empirical challenge and theoretical refinement.

The careful empirical discussions provided by our contributors offer ample material, through which the theoretical scholarship that formed our points of departure can be critically re-thought. What is more, those empirical discussions help re-inflect current discussions of socioeconomic crises. Repeating what has been stressed numerous times, several chapters offer powerful evidence of the timeliness and applicability of Polanyi's analytical categories or of Nancy Fraser's more recent, neo-Polanyian elaborations, including those of the socially disembedding effects of unregulated markets or the "double" or "triple movement", to which they give rise. Yet, certain historical and contemporary questions also require us to push beyond the theoretical frameworks that have informed many of our debates. And, of course, this is not primarily about the critical corroboration of relevant social theory; instead, at stake here are lives, futures, hopes and—especially in their current contexts—often their utter disillusionment.

Another (subtly) recurring theme concerns the very nature of capitalism. As shown by David Graeber (2012: 345ff), there is surprisingly little consensus as to capitalism's exact definition. Striking a similar chord, several chapters in the present volume hint or argue explicitly that the very idea of politically unconstrained markets is little more than ideological fiction; even the strongest drives toward deregulation conceive of markets as socially embedded, albeit of course in social and institutional structures very different from, and often diametrically opposed to, what the political left has in mind. The ability to analytically separate *different modes of embeddedness* is therefore vital. What is more, such competing models for embedding markets implicate competing discursive regimes, interpretative frames, and ethical orientations. Once again, Fraser's distinction between social protection and emancipation, on which we have built, provides vital analytical purchase here.

Crises, contemporary and historical, come in many forms and permutations. As we have seen, they include profound structural shifts and dislocations with the potential or, more often, real consequence of leaving collective life-worlds and individual life-chances in tatters. Other crises, as we also saw, are first and foremost about perceptions of decline, although this is of course not to deny that such perceptions often correspond to tangible and considerable social change. What unites the different settings and experiences of structural and/or interpreted crises examined above is the fact that the past comes to constitute an ideologically usable, and malleable resource in such circumstances. Often this is not "the past" in a historiographically verified, or even verifiable form, but a diffuse sense of *a past*, considered better than and hence preferable to the present. This is why and where the concept of nostalgia has played a central role—as both social phenomenon and analytical category—to several of the preceding chapters. As we stressed in our introduction, nostalgia assumes heterogeneous forms and can serve different political purposes. In any case, it needs careful scrutiny. Consider, for example, Theodore Roszak's outline of what he termed the "subterranean tradition of organic and decentralist economics":

> Reaching backward, this tradition embraces communal, handicraft, tribal, guild, and village life-styles as old as the neolithic cultures ... [I]t is not an

ideology ... but a wisdom gathered from historical experience ... [I]t has reemerged spontaneously in the communitarian experiments ... of the counterculture ... How strange that this renewed interest in ancient ways of livelihood and community should reappear even as our operations researchers ... conceive their most ambitious dreams of cybernated glory ... [I]f there is ... a humanly tolerable world on this dark side of the emergent technocratic world-system, it will ... flower from this still fragile renaissance of organic husbandry [and] communal households. (Roszak 2010 [1973]: 5).

Dated and over-romanticized though this may appear, there can be little doubt that Roszak's account still resonates today, at least among those sceptical of multinational agribusiness, global market forces, and the hypercommodification and technological colonization of twenty-first century life. As a formulation of nostalgia, it could hardly be clearer. However, does this qualify as "reflective nostalgia" (Boym 2001), which rather than blindly glorifying "the past" puts the latter to critical, potentially progressive use in the present? Or are the historical oversights in the preceding account—concerning the injustices, hierarchies and more than occasional forms of oppression typical of many a "communal, tribal and village life-style"—too blatant to rescue such nostalgia for a progressive politics? Nancy Fraser (2013) importantly reminds us that, historically, many human rights struggles had to be directed at community itself, for a traditional, conservative design of social protection not only ignored but reproduced and enforced many injustices and marginalizations. And do we need to ponder the wider implications of what else such nostalgic utopianism, if implemented on a large scale, would entail? For example, and relating this to Piketty's (2014) aforementioned argument (that is, concerning r > g), would a "new" economic logic dedicated to low or no growth and local production for use only not risk further exacerbating existing inequalities, at least under present institutional arrangements? Clearly, these are complex, decidedly empirical questions that can only be answered in specific settings, in which *the particular past being invoked* and *the particular politics for which it is invoked* require and invite contextual assessments rather than generalizing statements. Such has indeed been the spirit of the present volume.

Crises, then, also crystallize competing conceptions of social order, of the political future, and of what a good life should entail. As this volume has demonstrated, the resulting discursive struggles have a distinctive, indeed defining temporal dimension: profoundly concerned about the present, and formulating their respective visions of the future, they simultaneously reflect and utilise their particular retellings of particular pasts, whether real or imaginary. Nostalgia, one may paraphrase, is the crisis-induced repackaging of the past, in the present, for the future.

What is distinctive about the present volume is our conceptual bringing together—in the service of sustained analyses of particular empirical settings and phenomena—of questions of (dis)embedding, commodification, and the politics of nostalgia. To stress what we think and hope is obvious, our intention has never been to restrict ourselves to academic debates only. There is indeed a lot at stake here, as shown by the subject matter of our respective chapters and the wider issues this volume addresses. The confluence of the forces of marketization/commodification with the invocation of various "communities", and hence, the (re)drawing of social boundaries, and the political uses of the past indeed never seems far away in the early twenty-first century: whether we concern ourselves with growing inequalities and rising unemployment; or with human rights, environmental degradation, or (forced) migration and the (moral) panics it all too often triggers among the relatively privileged, safe but immobile; or whether our focus rests on the future of welfare systems, of care or education, or on the renationalisation of political debate currently evident across large parts of the world—markets, communities and nostalgia indeed interface in all these areas.

Finally, crises can of course trigger further crises. The notion of a "post-2008 world" (Varoufakis 2015) raises further important questions: how do we know if we are still in the midst of a previous crisis, or already battling a new one? And whether old or new, how confident are we that existing institutions, explanations and strategies equip us to deal with the circumstances at hand? Or, and just as importantly, (how) can the competing responses being proposed and debated be reconciled? As we have seen, while there are significant historical precedents for this, these and related questions indeed define many challenges "we"—in our narrow life-worlds and as members of our only rarely recognized, let alone celebrated global, human community—face in the new millennium.

References

Adloff, F. (2014). 'Es gibt schon ein richtiges Leben im falschen'. Konvivialismus— zum Hintergrund einer Debatte. In F. Adloff & C. Leggewie (Eds.), *Das konvivialistische Manifest: Für eine neue Kunst des Zusammenlebens* (pp. 7–32). Bielefeld: Transcript.

Bourdieu, P. (1977). *Outline of a theory of practice.* Cambridge: Cambridge University Press.

Boym, S. (2001). *The future of nostalgia.* New York: Basic Books.

Fraser, N. (2012). *Marketization, social protection, emancipation: Toward a neopolanyian conception of capitalist crisis.* http://sophiapol.hypotheses.org/files/2012/02/Texte-Nancy-Fraser-anglais.doc. Accessed 22 July 2013.

Fraser, N. (2013). Between marketization and social protection: Resolving the feminist ambivalence. In N. Fraser (Ed.), *Fortunes of feminism: From state-managed capitalism to neoliberal crisis* (pp. 227–241). London: Verso.

Graeber, D. (2012). *Debt: The first 5000 years.* Brooklyn/London: Melville House.

Heise, A. (2014). Zwangsjacke Euro: Die Fehlkonstruktion des Europäischen Economic Governance Systems. *Wirtschaft und Gesellschaft, 40*(1), 17–31.

Les Convivialistes. (2014). Das konvivialistische Manifest. In F. Adloff & C. Leggewie (Eds.), *Das konvivialistische Manifest: Für eine neue Kunst des Zusammenlebens* (pp. 33–77). Bielefeld: transcript.

Piketty, T. (2014). *Capital in the twenty-first century.* Cambridge: Belknap/Harvard University Press.

Polanyi, K. (2001 [1944]). *The great transformation: The political and economic origins of our time.* Boston: Beacon Press.

Roszak, T. (2010). Introduction. In E. F. Schumacher (Ed.), *Small is beautiful* (pp. 1–10). New York: Harper Perennial.

Schumacher, E. F. (2010 [1973]). *Small is beautiful.* New York: Harper Perennial.

Varoufakis, Y. (2015). *Thoughts for the post-2008 world.* http://yanisvaroufakis.eu. Accessed 22 July 2015.

Index

Note: Page number followed by 'n' refers to footnotes.

© The Editor(s) (if applicable) and The Author(s) 2016   **355**
C. Karner, B. Weicht (eds.), *The Commonalities of Global Crises,*
DOI 10.1057/978-1-137-50273-5

Printed by Printforce, the Netherlands